FEASTS OF BLOOD:

The Forgotten History of Welsh Prize Fighting

JOHN F. FRANCIS

cappaPress

While every precaution has been taken in the preparation of this book, the publisher assumes no responsibility for errors or omissions, or for damages resulting from the use of the information contained herein.

FEASTS OF BLOOD: *The Forgotten History of Welsh Prize Fighting*

Edition

Copyright @2020 John F. Francis
Copyright front cover illustration @2020 Helen Sandford

ISBN: 978-1-393-88117-9

Written by John F. Francis

For Barbara, Luke, Laura and Sophie for their help and support.

Contents

INTRODUCTION 1

FIGHTING THE LAW 7

PRIZE FIGHTERS 41

GOLDEN AGE? 85

FIGHTERS TO MID-1820S 103

DECLINE? MID-1820S - 1860 123

FIGHTERS TO 1860 141

REVIVAL? 1861 - 1900 167

FIGHTERS TO 1900 201

FEMALE FIGHTERS 229

FAIRGROUND BOXING BOOTHS 239

MOUNTAIN FIGHTERS 273

THE RING IS DEAD? 287

INDEX 315

FIGHT RECORDS 333

BIBLIOGRAPHY 389

The deliberate arranging of a feast of blood – the backing, the seconding, the journey, the prepared ropes and stakes, the fighting cold blood for money – all this is so horrible it is a disgrace to our country and our time.

(*Aberdare Times*, 2 November 1861)

Introduction

In 1811, the death was recorded at Cloddiau, near Welshpool, 'at an advanced age' of John Williams, 'better known as 'Jack of the Wern', who, 'In his youthful days he practised, with so great success, the art of pugilism, that the renowned Glau Brace, and several Cambrian heroes, yielded to his superior strength and dexterity'.[1] Williams would have fought in the second half of the eighteenth century and this reference indicates he was one of a number of well-known practitioners, and that prize fighters were celebrated.

There have been considerable changes in the sport over the succeeding two centuries, in its organisation, in fighting techniques, and in its perception by the public, but, in some respects, nothing has altered. It continues to thrive, and Welsh fighters, past and present, are still revered and talked about avidly.

But, 'past' in this context refers only to the early years of the twentieth century, when Jimmy Wilde, Percy Jones, Freddie Welsh and 'Peerless' Jim Driscoll, dominated world boxing. They are Wales' earliest remembered ring heroes.

Their feats and those of their successors have been well-chronicled, but the deeds of Williams and his contemporaries have long since disappeared into the mists of time. Their nineteenth century successors have been forgotten as well. Men who were, in their own era, just as feted as Wilde and company. Many were regarded as the best in Britain, which, given that Britain was then pre-eminent in the sport, meant the best in the world.

They are part of the forgotten history of Welsh prize fighting. Forgotten, that is, until now.

Pugilists have traditionally been depicted in art and literature, from images on a Minoan vase from Crete c. 1500 BC through Greek and Roman representations, continuing when the sport revived in 17th-century England and attracted the attention of artists such as Constable and Hogarth and, to a greater extent, the notice of writers. Shaw, Conan Doyle, Scott, Collins and Hardy refer to the sport, Thackeray wrote a poem about a big fight in 1860, and Hazlitt wrote an essay *The Fight* (1821). Other writers, Pope, Swift, Keats and Byron were also fight fans.

Modern contributions include a late Victorian bare-knuckle murder mystery and a novel set in the world of female pugilists and their patrons in late 18th-century Bristol.[2] Boxing's dramatic qualities have also appealed to filmmakers; the first motion picture using actors was a boxing exhibition in 1894, and in 1897, the championship fight between Gentleman Jim Corbett and Bob Fitzsimmons became the first sporting event to be captured on film.

English prize fighters have been well-documented. In addition to fighters in fiction, biographies abound, including one by a Monmouthshire man. Thomas Morgan Wintle (1855 – 1926), born at Pontnewynydd, wrote *'The Story of Bendigo,'* Champion *Prize Fighter of England.* Some of the information in Wintle's book came from the governor of Usk prison who had been chief warder at Nottingham gaol where Bendigo had been a frequent resident because of his drunkenness.[3]

Not so Welsh fighters from the nineteenth century, who live on mostly in fiction in the coal mining novels of, among others Jack Jones and Richard Llewellyn. The fighting tradition features frequently in other novels of the gen re, although mostly as local colour and period background.

Introduction

Encouragingly, in recent years that Welsh shortcoming has begun to be addressed. One publication (celebrating fighters from the twentieth century) includes a chapter providing an overview of the previous one hundred years.[4] Another author has recorded affectionately the main contests involving some Welsh prize-fighters of the nineteenth century, while a compilation of the ring records of mainly twentieth century boxers, includes one or two from slightly earlier years.[5]

The present work, which identifies almost one thousand Welsh prize fighters of the nineteenth century, is the first in-depth study of a significant activity, a major part of Wales' recreational culture. Prize fighting attracted crowds in their thousands, men, women and children, who would have travelled many miles to watch their ring heroes, and as such it might be considered to have been Wales's first national sport.

The sport, considered illegal, operated amidst constant debate, over its contribution to Britain's national image (fair fighting with fists showing manly British courage, as opposed to effeminacy of foreigners using knives in arguments), its military usefulness, influence on public behaviour, which activities were more acceptable, more dangerous or cruel, its place in a growing industrial society and in a supposedly enlightened age.

For most of the nineteenth century bare knuckle fighting (or using the 'raw 'uns', as it was known) was viewed as different from boxing with gloves, which was legal and generally looked on favourably.

It later morphed into glove contests which themselves became the subject of debate. Had it commandeered the name 'boxing' and was now merely prize fighting with gloves? Were gloves less injurious to health than bare knuckles? Was it more exciting for spectators? The biggest debate concerned its very existence. Should it be eradicated? If so, how? Should the law interfere with personal freedoms, or should prize fighting die a natural death through public opinion?

Even British prime ministers were in opposite corners. George Canning stated that the only satisfaction which he derived from a prize fight was the certainty of two blackguards obtaining a good thrashing, while Lord Palmerston, when asked for one guinea, the limit of each subscription to a Parliamentary collection for a triumphant Englishman, asked if he could instead donate five.

Female Members of Parliament squared up, too, in the second half of the twentieth century, Bessie Braddock championing the cause and Edith Summerskill trying to ban it just as determinedly.

Yet, despite its uncertain legal status and strong opposition, these 'festivals of the common people' flourished.[6] How they managed to do so and the mechanisms employed to sustain them, reveal much about attitudes, culture and the class system during Georgian and Victorian times.

Because prize fighting was considered illegal and was not controlled by any organising body, there are no official records to examine, and thus no inclusive statistics to be accumulated. Nevertheless, complete or partial career records of more than 800 Welsh fighters are revealed here, with more than one hundred others identified, although with no attributed contests.

This study, fully referenced and indexed, begins by examining the sport's legal status, which governed most aspects of the prize ring. It looks at why prize fighting was regarded as illegal, what action was taken to try to curtail it, the punishment meted out to those brought before the courts, and the considerable subterfuge engaged in by the participants to evade the law.

The following chapter focusses on the fighters themselves, challenging some of the popular perceptions about these ring warriors by revealing their

Introduction

colourful 'civilian' lives , their legendary drinking, their violence outside the ropes, and their careers on other stages – one became a Shakespearean actor and another, who was later a war hero, performed at the Folies Bergere nightclub in Paris. The chapter also considers, the money they earned and the health risks they faced in the ring.

Histories of prize-fighting in Britain divide the 19th century into three periods – a 'Golden Age' for approximately the first quarter, a decline until about 1860, followed by a revival.

This model had been applied to the London Prize Ring, where most of the leading Welsh fighters operated, and because of that association is considered at length, alongside to what extent it was applicable to Wales. In each period the sport's development is examined, the effect of alterations in its rules, how it fitted in with changing attitudes of the public, the authorities, newspapers and religious organisations.

Interspersed with each period are chapters detailing contemporary Welsh fighters, their important contests and career trajectories. Also included are chapters on female involvement in the sport, fairground boxing booths and the Welsh phenomena of mountain fighters.

The final chapter assesses the state of the sport since the end of the nineteenth century, including the long-lived colour bar in the professional ranks in Britain, and the sport's prospects.

Wales is treated here as including Monmouthshire, although the county, whose status had been a point of debate ever since the Acts of Union in the sixteenth century, was officially English until 1974. The Welsh/English issue was even raised in a fight report. After Bill Benjamin's battle for the Championship in 1859, the sport's newspaper, *Bell's Life,* was prompted to backtrack on his previously-reported Welsh credentials, stating: 'He is, we are informed, a native of Monmouthshire, and not a Welshman'.[7]

Here, though, admittedly with a personal interest, the preference is for the view of, among others, Sunday Closing campaigners in 1881, who insisted Monmouthshire was 'Welsh in language, religion and feeling'. [8]

---

[1] North Wales Gazette, 16 May 1811. Sporting Magazine, Volume 38, cited in Cambrian, 11 May 1811.
[2] Peter Lovesey, *The Detective Wore Silk Drawers* (England, Chivers Press, 2000), Anna Freeman, The Fair Fight (London, Weidenfeld & Nicholson, 2014).
[3] W. J. Townsend Collins, *Monmouthshire Writers* (Newport, Johns, 1945), p. 82.
[4] Peter Stead and Gareth Williams (eds.), *Wales and its Boxers: The Fighting Tradition* (Cardiff, University of Wales Press, 2008).
[5] Lawrence Davies, *Mountain Fighters: Lost Tales of Welsh Boxing* (Cardiff, Peerless Press, 2011). Gareth JonesThe Boxers of Wales. Volume 1: Cardiff (Cardiff, St. David's Press, 2009).
[6] G. M. Trevelyan, *English Social History*, (London, Longmans Green and Co., 1947), cited in David Thompson, England in the nineteenth century (1815-1914) (Harmondsworth, Penguin, 1964), p. 19.
[7] Bell's Life, 10 April 1859
[8] Hansard Vol. 262. 15 June 1881 cols, 614-616

1

Fighting the law

Prize fighting, i.e. fighting with bare fists for money until one combatant surrendered, had been *considered* illegal ever since the Riot Act of 1714 empowered local authorities to declare any group of twelve or more people to be unlawfully assembled, and thus to disperse or face punishment. Boxing with gloves for points in a display of skill, however, was viewed as an acceptable, manly exercise.

Everybody involved in a prize fight risked prosecution, with the courts gradually extending liability beyond the combatants to ring officials, spectators (including ringside reporters – a journalist was gaoled for ten days for being present), publicans who permitted such events to take place on their premises, police who allowed them to go ahead and members of the public who refused to help if police called for their assistance to halt proceedings. Spectators continued to be taken to court even after *R. v Coney* (1882) finally established that mere attendance at such an event was not an offence,

It was not even necessary for a prize fight to have taken place for a prosecution to be brought. Police often acted on nothing more than a rumour of an intended contest. Simply agreeing to take part was enough. Edward Turner, based in London, was forced to train in his family neighbourhood in mid-Wales to avoid a warrant before a fight in 1817, Henry Stephens was arrested while fleeing from a Cardiff pub, *The Swan*, the night before a proposed 'pitched battle' in 1853, and Griffith Watkins was dragged from his bed in Aberdare's *Railway Inn* in 1866 during a police raid which also netted six would-be spectators hiding in the pub's cellar. James Coghlan ended up in court in Cardiff in 1859 after being found lying down in a field where a fight was intended to come off. Among many other similar instances, Morgan Crowther and two associates were bound over in 1890 for attempting to commit a breach of the peace by training for a prize fight. They had been caught at Cowbridge 'running with heavy clothing and exerting themselves to great extent'. One of the combatants in a fight that took place near Monmouth in 1827 had been arrested beforehand, but he jumped out of the coach taking him into custody and ran off, eventually fulfilling his engagement.

Police might bring an alternative charge if they were unable to prove there had been a fight. If the alleged battle had been in a field, those concerned might be charged with damaging grass or trespassing. It might even be an additional charge, as three noted Welsh pugilists discovered. Bill Benjamin, Dick James and Ned Llewellyn, as well as being bound over at Tredegar police court in 1864 for aiding and abetting a prize fight where they were seconds, were also charged with damaging the fences and grass where the battle took place and were fined.

* **

AS the century progressed, increased policing resulted in the emphasis in prosecutions switching away from unlawful assembly and riot to personal injury.

After *R. v Hunt, Swanton and Others* (1845) which dealt with a prize fight where there was no affray and no riot, the courts became more focussed on how much harm that people could consent to in a fight. Courts began to hold that fighting with the 'raw 'uns' was punishable also as mutual assaults, even though there was neither death nor rioting. Fighting with gloves became increasingly viewed in the same way.

Reminders of the perceived legal position were given regularly, from Lord Chief Justice Lloyd Kenyon (born at Gredington, Flintshire, declaring in 1789 that 'Such battles were proper objects of the most severe prosecution', to fellow Welshman, Home Secretary Sir George Lewis (whose family seat was in Radnorshire), telling Parliament seventy years later there was not the 'slightest doubt' that they were illegal. In 1888, Home secretary Henry Matthews said in the House of Commons that prize fighting, boxing and sparring in gloves were all illegal. Winston Churchill, was to say much the same when he was Home Secretary in the first quarter of the twentieth century.,

Lawyers immediately challenged Lewis' statement, arguing that judges had 'assumed rather hastily' that prize-fighting was illegal, and that their decisions appeared unsupported by authority or principle.[1] The activity, lacked the chief elements of a riot, or of an assault, leaving its legal status uncertain and inconsistent. While boxing with gloves was viewed as acceptable, there was no written or unwritten code which permitted it and yet prohibited boxing without gloves. The lawyers urged that if boxing without gloves was illegal, it needed to be declared so by Parliament.

A Bill had been introduced into the House of Commons in 1816 by which participation in or attendance at a prize fight would be a distinct offence, but it never reached even its second reading. Despite proclamations by Government officers over the years, Parliament's only such moves came with the *1861 Offences Against the Persons Act* which declared that encounters which occasioned actual bodily harm were assaults and unlawful wounding, notwithstanding the victim's consent to the acts inflicted on him, and in

1868, when railway companies were banned from carrying prize fighters or other persons to the place where such a contest was to take place.

The Recorder at Manchester in 1893 added further weight to the 1861 ruling, when he stated that every fight in which the object and intent of each of the combatants was to subdue the other by violent blows was, or had a direct tendency to, a breach of the peace; it did not matter whether the fight was a hostile fight begun and continued in anger, or a prize fight for money or for advantage.

Before and after this pronouncement, it was stressed that it was for a jury to decide whether there had been an exhibition of skill (boxing) or a malicious contest with intent to do harm (prize fighting).

The Manchester ruling was soon acted upon, police stepping in to halt a glove contest in a booth at the World Fair in Cardiff in 1894 which was stopped after six rounds with both boxers exhausted. But that interference at Cardiff was a rarity; for over a year, glove fights went on comparatively unhindered in Wales, whereas bare-knuckle affairs continued to be interrupted by police, The day after the Swansea Stipendiary reiterated the decision in 1895, however, many spectators stayed away from a glove fight promotion in the town, and the principals were charged with 'striking determinedly at each other, intending to do as much damage as possible for a prize'.

***

THE Riot Act had been introduced at a time of civil disturbances, among them the Sacheverell riots (1710), which broke out in London and spread across the country, notably to Wrexham, north Wales.[2] The riots were a series of outbreaks of public disorder in which supporters of the Tories attacked Dissenters', particularly Presbyterians', homes and meeting-houses, whose congregations tended to support the Whigs.

The warning was read out rarely at prize fights in Britain, and, apparently, never in Wales, but the threat which it carried drove the activity underground, with supporters adopting a series of protocols to attempt to outwit the law.

Contests would be arranged in secret, and only basic details would be released initially – little more than the combatants' names, the amount of stake money, the date plus an approximate time and a vague location. Typically, a match in 1827 involving Monmouthshire man Bill Charles was advertised to take place 'within five miles of Newport', between the hours of twelve and two in the afternoon'.[3]

Information would be passed to supporters, usually in public houses, which were often run by current or ex-fighters, hostelries such as the *Old Red Cow* at Newport, the *Old Pine Apple* in Cardiff, the *Dynover Arms*, Pontypridd, the *Butchers Arms* and the *White Swan* at Monmouth, the *St. Ives Inn*, Neath, and the *Bell Inn*, Merthyr Tydfil.

Precise information would be disclosed only at the last moment to a small number of trusted followers, mainly those with a betting interest in the forthcoming event. Even then, details were subject to amendment if law officers were believed to be on the trail. If that happened, fight parties would often fragment and set off in different directions to throw police off their scent or, in 1887 in South Wales, pretend to be a hunting group, complete with guns and dogs, to allay suspicion. Fight supporters outwitted police near Cardiff in 1895 by setting up a counter attraction of a trotting match in the area at the same time, enabling a fight to go on uninterrupted.

For most of the century, permanent indoor venues were not feasible because such premises would be easy for the authorities to monitor, so fights were almost always in the open air, in remote locations, and during the early hours.

Preferred sites were secluded spots in the Welsh countryside, such as hill tops, particularly those enclosing the South Wales valleys, and the moors between Cardiff and Newport. The *Perrott Inn* near Quaker's Yard, in north Glamorgan, was a favourite resort. The inn was a long distance from the nearest police station, and the fight crowd would congregate there on a Sunday night so that 'early next morning they could 'enjoy their little gamer unmolested...detection in most instances was next to impossible'.[4]

An area near Rhymney was said to be a 'complete nursery for would-be champions' in the 1860s.[5] In and around Merthyr, claimed to be one of the last bastions of the sport in Britain in 1870, were hotspots such as Penydarren Park, the side of the tram road leading from Gwaunfarren to the Goitre pond, the Rhydycar Tips, and Giants' Cave, between Merthyr and Aberdare. At Treharris in the late nineteenth century, 'there was an area known as 'Bloody Island' owing to all the arranged pugilistic encounters for miles around being fixed to come off there'.[6] Land at the Gold Tops, not far from the centre of Newport, was known as the Bloody Fields 'from the number of sanguinary contests taking place there', while another popular site was Cooper's Fields, Cardiff.[7]

Pugilists got to grips on the side of the Monmouthshire and Brecon canal near the Fourteen Locks outside Newport, where two Englishmen, who had established contact at nearby Caerleon racecourse, came to blows in the early hours of one morning in 1900. They also fought on the beaches; 'Bruiser' and 'Young Fellow' battled on the Swansea Sands in 1891, and another local

Fighting the Law

Fight night (Illustration by Helen Sandford)

pair, Pedlar Palmer and 'Tubby' Dougie, also met there in 1899, while David Pierce and Sam James swapped punches on the sands at Aberavon in 1891.

Those involved were occasionally brazen by choosing the centres of towns. In Usk's New Market Street in 1823, over 100 watched as two local men battled away, another pair fought in Neath's Wind Street in 1878 'in order to have the benefit of the lights from an ornamental fountain', and a contest in the middle of the day in Adam Street, Cardiff, in 1886 was watched by nearly four hundred men, women and children, 'including a helpless-looking Bobby', which held up the traffic'.[8] In 1894, Watkin Edwards and Evan Llewellyn, stripped to the waist, were caught fighting in the playground of a Catholic school at Aberdare in front of between fifty and sixty on a Monday evening, and William Hughes and Richard Thomas were found exchanging punches on a bowling green at Ynysybwl in 1896.

The back rooms of public houses were used frequently, one contest featuring Michael Collins and David Evans taking place in the *Punch Bowl*, Blaenavon, in 1868.

***

SPECTATORS, and the combatants themselves, would usually disperse quickly if grudgingly when law officers arrived, much like the 'general stampede' on the Blaencaerau Mountain, between Maesteg and Cymmer, when Thomas Davies and David Thomas were interrupted.[9] Monmouthshire magistrate Joseph Davies praised fight followers for immediately obeying his orders with 'not a frown nor a cross look from anyone' when, unaccompanied by police, he intervened at Bedwas in 1855.[10]

But dispersal, as in this instance, was frequently only to another site. The fight party adjourned to the *Rising Sun*, Machen, and when Davies told them the fight could not take place in Monmouthshire, they went to the Glamorganshire part of the village where they battled for fifty rounds over an hour and eighteen minutes.

William Jones, of Sowhill, Pontypool, and John Morgan (Redbrook), were forced to adjourn their 1865 encounter at the Glyn Ponds on the Crumlin road near Pontypool, but after waiting for a short spell at the *Mountain Air Inn*, they resumed hostilities not far from the ironstone scourings in the hills above Penyrheol, only for the police to turn up again and arrest them. Police near Quaker's Yard in 1874 ordered several hundred men near the new pits to move away, but they went only as far as the top of Gelligaer mountain. On again being discovered, they moved on to Pengam, where they took train for Rhymney, in the next county, thereby evading the police. Police persistence also thwarted runaways in 1876, officers first dispersing a fight crowd near the Cwmbargoed railway and then again when the fight resumed near the Plymouth works; when the party ran off towards the Hare mountain.

***

A favourite site would be near a county border, so that if the law interfered, the fight party could cross quickly into the adjacent shire, where magistrates and police would have no jurisdiction and carry on. A battle took place in 1825 on the Lache-Eyes, an armlet of the Dee, near Chester in front of at least 8,000 after magistrates from Flintshire failed to halt it in their territory. In 1827, another, intended for the Hereford area, finally 'came off' 13 miles away at Monmouth Cap after local magistrates chased the fight party and an estimated four thousand would-be spectators out of Herefordshire. In 1828, Fiddler's Green, Radnorshire, near the junction of the counties of Montgomeryshire, Shropshire, and Radnorshire, was chosen so that 'should the combatants be disturbed by the vigilance of the 'Beaks' of one or two counties, they might retire to another'.[11]

This ploy did not always work, however. In 1833 a contest was entering its nineteenth round at Holt Castle Green, Denbighshire, when the Marquis of Westminster galloped up, strode into the ring and ordered the combatants to stop. One said that the site was outside his jurisdiction, but the marquis replied that he was a justice of the peace for Cheshire, Denbighshire and Flintshire so he did, indeed, have the power.

In later years, neighbouring police forces combined to thwart similar forays. A joint effort prevented 'two well-known 'roughs', 'Shony Isaacs' and 'Yanto Glatchen', coming to blows near Merthyr in 1863. Glamorgan police had driven several hundred fight followers out of the county towards the Brecon Beacons, where they were again routed by the Breconshire force and had to return to Merthyr unrewarded.

The intended 1865 clash between Ned Llewellyn (Aberdare) and Jack Portobello (Newbridge) was similarly foiled near Cardiff, when Glamorgan police were alerted by hundreds of 'men from the hills', disgorged by the last Taff Vale train into Cardiff, moving through the town at four in the morning to a spot near Rumney bridge. As hostilities were about to begin, a large body of Monmouthshire police appeared, forcing the party back towards Cardiff and on to the Caerphilly road. But Cardiff and Glamorgan police, who had been watching, chased them into the town, where 'finding it impractical to have a fight that day the groups wandered about the streets, some getting drunk'.

Later that year, police broke up a contest on Hirwaun mountain, and everybody dispersed, the court commenting 'with a discretion which we must commend', but only to the adjoining county of Brecon, where they remained for several hours under police observation before returning to Merthyr. Soon after, the supporters were on Aberdare mountain, where ten rounds passed before police forced a halt.

Further attempts to get around the law were made by including the fight in an 'assault at arms', which was a programme featuring single-stick and fencing bouts as well as supposedly harmless boxing matches. All these ploys were present when Monmouthshire man Morgan Crowther fought in a hall at Bath in 1890. All involved were found guilty, but the confusion persisted, with the Recorder insisting it had been a prize fight, only for the jury to disagree.

***

DESPITE the best endeavours of fight people, it was often difficult to ensure secrecy, for, despite the subterfuge, word invariably got out. Noisy followers in towns, or large processions moving through the countryside or trekking up the sides of hills tended to alert the law.

Police were drawn to a fight in Cooper's Fields, Cardiff, in 1851 'by the shouting of an immense crowd' at two o'clock on a Sunday morning, and to 'a fierce and sanguinary battle' in a dingle between Newport and Pontypool early one morning six years later after groups of men were seen on the road 'and from their description police believed they were the bruisers they had been on alert for all night'. Again, strangers prowling Merthyr streets at an unusually early hour in 1874 prompted police to follow them towards Fochrhiw, where there was already a large gathering.

Farmer and publican Joseph Teague, well-known in the fight business, was understood to be about to host a contest at his country residence, the Kimla, Neath, in 1862, but police were alerted by the number of people in his pub, which was the fighters' headquarters.

Around thirty tough-looking men arriving at the small railway station at Lydney, Gloucestershire, by a 1.23am train in 1889 alerted local police, who were able to halt a fight in a nearby field involving Crowther. Police at Pencoed near Bridgend in 1891 staked out a public house in the early hours as horse-drawn vehicles arrived constantly. They later followed the party to a pub at Coity, where the two fighters escaped over a wall, one of them, Jack Northey, being picked out of a crowd at the nearby railway station.

Police were tipped off that a prize fight was going to be held at Penarth in 1894 and officers on alert around the town spotted a large number of local pugilists and bookmakers sneaking into an empty shop just two hundred yards from the police station. Finding that the windows had been whitewashed and the crowd appeared likely to remain inside police raided the premises and discovered a ring had been set up, and coal-trimmer Albert Jones and John Williams, a butcher, were ready to fight.

A body of men on their way to a prize fight were profiled against the sky on the mountain beyond Pengarnddu and were spotted by a police inspector using a telescope in 1888, Another group, climbing the hillside at Dinas in 1897, alerted a police officer lying in bed who followed them and interrupted their plans. The same year police saw about 200 people climbing Gelliwion Mountain above Pontypridd and there forming a ring with William James and John Wills, two colliers, getting ready to fight.

These frequently noisy pilgrimages were another reason, apart from it being impossible to charge entrance fees, why the public were not particularly welcomed around a prize fight.

More often, the authorities were tipped off by anonymous letter and by farmers fed up with spectators trampling their crops, such as at Ynysybwl in 1876, when five hundred spectators had their enjoyment curbed by police turning up. A farmer, thought to have called in the police who halted a contest near Cwmavon in 1896, 'had his whiskers pulled, and other indignities inflicted upon him'.[12] But, another who discovered a prize fight involving Shoni Engineer taking place in his field did not order them off or contact the police. Instead, he told a court that after the fight he collected money from the crowd and gave it to the local hospital, explaining: 'I collected it because I allowed them to have their pleasure in my field'.[13]

Before Bill Savage's clash with Jack Branstonn ('Jack of Finchley') Branstonn's wife swore, slapped her husband's face and refused a bribe in a vain attempt to stop the fight, finally resorting to asking Savage to 'give him a good hiding'. The wife of a fighter battered in an Abersychan pub in 1857 went for the police after she was prevented from taking him home by the landlord, who was getting two more men ready for action.

A stranger lurking nearby was warned off by fight people at Pencoed in 1887, but when they realised that he might inform the police they escorted him to ringside where they plied him with whisky to keep him friendly.

A hasty change of venue was, however, needed at Cardiff in 1895 because of

> disquieting rumours which reached the ears of he principals to the effect that a hostile faction had lodged a couple of dogs possessed of big jaws, and as big a reputation for using them, in the Barrack Field for the purpose of spoiling the sport.[14]

Occasionally, even the fighters themselves, or their backers, alerted the authorities. When Aaron Jones took on Harry Orme at Newmarket in 1852, it was claimed that Orme's backers saw their man was on his way to defeat so they sent a well-known runner off to the nearest police station. In 1860 in Monmouthshire, in front of 2,000, a fight at Rhymney Hill reached its seventieth round when one man wanted to give in, but his supporters persuaded him to hold on for a few more rounds 'when a policeman would appear to the rescue; this was secretly arranged, and at the 75th round Mr. Bluebottle made his appearance'.[15] Dan Thomas, complained that he was 'coolly and impudently robbed' of his money in 1862 after his opponent's backers realised their man was going to lose and sent for the police to stop the fight.

One would-be exponent was let off scot-free by a court - and was unhappy about it. He was alleged to have instigated a prize fight and then, because he feared he would be hurt, told the police so they would intervene. Aberdare magistrates told him: 'We shan't bind you over for we don't think there is much danger to be apprehended from you'.[16] The report added that the man 'looked very much as if he would rather have been bound too than to have had such a doubt cast upon his prowess'.

***

LAW enforcers were known to take firm action to halt prize fights, police at Llandovery, for instance, being awarded a bonus by the local Corporation for doing just this in 1838. Superintendent Henry Wrenn, who proved proficient with bare fists by regularly getting to grips with the hard men of Merthyr's notorious 'China' district, dispersed around five hundred spectators by galloping his horse at them in a field at Abercanaid in 1848.

Several hundred 'blackguards' were reduced to 'growling savagely' as Newport's police chief, complete with sword, staff and handcuffs and assisted by a few colleagues and magistrates, herded them away from the site of a proposed 'series of low, blackguard prize fights' on Thanksgiving Day on the outskirts of the town in 1849. In south west Wales in 1889, the arrival of Tenby's head constable led to both fighters, their entourage and a large following taking to their heels and a chase ensued, after which those participating were captured.

Some arrests came at the end of long, mountain-top pursuits. In 1894, police captured collier Edmund John, who had been fighting near Pontypridd, after a mile-long chase. In 1898, John Bowen and Thomas Davies were the principals in an intended set-to at Clydach Vale. Police surprised onlookers who had formed a ring on the mountain top and captured Bowen and Davies after a three-hour chase. When Thomas Williams and Abraham Evans, colliers from Treorchy fought on the Forch Mountain, Treorchy, in 1900 police tracked them over walls and fences, 'which they managed to clear at first, and to do credit for themselves in an obstacle race'.[17]

Their ring exertions, they had just completed 16 rounds, slowed down fleeing fighters Joseph Thomas and William Gimlet on Brithwaunydd mountain in 1891, allowing police, who were two hundred yards behind them when the chase began, to catch them 'out of breath and gasping' at the foot of the steep hill at Trealaw.

Officers were left behind, however, when they tried to follow 'a number of persons well-known for their pugilistic propensities' seen leaving Cardiff in horse-drawn carriages in the early hours of the morning in 1869. Officers tried to follow on foot, 'but the horses were put to the gallop, and they soon disappeared over the brow of the hill. The run up-hill completely took the wind out of the constables, and on reaching the top not a vestige of the pursued could be discovered'. But, luckily, the marks of the wheels enabled the police to follow and the fight party was tracked to a wood near Lisvane, where two Cardiff pugilists were performing.

A police officer showed just as much determination during an hour-long 'tussle' with a Cardiff prize fighter at St. Mellons. He recalled proudly later in his career

> We closed and clinched for over an hour on the highway, and a crowd of 600 or 700 gathered to see the result. They made big gaps in the hedges on both sides to see. I got out my staff but some of the crowd took it away. Well, I fairly wore him out, although he was a trained man, and at the end of an hour's hard struggling, I got him handcuffed.[18]

Police would often turn up in disguise to make an arrest. Tipped off, they were on Blaenavon Mountain an hour before a fight party arrived in 1894, and, dressed as navvies, were close to the fighters, 'Daniels and Tar' while the fight was in progress. At the end, as the men shook hands, they were both arrested. A total of 46 rounds of 'a bout in the old style' took place on the Neath mountains in 1896 before 'four strangers, dressed in civilian attire, burst upon the scene. Someone recognised them before they reached the ring, for the cry of 'police' was raised, and the principals, and most of the company ran away.

Magistrates earned plaudits as well. Justices in Montgomeryshire in 1829 acted with 'laudable interposition' in preventing prize fights, and when Jones fought Young Brag in 1833, 'a Beak with a retinue of constables on horseback rode up to the ring and put a stop to the combat'.[19] The 'worthy Magistrate' then ordered a local pub landlord to stop serving spectators.

As well as acting decisively at the scene, the authorities could bide their time when bringing offenders to justice. A collier who assaulted a police officer trying to stop a contest at the Green, Brymbo, and then absconded, was arrested more than two years later in 1889; Newport magistrates waited more than a year to collar Jem Mace, a second in a prize fight at nearby Peterstone, pouncing when the English bare-knuckle champion returned to the area as an attraction with a circus in 1868, and Felix Scott, who escaped after wounding a policeman, was ultimately arrested twelve months later in 1888 - as he was leaving a prize-ring.

***

THESE examples of resolute law enforcement failed, however, to diminish a general perception of deliberate inaction by the authorities which was believed to have played a big part in keeping the sport alive and well.

It has been argued that, more often than not, prize fights were ignored or only half-heartedly prosecuted because of much sympathy with both the 'sporting' aspect of prize-fighting, and with 'manly English fist-fighting' in general, as long as it stayed within certain bounds.[20]

Governments, manned by regular fight-goers, were 'a conniving executive' which had never prosecuted in such cases, instead leaving the task it to local law enforcement, often seen in the same light.[21]

In regard to the highest-profile events, which were confined to England, the authorities either sought to dissuade the principals beforehand, or intervened when the action was over, rather than risk provoking the often massive crowds.

It was a pragmatic approach, allowing spectators their dubious pleasure and ensuring that the authorities were seen to be doing their duty by seeking to punish the performers. There was enough serious disorder to deal with without cracking down on spectators who, for all their boisterousness, did not threaten civil peace.

Determined interference was usually confined to local, smaller gatherings where such action was more likely to prove successful. Cardiff-based Patsy Reardon would have been more aggrieved than most, having had his fights with John Rooke and Jem Dillon both halted by police just weeks after major clashes involving Sayers v Heenan and Mace v King went ahead without interruption.

The grievance persisted that there was one law for the rich and another for the poor. The aristocratic members of the Pelican Club in London were able to enjoy prize fighting 'under police protection and the paternal patronage of a Tory government' while police would halt shows in working class venues.[22] Bob Dunbar, bound over for taking part in a glove fight at Newport in 1888, complained that one had been permitted at the Royal Albert-hall, London, the previous week.

Referred to variously as 'Blues', 'Bobbies', 'Peelers', 'blue coats', 'Boys in blue', 'Mr. Bluebottle' and 'slops', police were condemned frequently for not being present to halt the action. A newspaper thought it 'amazing' in 1887 that with the countryside 'dotted' with police stations, and communication by telephone and telegraph 'so complete' that Monmouthshire police should be unaware of a much-publicised two-hour battle near Tredegar. A prize fight which went undisturbed in the Gellygrove woods near Tonyrefail prompted a newspaper to ask 'Would it not be well to invest the reporters with the policemen's cloaks?'[23]

At other times, police were criticised for being at the scene but doing nothing.

Two men charged with fighting on Blaenavon Mountain in 1865 said they did not know they were doing wrong as there were five police looking on without interfering. The court heard that the battle had taken place forty yards outside the Monmouthshire boundary, and Monmouthshire police said they did not interfere because if they had been assaulted as public officers they would have had no redress. A prize fight at Merthyr in 18 74 went off under the noses of apathetic local police, it was suggested; the stakeholder lived a few yards from a police station and less than an hour after the fight, the stake money was paid over and a good part of the £200 bets were distributed in a pub across the road from a police station 'while the police-sergeant…stood sunning himself at the station door'.[24]

Magistrates or 'beaks', were accused of neglecting their duty to stop prize fights, even turning a blind eye to them, prompting a judge in 1824 to threaten a crackdown on those found wanting. They could not plead ignorance of fights, nor of the scenes that took place at them, it was claimed; they had been seen at fights and had even been robbed at such events, only 'to have their watches and purses politely restored to them, in gratitude for their permitting such exhibitions'[25]

Magistrates were even condemned when they did their duty, being accused of stretching the law to suit themselves, or blamed when their efforts were frustrated by a jury.

The decision to interfere, however, depended largely on a magistrate's own opinion of the sport, and, according to the memoirs of one, some were avid fans.[26] The magistrate in George Borrow's novel, *Lavengro* (1851), confessed that although 'of course, I cannot patronize the thing very openly, yet I sometimes see a prize-fight'. Welsh Davis's backers chose a site in 1831 for his fight with Deaf Burke, but they had forgotten that the sympathetic justice they were relying on had died and that his place had been filled by a fierce opponent who warned them away.

Judges indulged their own preferences as well. Some insisted that glove fights were illegal and at least as brutal as bare knuckle affairs, while colleagues said that judges themselves, rather than the police, should be blamed for the 'recent proliferation' of glove fights, a 'recrudescence of barbarity'.[27] Some judges gave implicit consent to the practice by accepting gambling contracts and issuing judgements on boxing wagers, but, illustrating the uncertainty among the legal profession, others were not so compliant. John Morgan, who had recently fought near Pontypool for £1 a-side won a court judgement in 1866 for the sum against the holder of the stakes, but the judge refused him costs because he could not allow expenses to a man who fought for money.

The whims of juries, who were known, collectively, to go against the guidance of judges, were important, too. A member of the jury for the Crowther v Hayman trial at Bath in 1891 had decided on a not guilty verdict before proceedings had even begun and remained steadfast against the eleven others. He said it was Saturday, he had already made sure of his Sunday dinner and would sit out his companions, who decided they were guilty, all day. As a compromise the jury found the fighters guilty only of assault.

***

JUST as it was difficult to ensure secrecy, a newspaper conceded that it was hard to stop the practice, the adroit and cunning tactics which enabled contests to take place 'shows us how difficult it is to extirpate old customs – how hard to hide the sparks of nature!'[28]

Such difficulty was aggravated by several other factors, among them a shortage of police. There were only a few paid and unpaid constables in the early years of the century on the south Wales coalfield, and when police forces were set up in Wales, those at Cardiff and Newport in 1836, their numbers were thought inadequate even for the population and the level of street violence, let alone for any other demands. Even at the end of the century, Wales had only half as many policemen in proportion to Britain as a whole, while Wales' rural counties had only half as many as the South Wales towns.

As well as being understaffed, police were poorly paid – Cardiff's first police chief needed to run a pub, the *Cardiff Boat* in Womanby Street, to supplement his meagre salary - and this was reflected not only in their low numbers, but also in their poor quality. Many were as disreputable as the worst of the fighters, being drunkards, thugs and of loose morals themselves.

A leading rioter in the thick of fighting during the Newport election troubles of 1852 was found to be 'a constable from the hills', and one who refused to help a fellow officer arrest Cardiff fight figure Jack Matthews in 1863, even restraining his colleague so that Matthews could strike him, was invited to resign for a lack of moral courage. A police-constable at Merthyr in 1865 was drunk on duty, the offence aggravated by the fact that that night police were short-staffed because a number had been sent to deal with a prize fight. In Monmouthshire, after several officers had been fined for assaulting suspects, the Chief Constable 'felt the need to remind his men that they were employed as 'guardians of the peace and not prize fighters'.[29] Some police officers were, indeed, prize fighters themselves; Thomas Thorn, who had been a member of the Cardiff police force, died from injuries received while fighting on the moors in 1869.

Another obstacle to enforcing the law was that as the century progressed, interfering in prize fights became more dangerous, 'crowds could no longer be relied upon to be as compliant as in the past, and there could be ugly scenes once they had been allowed to assemble'.[30]

In England, officers and magistrates regularly risked their lives, and occasionally paid with their lives when trying to halt prize fights. A constable was kicked to death, another, found dead on a beach, had been thrown over a cliff, while others were thrown into a canal and nearly cast off a steamer into the river Thames.

Nothing as serious occurred in Wales, but police were frequently attacked and threatened. A constable who had tried to disperse spectators near Usk bridge in 1839 was knocked to the ground by three men, who then ripped apart his clothing. Five police were hurt when fight fans, 'armed with sticks and bludgeons' and with a truncheon seized from an officer, turned on them at Llantwit Fardre in 1855 demanding the release of two fighters. One of the officers suffered a serious head injury and had to retire early from the force. In 1856 at Swansea a constable was forced to release one fighter when between two and three hundred spectators threatened to 'break his head'.

Similar threats and assaults from crowds in their hundreds prevented a police inspector near Rumney in 1861 from making arrests, and forced a constable near Risca a year later to release his prisoner, one man warning him 'Let him go or I will knock your – head off'.[31]

Police were stoned by spectators at Aberdare in 1872, and at Gatewen, near Wrexham in 1888. In the latter incident onlookers had been threatened with a revolver to stand well back from the combatants, but when police arrived, the crowd of around 300 colliers turned on them, and while the fighters got well away, the colliers pelted the police with stones as they chased them along the branch railway tracks.

Small wonder, then, that police sometimes took the view that discretion was the better part of valour. They held back from intervening in a glove match in the centre of Newport in 1888, partly because they were not sure if it was illegal, but also because, a court was told, they were outnumbered and would have been attacked by the irate crowd. Likewise, officers near Chepstow in 1856 who remained on site only to take note of who was present. Magistrates at Merthyr in 1866 had no sympathy with that standpoint, however, and after a policeman declined to antagonise a two thousand strong crowd because it was too dangerous; fined him £1 for neglect of duty.

Fighters also resisted interference, but only occasionally. A watchman who attempted to order all concerned out of a field near Merthyr in 1867 was threatened with assault by one of the combatants. Although most fighters were of a smallish, wiry build and not a physical match for burly policemen wielding truncheons, some reacted aggressively. Charles Thomas, 'finding he was getting the best of his man, and probably, therefore, would carry off the stakes', attacked the police constable who tried to call a halt at the Sandfields, Swansea, while Thomas Arundel assaulted the police sergeant who arrested him for taking part in a prize fight at Henllys in Monmouthshire.[32] When Jack Northey was arrested at Cross Vane, he made it clear he would not be going willingly, telling police 'I know very well I was fighting, but I am b- if I am going with you, though'.[33]

At a prize fight on the mountain near Dowlais in 1888, the two principals disappeared on horseback in the fog. Escapes, though, were often only temporary. Police saw George Jones stripped for action and surrounded by a large gathering on Llanwonno Mountain in 1891, but although he and the others ran off, he was arrested in a pub that night. The fighters in their hurry left their clothes behind on a hill near Resolven in 1897, so there was no difficulty in identifying them. Thomas Davies and George Brown hurried away when police approached on Gilfach Mountain in 1898, only to be caught in a field soon afterwards, both pretending to pick mushrooms. Police arrested two men on a mountain in the Rhondda in 1894, and locked them in a hen house on the farm where they had been fighting while they went looking for others whom they caught further up the mountain, playing cards. Morgan Crowther took off after his fight with David Cook at Bedwellty in 1888 and hid in a cornfield, only to be arrested a few hours later in bed at his mother's house.

Police were too late to prevent a mountain battle at Merthyr in 1897, but managed to intercept two carts being driven away from the spot, and found Redmond Coleman lying in the bottom of one, while his opponent was in the other.

A newspaper man could hardly believe it when spectators at a Rhondda prize fight, and even the seconds carrying the pugilists' clothes, joined in the police chase to try to capture the fighters. He asked 'Is not this very much like the pack of wolves who promptly set upon a wounded companion?'[34] But, far from aiding the police, this was more likely an attempt to help the fighters lose themselves in the middle of a fleeing crowd.

***

DESPITE dire warnings, those involved in prize fights had little to fear about being brought before the court.

There was a grudging admiration in the Press for fighters for their courage and perseverance, and for being prepared to stand up and use their fists fairly. The activity was regarded more favourably than brawling in the street, 'where unfair advantage was often taken in a cowardly attack of one man upon another'[35]

There was contempt for everyone else, though. The fighters' seconds, referees, timekeepers and others who aided and abetted were considered more culpable because they had fewer or worse reasons to be present, and they encouraged others to violence while they themselves kept aloof and had time to think about what they were doing.

Spectators, for their part, were despised for 'gloating over the blood, and urging the combatants on with fearful oaths to inflict blows from the smallest of which they would themselves 'recoil in terror'.[36]

The reputation of spectators could not have been enhanced when a match on Wimbledon Common in 1803 was called off. Instead, 'for amusement' they cut down the remains of a notorious highwayman, 'many of them observing he was an old acquaintance', sent to the gallows several years previously.[37] He was Louis Jeremiah Abershawe, better known as Jerry Abershawe, who was hanged and his body afterwards set on a gallows, the last hanged highwayman's body to be so displayed. The report went on: 'His bones were distributed and contended for with the utmost eagerness. Those who obtained his fingers, said they would make tobacco stoppers of them'.

Although the different actors were accorded different levels of blame, in court they were usually treated equally leniently. Most cases were dealt with in police court (later known as magistrates' court) as breaches of the peace, when the usual punishment was to be bound over, although a fine of approximately one week's wages might be imposed instead of, or in addition to, a binding over.

Relatively light fines suggested recognition of the sport as 'a manly and British practice'.[38] A possible fine would have been no deterrent to one of the combatants near Abergavenny in 1898 who told the court he wished the police had held back a little longer, as he thought he should have beaten his man, and would have been able to pay a good fine.

Gaol sentences were handed down occasionally, but mainly only after an outcry over leniency, which was feared to encourage the sport, or when it was felt that prize fighting was on the increase. David Thomas and Thomas Davies were given two months with hard labour at Maesteg in 1884, the court telling them that an example had to be made of them so that fights 'should be put down'. Morgan Crowther and David Cook, as well as two seconds, the time keeper and the stakeholder were all gaoled for one month after a prize fight near Bedwellty Church in 1888, when it was reported that prize fighting had been frequent in the district.

Imprisonment, usually of up to a month, could be expected, however, if defendants failed to pay fines, and a prison sentence might also be imposed when police were assaulted. Two colliers were gaoled for eight months and six months respectively for attacking a police constable with a boot and a stick after he broke up a contest at Gelligaer in 1867.

Eleven spectators at Abersychan were bound over in 1856, but that same year, twenty seven Chepstow men, charged with aiding and abetting by being at the scene, saw their cases dismissed after the magistrates stated, illogically, that there was no direct proof that they knew a prize fight was due to take place.

The *R. v Coney* ruling did not carry much weight in Wales, as spectators continued to be bound over, six for being present at a fight near Aberdare two years later, and eight after a set-to near Bedwellty in 1888.

Publicans found it lucrative to supply alcohol to fight parties, which is why they tended to give free board and lodging to a man in training in return for the custom he brought to the establishment. But fights were most likely to take place outside permitted hours of sale of alcohol so, facing a fine if police turned up, the relationship was a mixed blessing. This proved the case for three landlords at Llantwit Vardre who allowed drinking during the early hours of Sunday morning in 1870, while seventy-five men spotted inside the *Pleasant View Inn*, Aberdare Hill, at 5.30 in the morning in 1881 cost the landlord dearly.

Fines were also imposed on publicans who permitted pugilism on their premises, among those to suffer being the landlords of the *Sunderland Bridge*, Cardiff, in 1853, the *Railway Inn*, Abersychan, who cleared away furniture in the bar to allow space for fights in 1857, and the *King's Arms*, Blaenavon, in 1866. In 1869, the landlord of the *Mason's Arms*, High Street, Swansea, was fined with the alternative of gaol for allowing disorderly conduct – 'cursing, swearing and challenging to fight for money' - on his premises.[39]

Publicans also faced losing their livelihood; Swansea magistrates refused in 1855 to renew the licence of the *Golden Lion*, Devatty-street, after two pugilists had taken a joint benefit there. But landlords had little choice, apparently, as a North Wales newspaper carried a claim in 1872 that publicans were being forced to let their rooms for boxing to help pay the rates.

***

WHERE fatalities were concerned, a 'Welchman' due to fight for £100 a-side in London in 1790, was among those warned by the courts that if men came to blows immediately after angry words, a death would lead to a charge of manslaughter, whereas two men fighting for money at a distant given time, after, for example a night had elapsed, in a ring would be liable for murder.

But as the nineteenth century progressed, courts increasingly softened their stance to state that a fighter in such a case must be held guilty of manslaughter.

After ring deaths, calls from opponents for severe punishment, such as hanging, long gaol sentences or transportation, went unanswered, and threats from judges carrying the same sentiments proved hollow. Less than a month after warning of transportation in 1824, the emptiness of the words was exposed when the same judge sentenced a surviving fighter to just one month's imprisonment.

Nobody was convicted of murder, as judges and juries appeared at pains to avoid imposing its mandatory penalty, preferring to interpret the evidence as to merit, at most, a manslaughter verdict. No prize-fighter was transported. In 1794, Thomas Peak was sentenced to be burned on the hand and gaoled for one month at Wrexham, and, also in north Wales, Thomas Pugh was gaoled for 12 months in 1861, but such punishments were rare.

This study identified 30 Welsh ring deaths during the nineteenth century, and in 13 instances the surviving fighter was not convicted.

The fortunate flock comprised: John Robinson, (v Unknown, north Wales, 1812), Thomas Watkins (v Richard Davies, Presteigne, Radnorshire, 1818), Thomas Zacharias (v M. Williams, Penderyn, Breconshire, 1827), Thomas Price (v Richard Humphreys, Llanbadarn Fynydd, Radnorshire, 1829), Samuel Vaughan (v ? Williams, Hay. 1833). Philip Nicholas (v Thomas Thomas, Llandeilo, Monmouthshire, 1836), John Davies (v Walter Morgan, Quaker's Yard (1857), John Richards (v Roger Williams (Sirhowy,1859), William Davies (v Peter Mitchell, New Tredegar, 1869). Thomas Edwards (v David Rees, Aberdare (!894), Richard Ambrose (v Thomas Davies, Swansea (1896), Ivor Thomas (v Sam Mandry, Tonypandy, 1897), Edward Craddock (v Thomas Evans, Merthyr 1897).

Another 16 convicted of manslaughter received punishment ranging from a binding over order to 12 months gaol, three months (5) and one month (3), the most common sentences. Bindings over: Henry Lewis (v Arthur Vaughan, Mountain Ash. 1895). One day's gaol: Jenkin Morgan (v Rees Hopkin, Tondu 1846). Fortnight: William Price (v Thomas Evans, Aberstryth, 1859). One month: Jones (v Enoch Davies, London, 1819), Edward Lewis (v David Thomas, Aberstryth, 1858), Thomas Beynon (v Rowland Thomas, Merthyr, 1868). Two months: Edward Turner (v John Curtis, London, 1816), William Amesbury (v John Davies, Dowlais, 1891). Three months: John Williams (v Isaac Latcham, Abertillery, 1873), Walter Roberts (v Henry Lewis, Newport, 1874), Cornelius Collins (v John Hopkins, Mountain Ash, 1890), Lewis Price (v Trevor Roberts, Penrhiwceiber, 1890), John Thomas (v Edward Collard, Pontypridd, 1897). Eight months: William Davies (v Frederick Stephens, Pontypridd, 1888). Nine months: Evan Evans (v John Jenkin James, Porth, 1886). Twelve months: Thomas Pugh (v David

Richards, Cefn Mawr, 1861).[40] What happened to the remaining surviving fighter, reported as being killed 'at Wrexham, June, 1813', is unknown.

Some coroners and their juries acknowledged the afore-mentioned distinction and returned murder verdicts accordingly, but, a more sympathetic approach prevailed before a judge and jury, even though there often seemed little mitigating evidence. However, what might have influenced the judge in 1861 into handing out a twelve-month sentence was the fact that Pugh and his victim Richards had been bound over twice for fighting each other in previous months. An even more aggravating feature earned William Davies only an eight months term in 1888; he had killed Frederick Stephens, of Pontypridd, by kicking him several times in his private parts.

Usually, the verdict and any sentence appeared to depend on the luck of the draw, on whether the judge and jury were for or against prize fights. Both frequently appeared determined even to avoid a conviction for manslaughter when the evidence warranted it.

After the death of David Rees at Aberdare in 1894, the inquest jury returned a verdict of manslaughter, believing the match to have been a prize fight, but their counterparts at the Glamorgan Assizes decided it was a sparring match for points and cleared those involved. The grand jury at Swansea Assizes in 1896 threw out the bill for manslaughter against Richard Ambrose and eight others concerned in the glove contest at Swansea in which Thomas Davies died. The judge said the fight was 'conducted in complete fairness', 'the parties were friendly', 'there was no evidence of any unlawful act', and 'he was calling attention to those cases where there were grave doubts as to whether those cases should be sent for trial.'[41]

The assize judge thought the fight that led to the death of Sam Mandry/Mainwearing at Tonypandy in 1897 was for money and therefore illegal, but he said the key point was whether death was caused by a blow or from Mandry's own frailty and injury received by falling through the weakness of his knee. The jury after a few seconds and without leaving the box, returned a verdict of not guilty.

Sometimes juries declined to convict of manslaughter, despite being instructed to do so by the judge, probably because, as has been suggested, like poachers and smugglers, boxers 'were not perceived as criminals by customary views'.[42] At Brecon Assizes in 1859, the jury cleared John Richards of manslaughter following the death of Roger Williams in their fight near Dukestown, Sirhowy, prompting the judge, unimpressed, to inform them: 'I am thankful that it is your verdict and not mine'.[43]

Surviving boxers were mostly treated more mercifully than persons who killed in a street brawl where manslaughter and serious injury in Wales commonly earned a six or twelve-months gaol sentence.

This tendency was confirmed by a Welsh coroner. He was replying to criticism that remarks he had made at the inquest on Edward Augustus Collard the previous month had made light of the tragedy. He said he had committed more than thirty persons for trial on charges of manslaughter in connection with similar fights, the majority having been acquitted, and when there was a conviction the punishment was 'very slight, often merely nominal'. In cases where death had been shown to be due to kicking or stabbing, the sentences on conviction had been 'severe, often extending to a long term of penal servitude'.[44]

The issue was brought into sharp focus when the surviving fighter, John Thomas, went to trial. A newspaper positioned side by side reports of cases from the same day under the same judge at Glamorgan assizes. One stated that two men were given seven year's gaol for malicious wounding during a labour dispute at Cardiff docks, a sentence which 'created a sensation in court', and the other that Thomas received three months for the manslaughter of Collard, a collier, in a prize fight.[45]

The surviving fighter involved in a ring death usually included in his defence an excuse of long-standing which was difficult, if not impossible, to disprove. He claimed to have been a reluctant participant who had been provoked by his now dead opponent.

As early as 1811, this tactic of claiming 'the *deceased* was to blame' was so widespread that it was stated that the 'benefit of boxing' was thought likely to become as accepted in law as the 'benefit of clergy'.[46] The benefit of clergy was originally a provision by which clergymen could claim that they were outside the jurisdiction of the secular courts and be tried instead in an ecclesiastical court under canon law. It evolved into a legal fiction, where a basic level of literacy was often enough for someone to be considered a clergyman for this purpose and be treated more leniently.

Edward Turner told the court in 1816 his 'aversion to prize fighting was great', he had entered the ring with the greatest reluctance, 'but was induced by the assaults and pursuits, with most unremitting vigilance, of the partisans of Curtis'.[47]

Although the legal fiction was abolished in 1827, the defence continued to be forwarded (successfully) by most Welsh fighters in this predicament in the hope of a light sentence. Aiders and abettors usually received the same, but sometimes heavier, punishment after a fatality, with seconds seen as failing in a duty to intervene. An extreme example came at an Old Bailey trial in 1829 when two seconds were transported for life while the surviving fighter was gaoled for 12 months. In 1819, Jones was given one month's imprisonment for killing fellow Welshman Enoch Davies, while the seconds for the fighters received two months.

A judge in 1844 told an 'astonished' spectator at a fatal prize fight that he was liable to be indicted for manslaughter. But as time wore on, it was regarded as a waste of time charging large numbers of those present.

Edward Turner

At the inquest into the fatal fight on Llanwonno mountain in 1895, the coroner said he would not send for trial a great number of those present as it almost brought ridicule on the case and it would be laughed out of court. He had seen that done. There would not be the same difficulty in getting a conviction if only men who were clearly implicated and were undoubtedly taking an active part were sent for trial. That would act as a deterrent.

Earlier confidence that binding over orders would 'no doubt, soon put an end to the demoralising practice' of prize fighting, proved misplaced, and over the years, attitudes hardened, with increasing calls for more severe punishment, such as 'the tread wheel for a few months', or the lash, 'so happily banished from the army'.

The authorities remained tolerant, however.

---

[1] Law Times, 28 April 1860, cited in Bell's Life, 20 May 1860

2 Sharon Howard (unpublished Ph.D. thesis, University of Wales, Aberystwyth, 2003) Crime, Communities and Authority in Early Modern Wales: Denbighshire, 1660-1730, pp. 167-173
3 Bristol Mercury, 15 October 1827
4 Merthyr Telegraph, 9 August 1872
5 Merthyr Telegraph, 7 June 1862.
6 Merthyr Express, 4 September 1915.
7 Monmouthshire Merlin, 1 May 1841.
8 Margaret. Gregory, A Policeman's Lot: The Nature and Dynamics of the Monmouthshire Constabulary 1857 – 1914 (unpublished PhD thesis: Cardiff University, 2009), p. 38. Cambrian, 19 April 1878. Western Mail, 13 November 1886.
9 Western Mail, 7 October 1884; 27 December 1887, 23 Oct 1888. South Wales Echo, 4 March 1886.
10 Monmouthshire Merlin, 21 July 1855
11 Bell's Life, 10 August 1828
12 South Wales Echo, 1 September 1896.
13 Bristol Mercury, 21 June 1888.
14 Western Mail, 17 Aug 1895.
15 Bell's Life, 22 January 1860.
16 Merthyr Telegraph, 24 July 1874.
17 Evening Express, 17 September 1900. Rhondda Leader, 22 September 1900
18 Evening Express, 1 February 1899.
19 Cambrian, 26 September 1829. Bell's Life, 19 May 1833.
20 Martin J. Weiner, *Men of Blood: Violence, Manliness, and Criminal Justice in Victorian England* (Cambridge, Cambridge University Press, 2004), pp. 47,48.
21 Times, 4 July 1834;21 April 1860. Morning Post, 7 August 1834
22 Lloyd's Weekly, 17 November 1889. Reynolds News, 17 November 1889.
23 South Wales Star, 12 February 1892.
24 Western Mail, 7 Sept 1874.
25 New Monthly Magazine, cited in Monmouthshire Merlin, 12 April 1834.
26 Hawkins, The Reminiscences of Sir Henry Hawkins (Baron Brampton), pp. 23-25, cited in Boddy, pp. 76.77. *Boxing, a cultural history* (London, Reaktion Books, 2008).
27 South Wales Daily News, 25 January 1895.
28 Cardiff & Merthyr Guardian, 30 November 1872
29 Gregory, *A Policeman's Lot*, p. 132
30 Dennis Brailsford, Bareknuckles: A Social History of Prize-Fighting (Cambridge, Lutterworth Press, 1988), p. 100.
31 Cardiff and Merthyr Guardian, 8 June 1861; Monmouthshire Merlin, 8 June 1861; 11 October 1862.
32 Bristol Mercury, 4 April 1868. Western Mail, 21 September 1886.
33 Western Mail, 6 June 1895
34 South Wales Daily News, 5 May 1891.
35 Wrexham Weekly Advertiser, 8 April 1871
36 Glasgow Herald, 20 April 1860.
37 Morning Post, 19 January 1803.
38 Ruti Ungar, The Boxing Discourse in Late Georgian England, 1780-1820: A Study in Civic Humanism, Gender, Class and Race. Pugilism and the legal system.
39 Cambrian, 19 February 1869.
40 Some publications have recorded Charles Hall as having been involved in a prize fight at Connah's Quay, Flintshire, in 1825 which resulted in the death of Thomas Orford. However,

the death, reported fully in the *Chester Chronicle*, 18 March 1825. followed an argument which turned quickly into a street brawl.
[41] Evening Express, 23 June 1896.
[42] Ungar, The Boxing Discourse.
[43] Welshman, 5 August 1859
[44] Barry Herald, 4 June 1897.
[45] Evening Express, 6 July 1897
[46] Jackson's Oxford Journal, 26 October 1811. .
[47] Times, 2 November, 12 November 1816

2
Prize fighters

Ben Lloyd fled from the Rhondda to South Africa to avoid a court appearance after a fight. But his was an extreme reaction. Prize fighters were rarely discouraged by the consequences of being caught. Most were repeat offenders, who treated legal punishment as a minor occupational hazard.

Redmond Coleman, after being handed a month's hard labour at Merthyr, 'accepted the sentence coolly, exclaiming as he left the court, 'Another holiday again'.[1] Morgan Crowther, while waiting for the court outcome after a contest, fought three times, also once while waiting to be punished for another battle. Fighters continued to ply their trade even after being involved in ring deaths. Edward Turner returned to action straight after his release from prison, and Englishman Owen Swift took part in three fatalities before plying his trade in France.

These men were more concerned with how their fight could go ahead and with the financial rewards from betting and side stakes than with any penalties which the courts could impose. They had a good chance of going about their business undisturbed, and if they were apprehended, the legal sanctions were comparatively lenient - they were used to far more severe repercussions arising from their behaviour outside the ring.

George Borrow, author of *Wild Wales*, the account of his tour of the country in the middle of the century, classed fighters as 'men of renown

41

amidst hundreds of people with no renown at all, who gaze upon them with timid wonder'.[2]

Their fistic ability in the ring was admired, huge numbers flocked to watch them in action and supporters showed their appreciation with gold and silver baubles. Tom Sayers received several thousand pounds from subscriptions from all parts of Great Britain, including a purse of gold in Cardiff after his fight with Heenan in 1860, Bill Benjamin was given a silver cup after a visit to Swansea, and Morgan Crowther was presented with a gold scarf-pin at Cadoxton in appreciation of his performance in a fight in London. Patsy Reardon's supporters gave him a belt to commemorate a performance, as did the admirers of Dan Thomas who presented him with a belt 'of much value' after his fight with Nolan in 1862.

Sadly, many did not confine their talents to the ring, and they would be given a wide berth on the streets, having proved to be just as violent outside the ropes. The public were wise to keep their distance. Some of Merthyr's bare knuckle fighters were 'legendary', but, and there were many more like them throughout the country, 'They were also vicious criminals'.[3] Coleman, for example, was reputed to need only to stand silently by a bridge at Merthyr, holding out his hand for money to be placed in it, donors obviously fearing what might happen if they did not oblige.

If they did not know about these men from personal experience, then the public received plenty of warning in the Press. It has been claimed that newspapers in this period invariably 'portrayed the virtues' of sports stars, not the 'private reality'.[4] But prize fighters' indiscretions were reported fully, with local publications highlighting their ring trade in court reports as a further way of discrediting them.

Many were identified as prize fighters only in court reports which had no connection with the ring. Swansea man Richard Ambrose complained that whenever he was in court he was always advertised as being a pugilist. 'The local newspaper would put him at the top of a contents bill as if he was the biggest thief or blackguard in the county', he grumbled.[5]

British pugilists were hanged, transported or gaoled for murder, highway robbery and bodysnatching, and while no Welshman received the ultimate punishment, several were lucky to escape the hangman.

William Edwards, better known as 'Will Gwas y Doctor', was one, having been alleged by a local magistrate to have been a ringleader in the 1831 Merthyr Riots. Another, William Thomas, known as 'Crib' 'through his skill and daring as a boxer', was prominent in a racist killing in the 'Little Ireland' Greenhill area of Swansea in 1842. Irishman John Bowling was struck on the forehead with a hatchet, kicked and beaten, stabbed in the neck and had a lighted candle pushed into a nostril to extinguish it. The judge called it as bad a case of murder as he could conceive, but the jury decided it was manslaughter, for which the gang of six received the maximum punishment for that offence, transportation for life. London-based habitual thief John Lewis, usually referred to as 'the well-known pugilist' and 'the Welch champion', was also transported, in his case for a shorter term, either side of which in the second quarter of the century he had spells in prison.

Richard Crowther, Morgan Crowther's elder brother and also a prize fighter, was gaoled for 15 years, later reduced to 12, for manslaughter. Crowther had been refused beer at the *White Hart Inn*, Pentwynmawr, and a disturbance which followed ended with his stabbing a man in the eye.

John Wilde was suspected of beating to death a woman in the rough 'China' area of Merthyr Tydfil in 1849. The inquest on the woman, known as 'Buffalo', had to determine whether she died from cholera or from being beaten up by Wilde when she returned home drunk, and the jury decided on cholera. John Judson, from Wrexham, a member of a gang of poachers who shot a gamekeeper, was gaoled for three years in 1894. Jack Grant (otherwise known as Henry Williams), who had been beaten over 64 rounds in 1852 by Tom Sayers), and a fellow burglar tried to escape from Cardigan gaol in 1860. They overpowered the turnkey, but were thwarted by the governor, armed with a sword, and his wife, who carried a loaded revolver. Grant and his accomplice were acquitted of attempted murder but were gaoled for four years for burglary.

Jack Northey was another who might easily have found himself at the end of a rope; as it was, the Rhondda fighter served substantial gaol time for highway robbery with violence, indecent assault and malicious wounding as well as shorter terms for theft.

Among the everyday offences, beating up their wives and other women was a favourite pastime for some pugilists.

Coleman was in court three times in one year for attacking women at Merthyr, including once after he threw one into a canal overflow, while another victim was his own mother. When he was gaoled for a month for assaulting one woman, the court warned him that the sentence 'would have been very much more' if she had had a good character.[6]

After being found asleep on the last train from Cardiff in 1886, William Jones knocked the Brynmawr station master's wife down (he also kicked and punched the station master, the ticket collector and a porter), and two women tried to jump off the moving train to get away from him. At Newport in 1876, Richard Glancy assaulted a man who found Glancy beating his mother in the street. Edward Basham, father of future Newport ring hero

Johnny Basham, served gaol terms for assaulting his wife, Ellen, and police officers, and received lesser sentences for assaulting other women. Felix Scott appeared in court more than once for assaulting his wife and also served three months in gaol for ill-treating his two young daughters.

Pub employees were also considered fair game. In one violent spree in 1895, John Henry Harris attacked the landlord of the *Hare and Greyhound*, in Newport's High Street, and also mine host of the neighbouring *Lord Raglan*, then a police officer on the way to the police station, and at the police station again struck the landlord of the *Lord Raglan*.

In 1891, Ted Pritchard and another man were sentenced to a month's gaol for what was described as a 'cowardly' assault on a pub doorman, Pritchard first striking him and then holding him while his companion hit him. He appealed unsuccessfully and began his sentence the following January, after which a newspaper diplomatically stated 'Ted Pritchard, after a customary rest, is again willing to meet any aspirant to the title'.[7]

Assaults on the police were 'a fact of life' on the south Wales coalfield in the second half of the century.[8] Fighters were among the worst offenders.

Daniel Desmond knocked one officer out with a stick and hit another with a brick at Abersychan, Ben Lloyd launched an attack at Pontypridd, while John Henry Knight was an habitual offender in the Tredegar area with five strikes on his record.

Police were perennial targets also in other parts of the country. New police in the village of Cefn Coed in the 19th century would have to fight 'the local idlers' – they called it his first milling – to test his mettle.[9] It was also a tradition among the tough men of late nineteenth century Newport to provoke policemen into a beating. Police told the local court in 1894 that

'Old hands in the town were in the habit of giving new officers what they called an 'invitation', and then giving them a thrashing'.[10]

In Cardiff, fight figure Jack Matthews had a string of convictions over three decades for assaulting and threatening officers, twice with a sword and once also with a pistol. Police were said to be terrified of him. Matthews wasn't particular, though, he also attacked women, fellow pub landlords, journalists who wrote unflatteringly about him, his own solicitor, and even a crippled boy. John O'Brien, after pouncing on two strangers in a Cardiff street, punched and kicked two policemen who arrested him.[11] Felix Scott, was gaoled for 18 months in 1888 for biting off part of a policeman's ear.

For these men, well-used to gaol for their out-of-the-ring activities, fines or binding over orders for taking part in prize fights was nothing to lose sleep over.

Apart from targeting 'civilians', prize fighters attacked each other outside the ring as well. An argument in a London pub in 1825 started by Edward Savage led to his punching a fellow pugilist, whereupon a space was cleared, both stripped for action and a proper fight took place for thirteen rounds, during which Savage, swinging wildly, flattened a spectator with one punch. Patsy Reardon and fellow prize fighter Thomas Scannell were fighting in a Cardiff beerhouse in 1858 and when police arrived they stopped punching each other and turned on the law officers. Four years later, Reardon was involved in fights among boxers in a London pub. He was disorderly in the bar and was struck by the landlord, a boxer, whereupon another publican, also a boxer, attacked the first landlord with a broken glass.

David St. John was in London in 1894 issuing challenges, and when the Australian fighter Frank Slavin dismissed him as an unknown they began to argue. Slavin made a move towards him, but St. John landed a right-hander on the head, sending Slavin sprawling upon the floor.

Bill Samuel had more reported set-tos with fellow pugilists in Swansea's High Street than in the ring itself, clashing with Thomas Pearson, Bob Dunbar, and with Patsy Perkins.

Shamus Warner and Tom Hooligan had a swift series of brawls in 1895, first in a pub in Wind Street, Swansea, then out in the street, and again two nights later in the same street. The local newspaper suggested that if they were 'to settle their differences with the gloves they could do it properly, and by charging for admission get something for their trouble'.[12]

But, despite street skirmishes, pugilists generally got on well with each other outside the ring. They formed a close community; although there were hundreds of fighters, actual ring officials for glove contests seem to have been few. The same men, some active boxers, tended to feature as seconds, referees, timekeepers and promoters, opponents one month, then each other's seconds soon after. O'Brien and Shoni Engineer fought near Cardiff, but days later, O'Brien seconded Engineer against Enoch Morrison at Pontypridd. David St. John and Tom James fought each other twice, and then acted as seconds for Sam (Butcher) Thomas.

Mutual support manifested itself in regular benefit events for fellow fighters, particularly useful in times of special need, such as for Turner and Richard Ambrose for help with their legal expenses over their ring death trials, and to raise money for a sick O'Brien's medical expenses, while a benefit was held to pay for Enoch Morrison's funeral.

Occasionally, these hard men bit off more than they could chew. Richard James gave the landlord of the *Beaufort Arms*, Aberaman, two black eyes, but he himself was nearly throttled in return. He appeared in court in 1866 with a deep red mark around his neck, his victim being a former wrestler. Thomas Maroney emerged from a Rhondda pub in 1882 to find a fellow Irishman fighting a Welshman in the middle of a large crowd. Maroney immediately stripped to the waist and offered to fight anybody, whereupon eight men rushed from the lines and kicked and punched him severely.

John Judson got the better of a navvy in a pub fight in Wrexham in 1887 and then again when the man attacked him near his home, only for the navvy to pull out a knife and stab him eight times in the breast and back. William Hooligan was also stabbed after he threw a lump of sand and hit a man in the face 'for fun,' in Swansea in 1895, the man not appreciating the joke. During a dispute over cheating in a game of dominoes that same year, Jack Northey threatened to 'polish off' both his accusers if they would step outside the Rhondda pub, but, during the ensuing fight, Northey fell to the ground and was kicked several times in the face.

London-based John Lewis tried to break up a fight in 1832 between his wife and a woman neighbour and was stabbed in the head and body by the neighbour for his trouble. The next year he bit and punched the police officer taking him from court to gaol, so the officer, telling his colleagues to stand back, said to Lewis

> Jack you are a cowardly scoundrel, and as you have often said you could lick me, I'll see who is the best man. He then doffed his coat, and pitching into the champion right and left, gave him such a thrashing that the said champion was compelled to cry 'Enough'.[13]

And pugilists could find their reputations working against them when they themselves were the injured party. Henry Jones was described by defence counsel of a man who fired a shotgun to deter him at Swansea but hit him 'accidentally' as 'a great hulking bully' and the grand jury at

Glamorgan Assizes in 1897 agreed, throwing the case out. Similarly, Billy Morgan was shot in 1904 by a Swansea club steward when he caused a disturbance and refused to leave the premises from which he had been banned. The court heard that everybody in the Swansea club was afraid of seasoned fighter Morgan because of his violent character, and the grand jury ignored the bill against the steward.

Some fighters were, however, approachable outside the ring, and were praised for their geniality and generosity; Londoner John Knifton more than once gave money to the Merthyr Tydfil Orpheus Society, while others (admittedly some black sheep among them) flocked to take part in the Nazareth House charity evenings in Cardiff, and also for the Barry Nursing Association and Accident Hospital.

One renowned fighter kept order against an armed mob when an important foot race was staged at Llantrisant in 1843. The followers of one runner turned up brandishing 'bludgeons' and indicating they were ready to use them, but as the local newspaper reported, 'that great champion of Wales, as a prize-fighter, Shony Skibbor y Fawr,' warned them to behave themselves, otherwise they would 'feel the weight of his fists. They one and all were struck with terror, and dropt them immediately'.[14] Wisely, for the noted pugilist was blessed with 'a magnificent physique' and had used his giant's strength like a giant. He was a native of Merthyr, and a brass-fitter by trade'.[15]

***

CRIMES were usually drink-fuelled. Wales had a reputation for serious drunkenness throughout the century, and prize fighters played their part in maintaining that perception. But they were by no means the only or worst violent drunks in the community; they stood out because their ring exploits made them celebrities. When Redmond Coleman received his 38th conviction for drunken behaviour (still only his mid-twenties) the *Merthyr Times* commented that 'it was 'not a large number, as numbers go nowadays'.[16]

A judge in Cardiff in 1805 remarked that the 'rage for pugilism', particularly in the south of the country, was due to drinking to excess, 'a most prevalent impulse of the Welsh'.[17] And these men were among the hard drinkers who were the archetypal criminals of late nineteenth century Wales. The late 1860s until the early 1880s were 'the high-water mark for drunkenness in Wales'; in 1871; it was estimated that three-quarters of crime was caused by alcohol abuse.[18] Another judge in 1897 at Glamorgan Assizes, where a ring fatality was to be tried, commented: 'Drink, of course, in many of these cases, as in other districts, was, to a large extent, the cause of the crime'.[19]

Pugilists ticked most of the boxes for alcohol-inspired violence, being based in industrial and urban areas, particularly the coalfields, which were considered much worse for drunkenness than their rural counterparts and were from the unskilled working class where the problem was considered greatest. They had the same lack of access to good drinking water as most other people; in these circumstances, a sterilised drink such as beer, the alcohol of choice for fighters in Wales, was a popular, perhaps necessary, alternative throughout the community.

Beer was believed to be beneficial to fighters; 'old home-brewed beer is particularly recommended, drawn from the cask and not bottled', which was far better than the 'half-fermented, adulterated *wash* found in public houses'.[20]

Public houses could sell all types of alcohol – beer, wine, spirits – but beer houses sold only that beverage. The intention of the *Beerhouse Act* 1830 was to increase competition between brewers and it resulted in the opening of hundreds of new beer houses, public houses and breweries throughout the country. It was hoped that by increasing competition in the brewing and sale of beer, and thus lowering its price, the population might be weaned off more alcoholic drinks such as gin, which had previously been the choice of the lower classes

Spirits, beer and wine all poured down the throat of Newport's Bill Charles. Before one of his fights, Charles's friends were worried that 'he had made too free with the exhilarating drops......It is said...that on the morning of the fight he drank two quarts of strong beer, and sundry glasses of brandy and water and negus'.[21] The last-named was a drink made of wine, most commonly port, mixed with hot water, spiced and sugared. Another serious imbiber was one of Dan Thomas' opponents who could be kept sober before their 1862 clash only by being handcuffed and chained to his trainer at night.

Spirits were used regularly to energise fading fighters, even, for example, in one of the regular prize fights among pupils at Eton, a contest which ended in a death in 1825. Both boys were constantly plied with brandy to revive them, the deceased having consumed more than half a pint.

Spirits were the chief tipples as well outside the ring for Welsh fighters in the London area, gin proving to be Edward Turner's downfall, as a preview of one of his fights explained 'his application to the *daffy* bottle has been so frequent, as almost entirely to undermine his constitution'.[22] Daffy's Elixir was a patent medicine invented by a clergyman, Thomas Daffy, in the mid-17th century, and made largely from alcohol. One of the most common forms of alcohol used was gin; hence the slang name 'daffy's' for gin. An elegy about Turner stated that

The best blue ruin

Was his undoing.
....
With full proof gin
He filled his skin,[23]

Beer was the favourite beverage of Wales-based fighters, and each area of the country boasted pugilists as champion drinkers. At Merthyr he was Coleman, while just as notorious were Desmond (Pontypool), Morgan (Swansea), Matthews and Sam Gulliver (Cardiff), Richard Evans and Northey (Rhondda Valley), Judson (Wrexham), and Bob Dunbar (Newport).

They appeared so often in court that newspapers treated them as celebrities, headlining reports with 'AN OLD ACQAINTANCE', or '(name of fighter) AGAIN!

Billy Morgan continued to be a regular in court on drink and violence charges at the turn of the twentieth century, clocking up more than fifty visits and a few prison terms. Morgan made his 53rd court appearance in 1914 for being drunk and disorderly in Swansea.[24]

The sequence was interrupted by (impressive) army service in the First World War, but back in civvy street, Morgan reverted to his old ways. In 1917 he was gaoled for a total of four months for assaulting two tram employees and a milk seller, and fined, with the alternative of 14 days gaol for being drunk and disorderly and for being drunk in charge of a child.[25]

Morgan 'struck the conductor a very severe blow on the cheek' and when the tram inspector intervened swung at his head with a spade, catching him on the shoulder. Morgan asked the street trader for milk for his little girl; this was provided and when Morgan was asked for one penny for the milk, he struck the milkman across the face with a spade. Twice wounded in the trenches, Morgan told the court he had been 'overcome by the sun'.

Referring to his wounds he said: 'I was not altogether in my senses before, but this has made me worse'.

Like Morgan, Coleman renewed his acquaintance with the courts once free of army discipline. His court appearances were treated in headlines like cricket scores, the milestone, although far from the final score, being '100, NOT OUT'.[26] He made his 131st appearance in 1923.[27]

A practical joke played on Coleman enabled him to get off charges of drunkenness and breaking a pub's windows. Coleman, 'blind drunk', staggered into the *Parrot Inn*, Merthyr, and stretched out on a table, where he was laid out fast asleep in a mock wake by other customers. Pillows were placed under his head and feet, a winding sheet thrown over his body and lighted candles placed near his head. The magistrate said in view of the severe prank and the landlady not being present to supervise, Coleman would be discharged.[28]

When a drunk and disorderly charge was read out against Daniel Desmond, a magistrates' clerk asked whether it was '*the* Daniel'; the police replied that it was '*the* Daniel, alluding to the notoriety that attached to defendant's name from the many times he had been convicted for drunken and disorderly conduct'.[29]

Old foe Thomas Fletcher remembered Desmond admiringly. 'Pontypool was a very rough shop in them days and Daniel Desmond was the roughest of the rough', he said. Desmond was 'the terror of the neighbourhood' whose 'favourite trick was to enter a public house and drink up the beer from the customers' pints, and such was his reputation that hardly anyone dared oppose him'.[30]

Former prize fighter George Rowlands, better known as Gipsy George, amassed sentences of hard labour for drink-related offences for twenty years all over south Wales and once was even bribed to leave the town of Brecon.

Cardiff man John O'Brien, once the best in Britain, was out of condition frequently due to heavy drinking. He was once drunk in court and had to be removed forcibly and was in an even worse condition for a big fight in London which proved to be his last in the ring. And O'Brien had been drinking before he gate-crashed a wrestling match at the Colonial Hall, Cardiff, demanding to take part. He wanted to fight or wrestle either Greek George or his opponent, 'a Scottish giant called Blair'. The local reporter commented 'The Greek is quite prepared to wrestle O'Brien, and the latter would stand about as much chance as I would', adding, however, 'In a fight the result might be different'.[31]

Other old time fighters who appeared in court in the new century for unruly behaviour included Morgan Crowther, in 1901 for assaulting the police and using obscene language and in 1903 for assaulting police after being ejected from a Cardiff hotel, and in the same year Ambrose for fighting in the street, and months later for resisting the police, George 'Punch' Jones for being drunk in charge of two young children. In 1906, Sam Gulliver, who, with 12 previous convictions, six for assault, was gaoled for six weeks for a 'cowardly' attack on a man who had given evidence in a poaching case against friends of Gulliver, and John Owen (Aberaman), was gaoled for two months the following year for beating up his former landlady. Dai 'Buller' Rees, of Cwmavon, was fined at Aberavon in 1913 for intimidating a collier who refused to go on strike. Rees punched the man several times in the face and another man dragged the semi-conscious victim off the train by his feet.

Alcohol not only cut short ring careers, but it was also a contributor to an early death for some Welsh exponents, following in the tradition of Turner and Charles, who succumbed in their thirties, the latter said to be 'a victim, in the prime of life, to those habits of intemperance in which pugilists too frequently indulge'.[32]

William James, a Gelligaer miner, was drunk in a boxing match in 1833, swayed out of the way of a punch and fell on some wood, a sharp stake entering just below his left eye and into his brain, killing him. Aaron Jones died in the USA aged 38, claiming to have been poisoned, but the signs pointed to his heavy drinking. The inquest on Thomas Davies in 1896 heard that he was addicted to drinking which could possibly cause his organs to be more easily ruptured. Sam Mandry / Mainwearing had been drinking heavily for a fortnight before his ring death in 1897 and on the day of the fight he rode from the Rhondda to Llandaff on his bicycle to sweat the beer out of him.

Drink led to the death in 1892 of 23 year old William Morgan, from Ferndale, who had been found floating in the North Dock, Swansea, while alcohol nearly proved fatal to Rees Mazey, who fell over the quay into the mud near Swansea's New Cut Bridge in 1896, similarly to Patsy Reardon, who had narrow escape from drowning in 1865 when late at night he fell off the bridge over the Plymouth feeder at Picton Street, Merthyr. Reardon was carried by the strong current under a series of bridges until he arrived opposite Mill Street, where there was a lamp and a man jumped in and pulled him out. Another, even more fortunate to survive was Donoghue (Dennis) O'Shea, who shot himself twice in the head at Swansea in 1895 after drinking heavily.

And a liquid intake nearly proved the downfall of George Dixon in 1895 – but for the Merthyr man it was not alcohol. Dixon, 23, was prevented from drinking carbolic acid, and afterwards was found lying unconscious on a railway line.

***

A MID-CENTURY newspaper article claimed that the average pugilist retired from the ring at thirty, but many died before they reached that age.[33] Reardon, and Patsy Vaughan, of Chepstow, died from tuberculosis aged 34 and 25 respectively, while another scourge of the time, cholera, claimed the life of Jemmy Robinson, from Denbigh, aged 20. Mining accidents were another common cause of death, with Tom Lambert among those killed in the Pontypridd disaster in 1893, and John Collins, 27, one of 57 fatalities at the Tylorstown colliery disaster in 1896. Smith Sage, was crushed severely' in a fall of coal at Colynos coal-pit, Garndiffaith, just days before a proposed fight and the local newspaper saw a potential silver lining, commenting 'we trust he will be dissuaded by his late accident, from cultivating this brutal propensity'.[34] Shamus Warner was found dead in bed in the pub where he lodged, the Vivian Arms, Ferryside, asphyxiated by gas, and another untimely death of a pugilist was in 1906, when Dai Jenkins, aged 23, from the Rhymney Valley, was reported to have been shot in a dispute over cards in South Africa.

***

FIGHTERS tended to have short careers, either in terms of years - no more than four or five at the highest level, according to 'the best judges' - and/or the number of fights – most bare knuckle men had only a small number, Turner, for example, averaging just one fight a year in a 14-year career.

Condensed careers and long intervals between fights were more often than not the result of dissipated lifestyles and physical damage sustained in the ring.

Prize fighting represented a major health risk. Powerful men 'could fracture eyebrows, noses, rip off ears or lips, break teeth and smash jaws', while a blow to the neck could fracture the windpipe and the voice-box just above it, causing suffocation and bleeding into the neck, while a fractured rib spike could puncture the lung, causing an air leak and bleeding into the chest.[35] Aaron Jones knocked out the left eye of William Haines 'with a right hand punch.

The fighter throwing the punch could just as easily injure himself severely. Damage to the hands would have been common; they would have been disfigured, with injuries taking several months to heal. A hard blow to the head carried the risk of fracturing the bones of the hand and wrist and injuring the joints, leading to the onset of early arthritis and bringing careers to a premature end.

Turner emerged from a fight in 1824 with a bone in his left hand broken and one end of the fracture nearly protruding through the skin. In 1822, George Davis and his opponent 'exchanged hit for hit ...till their hands were swollen as round as dumplings'. Tom Spring's hands were 'dreadfully disfigured from coming into contact with Langan's 'hard nob' in their 1824 76 rounds in 1 hr, 48 minutes clash, and straight after the fight, Spring announced his retirement. Shirenewton fighter Harry Evans' hands were 'so knocked to pieces' that he had to give in against Edward Lake, of Newport, after twenty rounds over 59 minutes.

During a prize fight at Gabalfa, Cardiff, in 1895, one man had the knuckles of his right hand broken in the eleventh round, in the next round his opponent suffered a broken collarbone and they battled on until the end of the seventeenth before both retired.

Not every fight was brutal, however. A tame contest in 1862 involving Patsy Reardon prompted *Bell's Life* to complain 'they would have done almost as much damage if they had been hitting each other with balloons'.[36] The pair killed time by

> advancing, retreating, shifting here, pausing there, now putting their arms down, then putting them up again; now rubbing their chests, then their hands; now pulling up their drawers, then looking at their feet, as though intensely interested in the tie of their boot, until everyone was sick......after they had remained for fully 35 minutes without striking a blow, the referee told them that, unless a blow was delivered within six minutes, he should pronounce it to be a draw.

There was no blow delivered on either side within the given time, and the referee at once left his seat, and told the men that the affair was over, they having been at it one hour and fifty-two minutes. The journal, calling it 'one of the most farcical and ridiculous displays we have for some time had to record', said it was another blow to the Ring and 'a few more will floor it altogether'.

During their Cardiff fight in 1898, the referee repeatedly warned Mike Flynn (Ogmore Vale) and Aaron Davies (Rhondda) for clinching before stopping and declaring a draw, because the men were 'getting too loving'.

Prize fighting was even more dangerous because no sets of rules prescribed medical supervision, nor did they encourage much concern for the health of participants. It was only in 1898 that an inquest recommended that a doctor should be present at future contests.

Ring umpires had a duty to intervene if they were convinced that a man could not continue a fight with any chance of success, to prevent a repetition of punishment, which might prove fatal. But 'this discretionary power that renders prize-fights less objectionable than the casual turns-up in the street', was not used very often.[37]

Contests could go ahead despite there being substantial weight disparities between opponents. Differences of one or two stones were common and were barely remarked upon. If a boxer was willing to fight another several stones heavier, there was nothing to stop him. Turner, who stood 5ft 7 ins and usually weighed 10 stone 4 lb., gave away three stones and six inches in height in one of his early provincial bouts.

An extreme case occurred at Llangollen in north Wales in 1827, when Thomas Edwards, weighing about 17 stone, fought James Benbow, who tipped the scales at just 9 stone. As it happened, the additional weight was no advantage in a fight which lasted only four rounds, the lighter man flooring his opponent 'in great style'. Likewise, Tom Flynn, despite conceding almost three stones and being floored twice in the first round, punished Sam Davies 'severely' to force a fifth-round stoppage at Neath in 1895.

It didn't work out that way, though, for Jack Jenkins (8.st. 13lbs), who gave nearly 3 ½ stones to Dai 'Buller' Rees (12 st. 6lbs) and lasted just one round in 1900. The weight discrepancy proved insurmountable also for Enoch Morrison, who explained a second-round defeat to his local newspaper: 'My opponent was 12st. 4lb and my weight was 9.st. 11lb which means a big advantage on my opponent's side'.[38]

Men fought who were obviously not physically fit to enter the ring in the first place. Some had only one eye, like Tom Spring late in his career, John Richards, of Merthyr, and Newport's Bob Dunbar, while John Judson was back in action only weeks after being stabbed eight times.

Superficial injuries were reported in the Press in graphic detail, but potential long-term health problems, particularly the effect on the brain of repeated blows to the head, were not considered. Health issues prompted comparatively little debate. Comments came not from a health perspective, but rather from a moral one as they portrayed the brutality of the ring which was seen as an attraction for 'depraved' spectators.

What was also thought a priority was that injured pugilists might be unable to work, leaving their families a burden on the community, thus damaging the health of society as a whole. It was the same even after a ring death. When Richard Humphreys, from Betws Cedewain, Montgomeryshire, died in Radnorshire, in 1829, the concern was that his wife and four children had become 'entirely dependent upon the parish.'

The illegality of the sport was based initially on charges of unlawful assembly, and not on the question of physical risk; 'it wasn't until the end of the century that the courts felt the need to elaborate on the reasons why prize fighting should be declared illegal and dangerous as opposed to an initial desire to simply keep the lower classes, and their disruptive activities in their place'.[39]

Weiner remarked that the importance Lord Ellenborough placed on the harm to the individual in 1803 was 'something rarely before complained much of.'[40] Sporting equivalents to the Victorian friendly societies allowed sportsmen to insure against injury or death, though the Pugilistic Benevolent Society in 1852 catered only for the leading pugilists.

Injuries were claimed not to be as serious as they appeared, and this disregard allowed fights to continue long after they should have ended. When Curtis fought Turner, Curtis's head was beat in a dreadful manner....the blows he received on the head were the cause of his death..... blood poured from every pore in his head, his eyes, nose and mouth were running with blood in streams.[41]

When Edward Savage fought Spring the Conjuror, after 120 rounds both his ears 'swelled to four times their original size, his right eye was closed and his forehead was cut'.[42] Another fighter, in 1800, had his nose broken in the 12th round, his collarbone in the 20th, his jawbone in the 25th, and his breast bone in the 29th, and was encouraged to fight for two more rounds. Two men who pummelled each other for two hours and twenty minutes on the Rumney Moors near Cardiff in 1856 were so much punished that neither was able to leave the place without assistance, and their faces were 'so swollen as scarcely to retain the semblance of the human face'.[43]

In a fight near Cardiff in 1895, one combatant broke the knuckles of his right hand in the eleventh round, in the next round his opponent broke his collarbone, but the fight nevertheless continued for another five rounds before both fighters had had enough.

Prize-fighting was, in fact, championed as being safer than other forms of combat, including duelling, and Lancashire 'up and down fighting', where biting, eye-gouging and kicking with wooden clogs were the required skills. It was even claimed to be safer than rugby. Boxing booth owner Bill Samuel stated 'No one has ever been taken from our boxing salon to the hospital, but three Swansea footballers have been seriously injured this season.'[44] He spoke too soon, however, for, a year later, Thomas Davies died in Samuel's Swansea booth, and Samuel was among those charged with his manslaughter.

Such a cavalier attitude towards health was highlighted after a ringside collection following a particularly brutal fight in 1811, when 10 guineas was subscribed to the loser 'or his next of kin!' A similar light-hearted response came when *Bell's Life* looked back on the year 1827 and listed the ring heroes who had 'dropped off their perches' in the preceding 12 months.

The same mindset was behind many ring deaths, the fights having taken place despite warnings from outside health professionals. Curtis had just spent a month in hospital before taking on Turner. A prize fight in the Merthyr area in 1869 claimed the life of Robert Fletcher, a 28-year-old blacksmith with heart disease, who had been warned by his medical advisers not to drink alcohol or fight. Thomas Davies fought at Swansea despite heart problems and having suffered 'sunstroke' which left him with a speech impediment. Davies' health issues were known; Samuel, who staged the fight, was asked afterwards whether Davies had mentioned his heart disease, and replied: 'Oh yes, he has told me that he suffered from heart disease, and also weakness in the legs. He was rather flabby'.[45]

***

PUNISHMENT in the ring caused many fatalities, although the extent was disputed at the time and has been downplayed since. In an age when violent death was commonplace, those from prize fighting were regarded as merely 'unfortunate.'[46] The provincial press, or 'yokel writers', were wrong, it was claimed, to describe most fight fatalities as 'death by pugilism'; fewer than one tenth involved recognised pugilists; the rest arose from accidental meetings or quarrels involving men who were drunk (pugilists were rarely drunk before or during prize-fights), and most took place on days which were not recognized days for prize-fights.

It was claimed then, and since, that ring deaths were 'mercifully rare'.[47] But to contemporary newspapers they were commonplace. They regularly reported 'Yet another ring death.' The *Royal Cornwall Gazette*, urging

Parliamentary action, said in 1824 that in the past year it had recorded more than one dozen prize fight fatalities.

The present research has identified in Britain more than two hundred ring deaths during the nineteenth century, including the afore-mentioned thirty in Wales.

Two thirds of reported Welsh deaths occurred in the second half of the century, when more newspapers were around to report them. Previously, it can be reasonably assumed, others went unreported. Furthermore, prize fighting being regarded as illegal, more fatalities would be kept quiet, so the true number of ring deaths was probably much greater. Jones recognised the situation in *Black Parade* when he wrote 'nothing came' of a ring fatality after a fight on Aberdare mountain, the fighter had died in one of the 'common lodging houses, and people who died there were seldom fussed over'.[48]

Most ring deaths resulted from head trauma, from the type of blows which killed David Thomas, who sustained a ruptured vessel in the brain in the parish of Vaynor in 1858, and Edward Augustus Collard, killed near Ferndale in 1897, who died from pressure from a blood clot on the brain. Arthur Vaughan, fighting on Llanwonno mountain in 1895, died from 'the shaking of the brain and the failure of the respiratory nerves.[49]

Often, it was unclear whether death was caused by a punch to the head or by the head striking the ground when the fighter was knocked or thrown down. Isaac Latcham died at Abertillery in 1873 from compression of the brain, produced by a blood clot, John Hopkins' head struck the ground and he died from a brain haemorrhage near Merthyr in 1874, and John Jenkin James died near Porth in 1886 after he fell backwards, the back of his head coming into contact with a stone, death being caused by a clot on the brain.

When David Rees died at the Market Hall, Aberdare, in 1894 the stone floor on which he was fighting was covered with sawdust two to three inches deep. He appeared to have been struck an ordinary blow, and, falling heavily, his head hit the stone slabs of the floor, which had probably been scraped clear by the feet of the fighters themselves. He had a fractured skull, also a fractured dislocation of the first and second vertebrae.

Rowland Thomas' death after 2 ½ hours and 74 rounds in 1868 was caused by severe congestion of the brain, the result of excitement rather than of any specific act of violence, a surgeon told the court. The congestion might have been caused by drinking and excitement irrespective of any blows.

Likewise, when Patsy Reardon moved to the USA he fought Thomas McCann, who died during their contest in 1868 in Illinois. The *Chicago Tribune* reported that the fight, between 'two young men, 'lesser lights' in the world of 'fancydom', took place on the historic track of land across the river known as 'Bloody Island'. Reardon was sentenced to one month in the county gaol, the light punishment due to McCann's death resulting more from over excitement than from the severity of blows administered.

Roger Williams was killed at Sirhowey in 1859 by a blow on the jugular vein. Thomas Evans died after a prize fight at Merthyr in 1897 during which he fell against a wall and suffered a fracture of the spinal column. Others died from being struck in the body. At Quaker's Yard in 1857, Walter Morgan, aged 32, died after a blow to the pit of the stomach.

Some other deaths followed the victim's being thrown and his opponent landing on top of him, a wrestling move that was within the accepted rules at the time.

***

Prize Fighters

FIGHTERS were well-paid, according to the *Western Mail*, which, in 1888 claimed, with what has become the customary value judgement by the Press, that 'pugilists continue to earn the incomes of Prime Ministers'.[50] At least one fighter is believed to have matched the Prime Minister's wage of £5,000 a year (from 1830 to 1930); that was the American, John L Sullivan, who 'cleared five thousand pounds' on his exhibition tour of Britain around this time.[51]

But that was probably more than even the top British fighters could manage. It would be impossible, though, to discover exactly how much fighters earned as no records were maintained and newspaper reports did not reveal much detail. But as the top British fighters fought fewer than a handful of times a year for sums in the hundreds of pounds, it is unlikely that fight purses alone would have put them in the Premier's pay bracket. Winnings from fight bets might well have done, however.

Press coverage was vague, especially early on, regarding fight earnings. Reports rarely indicated what, or even if, a purse was to be contested in addition to a side stake, and even more rarely how, or if, the purse was to be shared. The only information released when Mendoza fought Humphries in 1788 was that the fifty pounds purse and the takings from the admission price of half a guinea a head, would be shared, as was 'generally the case', by both sides.[52]

In the early part of the century, the purse split might be between 4 and 10:1. Suggestions made in 1844 to decide how money should be divided indicate there was not a standard disposal other than the loser usually receiving nothing.

Gate receipts, on the infrequent occasions they could be collected, were regarded as a bonus, although the only spectators who could expect to be

The fatal fight involving Edward Augustus Collard
(Illustrated Police News, 29 May 1897)

charged were the better-off who paid for the best vantage points immediately surrounding the ring, an area which could be controlled by the organisers even at short notice.

A rare example of precise details being reported arose out of a fight in 1820 in Hampshire involving 'Gillan, a Montgomeryshire man', the admission price binge 'a tanner', the popular name for sixpence.[53] At Warwick racecourse in 1824, admission money from the grandstand which could hold more than one thousand spectators at ten shillings each was to be divided, with the organisers receiving one third for expenses and two thirds to the fighters. At that event, there were also two circles of wagons, containing about 130 spectators who were each charged five shillings, although the destination of that money was not mentioned. Wagons would be hired to form an outer ring, where

> many, who, for personal safety from thieves, and from a dislike to mix with the scavengers, and filthy wretches that compose the majority of the mob, will pay from 2s 6d to 10s for a standing-place in a cart to see the fight.[54]

But even those spectators who paid were not always guaranteed a view. When Turner met Scroggins in 1817, hundreds who had paid three shillings and five shillings for seats in wagons had no chance of seeing the fight because of disorderly scenes at the ringside. It was reported that 'Only those brave enough to withstand the heaving mass as well as 'the lashes of whips …flying to keep out marauders', caught a glimpse of action inside the ring.[55]

More details of fight purses emerged later regarding glove contests, which would usually be held indoors and had a promoter. They tended to be for purses, but the amounts were again publicised infrequently. Those reported show a split for the winner and loser of between 4 and 5:1.

When John O'Brien beat Felix Scott in Liverpool in 1890 for a purse of £50, £40 went to O'Brien) and £10 to Scott, who was having his first fight shortly after his release from a long prison sentence. In 1891, when O'Brien beat fellow Cardiffian Alf Mitchell at the National Sporting Club, London, for a £300 purse, he received £200, and Mitchell £50 with £25 going to each for expenses. Morgan Crowther met Arthur Wilkinson in a glove contest for £350 in London in 1891, with Wilkinson, the loser, given £75. Patsy Perkins, who had hired the room for the fatal glove contest in 1894, told police the gate money was to be divided into three equal parts between the two fighters and himself. Booth owner John Stokes revealed that he had paid £3 to the winner and £2 to his opponent after a fight in 1895.

By the early 1890s, London had become 'quite a favourite place' for Welsh boxers, the main reason being 'the inducements in the shape of liberal purses given by the capital's clubs'.[56] This was what persuaded Bob Wiltshire (Cardiff) and Perkins (Merthyr) to box the best of twenty rounds for £50 a-side and the 10 st. championship of Wales in 1895.

Fights were usually for side stakes. At the local level, where combatants themselves or their backers issued challenges directly and fights were arranged on a handshake, stake money would be deposited with a trusted third party mainly at a public house such as the *Bute Arms*, Cardiff, the *Castle*, Newport, Monmouthshire, and the *White Swan*, Monmouth.

Considerable business, chiefly challenges, was conducted through the columns of *Bell's Life*. In 1826, Philip Lewis, alias Portobello, 'the Glamorganshire Champion', used its columns to seek fights with leading men, as did Jonathan Williams, alias Grog, the Welch Champion, who had been described in a court report, as 'a person who has acquired considerable provincial notoriety as a pugilist'. Williams issued a general challenge in 1847, saying he was fighting at 11st. 7lbs. and could be contacted at the *Three Horseshoes*, Newport.

Arranging contests could prove less straightforward for Welsh fighters, whose backers might have to pay a premium to secure home advantage, as. Andrew Jones could confirm. 'The Welsh Champion' was matched In 1843 to fight his opponent 'anywhere in Wales' the other man needing to be paid all his expenses 'in consideration of his fighting in Wales'.[57]

Even an additional sum might not close the deal, however. *Bell's Life* reported in 1839 a challenge to leading fighters from someone who signed himself 'Cornelius Smith', for from £50 to £125 a-side, any bout to take place 'on Welch ground'. The journal warned that 'Taffy cannot hope for a customer on such terms. The backers of a man usually wish to sec him fight, and the distance would be rather too far, as well expensive, for the Cockneys'.[58]

Swansea fighter Samuel Ellery accepted Smith's challenge straight away, but he had his own conditions, one being that Smith weighed no more than 14 stones – he had weighed seven pounds more in his previous fight. Ellery's money was. He said, waiting at the *Hope and Anchor Tavern*, Swansea.[59]

For bigger contests, there would be contracts, known as articles of agreement, that would stipulate the size of stakes, how they would be paid in instalments, who was to hold the money, and who was to appoint the referee, approximate venue and date and penalties for failing to comply.

If a deposit was not made on time, a forfeit would have to be paid. Edward Savage's backers missed the deadline with their £20 fourth deposit for his match with Peter Sweeney, so, seven minutes after the deadline, Sweeney was allowed a forfeit. The money arrived five minutes later, 'but it was then too late unless Sweeney agreed which would certainly be honourable but is entirely optional'.[60] In 1864 Henry Batch received a forfeit from William Anthony after they agreed on £5 a-side at catchweight. They had fought 12 rounds near Swansea when the police interfered, and a meeting was appointed for next day, but Anthony did not show up and Batch received the stakes.

Stakes in Wales ranged from 2s.6d up to a rare £50. Mostly they were between £1 and £10, and they stayed that way throughout the century, In the industrial south stakes were bigger than in other parts of Wales, while in the provinces they were higher, and in London even more so.

Edward Turner began fighting in the provinces in 1813 for five guineas a-side, progressed to 50 guineas on his debut in the London ring, and was competing for 150 guineas in 1817. Even lesser London fighters at the time, such as the Savage brothers, fought for between £25 and £50.

Press reports usually mentioned only the amount, not what, if anything, went to the fighters. If they put up the stakes themselves, as they might do for low profile local contests, it would be winner takes all, but what they received on most other occasions, especially for the bigger events, when backers were needed, depended on the generosity of the latter.

Turner was three times handed all the opposition's cash, all involving £100-plus, but the fact that these gestures were remarked upon suggests that backers were not usually so generous.

Due to the secretive nature of the sport, gate takings were a non-starter as it was difficult if not impossible to charge admission to fights, so the vast majority represented a free show for spectators with consequently little or no gate money to be shared out. The losing fighter could expect to receive nothing unless a hat was passed around after a spirited performance, auch as when a 'handsome collection' was made for Edward Savage in 1825.

Prize Fighters

***

FOR all the fight purses, side stakes, and ringside collections, gambling was the main motivation for the sport's existence. Betting provided most reward for backers and fighters alike, and relevant information was a key element in early newspaper reports. A report of a fight at Llandaff near Cardiff in 1811 focussed on the changes in betting odds at every significant stage in the 27-round contest.

Large sums could be won and lost, with fifty thousand pounds, the purchasing power of more than five million pounds today, resting on one early contest. A pugilist was even bought out of debtors' gaol in 1803 so that gamblers could bet on him in a forthcoming fight. Pigeons were sometimes used to carry early news to London of boxing matches 'to enable the initiated to entrap the unwary in laying wagers'.[61] Turner against Jack Randall in 1818 was believed at the time to be the biggest-ever fight in terms of betting and staking, with much of the money coming from Wales, where betting was said to be widespread.

The *Aberdare Times* reported 'heavy betting' on the James v Benjamin contest in 1861 with 'hundreds of workers' putting money on local man James.[62] After the telegram 'which doomed James's friends to disappointment' arrived, however, the newspaper said that the losses were their own fault and it hoped they had learned their lesson, and would now act more responsibly, because

> There is a contest – a struggle- a fight, being carried on every day in Aberdare between hundreds of poor families, where their money could be much better applied.

71

Feasts of Blood

Other sports banned competitors from betting, so for them it would have to be in secret. But there was no governing body for pugilists, therefore, having nobody to answer to, fighters were able to bet openly.

None more so than Jones, the Welsh Champion, before one match in 1833. Jones, it was reported, 'previous to shaking hands, ... put his hand into his inexpressibles, and brought out a crown, and cried aloud, 'I win the battle in 40 minutes'.[63]

Morgan Crowther and James 'Chaffy' Hayman agreed in the ring on a £10 bet before their fight in a Lydney field in 1889. Months later, in the ring in a London club, Crowther offered to back himself for 'a couple of ponies' [£50 – a pony being £25] but opponent Arthur Wilkinson declined. Similarly, just before the start of their Welsh title fight in 1894, John O'Brien crossed to the corner of David St. John and offered to bet £25 on the result, while at his 'title' fight with Jack Burke in 1891, Ted Pritchard walked across the ring and offered to bet a level 'century' which was immediately accepted.

Jack Northey revealed the potential of such wagers when he told police after an aborted contest at Swansea in 1891, 'We were going to fight for a couple of quid, and if I had won, it would have been about £150 in my pocket'.

Betting odds around the ring changed constantly and could be manipulated during the contest. Thomas Thomas had thrown out a challenge in 1898 which was accepted by Joe Priddy and as their fight near Cardiff progressed, with Thomas appearing untroubled, his confident backers gradually lengthened the odds offered, Priddy's backers accepting eagerly. But Priddy had been holding back in the early rounds, and once the odds were at their most favourable, he took complete control and hit Thomas 'where and when he liked' for a ninth-round finish.[64] 'As one of his

72

friends expressed it, 'the fight was not only a surprise, but a tremendous take in'.

Fighters would bet on their athletic ability outside the ring as well. . Lightweights Crowther and Bob Wiltshire both took on top runners in 1893 for money in 120 yard sprints, along Marshes Road (renamed Shaftesbury Street), Newport, and in Cardiff, and, receiving five and ten yard starts respectively, both beat the favourites comfortably It was also reported that 'several smart sums of money changed hands' when John Jones (alias Shoni Castell-Nedd) competed in a foot race at Hirwaun in 1847 for which he had been training for several weeks.

Heavyweight Bill Benjamin accepted a challenge in 1862 to run 11 miles in one hour 30 minutes, staking £5.10s. against a pig of equivalent value by running from the *Butchers Arms*, Shirenewton, where he was the landlord, to the *Rock and Fountain*, Penhow, on the Newport road, and back. He was reported to have completed the run in one hour and 14 minutes.

On the face of it Benjamin's run was an impressive performance, but even more so (if true) was that of a boy 'about seven years old' who, for a sovereign, reportedly undertook in 1839 to run from Risca to Newport with the Tredegar stagecoach and reach the post office before it. The *Monmouthshire Merlin* stated that the boy kept up with the coach until it reached the top of Newport's Stow Hill 'when he quickened his pace down the steep descent and outstripped the coach, winning the wager'. The distance of about seven miles was completed in 45 minutes, according to the paper.

People would gamble on almost anything. For a bet, a 97-year-old man in the London area in 1807 agreed to walk four and a half miles in an hour and beat the time by three minutes. More exotic wagers involved, for a bet of one guinea, in 1809 a London man eating, in 15 ½ minutes, six pounds of tripe, two dozen large onions in sauce, two loaves, three pounds of potatoes, and drinking three pots of porter. Another man in the capital in 1819 consumed a dozen live wasps and two pounds of raw salmon in ten minutes for a small bet; he then offered to eat wasps wholesale at the rate of six pence a dozen, but after two dozen his throat and mouth became so swollen that he had to stop.

***

MONEY was more important for fighters than titles. After Wiltshire lost the 10 stone championship of Wales to Perkins, a newspaper commented: 'Titles, especially championships, go for little any way …..a good deal more to the point, was a stake of £50 a-side, while another important matter was a purse'.[65] Ted Pritchard said he did not want to fight John O'Brien for the championship belt, which was a contentious issue between them; O'Brien could keep it 'as it is not for such presents I want to box him, but for as much 'brass' as he can find'.[66]

Fight earnings, even for the lowest paid pugilist, were a welcome supplement to wages from his day job. Industrial workers in Wales rarely earned more than thirty shillings a week during the century, those employed in agriculture barely half that. Edward Augustus Collard, a Rhondda collier, who died in 1897 while fighting for £1 a-side, was one of the better paid workers, police finding a pay ticket on the body showing he had earned £4 2s 8d in the previous fortnight. The victor in a clash near Porth the previous year was able to enjoy a seaside holiday on the opposite side of the Bristol Channel at Ilfracombe on his winnings.

***

Prize Fighters

IT was claimed that prize fighters were 'almost invariably idle dissolute blackguards, who prefer being trained and pampered with rump-steaks and brown stout, to getting their living by honest labour'.[67] But they did not need to be reprobates to prefer that lifestyle; most professional athletes of modern times say they need full time training and expensive diets to achieve their potential, but in by-gone days, few could find others willing to pay them to do so. It was either work or starve and, consequently, most Welsh exponents had full time jobs throughout their ring careers.

Turner's rise to prominence, though, enabled him to switch from being a tanner to full-time fighter, and late in the century, former miner Crowther, by the age of twenty, could describe himself in the 1891 census as a 'professional athlete'. In the middle years of the century, Aaron Jones was a footman to an MP in London but was sacked when his employer learned of his prize fighting and he became a full-time ring performer.

Fighters were usually manual workers in the coal, iron and steel industries or in the docks of South Wales, but there were plenty of town tradesmen among them. The best early Wales-based men either worked in the growing southern ports, or on the rivers, canals and railways. Miners were in the majority in the second half of the nineteenth century when they comprised roughly two thirds of those identified in the present research.

***

NICKNAMES often revealed fighters' day jobs, Thomas Pearson being known as 'Tom Cloggy' because he was a clog maker, Tom Davies was 'Tom the Cleaner', Richard Evans was 'Dicky Puddler', a puddler being a trade in the iron industry, and Richard Matthias was better known as 'Dick the Thief', a newspaper claiming he fought only because he could not make any money by stealing. Some fighters were better known by their nicknames; when

'Shoni Engineer' died, the *Western Mail* remarked that few people knew that his real name was John Jones, who had been a colliery blacksmith.

Some nicknames indicated where fighters lived or came from originally, such as John Bevan ('Shone Castellnedd' (trans. Neath Johnny), and Edward Williams ('Ned Top of Cefn'), Daniel Davies ('Swansea Dan'), and Peter Burns ('Dublin Tom').

Tom Davies was known as Tom Books because his father was a bookseller, while Thomas Thomas was known, for obvious reasons, as Tom Twice.

John Isaac, a river haulier at Swansea, was better known as Shony Sherai. Evan Morgan (Risca) fought under the cognomen of Yanto Clathes. John Davies was known as Shoni Sailor; Thomas Morgan (Twm Kitty), and Morris Rooke was known as 'Morris Dido'. Charles Jones, alias Charley-the-Well, and William Williams, alias Bill-the-Coal, were prize fighters in the Wrexham area.

Others, for their own reasons, fought under aliases, such as The Sowhill Chicken, The Tredegar Infant, Stitcher Bach and Dick the Devil.

***

WHEN a pugilist eloped with the wife of a Swansea publican, a surprised local newspaper commented 'Men who practise the noble art for the sake of a livelihood are not generally credited with possessing the gifts of a soft address and a flattering tongue'.[68] Fists were the easiest means, it would appear, of securing that prize, and, occasionally, money was not the main motivation for combatants, rather there was a romantic prize. In 1846, Rees Hopkin, of Tondu Works, died after one such prize fight, when both he and his opponent employed seconds and which lasted one and a quarter hours. In 1862, crowds of people were seen on the side of Aberaman mountain, where two young men, named Pendry and Harris, fought 97 rounds in two hours and forty minutes over a woman – plus £1one pound a-side. The local paper commented

> It is said that Pendry was her favourite, but unfortunately Harris was proclaimed the winner of the fight. We hope the young woman will now see the propriety of discarding both of her pugnacious lovers.[69]

Two men fought at Rhymney in Monmouthshire in 1874 to decide which of the two was to become the husband of a young woman, who was waiting in the neighbourhood for tidings of the result of the battle. Side stakes of £10 were involved this time. A similar fight took place near Wrexham in 1894, but the prize was reported to be 'anything but flattered at the absurd spectacle which resulted, two lovely black eyes' being not the only damage.[70] The newspaper added: 'It's really no use to attempt to bring back the days of chivalry in this manner'.

The addition of a money prize detracted from a romantic gesture, but it made sense. The combatants would want all the trappings of a prize fight – money, seconds, etc to avoid any suggestion of a brawl which, as we have seen, could lead to more serious legal consequences than a prize fight which would be, comparatively, tolerated by the law.

Other non-monetary prizes included silver watches, a flitch of bacon, lottery tickets, what was 'elegantly termed a belly full', a leg of mutton, and a bottle of whisky.

***

THERE were money-making opportunities outside the regular ring, from taking on all-comers in the boxing booths attached to travelling fairs, to merchandising; early fighters sported coloured kerchiefs (Welsh fighters favouring the blue bird's eye, blue with white spots) and sold replicas to supporters after fights. Pugilists taught self-defence; Phillip Dixon travelled throughout Wales, 'teaching the art of boxing', Luke Horner gave lessons in Newport, Harry Jones and Pat Donovan gave 'sparring lectures' in south Wales towns including Newport and Brecon and in 1848 a large room in Orange-street, Swansea, was let to a travelling group of pugilists who entertained 'an admiring throng'.

Some fighters were employed for their intimidating presence. Eighteen were used as bouncers at King George IV's coronation in 1821, and the Tories at Stroud during the 1834 Parliamentary elections employed 'the notorious Luke Rogers', a frequent visitor with boxing booths to South Wales, in 'an unprovoked attack' on several townspeople. The 'notorious fighting man' Bill Richards, known as the Welsh champion, was one of the leaders of the election riots of 1852 at Newport.

Bill Benjamin was engaged by an innkeeper at Sharpness to keep order among 'the large number of navvies' in the area which he did 'far more effectually than the whole of the country police could have done'.

Tom James became a bailiff, while Salvation Army leader General Booth, whose followers were often attacked in the streets, employed 'Ben, said to be 'the champion Yorkshire prize fighter', as a bodyguard on his tour of South Wales in 1883. Ben was a 'muscular Christian of over six feet, whose huge form appeared the more ponderous by the wearing of a tight and white jersey.'[71]

Some pugilists became circus or theatre stars, the best-known able to command the salaries of top-billed stage performers. One of the earliest was Jem Belcher, whom a Bristol theatre in 1802 paid ten guineas a week to demonstrate his boxing skills on stage; he took an old opponent with him who was paid three guineas a week, 'being only a second-rate performer.'[72]

Prize Fighters

A lion tamer going by the name of Captain Marco saw his circus career interrupted in 1897 when police pounced at Ebbw Vale, recognising him as Cardiff fighter George Osborne, who was wanted at Chester on a charge of horse stealing.

Fighters might embark on touring exhibitions, among the earliest ones to do so being Tom Cribb and Tom Spring, who performed throughout South Wales in 1819, and Turner, who toured across Essex and in mid-Wales around the 1820s, These fighters 'were the precursors of the general move of spectator sport into its eventual ambit of show business. The star pugilists had now the air of popular entertainers'.[73]

***

ALTHOUGH fight figures continued to be the most loyal customers of public houses in their later years, many veteran or retired men could be found behind the bar. They were following an old tradition which in the early part of the century was already causing concern, and, it was said, should be looked at by magistrates. It was claimed that

> The mischief arising from clerks, shopmen, and others, associating at these houses with what are termed sporting characters, is incalculable. Idle habits, and a spirit of gambling, are produced, end employers are plundered.[74]

It was alleged that the only ambitions fighters had were to keep a brothel, a gambling house or a pub, places where their friends collected and where fights and 'all their collateral villainies, were arranged'[75]

> More than one retired prize-fighter was keeping a public house in London at this moment who had killed an antagonist, and who believed that a period of imprisonment for the 'manslaughter' had settled the awful account.[76]

The writer was more than likely referring particularly to Owen Swift, the survivor in three fatal prize fights, whose London pub was where the final deposit for the Sayers-Heenan fight was paid.

There were, after all, strong links between pubs and prize fighting; they were centres for organising the sport and also operated as betting shops for the activity. Public houses were even pioneer travel agencies for fight fans. In 1865, it was advised in the Press that an information and travel escort service was available from Dan Thomas, of the *Old Pine Apple* in St. Mary Street, Cardiff, and from the landlord of the *White Hart Hotel*, Pontypridd, who would be 'most happy to escort gentlemen to the scene of action'.[77]

Alf Mitchell was mine host of the *Gun and Tent*, Spitalfields, London, Jerry Morgan the *Red Lion*, Cardiff, while Bill Samuel was landlord of the *Kings Arms*, Swansea. Other pugilistic publicans included Bill Benjamin, *Butchers Arms*, Shirenewton, *Kings Head*, Chepstow, and *Cross Hands*, Mynyddbach, Shirenewton), Richard James (*St. Ives Inn*, Neath), and John Richards (*Lord Raglan Inn*, Aberdare). In Cardiff, Jack Matthews ran beer houses, namely the *Forester's Arms* in Adam Street, and the *Flying Eagle* in Charlotte Street. John O'Brien and Peter Burns both ran illegal shebeens in Cardiff, and former Rhondda fighter Charlie North also dispensed liquid refreshment – from a water cart, or as it was advertised, a 'moving reservoir'. The tavern-keeping tradition even spread to the USA, where Aaron Jones kept a 'flourishing' bar in Philadelphia.

Running a pub was an occupation in which their special talents would be useful in dealing with disorderly customers, a factor which helped Morgan Crowther to gain a temporary licence to take over the *Moulders Arms*, Newport, in 1893. Crowther's application was granted, despite police objecting over his prize fighting and bookmaking activities and because of his conviction for being drunk and disorderly – he was only 13 at the time, his solicitor claimed in mitigation. But, after the issue was raised in the House of Commons, Newport magistrates, the bench packed with temperance men, refused to make the licence permanent.

Never mind this decision 'taking the biscuit', according to the *Western Mail*, questioning Crowther's rights to a licence 'fairly annexes the whole blooming bakery'. In a ringing endorsement, the newspaper said that 'If ever there was an exponent of the 'noble art' who behaves himself as a gentleman that man is Morgan Crowther....in fact, he is the one man in a thousand who elevates instead of lowers the art of which he is such a capable exponent'.[78]

Despite strong support from leading police officers, Bill Samuel was at first refused a pub licence in 1887 for the *King's Arms*, Swansea, after the stipendiary said that a professional boxer Samuel 'would be the very last man he would hand a licence to'; the bench 'wanted a higher class of men than professional boxers to hold licenses in Swansea.'[79] A week later, after the court heard that Samuel would retire from boxing (which he failed to do), would not tolerate betting on his premises and would not give boxing lessons there, his application was granted.

***

A select few Welsh fight figures were shrewd enough to make themselves comfortable financially in retirement. Jerry Morgan used his savings, after quitting the ring at 28, to buy a pub in Cardiff and also the Premier Boxing Academy in the town, both businesses said to have been successful. Dan Thomas, as well as running several Cardiff pubs, also invested in collieries, and 'became a man of means', leaving £12,704 in 1910, worth around £1.5 million today.[80] Morgan Crowther, a bookmaker, could afford a string of racehorses, including a Grand National runner, and Jack Matthews left an

Aladdin's Cave of jewellery and antiques in Cardiff, his wealth the proceeds of his career as a publican, brothel owner and major handler of stolen goods.

Morgan, in looking after his earnings, was said to have 'acted in a manner quite contrary to that of the pugilistic fraternity'.[81] Whatever money the majority earned was most likely spent on alcohol. Thus, Turner was left dependent on public collections in his final years, while others ended their days in the workhouse, among them George Rowlands in Cardiff, Daniel Desmond, who slept in brick kilns, at Pontypool, Patsy Cummings, 'a once famous prize-fighter, for some time acknowledged as the lightweight champion of England', at St. Asaph, and Redmond Coleman at Merthyr.

Bob Dunbar finished up in a mental hospital aged 79. Dunbar, blind and previously reduced to selling matches in the streets of Cardiff and Newport, died in disturbing circumstances. An inquest in 1938 at the Monmouthshire Mental Hospital, later renamed Penyfal, heard that Dunbar had fallen out of bed. Death was due to heart and lung damage following fractures of the ribs, five on the right side and two on the left. A doctor said enquiries failed to show when or how he received the injuries; they could not have been the result of the fall.[82] Dunbar's injuries might well have been caused by a beating, but the truth will probably never be revealed, as newspaper reports offer the only available account.

Coroners' records were not designated as Public Records until the Public Records Act 1958. Before that date (with the exception of some 19th century coroners' records which were registered with the Court of Quarter Sessions) there was no requirement for the records to be kept indefinitely.

---

1 Western Mail, 2 Feb 1897.
2 George Borrow, Lavengro. The Scholar, The Gipsy, The Priest (London: Oxford University Press, 1914), pp. 183-4).

3 Joe England, *'Merthyr's Rich Heritage'* delivered at conference 26 November 2010.
4 Mike Huggins, The Victorians and Sport (London: Hambledon, 2004), p. 174, p. 177.
5 Cambrian, 27 September 1901.
6 Merthyr Times, 24 December 1895.
7 Morning Post, 10 October 1891. Evening Express, 27 February 1892.
8 David J. V. Jones, Crime in Wales, p. 84.
9 Merthyr Express, 22 January 1910.
10 Monmouthshire Merlin, 3 August 1894
11 Western Mail, 12 May 1890.
12 South Wales Daily Post, 8 August 1895
13 Weekly Dispatch, 3 November 1833.
14 Glamorgan Gazette, 1 April 1843.
15 Red Dragon, Vol. XI No. 4 April 1887 1 April 1887.
16 Merthyr Times, 8 July 1898.
17 Cambrian, 7 September 1805
18 W. R. Lambert, *Drink and Sobriety in Victorian Wales c.1820- c.1895* (Cardiff, University of Wales Press, 1983), pp. 47, 48. Jones, Crime in 19th Century Wales p. 54.
19 Weekly Mail, 20 November 1897.
20 Morning Post, 29 September 1827
21 Monmouthshire Merlin, 9 June 1832.
22 Morning Chronicle, 21 April 1824
23 Bell's Life, 30 April 1826
24 Cambria Daily Leader, 11 May 1914.
25 Cambria Daily Leader, 25 June 1817.
26 Weekly Mail, 25 April 1908.
27 Merthyr Express, 25 August 1923.
28 Illustrated Police News, 19 November 1898.
29 County Observer, 18 January 1868.
30 Western Mail, 28 January 1928.
31 Evening Express, 26 January 1892.
32 Cambrian, 14 January 1837
33 Morning Post, 16 September 1845.
34 Illustrated Usk Observer, 2 April 1859.
35 Mick Crumplin (Fight Night, Yesterday TV, October 2012).
36 Bell's Life, 30 Mar 1862.
37 Morning Chronicle, 17 November 1824.
38 Evening Express, 11 April 1895.
39 Jack Anderson, 'Pugilistic Prosecutions: Prize fighting and the courts in nineteenth century Britain', The Sports Historian No. 21 (2), p. 35.
40 Martin J. Weiner, *Men of Blood: Violence, Manliness, and Criminal Justice in Victorian England* (Cambridge, Cambridge University Press, 2004)
41 Morning Chronicle, 26 Oct 1816.
42 Morning Chronicle, 16 January 1828. Bell's Life, 20 January 1828.
43 Monmouthshire Merlin, 19 July 1856
44 Western Mail, 16 Mar 1895.
45 Evening Express, 21 March 1896
46 Morning Post, 18 September 1829
47 Bob Mee, Bare Fists (London, Collins Willow, 1998), p. 76.
48 Jack Jones, Black Parade (Cardigan, Parthian, 2009) p. 54.

[49] Western Mail, 19 Sept 1895
[50] Western Mail, 3 January 1888
[51] John L. Sullivan, Life and Reminiscences of a 19th century gladiator (London, Routledge, 1892), p. 195.
[52] Times, 9 January 1788.
[53] Morning Chronicle, 14 October 1820
[54] New Monthly Magazine, cited in Monmouthshire Merlin, 12 April 1834
[55] Morning Chronicle, 27 March 1817
[56] Western Mail, 6 April 1893
[57] Bell's Life, 19 February 1843.
[58] Bell's Life, 31 March 1839.
[59] Bell's Life, 7 April 1839.
[60] Morning Chronicle, 18 September 1828
[61] Examiner, 29 May 1831.
[62] Aberdare Times, 3 August 1861.
[63] Bell's Life in London and Sporting Chronicle, 19 May 1833.
[64] South Wales Echo, 15 January 1898.
[65] South Wales Daily Post, 25 March 1895
[66] Western Mail, 3 Mar 1892.
[67] Times, 30 July 1828.
[68] Evening Express, 6 April 1891.
[69] Aberdare Times, 17 May 1862
[70] Llangollen Advertiser, 21 December 1894
[71] Cambrian, 4 May 1883, Weekly Mail, 5 May 1883
[72] Times, 1 January 1802.
[73] Brailsford, pp. 153,154.
[74] Times, 30 July 1828.
[75] New Monthly Magazine, cited in Monmouthshire Merlin, 12 April 1834.
[76] Bury and Norwich Post, 28 February 1860.
[77] Bell's Life, 25 March; 1 April 1865. The secret was not kept on this occasion, as 'a strong posse of police' were waiting at the proposed site at Rumney Bridge.
[78] Western Mail, 5 July 1893.
[79] South Wales Daily News, 28 January 1887.
[80] Glamorgan Gazette, 15 July 1910. Cardiff Times, 10 September 1910.
[81] Evening Express, 17 September 1892
[82] Western Mail, 12 March 1938

3

Golden Age?

If prize-fighters were able to prevent the Queen of England from attending her husband's coronation, then they must, indeed, have been a well-connected group.

When King George IV was crowned in 1821, his estranged wife, Queen Caroline, turned up at Westminster Abbey demanding admittance, only to be turned away by pugilists hired as doormen for the occasion. Anticipating trouble, Lord Gwydir (whose title came from a north Wales estate) had appointed some of the leading pugilists in the land as bouncers.

The prize fighters acted as if very much at ease amongst the assembled aristocracy attending the Coronation, to such an extent that the *Times*, which had earlier remarked on the irony of employing 'avowed Peace breakers to keep the peace', sniffed that during the build-up, these 'notorious persons moved backwards and forwards in the hall with a mimic air of official confidence', and that one of them cut across a procession by the canopy bearers 'with an ale jug in his hand'.[1]

The new King was so pleased with their performance that he sent them letters of thanks as well as a gold medal to share. This was the ultimate confirmation that prize fighters were a protected species in British society.

Unsurprisingly, the late eighteenth and early nineteenth century has been viewed as the 'golden age' of prize-fighting in Britain.

The sport, once so popular that King George 1 ordered a ring to be erected in London's Hyde Park for public use, had fallen into disfavour because of corruption, a lack of personalities in the ring, and the absence of royal patronage. It was able to flourish again because it regained royal favour when the Prince of Wales, later King George IV, became 'a warm friend'.[2]

This was true, but the general public were not encouraged to think he supported a 'blackguard's activity'. On the contrary; the *Times* phrased its report about his presence at a big fight in the following words – 'whether accidental or otherwise, we know not – we may, however, reasonably suppose the former'.[3]

The nobility, among them regular fight-goer Sir Thomas Apreece, whose family were descended from Gruffydd ap Rees, prince of South Wales, inevitably followed the royal lead. A civic dinner given in London in 1790 for leading pugilists, and a who's who of the aristocracy attending a party in 1811 for leading fighter Molineaux, proved that the upper classes were renewing their interest and that pugilism was becoming socially acceptable.

The activity thrived also because the upper classes formed an alliance with the lower orders ('the aristocracy and mobocracy'), sharing a love of its violence, of the drinking in the pubs which were the clearing houses of the sport, of gambling which governed it, an admiration for physical strength, ferocity and an ability to use fists which was considered manly, plus a love of other long-established blood sports.

Peers were 'the priests of the national cult, who presided over the ceremonies and held the rough and often turbulent multitude in awe'.[4] They attended and officiated in fights, shielded offenders from the law, and put up money for fights. For their part, the lower orders supplied the fighters and most of the spectators.

It was an 'almost unimaginable' relationship, according to the *Times*, which accepted that watching prize fighting would appeal to the 'lower orders of men' but believed more was to be expected from men of superior rank, who 'had responsibilities to the Crown and to Parliament and should not be engaged in breaking the King's Peace where their dignity, privilege and importance were compromised'.[5]

Prize fighting was said to be beneficial for the lower orders, as a diversion because it stopped them from becoming discontented and, unlike the French, turning their attention to revolution. A contrary view was that prize fighting was not the hobby of the lower classes, and only the support of men of influence and wealth' kept it going.[6] Whatever, a prize fight was said to be the Carnival of England.

> On such an occasion the distinctions of rank are laid aside; the decencies of society are forgotten. The pickpocket bets with the peer......and the dandy of the drawing-room is proud of a sly nod from the hanger-on of the Fives Court. All are vulgarized.[7]

When Edward Turner fought in London in 1819, a large attendance, ignoring heavy rain, included 'a chain of *drags*, from the Lord's barouche to the Westminster cabbage cart, filed half a dozen deep for many miles'.[8] Again, a Turner battle in the capital later that year attracted 'all orders, from his *Grace* and *Lordship* to the *bustlers* and *drillmen*', and 'A few Coronets gave an air of respectability' to a contest involving Turner in London in 1824.[9]

***

THE sport was thought to help fill a need for fighting men in Britain, which had been at war almost continuously during the preceding one hundred years, with hostilities continuing into the first quarter of the 19th century, although the major conflicts, the Napoleonic Wars and the war with the USA were over by 1815. However, the possibility of invasion remained a major concern (there had been a French incursion at Fishguard in South Wales in 1799).

In the first decade of the century, to meet this need press gangs in London began to round up fighters and able-bodied spectators, nabbing 'both the combatants with their seconds, and fifteen stout young men' one time, and 'about forty good hands' another.[10] The authorities clearly hadn't forgotten where they could find recruits for, one hundred years later, early in the First World War, there was the same need – and approach. It was reported then that three thousand men were at a boxing venue in London when a raid by police and soldiers, who demanded a show of identity cards, arrested 220. who were 'marched off for evading their duty under the Military Service Act'.[11]

While the authorities required fighting men in times of war, the public demanded them, it appears, in peacetime. It was claimed in a brief interlude between hostilities that

> After so long a war, people have been so much accustomed to battles and bloodshed, that they cannot brook a sudden stoppage of these interesting details. Boxing and Bull-baiting afford tolerable substitutes.[12]

The use of fists was seen as the manly British way of settling disputes, unlike that of 'effeminate' foreigners, who, with no knowledge of the sport, used knives in arguments with fatal results whereas an Englishman would only have knocked his opponent down.

It bore 'an affinity to national courage' as opposed to the 'cold-blooded inhumanity' in foreign practices such as the barbarous Parisian custom of 'throwing the bird' where a live goose was suspended from a pole and killed by sticks thrown at it. This argument was undermined, however, in Wales at least where the similar 'throwing at cocks' was a particularly brutal pastime'.[13]

***

PRIZE fighting proved so popular that towns would put up the money to attract a big event, aware of the business it would bring in from substantial crowds. In later life, Borrow longed for this period, the time in his youth,

> when a pugilistic encounter between two noted champions was almost considered a national affair, when tens of thousands of individuals, high and low, meditated and brooded upon it, the first thing in the morning and the last thing at night, until the great event was decided. . . . In the days of pugilism it was no vain boast to say that one Englishman was a match for two of T'other race. . . . what a bold and vigorous aspect pugilism wore at that time'![14]

Prize-fights were a regular occurrence at the opposite ends of the social scale. Government inspectors visiting Newgate prison 'saw a regular boxing match between two criminals, stripped and fettered, having their bottle holders, and sitting on the knees of their seconds as systematically as if they were fighting in a field'.[15] At Eton public school, a two-hour contest between two teenage pupils fought over sixty rounds, ended in the death of the 15-year-old son of the Earl of Shaftesbury; forty years after a similar tragedy at the establishment. A North Wales landowner, Thomas Assheston Smith, of the Vaynol estate at Bangor, who later became an MP, had been an Eton combatant, and, was 'long-remembered for his fighting skills' at the school at the start of this 'Golden Age'.[16]

Such fascination with the sport was noted abroad, the French viewing Britain as a nation not merely of shopkeepers, as Napoleon is supposed to have sneered, but as 'a nation of *boxing* shopkeepers'.[17] Foreign visitors who could not have helped noticing 'the walls of the Capital of England placarded with bills, announcing the publication of Portraits of two *well-known Bruisers'* made similar comments. Author Washington Irving informed his American readers of the upper classes' love of boxing and betting on the sport, and Grand Duke Nicholas, of Russia, asked 'to see the method of English boxing', and was a spectator at one contest in 1817.[18]

***

BUT, if there was, indeed, a 'Golden Age', the term would be more accurately confined to the London Prize Ring.

Previous studies of prize fighting in Britain have relied on capital-based publications, for which the rest of the country hardly existed. These journals reported almost exclusively on fighters appearing in London, which, to them, was the only place of significance for the sport. Provincial feats amounted to 'little until a boxer makes his *debut* in the London ring. In fact, a pugilist is not recognized till he has made this appearance'.[19]

***

THERE was not yet a 'Golden Age' in Wales, but prize fighting was certainly established by this time, and at least since the 17th century.

In the Aberdare area, a 17th century fight figure was remembered as the keeper of a tavern at the foot of Aber-cwm-y-bwcci hill, who was 'a great admirer of the noble art of self-defence and was wont to officiate at meetings of that nature wearing a red cap ('cap coch' in Welsh).[20]

He was the ostensible cause of the community changing its name over two hundred years later. Villagers at Capcoch in the Cynon Valley had complained that 'the origin of the name was very degrading' because of its association with him. Another reason put forward was embarrassment caused by disrespectful immigrants to the area – 'the monoglot Englishman was apt to give the last syllable of the word a silly and vulgar meaning'. The local council agreed to substitute Abercwmboi, but the primary school and local pub retained the name.

At Sirhowy and Tredegar, there were weekly bareknuckle fights at recognised spots such as 'the Back of the Stables, Cefn Golau, No. 2 Pit, [and] the Bloody Spot or Top Pitch, Sirhowy…the Bloody Spot being a favourite venue for these bare-knuckle bouts'.[21]

As well as 'Jack of the Wern', Tom Gibb, of Oxwich, in the Gower peninsula, was a formidable prize fighter in the eighteenth century, and was seen in action regularly at Penrice Fair. Thomas Hughes, from Mochdre in Conwy, was a boxer before becoming a Methodist preacher in 1771, and, also in the 18th century, another fighting sinner turned preacher was Robert Thomas of the Ffridd in Bala Deulyn, Caernarfonshire, (father of the puritanical Methodist preacher John Roberts, of Llangwm) who used to 'sing and string rhymes and tell tales in the inns-not to mention his prowess as a pugilist-before he found grace'.[22]

In 1791 'the hardest-fought battle ever remembered in that part of Wales' was reported to have taken place at Dolgellau, Merionethshire, featuring Ellis Pannwr, who for several years had been regarded as the Welsh champion, and Roderick Lewis; they fought for seventy guineas a-side, and, at a time before the law focussed on such events, the organisers were able to charge for admission, the pair sharing £17 entrance money.[23] The correspondent enthused

> Such display of gymnastic ability has not perhaps been exceeded by Johnson and Big Ben. The hard blows (without falling) re-echoed for thirty minutes and upwards: but to shorten the combat, the former hit his antagonist his favourite blow, under the left ear, which terminated the battle, and brought him to the stage apparently dead; and the umpires, Rees Meredith, and Rowlands Wemdu, Esqrs. pronounced him the conqueror.

In a sobering note, the report continued: 'We are sorry to add that Roderick Lewis has but little hopes from Dr. Dowtain of that town of recovering his left sight'.

In 1794, John Barlow issued a challenge in *The Welsh Harp*, Flintshire, to fight 'any man of his weight for a shilling', the gauntlet being taken up by Thomas Peak.[24] Around the beginning of the 19th century, Welsh Wesleyan Methodists at Tredegar used the house of Richard Evans 'one time a noted pugilist'.[25]

A poem celebrates a prize fight in the early nineteenth century featuring a Montgomeryshire man, 'Young Bloody'. It includes the lines

Come all you gallant boxers
In boxing take delight,
Draw near and I will tell you
Of a famous noble fight
It was as hard a battle, boys,
As ever yet was seen.
And now, for it was fought, my boys,
On Ludlow Castle Green.

Chorus
Success unto Young Bloody,
Let every hearty sing,
He is the conquering hero
And the champion of the ring[26].

The poem reveals a great interest in prize fighting (the combatants 'stood amidst thousands'), the mechanics of such events, with wealthy backers each nominating a champion, and the money that could be involved (the stakes were 'five hundred pounds in gold'; the betting odds, the fears of bribery and the flash language. Among the backers was a 'Squire Harrison', believed to be Major Robert J. Harrison, the grandfather of the first Mayor of Montgomery who is said to have wagered his carriage and pair on the fight.

Few references to prize fighting at any level in Wales during this period have been discovered. In 1812, *Cambrian* reported only that a 'pitched battle' was fought at Newport, Monmouthshire, 'between a Welshman known by the name of George the Sailor, and an Englishman'.

For a clash at Llandaff in 1811, *Cambrian* gave the names of the principals as well as the main incidents in the 27 rounds spread over 32 minutes. The *Carmarthen Journal* reported to a similar extent a contest at Haverfordwest in 1812, between 'Abraham Platt and Solomon Moseley, two travelling Jews', which lasted thirty-seven minutes and a half. This round-by-round account revealed that a 'considerable degree of science' was exhibited, and betting was involved. The following year, a contest was reported by a London newspaper to have taken place at Chepstow involving Molineux, (presumably the well-known American of that name) and a fighter called Horton.

The Welsh prize-fighting tradition was recognised outside the country, for, when it was suggested to the English champion Daniel Mendoza in 1796 that it might pay him to pass on his skills in Wales, he replied warily that he might 'find them *too knowing* already, and perhaps receive a *banging* for his pains'.[27] Nevertheless, Mendoza did give an exhibition at Neath the following year.

***

CROWDS in Wales were surprisingly large for such a covert activity in a country which had only a small and widely scattered population. Evans remarks that the most striking impression from an imagined bird's eye view of the Welsh countryside would have been that of the absence of people; in

1801 Wales had a population of only 587,345, 'fairly evenly spread' over the country'.[28]

There were no large towns comparable to those in England. At the beginning of the century, Swansea had the largest population (10,117), followed by Merthyr Tydfil (7,705) which eased in front by 1821. In 1801, Cardiff, with a population of 1,870, was a small market town and port, and by 1821, its population was only 3,521. Newport in Monmouthshire was only a small village at the beginning of the century with just 1,087 inhabitants. The prize fight at Llandaff in 1811 between James and Stephens attracted a crowd of nearly 500, equivalent to one fifth of the population of Cardiff, and up to 1,000 watched the fight the following year at Newport involving George the Sailor which amounted to almost one half of the population of that port.

Bando or bandy, an early form of hockey, has been proposed as the first mass spectator sport in modern south Wales, with games said to have attracted crowds as large as 3,000.[29] Yet, fight attendances were frequently estimated to be much larger. At least 5,000 was reported for a 103-round contest at Harewood End near Monmouth in 1824 between a Monmouth quarryman, Robert Parry, and Thomas Powell, a blacksmith, of Broad Oak, Herefordshire.

Taking advantage of this appetite for prize fighting, opportunists staged exhibitions in Swansea and Cardiff in March 1826 which drew 'numerous and admiring spectators who believed they were watching famous pugilist Barney Aaron'. But when the imposter was shown a news item stating that the real Aaron was due to fight in London the same day, 'he and his associate decamped suddenly' leaving hotel bills and bills for printing advertisements.[30]

Spectators travelled great distances, mostly on foot, as the majority owned neither a horse nor carriage. They were used to it. People 'thought nothing' of walking seven miles to visit relatives in another village, and many men walked even further to their places of work, with distances of 28 miles a day each way 'by no means freakish' examples.[31]

Welsh cultural icon Iolo Morganwg (Edward Williams), once walked from Flemingstone more than fifty miles to Bristol and then back home again the following day, while the future Bishop of Llandaff, Edward Copleston, often walked forty miles in a day. At the beginning of the nineteenth century, Copleston, in his younger days walked from Oxford to Marlborough in Wiltshire in one day, and also from Oxford to Ufton in Warwickshire, the first twenty-two miles in five hours.

***

THERE is little evidence of interference in prize fights by the authorities, who in South Wales at this time had bigger concerns. Troops were called in regularly from English garrisons at Bristol and Gloucester to crack down on unrest among coal and iron miners in the upper reaches of Glamorgan and neighbouring Monmouthshire over wage cuts, lack of work, and the truck system.

In 1816, cavalry was sent into the Monmouthshire and Breconshire border area, where more than 1.500 colliers and miners were said to be in 'open revolt' and there were fears for the security of the vast stock of firearms at the army depot at Brecon. In 1822 came the beginnings of the Scotch Cattle movement and a foretaste of the style of the Rebecca riots of south west Wales twenty years later. Magistrates offered a fifty pounds reward for the conviction of persons going disguised in women's clothes and with blacked faces, by night, intimidating workers, actions referred to as 'the terror of the night visitation from the 'black cattle' and the 'black ladies'.[32]

The trouble came to a head with attacks on a wagon train carrying coal and escorted by cavalry up the narrow, winding Western Valley of Monmouthshire to iron works at Ebbw Vale. Workers ripped up the tram road, hurled rocks down the steep hillside, burnt wagons and pushed others in the river and were only driven off when troops opened fire and used their swords.

***

WHAT the fight crowds witnessed would have been familiar today only to the extent that two men could be seen attempting to assault each other (eventually, that is, as they often spent many minutes sizing each other up before committing). Bare-fisted, stripped to the waist, wearing long pants, and, as practically all encounters were on grass, wearing spiked shoes to retain their footing, fighters would throw punches, attempt wrestling throws, kick and bite – and even pull each other's hair. Rather than move their bodies out of the way, bare-knuckle fighters stood toe-to-toe, attempting to block incoming punches with their forearms and elbows. Attacks to the body were preferred, because with neither gloves nor bandaging covering the fists, punching to the head carried a strong risk of injuring the hand.

Prize-fighting operated mostly under the rules drawn up in 1743 by Jack Broughton, the then champion of England. Broughton's rules outlawed only biting and gouging an opponent's eyes, nose, or mouth with fingernails. Attacks such as kicking an opponent in the belly were legal. The rules were based on those of Pankration, a blend of bare-knuckle boxing and wrestling, an event introduced into the Olympic Games in 648 BC.

Golden Age?

Under Broughton's rules, wrestling holds were allowed only above the waist, but such skills proved to be at least as important as punching ability. With this in mind Mendoza recommended that fighters should lean forward, hands well out in front, and with feet planted, rather than standing side-on and on their toes as in modern boxing. The squat stance was to maintain a good balance and make it difficult to grab and throw an opponent to the ground and then land heavily on top of him.

There were wrestling moves a-plenty in the fight in 1817 which established Edward Turner's reputation in the prize-ring. To close the first round, Jack Scroggins 'gave Turner a sample of his famous cross-buttock', and did the same to end every round until the 25th when the stronger Scroggins tired, allowing the more skilful Turner to return the cross-buttocks with interest. In another fight full of wrestling moves in 1822, George Davis 'threw his adversary a rattling cross-buttock' on his way to a six round win.

The ring was not the lonely place it is now, with only the referee and the two fighters allowed inside the ropes during each round. For big matches it might contain up to eight men, the two fighters and two seconds for each side, plus an umpire for each side, the referee remaining outside the ropes. Frequently, it became even more crowded. In Turner's chaotic clash with Scroggins, not even stewards using horsewhips 'with indiscriminate vengeance' could quell a riot; the ring ropes were broken down, the crowd burst in and the two men ended up fighting among their supporters, Turner himself being struck by a horsewhip in the confusion.[33]

To reduce the number of unruly spectators, contests including several of Turner's encounters, began to be held in even greater secrecy.

There was no points scoring system as in modern boxing, neither were there timed rounds; a round could last for a few seconds or for many minutes, each session ending when one man went to ground. He had half a minute to resume after a fall or be declared the loser. If he was able to stand and get to the mark, or his seconds could manhandle him to the mark, then he could continue the fight. The fighter, or more likely his seconds or his backers would decide when he'd had enough and could quit. Boxers could drop to the ground without taking a punch, to gain additional recovery time, and fights would often drag on interminably without many actual punches being landed. A fight ended when one of the pugilists was unable to continue. If the battle could not be completed, as in the case of Turner v Scroggins when the crowd wrecked the ring, the referee's first task was to declare all bets null and void.

It was not unusual for the crowd to decide themselves if a fight should carry on. A contest in 1821 ended when one of the combatants failed to come up to scratch, but after the crowd broke into the ring it was resumed and they fought three more rounds before the same man collapsed and died.

Broughton's rules were generally adhered to as well in 'amateur' contests which appeared to have arisen out of quarrels in pubs. Instead of the argument erupting into a brawl inside or outside the pub, arrangements would be made to settle disputes in regular prize fighting fashion with side bets, referee, seconds, timekeeper and other ring rules observed.

Adhering to these rituals suggests an immersion in the culture of prize fighting, and the idea that this was more respectable or creditable than mere brawling, and that credibility and reputation among the community would be maintained only if these rules were followed. Also, of course, it would be appreciated that a fair fight was looked on by the courts more sympathetically than a street brawl.

Although fighters commonly styled themselves as 'champion' of their operating district, there was only one popularly recognised champion and he was champion of England, which meant champion of the rest of Britain. Champion meant the best man that could be found; there was no qualification of the title, and none of the modern weight divisions.

Apart from Broughton's rules, which dealt only with the fight itself, there were no health and safety rules and no organisation.

***

NEWSPAPERS condemned prize fighting as 'brutal', 'barbarous' and 'disgusting', and urged Parliament to ban it, yet, when they could obtain a fight report, they provided comprehensive coverage, and by so doing played a big part in popularising it.

What also boosted the sport's popularity was the 'wicked ingenuity' of the jargon used by the Press. For example, Billy Owen's opponent 'shot out a sneezer which sprung the claret from Taffy's proboscis', and Owen took 'a tremendous discharge on his leek trap which made the ivories chatter' and received 'an awakener on his chaffing engine', another punch in the mouth.[34]

Such language, it was claimed, helped to sanitize prize fighting, draw together those from the highest and lowest classes, and by lessening the horror of such events, and the misplaced levity with which those details were given, could only excite ridicule and treat the subject as a joke.

There was probably sound thinking, it was suggested, behind the jargon because if reports were written in plain language, 'it would be impossible to avoid a decided feeling of disgust'.[35] A newspaper illustrated its point by comparing language in *Bell's Life*, which said that one of the combatants 'napped a slogger on his snuffer-tray', with that in the *Times*, which said 'the unfortunate wretch received such a tremendous smash on the nose that the blow resounded all over the meadow in which the fight took place'.

Newspapers justified their coverage by claiming that, as 'historians of the day', they were 'obliged' to give information to the public; and were sacrificing feeling and taste to the gratification of readers. More credibly, as one conceded, if they did not, they would 'infallibly' lose many of their readers.

By the 1820s, newspaper coverage had increased, with readers being offered much more than basic details. At the end of 1824, *Cambrian* even reported the build-up to the encounter between Parry and Powell, identifying the combatants, also the date of the fight, when, the amount of side stakes, and where (the *White Swan*, Monmouth), the side stakes were to be deposited, as well as commenting that 'Even betting to a considerable amount was made'. The newspaper's account of the actual fight, at Harewood's-end, was more fulsome again. Setting the scene, it reported

> Early in the morning, the crowd pouring in one continued stream towards the scene of the action, attested the interest which this contest excited in the neighbourhood; there was not less than 5,000 persons present.

The newspaper, which had already that year reported all 77 rounds of the Spring v Langan contest for the Championship, and all 76 of their second fight, as well as devoting space frequently to lesser fights, proceeded to describe individually all 107 rounds of Parry v Powell.

This increasingly almost blow-by-blow coverage suggested a golden age for the sport in Wales was on its way.

---

[1] Times, 18, 20 July 1821.

Golden Age?

[2] Harry Mullan, *World Encyclopaedia of Boxing: The Definitive Illustrated Guide* (London, Carlton, 1999), p8.
[3] Times, 27 March 1787
[4] G. M. Trevelyan, *English Social History*, cited in David Thompson, *England in the nineteenth century* (185-1914) (Harmondsworth, Penguin, 1964), p. 19.
[5] Times, 1 May 1788; 23 August 1805; 8 August 1778; 4 February 1804.
[6] Berrow's Worcester Journal, 15 January 1824
[7] Bristol Mirror, cited in Royal Cornwall Gazette, 12 January 1822.
[8] Morning Chronicle, 19 June 1819
[9] Morning Chronicle, 27 October 1819. Morning Post, 22 April 1823; Caledonian Mercury, 21 February 1824; Morning Chron., 10 November 1824.
[10] Morning Post, 1 August 1801; 24 July 1809.
[11] Merthyr Express, 9 September 1916.
[12] Morning Chronicle, 18 December 1801.
[13] Martin Johnes, *A History of Sport in Wales* (Cardiff, Univ. of Wales Press, 2005), p.4.
[14] George Borrow, *The Scholar, The Gypsy, The Priest* (London, Macmillan, 1900, First pub. 1851),
[15] Morning Post, 15 June 1814
[16] Caernarvon & Denbigh Herald, 17 February 1893.
[17] Journal de Paris, cited in Morning Chronicle, 20 August 1804.
[18] Clive Emsley, *Hard Men: Violence in England since 1750* (Hambledon and London, London, 2005), p.41. Washington Irving, 'John Bull', in The Sketch Book, 1820. Morning Post, 16 January 1808. Morning Chronicle, 14 February 1817
[19] Henry Downes Miles, *Pugilistica: The History of British Boxing* (Edinburgh, John Grant, 1906), p. 380, p. 366.
[20] Aberdare Leader, 14 October 1905.
[21] Oliver Jones, *The Early Days of Sirhowy and Tredegar* (Newport: Starling Press, 1969), p. 63.
[22] Y Cymmrodor the magazine of the Honourable Society of Cymmrodorion (1900-1951). Vol. 45 1 January 1938 Page: 115
[23] Kentish Gazette, 9 August 1791.
[24] National Archives of Wales, Crime and Punishment Database. http://www.llgc.org.uk/sesiwn_s.htm.
[25] Y Goleuad, 8 March 1884. Gower – Vol. 27, 1976. Bathafarn - Cyf. 19 1964 Methodism in Monmouthshire in 1851.
[26] Collections, historical and archaeological relating to Montgomeryshire Collections, Vol. 45 (1938), p. 183-185. The National Library of Wales.
[27] Times, 6 August 1796.
[28] Neil Evans, As rich as California…Opening and Closing the frontier: Wales 1780 – 1870, in (Gareth Elwyn Jones and Dai Smith, eds.,) *The People of Wales* (Llandysul, Gomer Press, 2000), p. 112
[29] Gareth Williams, 1905 and all that: Essays on Rugby Football, Sport and Welsh Society (Llandysul,1991, p. 114), cited in Johnes, A History of Sport in Wales, p. 3.
[30] Cambrian, 25 March 1826.
[31] Philip S. Bagwell, 'The Decline of Rural Isolation', in G. E. Mingay (ed.), *The Victorian Countryside*, Vol. 1 (London, Routledge & Keegan Paul, 1981), p. 32
[32] Bristol Mercury, 20, 27 April 1822.
[33] Morning Chronicle, 27 March 1817
[34] Caledonian Mercury, 21 February 1824.
[35] Glasgow Herald, 20 April 1860.

4

Fighters to mid-1820s

The most prominent Welsh fighters in the so-called 'Golden Age' were those appearing in the London prize ring who were generally born of migrant families in the capital.

Edward Turner was born in 1791 in London, in Crucifix Lane, Bermondsey, to parents from the Newtown area in Montgomeryshire, mid-Wales.[1] He began his pugilistic career in the 'sparring club or school for glove practice' that had been set up in the Bermondsey tanning yard where he was an apprentice.

> Here......young Turner greatly distinguished himself, by the quickness, natural grace, and intuitive steadiness of his style of sparring...and this was exemplified in Turner's first battle, with the foreman of the yard, John Baulch, from Bristol, who often spoke disparagingly of the Welsh and boasted he could beat Turner.[2]

It proved a vain boast, for, after an hour's battle, a badly beaten Baulch was led helpless from the ring.

Turner's first recorded contest was against 'a big Irishman' in the cock-pit at the *Huntsman and Hounds* public house in Lock's Fields, London, in 1813 which he won inside 25 minutes. His subsequent battles, as a result of his work taking him to Scotland and the north of England, included victories after half an hour in Glasgow, and in 45 minutes in front of 'thousands' on Newcastle racecourse against Blackett (6ft. 1ins and over 14 stone); on his return to London, Turner beat Youler, 'Davenport's Jew', in St. George's Fields in 35 minutes.

Turner was ahead of his time as far as his fighting style was concerned. For a start he was a southpaw, facing his opponent with his right foot and right hand forward, the opposite stance of nearly all of his contemporaries. On top of that, he did not stand toe to toe with his opponent in the usual manner but chose rather to hit and then move away out of range. This hit-and-not-be-hit style grew to be admired as the sport evolved, but in the early days some thought it unsporting. Not least some of his opponents, among them Blackett who,

> received so much severe punishment, without being able to return any milling upon Turner, that he swore, in the utmost rage. 'he would not fight any more, as Turner was not a fair fighter, and that he did nothing but make hits, and then jump away.[3]

Turner came to wide notice after his first outing in the recognised London ring in October 1816 at Moulsey Hurst. Few were present to see him take on John Curtis, an experienced man who was the clear favourite, Turner being only a novice as far as the betting crowd were aware. But Curtis was another who found Turner too difficult to fathom. Pioneering prize fight writer Pierce Egan explained

> His position was so formidable, and his mode of setting-to so different from pugilists in general, that Curtis could not approach him, with anything like safety, to make a hit.[4]

In a fight where 'it was all on one side from first to last', Curtis was so battered over the 68 rounds that he died shortly afterwards.

As well as enabling a likely betting coup, the anonymity of provincial fighters also worked to Turner's advantage when he subsequently appeared at the Old Bailey charged with Curtis' murder.

Turner claimed never to have appeared previously in the prize ring, no doubt intending the court to believe he meant any prize ring, rather than just the London Prize Ring. The court, like the capital's prize fight community, ignorant of anything happening outside their sphere (and/or privately supportive of the sport), duly obliged, and this 'fact', together with Turner's sporting behaviour during the fight, was taken into consideration when a lenient sentence of two months' gaol was imposed after he was found guilty of manslaughter.

As his reputation grew, Turner went on to appear regularly in front of crowds of twenty thousand in a career lasting until 1824. His successes in three meetings with Scroggins, all taking place in less than a year after his release from gaol, 'established his pugilistic fame'.

Their first encounter was in the London area in March 1817, when the unruly twenty thousand strong crowd broke into the ring, causing the fight to be abandoned in the tenth round.

Their second battle, in June at Sawbridgeworth, Hertfordshire, was subsequently held in comparative secrecy, and the site was switched in such a hurry to evade the law that hundreds did not have time to get there. They missed seeing Scroggins throw Turner with his famous cross-buttock move to end the early rounds, but what Scroggins gained by this move he lost

> by the severe up hand hits he received in his endeavour to break down Turner's impenetrable guard. Scroggins tired as the fight wore on and Turner was able to return the cross-buttocks with interest.[5]

Scroggins, again the betting favourite, suffered his first defeat after 33 rounds in 75 minutes.

Their third meeting was at Shepperton the following October. Turner, the favourite this time, had, by the 14th round, beaten Scroggins's head 'into stupidity', winning easily over 45 rounds in one hour and 29 minutes.

Scroggins said he was baffled by Turner's reach and manner of fighting and it was impossible to make a springing hit; with this acknowledged superiority he did not want any more to do with Turner, and any other fighter was now welcome to take him on.

An eagerly-anticipated match was made against the Irishman Jack Randall, at Crawley Hurst in Sussex in December 1818, and, in what was regarded as an Ireland v Wales clash, Turner was beaten in 34 rounds over 2 hours, 19 minutes and 30 seconds. A poem paid tribute to his bravery which included the lines

> Back'd by the Welsh, Ned stood his ground,
> A better man could ne'er be found,
> Showing fine science every round,
> And not a flincher he![6]

Apart from Turner's lack of punching power, in what was a portend of things to come, his relaxed fitness regime - he was a typical prize-fighter with regard to his dissolute lifestyle, at least - had also been a contributory factor in his defeat.

Turner won his next two clashes, forcing Cyrus Davis to retire in the 30th round, their battle lasting 53 minutes, and then in front of over 20,000 beating John Martin at the same venue, Martin retiring in the 42nd round after one hour and nine minutes.

But Turner was warned that his excessive drinking of gin might prove costly when he went into a second fight with Martin at Crawley Common on a hot June day in 1821; the sporting journal *Fancy* commenting: 'Lushington is evidently his master, and must be cut with'.[7] Near Drury Lane Theatre in London was the *Harp Tavern* where a club of hard drinkers called The City of Lushington had been founded in 1750. It is believed that the word 'lush', meaning a habitual drunk, originated here.

The same issue drew attention to Turner's 'womanising', advising

> 'Woman, likewise, is not only morally averse to the sports of the Fancy, but she is also physically detrimental to the ring, whether she wear the bauble so named or not'.

The unheeded cautioning was prophetic, as Martin's heavy blows to Turner's weakened body forced him to retire after 59 rounds over one hour and 28 minutes. Turner went on to lose his next two fights as well, Cyrus Davis avenging a defeat with a comfortable victory over a shadow of the former champion in February 1823 at Harpenden Heath, in fifteen rounds over 55 minutes and four seconds, and then Peace Inglis lowering his colours.

Turner had been given another chance by his backers for old times' sake when he was matched with Inglis in April 1824, but neither they nor anybody else thought he had a chance of victory because his drinking had so undermined his health. The local paper reported that when the 'celebrated pugilist' returned to Newtown for training, 'he had a severe attack of inflammatory fever, chiefly brought on by the intemperance in which he had so freely indulged'.[8]

Turner was, nevertheless, on top for most of the fight before tiring and being withdrawn in the 47th round after one hour and eighteen minutes. A newspaper remarked

> The matchless character of his science was best proved by the trifling degree of punishment which he received; while Inglis…wearing the laurels of victory has to confess they were dearly, very dearly, bought.[9]

Although Turner was now widely believed to be finished as a fighter, a second meeting was arranged between the pair. Beforehand, doctors advised Turner against continuing in the ring, 'but as the poor fellow's money was down, he had nothing left but to fight or forfeit the result'.[10]

He was advised to take the healing waters at Llandrindod Wells in mid-Wales, and 'the salubrious effects of these celebrated springs amply justified the confidence with which they had been recommended, and the brave little Welshman entered the ring in such condition as to render victory certain.'[11]

Turner's much improved condition 'astonished' a number of good judges, and 'proved he had, for a time at least, completely abandoned those enervating habits in which he had been too apt to indulge'.[12] It wasn't a mirage, Turner was back to his best; he was on top throughout and won by a knockout in the fifteenth round after 46 minutes, so recovering his lost prestige.

After this surprise victory, Turner returned to Newtown, where 'He was hailed with all the respect due to a hero in a more important cause', with a peal of church bells, a feast of two roasted sheep, with entertainment provided by Welsh bards.[13]

Sadly, the victory over Inglis proved to be a last hurrah. In the ensuing months, Turner was reported as being 'very unwell' and warned again to take care of himself. Less than a year later, he was 'sinking into the grave'. Ex-champion Tom Spring appealed for help for the stricken warrior and announced that a farewell benefit for him would be held later in the month, but Turner died of consumption on the very day of the fund-raiser, 18 April, 1826.

Tributes poured in, among them from *Cambrian,* which stated: 'As a boxer his fame will always stand high. He was by trade in the tanning line, which all his competitors bear marks of', and from Pierce Egan, who wrote: 'Of his weight – one of the bravest of the brave – as good as gold'.[14] *Bell's Life* marked his passing with 'Elegiac Stanzas on the death of Ned Turner'.[15] Part of it read:

Alas, poor Ned! –
He's floor'd – he's dead;
His fighting days are ended.
The Champion Death
Has 109oul'd his breath;
His bellows can't be mended.

Poor Ned is gone;
And now has done
His fist work as his mouth-work.
<u>The boast of Wales,</u>
"Odds splutter a' nails,"
And glory of all Southwark.

The tanner's trade
He always made
His business, and took pride in
A desperate fight
Because he might
By trade give folks a hiding.

And, reader, mark,

Though with oak bark
He work'd to tan his leather,
His heart, now broke,
Was heart of oak,
Yet light as any feather.

Too light, alas!
Since flesh is grass,
Because he was light-hearted;
The best blue ruin
Was his undoing,
And so he soon departed.

'Twas Deady's best
Laid him to rest;
He died, alas! Thro' Deady;
With full proof gin
He filled his skin,
And soon for Death was ready.

At thirty-four
(He was no more),
This noble-minded Tanner
Into a pit
Was put, to fit
His corpse in proper manner.

Now weep all you,
Who ought to do,
Well-scienc'd man, or learner;
And treel join
Your tears with mine,
To mourn for poor Ned Turner!

If honest worth,
Less priz'd on earth,
In heavenly choir should seat him;
To join him there,
Let all prepare,

For I should like to meet him.

Years after his death, Turner was remembered by a sermon rich in prize ring metaphors by 'one of the lower order of *Ranting Preachers*' hoping to persuade his audience to give him money, who complained 'I dare say you would all pay see a boxing match between Turner and Randall; yet you don't like to pay for seeing a pitched battle between me and *Beelzebub*.'[16]

***

THOMAS 'Paddington' Jones was another London Welshman. He had probably 22 fights around the turn of the century, the number inexact, with various sources failing to agree. He was born in 1771 in Montgomeryshire in mid-Wales, and was taken to Paddington, London, by his mother.[17]

Jones began in the ring at the age of 15. Most of his fights were minor battles, with Jones, just over 5ft. 7ins and weighing 10st. 5lbs., winning all but 5 often against far heavier opponents. *Bell's Life* described him as a

> perfect master of the science....He was a tremendous hitter, and could use left and right with equal effect. He was what is properly termed 'a fair, stand-up fighter;' went to the head of his antagonist, steady and firm – brave as a lion, and without a bit of 'flinch' about him.[18]

Jones' most important contest was in 1799 against rising star Jem Belcher, from Bristol, when he gave away two stones and acquitted himself well. He knocked future champion Belcher down to end the first round, but in the tenth Belcher 'put in some tremendous hits with the rapidity of lightning' to take control, Jones 'nobly contesting for 33 minutes for the space of 33 minutes before he gave in'.[19]

After his retirement, Jones seconded fighters for many years, among them Scroggins when he fought Turner.

Jones was remembered as

> one of the very best of the old school of pugilists – a man who although always poor, maintained a character for unimpeachable honesty, and unquestioned game – and whose good conduct on all occasions....gained him universal esteem. He was a bright example for the pugilists of his day.[20]

Jack Rasher was a Whitechapel butcher who had a short but hard-fought career in the London area in the early 1820s.. Limited in skill but with more than his share of gameness, he was in the second rank of performers and as such fought on the undercard of matches involving Turner and also Tom Spring. After Spring beat Burns on Epsom Downs in 1820, Rasher took on the exceptional physical specimen Charles Gyblett, who was said to be able to 'lift seven hundredweight and to jump over a five-bar gate with the utmost ease', and he proved his athletic ability after winning in 58 rounds over one hour and thirty minutes when he 'ran and jumped as high as five feet.'[21] One of his wins was against fellow butcher Joe Spencer at Crawley Down after 'a most desperate slaughtering fight between two of the cutting-up tribe' over seventy rounds in one hour and a quarter.[22]

Rasher, however, followed fellow Welshman Turner in his intake of alcohol and in his last appearance in the ring, turning up for a benefit evening for Turner, it was obvious he had been 'very busy with Mr. Lushington recently' and was derided when he sparred with three fellow pugilists.[23]

Robert Smout, from Welshpool, Montgomeryshire, fought William Shields, an Irishman, in Peckham Fields, London, in 1825, a report revealing

> It was as gallant a battle as has been witnessed for some time. Both men went to work fearlessly and smashed each other in the most finished style. Smout took the lead, but Shields was not to be told out – he was as game as a lion, and although severely

punished, he succeeded in reaping the laurels of victory in the twelfth round.[24]

George Davis, a promising fighter in the London area, was 'a Welshman who had fought his way up, and on whom the Deputy Commissioner had passed a promising opinion'.[25] Davis's clash at 'Green Meadows, on the Stanmore Road', in 1822 was full of wrestling throws, and he

> 'threw his adversary a rattling cross-buttock, while in round four they exchanged hit for hit more than a dozen times till their hands were swollen as round as dumplings.'

Davis won in six rounds. An impressed reporter commented 'Davis will be a sticker with some practice'.

A contemporary of the aforementioned fighters was Charles Williams, who styled himself the Welsh champion 'being a Taffy by birth', and whose day job was reported, by someone evidently paid by the word, to be 'a waiting gentleman upon that noble animal the horse'.[26] Williams and John Mahers who, 'although not much known in the sporting world, were of some note in their own neighbourhood', met at Stratchfield in 1825 with Mahers throwing Williams several times with cross buttocks before Williams retired after fifteen rounds in 36 minutes.

Passing reference was made to D. Jones, identified only as 'a Welchman', who fought in the Tooting area in 1819 and won in eight rounds. Another newspaper report in 1823 referred to a prize fight involving 'Lewis, a Welshman' at Blackheath on November 5 for £6 a-side and 2s. 6d. for a leg of mutton. That was more than likely John 'Jack' Lewis, who, the previous July fought 'a sharp battle and not without science' against Green, for £10 a-side in London's Copenhagen Fields, Green retiring with an injured finger.

In January of the following year, two overweight fighters – 'Griffiths, a Welch sailor, and Rogers, an old smuggler' both 'better calculated for feasting than fighting' met at Hongeham, near Deal, Griffiths losing in eight rounds. In 1825 a newspaper reported 'Scotch and Welch champions' sparring at the Tennis Court in Haymarket.

Spectators at a cock-fight at Cheltenham in 1826 had an unexpected treat when rival handlers got into a dispute and decided to settle it with a prize fight, the 'Welchman' losing in six rounds.

In 1838 in the Paddington area of London, Morgan Jones beat the two stones heavier George Davison in 38 minutes. Two years later William Jones beat John Greenstreet in ten rounds over 24 minutes on Woking Common, London.

***

TOM Spring 'may' have been the best Welsh fighter of the nineteenth century. He won the Championship in 1821, and that meant he was the champion of England at any weight. Spring, whose real name was Winter (or Wynter), was born in the Herefordshire village of Fownhope on the border with Wales, in 1792.

However, 'may' is the operative word here The only reference to his having a Welsh background occurs in the *Cambrian* newspaper which exclaimed proudly in 1824: 'We understand that Spring, the Champion of England, is a Welshman; his real name is Wynter, and his family are of Kerigkadarn, in Breconshire'.[27]

The source and veracity of the journal's information, which came days after his final fight, is not known. Spring's biographer does not refer to Welsh connections, neither does the fighter himself nor commentators at the time. That is persuasive, but not conclusive, evidence.

There is, though, a probability of a Welsh background. His mother Mary's maiden name was Davies.[28] There is a marriage documented for 01 August 1782 at Fownhope between Joseph Winter, the name of the fighter's father. and Mary Davies. There are also baptism records of several females named Mary Davies, who could have been Spring's mother, nearby in Wales, but no definite link has been established by this research.

Spring's ring career began at the age of 17 with victory over a local fighter, and after another success, he moved to London, where he built his reputation. Despite losing an eye in the only defeat of his career, Spring went on to be recognised as champion by beating Bill Neat before retiring at 29 to resume as a publican. Spring did not possess a strong punch so he worked on his defence and was considered one of the most scientific of the early boxers.

Another claim to fame, probably unique at that, was that he had a newspaper named after him, the weekly publication *Tom Spring's Life in London and Sporting Chronicle* (1841–4).

***

THE lack of Welsh references to Spring may be significant, however, because exiles in London usually maintained a strong sense of national identity, and there appeared to be a supportive network for pugilists among the estimated 10,000 to 60,000 people of Welsh descent in the city in the early nineteenth century.[29]

Turner regularly sang Welsh songs inside the ropes, while for a fight shortly after St. David's Day, he returned to mid-Wales to train or to recuperate. *Bell's Life* reported in 1825 that Turner chose 'the anniversary of his titular Saint, St. David, for his benefit, & in consequence, the Five's Court was crowded with the Knights of the Leek'.[30] Turner was also a backer for fellow Welshman Smout, when he fought in Peckham Fields, in 1825. The Turner and Smout families hailed from the same part of Wales, and both fighters were in the leather trade. Further evidence of the links, one of D. Jones's seconds in his 1819 fight in the Tooting area, was 'Old Taff', and after his eighth-round victory, Jones 'was carried off the ground by the Taffies in triumph'.[31]

The London-based publications emphasised their nationality whenever Welsh fighters appeared in their columns, Turner was often referred to as Welsh, usually with accompanying stereotypical references. The perception of the Welsh, which had given satirists, cartoonists and broad-sheet writers so much fun since Tudor times, persisted into the early part of the nineteenth century possibly because there were so few other 'foreigners' to attract attention.[32]

Their references showed an indulgent and amused attitude. 'Taffy', 'leeks' and 'goats' (suggesting the inhospitable terrain of Wales in contrast with the lowland South East of England – the poor, pastoral upland societies of Wales was one of the basic divisions between 'civil' and 'uncivil' societies comprehended by English commentators of this period.) were used regularly with reference to Welsh fighters. They also referred to the Welsh claim to be descendants of the Trojans, and reputedly the oldest and noblest inhabitants of Britain.

Turner was said to be 'descended from that warlike race of people, denominated ANCIENT BRITONS' and 'seems to have imbibed those true notions of valour, which so eminently distinguish that loyal and brave description of men', while Bill Charles was referred to as 'a disciple of the long-bearded mountaineers of Wales'.[33]

***

Fighters to mid-1820s

IN contrast to the level of attention their compatriots received in London, Welsh fighters elsewhere in Britain generally went unremarked upon, other than having their nationality noted. In a rare reference to an obvious dandy, a Scottish newspaper reported in 1824

> A superior combat took place on the glen near Arthur's Seat. The heroes were Billy Owen, a Taffy of some note, fancifully denominated Three-fingered Jack....Taffy, who in his way is a bit of a blood, figured in prime twig, with straw castor, swell cravat, smartish surtout, and shining padders.[34]

London-based Welsh fighters were given much less coverage in Wales itself. The *Cambrian* tended to reproduce reports in London papers practically verbatim, although omitting any indication of a Welsh connection – apart from the boast about Turner.

The limited Welsh Press coverage was partly because there were few Welsh newspapers. In 1804, the first weekly newspaper appeared in Wales when *The Cambrian* was published in Swansea, *The North Wales Gazette*, was established in 1808, and *The Carmarthen Journal* in 1810. The paucity of reports was also due to opposition to sport events from Welsh language papers – the first Welsh language weekly to be published was *Seren Gomer* in 1814 – which were 'by and large' controlled by Welsh Nonconformists who 'would not have approved of the betting or indeed of many other aspects of these communal gatherings'.[35]

English newspapers near the border at Worcester, Gloucester, Hereford and Bristol were more likely than Welsh publications to mention fights in Wales,

Turner's Welsh background surfaced in north Wales papers when they likewise lifted reports from London counterparts, although the accounts were hardly approving. He was dubbed the 'pugilistic prince of Wales' in the

North Wales Gazette in 1824, but far from this being the proud boast about a countryman, their report was copied from a London paper, and reluctantly at that the paper admitted, because 'the *fancy* in some of our readers demands such statements'.[36]

Furthermore, Welsh newspapers, even if they had the inclination, did not have the staff to seek details of local fights, and most reports were of battles in England regurgitated from London publications. *The Cambrian* relied for most of their material

> on what was brought by the incoming mails each day.....Local news was difficult to obtain at first, since the paper could not afford to maintain regular paid correspondents, and since the editor could not travel very far afield himself in search of it, he relied on gratuitously-sent paragraphs.[37]

The public, notwithstanding the limited availability of information, followed the career of Turner, and backed him with considerable money, it being reported that 'thousands were riding on the result of Turner's fight with Scroggins, much of it from Wales.[38]

***

MERTHYR man John Thomas made his London debut in 1825 when he sparred with the Scottish 'champion', name unknown, and it was reported that

> Taffy made his first bow...He is a fine young man, and, with instruction, would puzzle some of the vulgar....The round hitting of the Scotchman was well met by the straight muzzlers of the Welchman...Taffy retired as proud as one of his buck goats.[39]

The backers of Thomas, who referred to himself as the Welsh Champion, issued a challenge to 'any man in England of his own weight, 12st. 7lbs for

118

£50 or £100 in 1826. Replies were to be sent to the *Bell Inn*, Merthyr. The Scot itched to put the record straight, and set out his intentions in the columns of *Bell's Life* thus

> The Scotch Champion challenges Mr. Taffy Thomas 'and would be pleased to draw a little of his hot Welch blood at the earliest occasion. The Scotch Champion was in bad condition when he set-to with Mr. Ap Shankin Thomas or he would not have had to boast or vaunt about what he did that day with the gloves. Taffy will not talk so lightly about the knuckles. The Scotch Champion means to visit Glamorganshire in a short time and will be happy to make a deposit of 20/ at the Bell, Merthyr.[40]

The Scot travelled to the Welsh iron town to back up his words. Recently-married Thomas – in his own words 'I am, at last become a Benedict' – said he had promised his wife to give up fighting but would delay his retirement for three months if a fight for one hundred sovereigns a-side was arranged. The clash, however, did not materialise.

In the early part of the nineteenth century Edwin Hughes was a prominent north Wales fighter who later became a publican at Denbigh, keeping 'the Wine Vaults, known as 'Angels'. Another, Hugh Jones, alias Huwcyn Twyrch, was remembered as a 'remarkable character and pugilist' in the Denbigh area at this time.[41] A renowned ring warrior from the Conwy area in North Wales was 'Ned of the Green Hills'. In his later years, although am elderly man, he was still

> of Herculean frame, wide-shouldered, bull-necked and long-armed. One who had never heard of his fame needed but a glance at his bullet head, broken nose and square jaw to convince him that the man before him had been a bruiser in his day. Indeed, Ned of the Green Hills was once the terror of the whole neighbourhood; and his fame was spread through a pretty wide district as a pugilist.[42]

Robert Jones, printer and prize fighter who was born at Bryn Pyll, Trefrhiw in 1803 was 'known as Ceillog Ffair Llanbedr (the fighting cockerel of Llanbedr), and this arose because of his fame as a pugilist, particularly on his home ground at the pony fair of Llanbedr'.[43]

Around this time, George Heycock enjoyed a certain reputation in the Taibach area despite a childhood illness which left him with one leg shorter than the other. A shoemaker who became a preacher, he was known as Bruiser Heycock. Due to the static style of fighting at the time he did not, consider his handicap to be a hindrance. He explained:

> In those days, the opponents did not dance about the ring; throughout the fight they usually squared up to each other toe to toe, shifting their position by pivoting on one foot.[44]

---

[1] Times, 11 January 1790. Docklands Ancestors ref X097/224. Transcriptions of the Montgomeryshire Genealogical Society.
[2] Henry Downes Miles, Pugilistica: The History of British Boxing (Edinburgh, John Grant, 1906), p. 364.
[3] Pierce Egan, *Boxiana, from the Championship of Cribb to the present time*. Vol. ii (London, Sherwood Jones, 1824), p. 137
[4] Egan, *Boxiana,*, p. 135.
[5] Morning Chronicle, 11 June 1817
[6] Egan's Book of Sports, 1836, cited in Cambrian News, 10 August 1877
[7] Fancy, 21 April 1821.
[8] North Wales Gazette, 25 November 1824.
[9] Morning Chronicle, 21 April 1824
[10] North Wales Gazette, 25 November 1824.
[11] North Wales Gazette, 25 November 1824.
[12] Morning Chronicle, 10 November 1824
[13] Miles, *Pugilistica:* p. 380, p. 381.
[14] Cambrian, 29 April 1826. Pierce Egan, Book of Sports, (London, Tegg, 1832), p. xvii.
[15] Bell's Life, 30 April 1826.
[16] Examiner, 18 September 1831
[17] Bell's Life, 31 July 1833
[18] Bell's Life, 11 August 1833.
[19] Sportsman's Magazine Vol. 1, p. 173.
[20] Bell's Life, 11 August 1833.
[21] Sun, 17 May 1820.

[22] Star, 6 June 1821.
[23] Star, 6 November 1821.
[24] Morning Chronicle, 19 May 1825
[25] Morning Post, 28 June 1822
[26] Bell's Life, 18 December 1825.
[27] Cambrian, 19 June 1824
[28] John Hurley, Tom Spring: Bare-knuckle champion of All England (Stroud, Tempus, 2007).
[29] Emrys Jones (ed.), The Welsh In London (Cardiff, Univ. of Wales Press, 2001), p.91.
[30] Bell's Life, 6 March 1825.
[31] Morning Chronicle, 30 October 1819
[32] Jones, The Welsh in London, p. 90
[33] Egan, Boxiana, p. 135. Bell's Life, 3 June 1832.
[34] Caledonian Mercury, 21 February 1824.
[35] E. Wyn James, 'The Lame Chick and The North Star: Some Ethnic Rivalries in Sport as Reflected in Mid-Nineteenth-Century Welsh Broadsides', in Marjetka Goleż (ed.), *Ballads between Tradition and Modern Times* (Lubljana, Slovenia: Slovenian Academy of Sciences & Arts, 1998),
[36] North Wales Gazette, 18 November 1824.
[37] R. D. Rees, 'Glamorgan newspapers under the Stamp Acts', *Morgannwg transactions of the Glamorgan Local History Society*, Vol 3 (1959), pp. 61 – 94)
[38] Morning Post, 7 December 1818.
[39] Morning Chronicle, 20 October, 1825.
[40] Bell's Life, 15 December 1826.
[41] Llangollen Advertiser, 5 January 1883
[42] Welsh Outlook, October 1914: The life and opinion of Robert Roberts.
[43] North Wales Weekly News, 23 December 1976.
[44] Rev Edward Matthews, Siencyn Penhydd and George Heycock, translated by A Leslie Evans (Port Talbot Historical Society,1989), p. 73.

5

Decline? Mid-1820s - 1860

The claim that 'those brutal exhibitions are happily on the wane' proved prescient from the late 1820s – at least for the London ring, which promoted fewer fights and attracted smaller attendances than previously.[1] Major encounters in the capital still drew up to twenty thousand spectators, but run-of-the-mill matches were 'virtually ignored'; one, involving Edward Savage attracted so few spectators that it was remarked 'a moderate-sized tarpaulin would have covered the lot'.[2]

Many factors contributed to the decline. After the long war years, fighting men were generally no longer needed nor valued as there was no longer a threat of invasion and Britain would not be engaged in a major European conflict until the Crimea war in the 1850s. Even so, Britain's preoccupation with a potentially dangerous situation with France in 1851 prompted a warning that efforts to ban pugilism at home and a corresponding encouraging of the sport in France would make the French better warriors.

It might have seemed uplifting in this atmosphere for MPs to be seen to not be averse to fisticuffs themselves - two of them, Benjamin Oliveira (Pontefract) and Henry Butler Johnstone (Canterbury) brawled over a cab outside the House of Commons in 1852.

That apart, this was an age of enlightenment when old beliefs and practices were challenged and many abandoned. There were crusades against cruelty to animals, child labour, and excessive gambling and drinking.

Parliament tried to encourage the lower classes into 'manly' sports such as gymnastics, archery, quoits, athletics, and cricket. Cambridge University students were even warned that having boxing lessons or attending a prize fight could lead to suspension or expulsion.

It was claimed that 'No man of cultivated intellect would now think of laying 'Boxiana' upon his drawing-room tables', while thanks to the general spread of education, especially the establishment of Mechanic's Institutes, the 'English workman enjoys a prize fight less and a newspaper more'.[3] Satirical magazine *Punch* sighed: "Modern legislation is chiefly remarkable for its oppressive interference with the elegant amusements of the mob', adding 'The 'masses' see no pleasure now'.[4]

A Government select committee in 1833 looked at ways of providing more open spaces in increasingly crowded towns to improve the health and well-being of workmen, who were deemed to have no other pleasures, to 'wean them from low and debasing pleasures' among them pubs and prize fights. The opening to the public in 1839 of Hampton Court Palace appeared to be a step in the required direction, with thousands of men 'whose fathers would have made holyday at the boxing-ring' strolling contentedly in family groups, admiring the gardens, indicating 'a change in the popular mind in the course of one generation'.[5]

Pressure on the money side of the sport took its toll as well. The ending of Royal patronage and the upper classes' following suit, as well as a major commercial panic in 1825 with many banks failing, combined to deprive the London ring of much financial backing, resulting in smaller side stakes.

Apart from outside influences, corruption within the sport itself also contributed greatly to its decline – it was claimed that at Harpenden in 1825, 'the only honest bout' featured Savage. Bribery and betting were the chief culprits, but greed played its part as well, with *Bell's Life* blaming fighters who would not perform for less than one hundred pounds. Thomas Paddington Jones had no time for these pugilists; it was claimed 'he would polish off half a dozen of them in his younger days for a tithe of the sum'.[6] The journal added that the 'absurd practice of making large stakes has in fact ruined the Ring'; when a man wanted to boast but not to fight, he invariably fixed his price beyond the reach of 'his willing customer'.

Disorder in and around the ring didn.t help, either. Spectators breaking into the ring had become 'an evil of the greatest magnitude', raising fears that upper class support would dwindle if they paid for a reserved seat only to be trampled on and swept aside by an invading mob; a reporter was 'compelled to seek refuge within the ropes' during one contest in 1844.

After further crowd trouble, the Fair Play Club was formed in 1828 'to put an end to the disgraceful scenes which have of late characterised the milling fraternity'.[7] One of their earliest actions was to hire eight pugilists at 10s. each to keep order when Savage met Peter Sweeney. As it happened, the only interruption was by law officers who forced a halt after 16 rounds.

***

THERE were no signs, though, of a decline in Wales, rather there was a surge in popularity. In the provinces, the effects of the commercial crash were not as severe, prize-fighting's 'corruptive influences' were mainly absent, and there had been little upper-class support anyway, so it was not missed. As a result, outside London the sport 'rose into an importance and acquired a reputation which it had never known before'.

By the early 1830s, over a third of the fights were taking place in the growing industrial areas.[8] In 1849, it was estimated that 'Boxing for gain is practiced [sic] by 2,000 persons in the United Kingdom'.[9]

At the beginning of the period, South Wales, where most of the country's prize-fighting occurred, was yet to become a booming industrial area, apart, that is, from Merthyr Tydfil, which was at its peak as an iron making centre and the most heavily populated town in Wales. Lagging behind, Swansea was a growing centre for metallurgical industries, and also a seaside resort, while Cardiff was an insignificant coastal port in 1840, and in 1849 still only a 'third or fourth rate country town'.[10]

However, both towns gradually narrowed the gap on Merthyr, thanks to a great influx of population into the growing seaports of South Wales and into the iron and coal valleys - and in the opposite direction as far as Merthyr was concerned when the iron industry faltered.

Whether or not there was any call for fighting men in Wales, there were plenty of them around as the threat to national security from civil unrest and the danger to public order switched from abroad to concentrate even more on that part of Britain, mainly the south-east of the country which was regarded as particularly subversive.

- - Wales in the 1840s was regarded as the most militarised zone in Britain -- troops were brought in regularly to cope with industrial and political disturbances in the South Wales valleys which manifested itself in Scotch Cattle, the Merthyr Riots (1831), and the Chartist uprising (1839). There were also election disturbances (1852), as well as the Rebecca riots in rural south west Wales.

Criticism of Welsh morals and culture earned the controversial Commissioners for Education Report of 1847 the new name of the 'Treason of the Blue Books', but the sentiments expressed in the report were not new; they had been contained in a similarly-worded newspaper report four years earlier. Then, a fatal prize fight in Swansea was added to the mix.

The *Royal Cornwall Gazette*, despite being printed on the other side of the Bristol Channel, had a significant readership among Cornish migrants, some of them wealthy businessmen and industrialists, in south west Wales. It reported that Llanelli magistrate William Chambers, who played a key part in capturing Rebecca rioters, had seen buildings and haystacks on three of his farms burned down in retaliation. The newspaper used this and other violent incidents to launch a scathing attack on Wales and its people. It alleged high criminality and low morals among an ignorant and demoralized people, with the Welsh language being a serious bar to improvement, and religion the chief curse of the country. All of which was repeated in the Commissioners' Report.

The newspaper tirade included

> We remember a case near Swansea where death occurred in a low and brutal boxing match, and the jury brought in a verdict of 'Justifiable Homicide'! and a murder of a most savage and unprovoked character was committed within a mile of the same town, and though the Coroner's inquest returned a verdict of 'Wilful Murder', nobody thought it his business to pursue the offender, who was not even sought after.[11]

Chambers' family had now left the area, a few months after the birth of Chambers' son, John Graham Chambers, who went on to play a major part in the sport's development.

Industrial South Wales was a frontier society, containing migrants from all over Britain and beyond, the majority being young, vigorous males in the growing ports and coalfields. Davies notes that as they had often nowhere but the tavern in which to spend their leisure hours it was 'hardly surprising that the communities of the coalfield were inflammable'.[12]

Police dealt with considerable violence daily. In the Merthyr police district during the years 1842-59, between a third and a half of all charges were of assault and drunken and disorderly conduct.[13] It was no different in the north of the country; in the port of Amlwch in the 1850s, one of the regular sights was 'at least seven pugilistic encounters in the street between old Mrs. Roos' pub and Roberts' lodging house'.[14]

This was an environment in which the sport could thrive and, conversely, good reason for the authorities to be wary of large excitable crowds.

According to Jones, prize fighting seemed to have 'initially flourished in the growing towns' of Wales, adding, however, 'if contemporaries are to be believed, within a short time there was a 'revolution in habits'.[15] Opinion on this was divided at the time, some contemporaries insisting, for example, that prize fights 'rarely occurred in the Monmouth area', while others held that contests took place 'too frequently' in the Monmouthshire countryside.[16]

The latter view was the more accurate. Prize fights continued to be frequent and attracted large crowds in Wales, 4,000 when 'Gas' met Robinson at Monmouth Cap in 1827, an 'immense' crowd in the Sirhowy Valley near the Quarry Mawr later that year, around two thousand for the fatal battle between Price and Humphreys at Llanbadarn Fynydd, Radnorshire, in 1829, more than five thousand when Charles took on Trainor at Monmouth Cap in 1832, and around 3,000 for Charles' v. Bill Gardiner at Raglan the following year. In August 1840 an estimated 3,000- saw a battle between Harry Jones, 'a celebrated Cardiff bully and another bully' Shony Skibbor y Fawr forced by magistrates from Cardiff Heath to the Rumney area in neighbouring Monmouthshire, Jones retiring after twelve rounds with 'severe bodily bruising'.

In 1856 in a field near the *Rock and Fountain* inn between Chepstow and Newport, from 3000 to 4000 people saw Dan Thomas, fight Ingram, of Bristol. Spectators in their hundreds were present near Abercanaid in 1848 when Daniel Williams, a miner, took on haulier David Morgan, similarly at Town Hill Farm, near Swansea, in 1856 to watch John Brumingham, and also at a prize fight at Tredegar the same year.

There were also many low-profile, but just as fiercely fought, battles throughout the country. In 1828, the 'Tram-road champion' and another 'acknowledged good one' contested 104 rounds in one hour and 45 minutes until both succumbed to exhaustion at Talgarth. In 1829 Bill Pea beat George for £50 a-side at Knighton, Radnorshire, in 81 rounds over one hour, 25 minutes. In 1832, 'one of the most slashing fights that ever took place in Wales' occurred near Newport, between local man W. Williams, and Shaw, from Staffordshire, who endured fifty-eight rounds in one hour and twenty minutes. In 1835, 'a slashing contest of an hour's duration' took place 'during a tremendous thunderstorm' at Brecon between 'the Newton hero' and 'Scroggins the Welch champion'.[17]

A spot near Cardiff was the site in 1837 for a fight of 120 rounds over one hour and forty minutes between Spencer and Pike. Dick Hands (a butcher) beat Jack Howard (a runner) for a purse, over 9 rounds at Pontypool Racecourse in July 1840, In August that year at nearby Marshfield Bill Davis drew with David Jenkins over 52 rounds in 77 minutes in a display of 'Welch courage' with neither giving way and forcing their 'friends' to move in to separate them. In 1843, Bill Green beat Andrew Jones over 36 rounds in ninety minutes at Llangollen. The next year, there was a report of a 'capital encounter' involving Jack Perks, a native of Brecon. In 1844 Harris Birchell beat McIntyre for £5 a-side in 65 rounds over 108 minutes at Ormes Had, Caernarfonshire.

***

THESE occasions could get out of hand. Prize-fighting became a focus for tensions between Welsh and English workers and Irish immigrants. At Ferry Side in South Wales in 1851, Irish navvies employed on the railway line tried to arrange a bout between their champion, 'a notorious Irish boxer', against anyone from the ranks of the English navvies, among whom were 'two celebrated English bruisers' who were fighting in another part of the village.

The proposed contest did not happen, but, instead of bare fists, 'Pokers, large pieces of timber, handles of brushes, knives, and weapons of every description were used in 'a pitched battle between 150 English and Irish navvies, which continued for several hours'.[18] In 1858, an encounter between an Irishman and a Welshman at Rumney near Cardiff was halted when a reported one hundred Irishmen brandishing sticks broke into the ring to rescue their 'very much punished' countryman.

During one clash at Newport in 1853, the second of a fighter who was getting the worse of the punishment knocked down the opponent, kicked him and then threw him in a ditch. When a passer-by remonstrated, the second knocked him down as well.

***

THAT year, with Macarte's American Circus in town, Newport residents were treated to a 'mock prize fight' involving 'Tom Barry, King of Clowns, and Mr. Lenton, the India-rubber Clown'.

By 1860 in south Wales, the *Monmouthshire Merlin*, conceded 'The disgusting and brutal exhibitions called 'prize fights' were becoming frequent'.[19]

Further evidence of the sport's healthy state in this period was provided by the frequency of challenges flowing from all over Wales. Alex Cropley in

Haverfordwest, West Wales, announced he wanted a fight for £50 a-side in the London area in 1826 and would soon travel to the capital to finalise one. He was followed by novice M. Richards, from Welshpool in mid-Wales in 1829, and also that year by Richard Lewis, from Newport, looking for a match within fifty miles of the port and claiming to have up to £500 available in the *Noah's Ark Inn*, Newport. In 1841, John Pugh Smith, from Wrexham in North Wales, challenged any man of 9st. 10lbs. within 12 miles of the town or anywhere in Denbighshire.

Exiled Welshmen were just as keen for action, John Davies, responding in 1831 to a fighter's boast that he 'could lick any Welchman of his weight' replied that he had up to £50 stakes waiting in a London pub if the man was serious. Thomas Williams, alias Tom the Welchman, issued regular challenges in the early 1840s, money available in a Dudley pub.

Reports of the sport's demise in Wales were wishful thinking, as was the claim that it was over the border in England where the problem lay, a newspaper suggesting 'There must be great ignorance and brutality in England when such rural sports as these find countenance'.[20]

Both were symptomatic of a state of denial which lingered throughout the century in response to attacks such as that by the Education Commissioners.

***

COMMENTS in early newspaper reports were generally of apparent admiration, 'a 'slashing fight' becoming a cliché, interspersed with details of side stakes, deposits, weights, plus betting information. But condemnation intensified in the late 1830s, with encounters now routinely being described as 'disgusting', 'brutal', 'disgraceful', 'shameful', 'demoralising', 'scandalous', and efforts were made to embarrass spectators, who were labelled 'riff-raff'.

Occasionally, newspapers even publicly refused to report a fight. The *Cardiff and Merthyr Guardian,* angry that 'the quiet district of Pontsarn, always attractive for its seclusion and loveliness, was desecrated by one fight', said it would not 'weary its readers' with details.[21] The *Illustrated Usk Observer* reminded its readers that it did not normally give such accounts, but was making an exception because Bill Benjamin, who was fighting for the Championship, was a local man, 'consequently considerable excitement has prevailed amongst all classes in the county'.[22] There followed, nevertheless, the full *Bell's Life* report in the Usk newspaper's columns.

Likewise, the *Monmouthshire Merlin* intimated in 1857 that only readers of *Bell's Life* would be interested in 'One of those scandalous events …..known among them as a 'mill' that took place near Newport; but the newspaper nevertheless published a full report.[23]

***

MOST early disapproval of the sport concerned the heavy drinking that surrounded it - which was a feature of life in Wales generally. The British and Foreign Temperance Society in 1833 had 236 branches and 40,987 members in England and Wales; of these, Wales had one branch with 14 members. The 'industrious classes' were urged to forego such 'barbarous degrading amusements' and their 'old haunts of taverns, ale-houses, and houses of ill-fame' and flock to Mechanics Institutions 'for instruction in the arts and business of life'.

Not all followers of the sport were from the rough, lower classes, but any atypical ringsiders were remarked upon. There were many 'respectable, well-dressed persons' for Charles v Gardiner, while at a bout on the Rhyl Marsh in 1850, there were 'noticed some Gentlemen who are friendly to this kind of sport.'[24] At Thomas' set-to at Penhow, the *Monmouthshire Merlin* was 'sorry to learn that some persons from whose position in life a far better example might have been reasonably expected, encouraged the brutal spectacle by their presence'.[25]

Also condemned were the undesirables that the sport was said to attract, such as the pickpockets who followed spectators from Penhow back to Newport, where they continued 'abstracting money from several pockets, both at the railways stations and at public houses in the town'.

There were strong religious protests, particularly over Sunday prize fights. It has been claimed that Sunday 'desecration' was one of the few offences against decency from which pugilism always remained 'remarkably free'.[26] Contemporary newspaper reports, however, contradict this assertion as far as England, upon which previous studies have concentrated, is concerned; they point to frequent violations of the Sabbath.

Sunday prize fights were just as common throughout Wales. Reminiscing, an old man of Penrhewl, Denbighshire, said 'There was no proper Sunday observance, and it was a regular occurrence to have pugilistic encounters on the Common on Sunday afternoons'.[27]

Merthyr's already 'tarnished' image, with its 'exaggerated' reputation for crime, bad workmanship and loose morals; and for being a place 'where animal passions rage unstemmed, where all human laws are scouted, and all divine laws disobeyed', was aggravated by a fatal prize fight on a Sunday. A local newspaper was shocked that in 'a land influenced by religion', 'on the last Sabbath day...a crowd of men, young and old, assembled to take part in that brutalizing practice – a prize fight'.[28]

In north Wales, Methodist missionaries holding a service at Holt on a Sunday afternoon in 1847. observed that 'a great number of people had assembled near the cross to witness a pitched battle between two men. We were informed that it was no uncommon thing even on the Sabbath' day'.[29]

A *Merthyr Telegraph* reader, complaining in 1856 of the public drunkenness of youths, said the town had nothing to offer to its young people who worked hard and earned good wages; 'but the public house, and the eternal quart, varied at times with a low theatre, a boxing tent, and a shooting gallery.'[30] The town needed to follow the example set in Birmingham of forming a Public Recreation Society, which set up bands and choirs and board games.

***

THE old ways of fighting remained at the start of the period, as Broughton's Rules continued to govern. Punching was still with bare fists. Gloves had been used for many years, and there was a report of such a fight for a sovereign in London in 1845, but they were used mainly in boxing, training for boxing and in fairground booths. Fighters were still allowed to throw their opponents to the ground and try to land on top of them, winding them or injuring them, sometimes fatally, in the process.

Spiked shoes, worn to retain a fighter's footing on the bare ground, remained an important piece of equipment. One battler, having exceeded the stipulated weight, was forced to compete in the south of England without shoes, and his opponent, wearing spiked shoes used every opportunity to tread on his feet, 'mutilating them exceedingly', the umpires dismissing frequent appeals, deciding this tactic was within the rules.[31] When Edward Savage fought Kirkman, his opponent objected to the length of Savage's 'certainly anything but moderate' spikes and a hammer was used to make them acceptable and enable the contest between cab drivers, or 'heroes of the whip' to go ahead.[32]

Sometimes umpires and referee were by-passed when major decisions were made. When Hoddell and Humphreys met at Newtown in 1828, a desperate dispute' arose over an alleged foul blow, and the seconds and backers agreed to a draw 'and the men were to have ten pounds each'.[33]

All the old bad habits endured, as well – the heads of pugilists were still shaved 'as a matter of course' to prevent opponents seizing hair, even with their teeth, to gain an unfair advantage, and a 'cowardly practice' became popular of greasing men's necks, to prevent their opponents from grappling with them in close contact.[34]

Rounds could still drag on; the first round of one fight took 48½ minutes because the men were too wary of each other to throw a punch. For the greater part of the time, their seconds lay on the ring floor, and ringsiders jeered. Tom Spring, one of the seconds, and others began singing (probably to keep awake) a popular Irish song of the time.

Broughton's Rules were superseded in 1838 by the London Prize Ring Rules, which codified practices that had existed for some time, among them the use of a 24 foot square roped ring and a half minute time. These rules had been stipulated for a match near Huddersfield in Yorkshire five years earlier for a fight involving Welsh Jones 'alias the Welsh Champion'.[35]

The new rules banned falling down without being hit, a common tactic which was looked on with disfavour but not previously outlawed. One of Edward Savage's opponents had been advised that he 'must avoid falling without a blow to avoid punishment as this practice in strictness would lose him the fight.[36]

When Bill Charles beat Jem Bailey near Bristol in their third and deciding fight, Bailey was booed frequently throughout the two hours for dropping to the floor whenever Charles put in an attack. And when Charles lost to Bill

Gardiner in 1833, *Bell's Life*, while conceding that this tactic denied Charles 'the opportunity of doing his best in a stand-up fight', pointed out that Gardiner was 'not considered to have transgressed the laws of Boxiana'.[37]

Also forbidden by the London Rules were kicking, butting, biting, low blows, and the use of spiked boots. In addition, the fighter now had to walk to scratch unaided, to prevent those rendered unable to fight from taking further punishment after their seconds had carried them to the mark, 'such a barbarous practice having caused several deaths.'[38]

Tom Spring suggested solutions to improve the sport – a fair play association which would have disciplinary powers, regular benefit shows to raise money for the association's work and to help members who would be obliged to take part, and various rules about how fighters should be paid. Little came of them, though.

***

IN the absence of an official governing body, *Bell's Life* gradually assumed control at national and regional level. Challenges for the most prominent fights were made through its columns, its employees refereed fights, and the journal itself acted as stakeholder with money being sent to its offices in instalments. It was also a final court of appeal. For a proposed match in 1860 involving Wales-based Patsy Reardon, the latest deposit on his behalf arrived late, and the paper declared his opponent to be entitled to the forfeit.

The power of *Bell's Life* was feared in the business, with rival journalists wary of contradicting its fight reports, while non-compliance with its decisions could have serious repercussions since big fights relied on publicity from the journal. A pugilist who made an unsuccessful legal challenge to the paper's ruling on a fight purse saw his name banned from its columns 'until he has learned to know better'.[39]

Decline? Mid-1820s-1860

***

SPECTATORS early in this period continued to travel on foot or by horse or carriage. For Charles's meeting at Raglan against Gardiner which was to begin at 1pm, 'as early as six o'clock in the morning, numerous groups of hardy pedestrians were moving forward for the purpose of getting a good place to see the 'vight'(sic).[40] They were followed by 'every species of vehicle ….from the swell drag and four to the donkey cart and the number of horsemen was immense'.[41] Hundreds were on the road at 2 a.m. for the Jones v Brag clash in 1833, the start scheduled for five hours later. A 'great number' of spectators 'were seen at an early hour in the morning, trudging towards the spot about three miles from Wrexham,' to see Pugh and Foulkes battle it out in 1841.

Bad weather was no deterrent to these intrepid travellers. When a fight involving Edward Savage was forced from its intended venue in Middlesex over the county border into Hertfordshire, followers made their way through hail and rain, some falling into the river Brent as they tried to cross the swollen waters, after which they had to watch the action ankle deep in mud. The fighters battled for two hours and 27 minutes, 'ankle deep in slush, and as the men fell and were lifted to the scratch, they rather had the appearance of Ethiopians than of natives of our northern climes'.[42]

Fighters did not let much keep them from the scene of the action, either. When Welsh Davis set off to meet Burke on the banks of the Thames in 1831, the chaise in which he was travelling overturned, severely injuring two companions. Davis, fortunately, 'escaped without mischief, and appeared in the Ring with undiminished ardour'.[43]

There were dangers as well for those inadvertently caught up amongst the travelling armies of fans who frequently caused mayhem, offending common decency, unsettling and debasing the minds of the resident labourers, filling the neighbourhood with drunkenness, and causing an influx of bad characters, who seldom leave without some outrage upon property.[44]

In the same vein, a large fight crowd 'made free with people's orchards' in the Caerphilly area in 1866.[45]

By the 1840s, rail travel had enabled fighters and followers to be transported quickly across country, making it difficult for the authorities to follow. But, as has been pointed out, they rode on the ordinary time-tabled trains, whose schedules were inflexible. If a fight was prevented, it was difficult to move to an alternative site, especially as all the passengers found themselves suddenly reduced to walking on leaving the train.[46]

The answer was the special excursion train, following the example set by Thomas Cook, who had just begun to charter trains for his temperance trips. They provided a relatively flexible journey, allowing alternative sites to be chosen after police intervention.

It had always been difficult to charge admission money to fights, but when railways and steamers, frequently used jointly, began operating for distance travel, in addition to reducing interference from the law, they helped promoters to make money by charging for the journey, so that only those who bought tickets, usually costing between £1 and £2, would be sure of being at the ultimate venue.

Favourite steamer routes were, as far as Wales was concerned, on the Mersey from Liverpool and Manchester into north Wales, or across the Bristol Channel between south Wales and the West of England. When Charles travelled to fight on Bailey's home turf on the other side of the waterway in 1828, 'immense droves of the Welch *Fancy* crossed in the steamers' in support. They were able to do so because a few hours on the extensive port to port services that linked South Wales to the West Country, or by the Beachley to Aust ferries, made the excursion more practicable than the alternative of days by coach overland via Gloucester.

Boats on the Thames were often able to anchor near the ring in a remote spot, but, against that, other craft could compete for passengers, and there might be landing problems if there was no jetty available. After the Benjamin v Sayers fight in 1858, spectators had to 'wade almost knee deep in mud to the small boats destined to convey them on board the vessel'.[47]

River travel ended in tragedy in 1835, when forty people returning from a prize fight in Cheshire, drowned in the River Mersey when the two boats on to which they were crowded sank.

Former fighter Owen Swift believed that the only way to travel 'pleasantly by steam' was by boat, but he was a traditionalist at heart, admitting

> despite the additional time occupied, I love the poetry of travelling, and would rather go a hundred miles to a mill in "a slap-up-drag," than fifty to one by a railway or steam-boat. The journey in the post-chaise, or behind a fast trotter, to witness a mill, is the very charm of the event.[48]

---

[1] Berrow's Worcester Journal, 11 January 1827.
[2] Leicester Chronicle, 5 December 1829. Morning Chronicle, 24 December 1828.
[3] Daily News, 25 November 1847. Morning Chronicle, 31 December 1853. Sun, cited in Bristol Mercury, 8 October 1842; Morning Post, 29 May 1858.
[4] Punch. Cited in Kasia Boddy, Boxing, a cultural history, p. 76.
[5] Northern Star, 25 January 1840.
[6] Bell's Life, 11 August 1833.
[7] Morning Chronicle, 11 September 1828.
[8] Morning Chronicle, 19 October 1825. Licensed Victuallers' Mirror, 11 November, 1890. Dennis Brailsford, Bareknuckles: A Social History of Prize-Fighting (Cambridge, Lutterworth Press, 1988), p.118
[9] Derby Mercury, 9 May 1849.
[10] William Rees, Cardiff: A History of the City (Cardiff, p. 277. Rammell's report, p. 11.

[11] Royal Cornwall Gazette, 22 September 1843.
[12] John Davies, A History of Wales (London, Penguin, 1994), p. 351.
[13] David J. V. Jones, Crime in 19th Century Wales, pp. 68, 70
[14] Robert Roberts, Y Sgolor Mawr" ("The Great Scholar"),
[15] Jones, Crime in Wales, p. 96
[16] Monmouthshire Merlin, 6 May 1837. Glamorgan Gazette, 15 June 1839.
[17] Monmouthshire Merlin, 29 August 1835
[18] Cambrian, cited in the Morning Post, 15 December 1851
[19] Monmouthshire Merlin, 11 September 1858; 1860, cited in Rumney and St. Mellons. A History of Two Villages (Rumney and District Local History Society, 2005].
[20] Pembrokeshire Herald, 30 July 1847.
[21] Cardiff and Merthyr Guardian, 6 June 1857
[22] Illustrated Usk Observer, 9 April 1859
[23] Monmouthshire Merlin, 15 August 1857
[24] Monmouthshire Merlin, 30 March 1833. Caernarvon Herald, 23 February 1850.
[25] Monmouthshire Merlin, 9 February 1856
[26] Brailsford, Bareknuckles, p. 94.
[27] Denbighshire Free Press, 17 September 1910.
[28] Merthyr Telegraph, 25 September 1858
[29] The Treasury: A monthly miscellany of missionary reports in connection with the Calvinstic Methodist Churches. Vol. 1, 1864, p. 122.
[30] Merthyr Telegraph, 26 April 1856.
[31] Times, 13 March 1845.
[32] Bell's Life, 2 September 1827
[33] Bell's Life, 10 August 1828.
[34] Bell's Life, 18 June 1831.
[35] Bell's Life, 28 April 1833
[36] Bell's Life, 20 January 1828
[37] Bell's Life, 7 Apr 1833.
[38] Morning Post, 20 July 1843
[39] Era, 23 June 1850
[40] Monmouthshire Merlin, 30 March 1833
[41] Monmouthshire Merlin, 30 March 1833
[42] Bell's Life, 11 March 1827
[43] Morning Chron., 23 February 1831. Preston Chron., 22 November 1834, 24 January 1835.
[44] Essex Standard, 14 October 1842
[45] Cardiff Times, 24 August 1866
[46] Brailsford, Bareknuckles, pp. 100,101
[47] Bell's Life, 10 January 1858
[48] Owen Swift, The Handbook of Boxing (London, Nicholson, 1840), p. 14

6

Fighters to 1860

The most prestigious fights in this period with a Welsh interest featured Bill Benjamin, from Shirenewton in Monmouthshire. His debut in the prize ring 'came off' in 1858 and was for the world heavyweight title – as was his second appearance in the ring a year later!

Benjamin had challenged Tom Sayers for the Championship. Ostensibly, it was for the championship of England, but by common consent the champion of England meant the champion of the world. Official champions at national or world level did not exist; a champion was recognized by public acclaim after a notable victory and subsequent successes.

Money ruled here, as in most aspects of the sport, enabling Benjamin's backers to buy him his title chance. Custom required a champion to accept any challenge and cover the stake put up by an opponent's backers or forfeit the title. Benjamin's patron, who offered a side stake of £200, was Monmouthshire landowner James Carruthers, of the Gondra, a future High Sheriff of the county.

In a sport where nothing underhand could be ruled out, the match attracted all kinds of rumours, that Benjamin was far from being the novice that he was believed to be, that he was a well-known boxer fighting under a *nom de guerre*, that a betting scam was being set up with Sayers intending to throw the fight, or that a betting coup was being planned with the aim of making Sayers the non-favourite.

The fighters and their supporters travelled by special train to Strood in Kent where a paddle steamer waited to carry them to the Isle of Grain site in that county.

The fight, such as it was, took place on 6 January 1858. Sayers was 'a rattling favourite', but Benjamin,

> a fine-looking young fellow, possessing great muscular development, and a bright, determined countenance', at 5 feet 10 ¾ inches and 12 stone, was taller and heavier 'and looked from top to toe big enough to contend for the championship.[1]

Interest back home in Monmouthshire had been intense, as Benjamin's local newspaper reported

> The above affair caused a great stir in this neighbourhood and the demand for *Bell's Life* on Saturday was extraordinary and could not be fully supplied.[2]

That journal's fight report did not, sadly, contain uplifting news for Benjamin's followers.

Their man was a sturdy farmer, but the only fighting he had done previously was in local brawls, whereas Sayers was a seasoned performer with an impressive ring record. Benjamin may have looked the part, but he fought like the complete novice he was. In the first round, a left and right to the head knocked him down, and the trade newspaper reported

> the look of dismay upon his countenance as he glanced around was perfectly ludicrous. It was at once patent to all that he knew nothing of the business he had undertaken, and that the contest was virtually over.[3]

In the second round, another left knocked Benjamin off his feet. His seconds took him to his corner, and he appeared reluctant to continue but, on time being called, trainer Harry Broome pushed him forward. In the third round, Benjamin went down again from punches to the head, the report adding: 'He lay in the middle of the ring, and nothing could persuade him to come to 'time'.

Benjamin's 'puny effort' was labelled the worst challenge ever for the championship; he had not tried, it was claimed, but instead had 'heaped ridicule on himself and his party'. One newspaper commented after the briefest-ever fight for the championship that the result proved 'how ridiculous' it was to pitch an untried man in his first fight against the best man around.[4]

Broome, himself an experienced fighter, should have realised that, but afterwards he claimed to be 'disgusted, disappointed and betrayed' by Benjamin, who had brought 'dishonour' by his 'cowardice'; he regretted that Benjamin did not show more pluck and manliness'.[5]

Broome even challenged Benjamin to a fight, and, having held the title himself two years previously, would, on that performance, most probably have beaten him. Relations in the camp deteriorated further when Broome sued Benjamin's backer Carruthers for the expenses incurred in training.

Benjamin begged Carruthers to give him an opportunity for redemption with a second fight against Sayers. He insisted he was no coward and did not deserve the stigma attached to his name, he told *Bell's Life*, and offered the publication, which had urged him to give up boxing because he was so inept, a list of reasons for his defeat.

A catalogue of lame excuses included no proper training, sickness on the day, first fight nerves, he was unused to stripping in the cold, and was surprised at the suddenness and severity of Sayers' punches. Most excuses showed up Benjamin's inexperience, particularly the ludicrous explanation he gave to his gullible local paper.

He attributed his summary defeat to Sayers having hit him in the stomach without telling him. Nothing daunted, however, by this uncourteous trick, he was still ambitious to gain the champion's belt.[6]

The rematch in April 1859 was indeed advertised as being for the championship of the world. Nearly one thousand followers left London 'ostensibly for Dover, but this in sporting phraseology was 'a blind'; the fight came off at Ashford in Kent.[7]

As with the first encounter, rumours abounded, among them that Benjamin, now trained by two former Championship winners, Nat Langham, the only man ever to beat Sayers, and Bendigo, was really an excellent fighter and lost the first battle only by accident. But the public weren't fooled, because no one would accept less than 4 to 1 on Benjamin winning, and many laid 5 to 2 on Sayers winning inside 15 minutes.

Benjamin made a surprisingly impressive start, though, and by round seven was earning plaudits for his resolute performance, with Sayers, rumoured to have, understandably after their first clash, taken the return lightly, tiring quickly and becoming ragged.

Round eight proved the turning point. Benjamin tried to land a left but was knocked down and nearly out by a right counter. He was knocked down in the ninth and tenth rounds, and when his seconds 'threw up the sponge' he broke away from them and carried on fighting. In the opening seconds of the eleventh round, Benjamin missed with a left and stumbled forward, Sayers catching him on the nose and flooring him. He was helped to his corner, and his seconds retired him after 22 minutes; but even then, Benjamin, 'who was all but blind', still attempted to fight on.[8]

The return match was clearly not a debacle as was their first encounter, but, still, not everyone involved took it seriously. One of the seconds for this fight, 'the eccentric Mr. Noon',

> amused himself by performing Indian war dances in the middle of the ring, trusting to others to do his duty; and when the rounds were being fought, instead of keeping his corner, he pirouetted around the men, and sometimes interposed his person between the combatants, to the infinite disgust of all present. On one occasion he actually commenced sparring with Jack Macdonald, a second of his opponent.

The fight was celebrated in a printed poem, a form of memorabilia frequently sold at the time. It included the lines:

The country was all alive, and thousands on
  did run.
On the Ist. Round, on Sayers lads, the bets ran
  3 to 1;
He fibbed away like 1 o'clock, & as you all
  May think
He made poor Benjamin's claret run, like
  soap-suds down a sink.

It was in 3rd round my boys, you know without a
  doubt,
Ben's head got into chancery, and he scarce could pull
  It out.
A buxom farmer near the ring cried Ben is licked I see,
For Sayers he has knocked his nose down in his
  Breeches knees.

They fought 11 rounds my boys so nobly in the ring,
When Sayers conquered Benjamin and made him to
  Give in.
The loud hurrah's did rend the air, poor Ben's grieved
  to the heart
He got well lick'd that glorious day, while Sayers had
  scarce a mark.[9]

The *Bell's Life* verdict was that Benjamin had, without a doubt, redeemed his character, but, at 34, he was too old to be turned into a top fighter; had he begun many years earlier, that might have been possible.

'What he should do now is to retire, and we are glad that he has decided to do so', the journal commented.[10] Benjamin's local paper was blunt and less supportive than previously. 'We hope this misguided young man will now return to his agricultural pursuits, and that we may hear of no more such disgraceful proceedings'.[11]

Although, Benjamin, a publican as well as a farmer, should have been independent of the ring, he made a surprise return two years later, disposing of fellow Welshman Richard James in two rounds in three and a half minutes for his one and only victory.

Benjamin had probably needed the money. The following month, bailiffs warned him that unless he paid a debt, 'her Majesty was prepared to find him a certain quantity of food daily, and also bed accommodation'.[12] Benjamin did not pay promptly and had a spell in Usk prison.

His retirement was announced after the fight, but he stayed in the sport, was involved in James' later career, and was also active as a second, and as a referee. In 1894, when he was 69, he was challenged by Jem Mace, who had been Champion thirty years previously and was himself now 63. The fight did not come off.

***

DAN Thomas served a comparatively long apprenticeship before he fought for a 'title', in his case at lightweight. Thomas boasted ten successive victories in local contests, half of them at Dowlais, Merthyr or Ebbw Vale and those following further south at Pontypridd, Magor and Newport, before moving up a grade. His only defeat in 12 outings came in 1856, when he had to retire against David Ingram (Bristol) after 35 rounds in 50 minutes at Penhow.

But, in his next appearance, his debut in the London ring, in 1858, he beat Jack Brookes over 54 rounds in one hour and thirty-seven minutes. Thomas's victory over a strong favourite earned him a match with Charles Lynch, of the USA, the following January. Weighing 8st 6lb and 5ft.4ins tall, Thomas was a

> fine manly fellow; he has a bright keen-looking eye, a broad expansive chest, and this, combined with the advantage of height and reach, made him from top to toe look, as he really proved, the most formidable opponent that ever the gallant American had met within the twenty-four foot arena.[13]

And so it proved, Thomas winning with contemptuous ease over 56 rounds in one hour and forty minutes. The report stated that

> Lynch rushed in at every opportunity, with Thomas scoring heavily with his left hand, and pointing at his opponent and laughing several times at his vain attempts... in the last Lynch was knocked down by a fine cross counter, and although not out of time, his seconds found it would be useless to allow him to continue the battle any longer and threw up the sponge.

Thomas eventually became more immersed in religion and in a business career than in fighting. He announced his retirement in 1860 after beating Gillam, of Brighton, in 48 rounds over 165 minutes.

But he returned to the ring two years later against Joe Nolan for the 'lightweight championship'. The fight lasted one hour and thirty minutes, with Thomas well in control against a flagging Nolan, but it ended without a decision after being halted by the police at three different venues. Nolan's backers did not want another meeting, 'with the certain chance of losing', and paid Thomas £25 to agree to a draw.

That proved to have been Thomas' last outing, although he continued as a second, a trainer and a referee.

Thomas was rated 'the best and cleverest pugilist of his weight that has appeared for some years', and, like Turner forty years earlier, was celebrated in verse, alongside champion Welsh runner John Davies, known as 'The Lame Chick'.

> Nid oes gwiw i'r Saeson bellach
> A gwŷr Morgannwg i ymyrrath;
> Y Cyw a'u trecha i redeg gyrfa,
> Dan Pontypridd a dorra'u c'lonna.

> ('There is no longer any point for the English to meddle
> with the men of Glamorgan;
> the Chick will beat them at running,
> Dan Pontypridd will break their hearts.') [14]

Illustrating the close links between the two sports, Owen Swift had been the referee when Davies beat Thomas Maxfield in a mile race near Bath in 1846.

***

THE year preceding Benjamin's first challenge to Sayers, and immediately before Sayers became champion, Aaron Jones, born near Shrewsbury, Shropshire, in 1831 to Welsh parents, met Sayers twice.

Jones began his working life aged nine when he went to London as a page to the brother of the sixth Earl of Essex. 'but on account of his sparring notoriety', he was discharged after four years and returned home'.[15] He defeated several local men, beginning at the age of 15, before embarking on a career in the London ring, which began with a defeat, after 47 rounds, in 2 hours and 55 minutes against Harry Orme at Woking Common in 1849, and continued in the same unsuccessful vein.

Jones won just one of a handful of fights before meeting Sayers twice in a month early in 1857. Their two battles comprised 150 rounds over five hours. After 65 rounds in 3 hours and ten minutes, the first fight ended in a draw because of bad light, Jones having taken first blood and first knockdown in a purposeful start.

Sayers' backers were so sure of their man's chances in the return match that they agreed to double the stakes to £200 a-side, and their confidence was justified. In front of around 3,000, Sayers was on top throughout, with Jones not fighting with the same spirit as in the first meeting. The battle lasted 85 rounds over two hours, leaving Jones, 'much punished'; he had 'little chance for the last thirty minutes', and was eventually retired by his seconds.

***

BROTHERS Edward and Bill Savage, who appeared in the London ring in the late 1820s, were born in the city to parents from the Wrexham area. Unlike most prize fighters, who were from poor, working-class backgrounds, they had a father who was 'a man of considerable property, and the young Savages were reportedly well off when they came of age'.[16] However,

> gaiety, horse-racing, cocking, fighting and wenching, ultimately brought their Noble to *ninepence*; and they were compelled when all the *blunt* had toddled, to look out for a 'bit of work' to earn an honest penny.....Horse-dealing, cab-driving, and lastly, prize-fighting, were their successive pursuits.

The brothers fought at a lower level than Turner's, both losing more bouts than they won. They combined the ring with cab driving to earn their living,

Edward, who drove a cabriolet, a light, two-wheeled carriage with a hood, drawn by one horse, had four fights with Jem Kirkman, who drove a hackney coach, usually a four-wheeled carriage drawn by two horses. While the contests were of 'minor consequence' overall, the men were 'the champions of the rival classes to which they belong', and fought for honour rather than profit, for the stakes amounted only to 10/ a-side'.[17]

Their four meetings comprised about 300 rounds over more than six hours, the honours going to Kirkman, who won twice with one win for Savage and one draw. After 2 hours and 2 minutes, over 93 rounds, their third meeting ended in a dispute after Savage fell on his knees on Kirkman as he lay on the ground. The two umpires disagreed on whether it was a foul and appealed to the referee, after a draw was agreed.

It was said of Savage that 'Of science he possesses but little – his principal merit being that of endurance'.[18] He proved this in between these fights with two gruelling meetings with Jem Wallace, winning the first over 127 rounds in 2 hours and 27 minutes, but losing the second in 61 rounds over 1 hour and 20 minutes. Savage forced Spring the Conjuror to retire after 120 rounds in January 1828.

After his clash with Peter Sweeney in October 1828 was interrupted by police, Savage failed to turn up on the day appointed to renew the fight, and haggling failed to end in agreement, so Savage was paired instead with Sweeney's brother, Tom. Savage agreed to the match in irritation, but he thought the fight was a 'gift' because, although much heavier and younger, Tom was a novice who had never appeared in the prize ring before'. Savage thought he was a certainty to win.

As it turned out, Sweeney proved 'too young, too fresh, too active and too heavy' and forced Savage's seconds to retire him in the 26th round after 33 minutes.

Savage and Peter Sweeney met the following March and the fight lasted one hour and 55 minutes over 94 rounds, with Savage losing 'more by exhaustion and repeated falls than by serious hitting', one 'tremendous fall on his head' leaving him 'insensible'. Savage was now urged to retire, but before he did so he was well-beaten by a fighter named Gow over 23 rounds in the same number of minutes.

Bill Savage was skilful and 'a much better fighter than his brother', but this was not much of a compliment, as *Bell's Life* added that he did not 'stand very high in the estimation of the patrons of the Ring', had 'nothing decisive in his style of fighting, and is not a finishing hitter'.

Savage lost most of his handful of reported fights, some going unreported at the time, before his ring career was interrupted by a year's gaol with hard labour for indecently assaulting his step-daughter. On his release, his first contest was held behind Millbank prison, probably his recent lodgings, when he beat Griffiths in 23 rounds over 45 minutes. Savage appeared on the same bill when brother Edward had his third fight with Kirkman, proving much too skilful for 'Jack of Finchley', for a purse of forty shillings.

Keeping order around the ring was a major problem at this time, and during Savage's battle against Paddy Flynn,

> a strong feeling of indignation was expressed against a bulldog, which had broken loose from some of the *fancy*, and which, darting into the ring, first seized Flynn, then Savage by the drawers, while in the act of struggling each other against the ropes. Fortunately, he was taken off before he inflicted a flesh wound.[19]

After his next outing, against Harry Jones, when he was punished heavily throughout 56 rounds in one hour and 35 minutes, Savage 'was taken from the ring in a dreadful state, completely blind, while Jones had not a scratch', the *Morning Chronicle* commenting 'his day is evidently gone by'.

Savage fought at least one more time, losing to Pick at Battle Bridge in 1828.

Unlike the gentlemanly Turner, the Savage brothers were not well liked. Bill was loud and aggressive when trying to make matches, while Edward was seen as

> rather a foul fighter, and but too much disposed to take unfair advantages of his opponents – a trait in his character which has rendered him somewhat unpopular with the Fancy, who, very properly, set their faces against such practices.[20]

Edward was seen as 'a tough, game middleweight and a good boxer – when in the mood – but he was not averse to the odd nefarious dealing if it enhanced his financial position', one opponent alleging that Savage had offered to throw their fight. The Fair Play Club excluded Edward from all benefits of the club, recommended pugilists not to spar with him nor be matched against him and the public to discount him as a pugilist.

The courage of the brothers was questioned during fight negotiations. Bill was labelled 'cowardly' for refusing to fight after losing the toss for venue and then threatening that he and his brother would attack the opponent. Edward once turned up to a fight but then refused to go ahead. He claimed to have had an injury from climbing a tree, but it was generally thought 'he didn't wish to be thrashed'.

However, once they were in the ring, their bravery could not be questioned. They were reckoned to be 'game to the very echo'.[21]

The brothers made money from wrestling as well as from pugilism, so, naturally, this fighting tactic was very much in their repertoire. When Edward fought Spring the Conjuror, 'In the 117th round Savage fell heavily on Spring with his knee, and a badly weakened Spring lasted for only three more rounds before his seconds gave in for him'. Two years earlier, Savage had finished off a contest after two and a half hours over 101 rounds, by throwing his opponent, who was not able to rise for a minute.

Edward and Bill had one thing in common with Turner, though, they were also proud of their Welsh heritage, which was evident whenever they stepped into the ring. Before one fight, Edward turned up 'adorned with a leek, as an emblem of his country, singing 'Taffy he came from the borders of Wales'.[22] Welsh fighters had a reputation for being excitable, and, one time, Bill's 'Welch blood got warm, and he had lost his temper' while taking part in a wrestling match, adopted a boxing stance whereupon his opponent threw him for the victory.[23]

***

DAVID 'Welsh' Davis, 'a coach-body-maker in Birmingham from the land of leeks', was described as a 'very fine young man, about 12 ½ stone, has excellent science, and will certainly astonish some of the London pugilists', after his 18-rounds win over Manning at Wolverhampton racecourse in 1828.[24] *Bell's Life*, noted that 'game Welchman' Davis 'can hit very hard, possesses good science and courage, an admirable thrower, & can get away well from mischief'.[25]

Davis had moved to London by the time he met Deaf Burke, and although he showed 'first rate game', Burke was on top throughout, forcing his retirement with a broken nose in 12 rounds over 27 minutes. Davis's backers accepted he had done his best but had been over-matched yet was capable of beating Burke in the future. *Bell's Life* disagreed: 'As he has a good business, however, we would advise him to stick to it, and leave the ring to follow its own vagaries'.[26]

Davis ignored the advice and fought Preston in front of the grandstand on Wolverhampton racecourse watched by a crowd of almost ten thousand. It proved eventful, as an excited crowd twice broke into the ring, then, after twenty minutes of fighting, police intervened. A second ring was formed a mile and a half away and the men fought for another 35 minutes before the battle ended in confusion. Davis claimed a foul and Preston maintained he had won because Davis had not come up to scratch. The referee ordered them to fight on but only Davis agreed.

The fight earned the combatants a call to the Staffordshire Assizes where Davis was discharged because he had a wife and children to support and he expressed his determination to abandon the ring. He didn't forsake prize fighting, though, the pair having a return match in Staffordshire a year later, this time Davis retiring after 22 rounds in just under an hour.

***

OTHER Welsh pugilists in London, where the *Welch Harp* pub in the Edgeware Road was a popular meeting place for the prize ring fraternity, included David Morgan, who, at three feet nine inches in height, was known as 'the Dwarf Champion of Wales'. Morgan was 'under the care' of Edward Savage, for a victory in 1828 against the similar-sized Scot Peter McBean at Whetstone and was 'attended by a few from the 'Land of the Leeks'. After 27 rounds in 37 minutes, 'McBean's friends, seeing he had no chance and was dreadfully punished, took him away'.[27]

At the end of 1846, a fight in London involved Jordan, yet another calling himself the 'Welsh Champion' who was reported to be a 'wonder', having fought upwards of seventy battles with 'roughs'.[28] The native of Monmouthshire, a moulder by trade, went into a pub run by well-known pugilist Ben Caunt and offered to fight him 'or any other big-un' the next day for £20.

Caunt matched him with Nobby Clarke, and Jordan, despite showing 'unshrinking courage' was beaten in 15 rounds over twenty minutes, 'carrying away a head which it will require all his ingenuity to 're-mould' into its original shape'.

***

FIGHTERS based in Wales became more widely known in this period as London publications increased their interest, and there was additional coverage by their provincial counterparts and by English-language newspapers in Wales. Many English language weekly newspapers were now founded in Wales (particularly after the Newspaper Stamp Act came into operation in 1855, opening the way for cheap, mass-produced publications). Like their counterparts in the early years of the century, they regularly obtained local fight news from London sources and continued to print reports verbatim from the English provincial Press.

When a group of pugilists from Bristol, at that time a major centre for the sport, visited Newport to give exhibitions in 1827, they posted bills on behalf of one of their number, Jem Bailey, challenging any man in the town.

The locals responded by putting forward Bill Charles, who had had 'several turn-ups in his own neighbourhood, and always beat his man'.[29] Charles stood 5ft. 7ins, weighed 12st. 5lbs and possessed a reputation for durability, in ring jargon he was 'a complete glutton'.[30]

Bailey had taken part in a fixed fight three years previously, as a member of a group who conspired to bribe Steven Strong to lose against him, but he came unstuck this time.

The match took place close to the Newport docks, and the challenge proved to be a big mistake on his part, *Bell's Life* remarking, 'Never were the knowing-ones taken in more completely than in this fight, which lasted but thirteen minutes'.[31]

Against Charles he went down in each of the eight rounds to escape punishment and at the end of the eighth cried 'enough', prompting Charles to 'dance a hornpipe round the ring, amid the most deafening shouts'.

The journal remarked on Bailey's pre-fight behaviour:

> Nothing could be more disgusting than the taunting *chaff* he used before the fight; and we sincerely hope, if he goes further down the country, exhibiting the art of self-defence, that he may again and again pay for the insults he has offered to the Welsh.

Three weeks later, Bailey turned the tables in 'an unparalleled fight of 117 hard rounds' at Glascoed Common in Monmouthshire. Charles's supporters grumbled that he lost because the fight did not take place in an enclosed ring but on an inclined ground and in and out of the crowd. *Bell's Life* thought differently. 'It would be well not to urge him to meet Bailey again,' it remarked, 'even if they should make the conditions with the extra advantage of a 24-foot enclosure'.

But they did meet again, three months later, on Bailey's home territory of Gloucestershire. The ring was originally pitched at Kingswood Hill, 'and long before that hour the road was crowded with heavy drags, light traps, gigs, prads, and tramps, all hastening to the spot'.[32] But police were on hand,

and the entourage headed off to Chipping Sodbury, where a proper ring was erected.

Charles, who was 'considered another Glendower and is recognised as the Welch champion', proved the experts wrong by winning after 100 rounds, but *Bell's Life* could only remark sourly: 'Charles proved himself to be an out-and-outer at receiving; but he has no pretensions to fighting, and a clever chap would have beat either in half the time'.[33]

The meeting between Charles and the Irishman, Stephen Trainor, at Monmouth Cap in 1832, was regarded as a major international event with 'four distinguished characters, from the London ring, retained' as seconds for the fighters.

Irish pugilists in Wales enjoyed a strong following among their exiled countrymen. All of Trainor's fellow Irishmen, or 'potato eaters' in newspaper parlance, who, like him, hawked silks for a living, sold their wares 'at considerably reduced prices to enable them to back their *darling* boy. Some even put their packs in pawn'.[34]

Feelings ran high and dirty tricks were afoot. The day before the fight *Bell's Life* reported that an anonymous letter had been sent to Charles stating that the two men who were to be his seconds had been seen with Trainor at Bristol. But the journal claimed to 'have the best authority for stating, that the assertion is unfounded'.

In the build-up, the chief ring official, trying to clear the ring, exchanged punches with a spectator who refused to stand back.

The main fight, in front of more than five thousand spectators, lasted 14 minutes, and Charles survived without a scratch. Trainor, though, was very much punished, had three of his ribs broken, and was 'put to bed in a pitiful state'.

The act action wasn't over, however. A match was arranged between the two men who had scuffled previously, which the official won and then, in a melee, the official's second was thrown over a hedge into a ditch.

Celebrations were muted, however, the consensus being that Trainor was a poor fighter and that Charles, who had 'taken less care of himself within this last month than at any period of his life' (ring-speak for heavy drinking), could have easily beaten three more like him. Charles' local newspaper commented 'Charles gained few laurels by his victory. He had nothing to fight against. Had he any punching power he would have won in half the time'.[35]

A match with up-and-coming London fighter Deaf Burke, heavily backed by supporters of the defeated Trainor, then fell through because of the alleged intransigence of Charles' camp over money and the venue, the Newportonians allegedly wanting it 'within five miles of their own dunghill'.

Charles next took on Bill Gardiner, of Ross. They met in a field near Raglan watched by nearly three thousand. In almost every round Gardiner slipped down to avoid punishment after landing his own heavy blows. After 38 rounds 'it was now evident that Charles was losing fast, and, the half minute having expired, Charles extended his hand to his adversary, who cordially shook it, and then leaped over the ropes amidst the astounding buzzes of the Herefordshire men.'

***

NUMEROUS lesser fights in Wales were reported, among them clashes at Caerphilly, Newport, Cardiff, Llangollen, Vauneg and Abergavenny, but only a few in detail, and most only by *Bell's Life*. In 1828, Cowbridge youth John Davies beat John Newnom after seventy-nine rounds in a field behind the town's *Greyhound* public house, and it was reckoned that 'if 'picked up' by a good judge, might prove a little fortune, as he is equal to any man of his weight'.[36] It was probably the same John Davies who, responding to a boast in 1831 by Jem Bailey, of Bristol, that he could 'lick any Welchman of his weight', threw down a challenge for up to £50 a-side, his own stakes waiting in a London pub.

Later in 1828, at Fiddler's Green, Radnorshire, W. Hoddell met Richard Humphreys over 61 rounds, the fight lasting one hour and 47 minutes, and despite the contest ending in a draw, Hoddell 'assumed the title of Champion of Wales'. A local forge man, James Morgan, brought in the New Year of 1829 with a fight for £5 a-side in a field near Usk with a Gloucestershire navigator. After 43 rounds spread over one hour and three minutes, Morgan retired, his left arm rendered useless by a succession of blows. In the last weeks of 1829, a 'gallant' fight for £10 a-side took place in Montgomeryshire between Tom Jones and Tom Shenkin which, 'after 64 rounds hard milling', Jones won. Jones was the loser in two more gruelling fights in neighbouring Cheshire in the following years, however, both to Bill Hutch over 73 and 51 rounds respectively. On the latter occasion with one eye 'completely banged up and dreadfully beaten, he was carried from the ring in a state of stupor'. In the London area in 1834 Sampson Jones, 'a Welchman', was beaten in 18 rounds by Brandbrich.

Welsh newspapers carried reports of prize fights at Caerphilly, Neath and Abercanaid and in Monmouthshire, where a court at Pontypool sat in judgement on two fights on the same day. Smith Sage and John Tamplin fought in front of 'an immense crowd of people' between Blaenavon and Garndiffaith in 1859, and the following year, two employees of the Blaenavon Iron and Coal Company, Ben Andrews and 'Dai Strawhat' rang in the New Year by fighting for more than two hours and twenty minutes. Around this time, one fighter's appearance in court

> created a good deal of curiosity....The prisoner, judging from his appearance seems a half sane looking individual, and the thrashing he bore on the occasion of the fight appears to bear out the truth indicated in his physiogonomy.[37]

***

Randall 'the giant', based at Newtown, issued a challenge, not taken up, in 1842 to the 6ft. 11 ¼ ins. American Charles Freeman for £200 a-side. Randall's sparring gloves were said to 'measure eighteen inches long in the palm'.

Another of whom prize ring details are scarce, was Thomas Rees (Twm Carnabwth), from Mynachlog-ddu, Pembrokeshire, who, apparently, 'won great fame as a pugilist', before in 1847, aged about forty, in a drunken fight he lost an eye.[38] Rees was remembered as 'a great muscular pugilist, a frequenter of fairs and festivities, for rounds of fights etc.'[39]

He, apparently, played a major part in the Rebecca riots, indeed one account names him as the movement's first leader and the first to wear the movement's uniform of women's clothes.

> a gown large enough for the chosen leader could be found only with difficulty. At last the rioters came across a tall and stout old maid named Rebecca, and, after undergoing some alterations, her dress was made to fit Thomas Rees tolerably well. From this circumstance the name "Rebecca" was adopted, and not as we have hitherto been given to understand, from having taken the well-known verse in Genesis as a motto.[40]

Other fighters mentioned briefly include William Cole, based at the *Oxford Arms* Inn, Presteigne, Radnorshire, who challenged W. Hoddell in 1828, Luke Purcell, who was said to be 'prepared to fight Evan James, either at Brecon or Swansea' in 1830, David Howell, based in the Chester area in

1833, George Pick referred to as 'the Welch Champion' in 1837, and Bill Holwell 'the Welch Champion' in 1842.

**

COMBATANTS increasingly journeyed out of Wales, although again mostly to just over the border, in Cheshire, Herefordshire, the Midlands and some as far afield as Yorkshire, their exploits still reported almost exclusively in *Bell's Life* or in *The Era*, another London publication.

Between three and four thousand Midlands colliers were reported present when Thomas Williams, 'commonly called the Game Welchman', fought 28 rounds 'with manly firmness and unshrinking courage' at Northerton, near Dudley in 1829. Williams appeared on his way to victory until opponent Isaac Hadley rallied, according to the colourful jargon typical of *Bell's Life* correspondents, 'tipping poor Taffy a clink under the listener, tumbled him over as stupid as a cat under the influence of prussic acid'.

In Bristol the following year, Thomas Hamlet was beaten in 27 rounds over 35 minutes by John Callaghan, while Tom Jones lost in 73 rounds to Bill Hutch in Cheshire, a defeat that was to be repeated two years later in the same area, this time in 51 rounds with Jones having been 'knocked senseless'.

A 'slap-up fight was reported near Hanley in the Midlands in 1833 involving 'Evans, the Welch collier'. Evans' opponent, Jackson, was taller, 'but still the firm and beautiful appearance, and muscular power, of the Cambrian, were evidently in his favour'.[41] The report continued

> 61 rounds were fought with the greatest game on the part of Jackson, but to no effect against the Welch Champion, who floored him fifteen times in succession; in fact, he had the advantage of him in activity and science, against which strength, in a regular ring, cannot prevail. Jackson at length gave up, by the advice of the 'out and out Corinthian; who backed him.

Later that year, 'Jones (the Welch Champion)' fought Young Brag, the Yorkshire Pet near Huddersfield. Jones was certainly relaxed beforehand, stretching himself out on the ground until his seconds roused him for the action which lasted eight rounds before a magistrate and police officers rode up on horseback to call a halt. In other parts of England Tom Jones was beaten in forty rounds over one hour and eight minutes in Cheshire in 1842 by Matt Harrett, Tom Davis beat Keeney Malone in 54 rounds 'in a pitiless storm' near Liverpool in 1845, and Thomas Williams, based in Walsall, knocked out Tabberner, of Rushall, after 16 rounds over 35 minutes near Birmingham in 1847. A fight was reported at Acklam in north Yorkshire involving 'a Welshman' who fought an Englishman named Prior, 'after a series of rounds.....Taffy was declared victor'.[42]

***

TRAVEL and communication improvements after the mid-century developed an international dimension for the fighters as well as for those engaged in several other sports. Previously, crossing the Atlantic Ocean had taken anything from 26 days (In 1819 by the *Savannah*, a sailing packet with an auxiliary engine and collapsible paddle wheels), to just over 11 days by the *Britannia* in 1840. In 1856 the first iron Cunarder, the *Persia*, reduced the time to just over 9 days, and by the end of the century the *Deutschland* could cross the Atlantic in under 5 days.

And where communication between Europe and the Americas could only be via ship, the transatlantic cable sped up communication to within minutes, allowing an inquiry and a response within the same day. The first transatlantic telegraph cable was completed on August 5, 1858 but was destroyed the following month when excessive voltage was applied to it. A next attempt was undertaken in 1865 and a connection was completed and put into service on July 28, 1866.

R. G. Williams, born at Caernarvon, north Wales, was reported to have fought in the USA during this period. Williams, born in 1829, ran away from home and emigrated to America in 1843. 'He fought his first prize fight in New York in 1850 'putting Mike Trainer, the then champion of New York State, to sleep in a few rounds'.[43] He was, however, better=known for his activities outside the ring, as an 'evangelist, reformed drunkard, [and] gambler', a former inmate of New Jersey State prison, and a Shakespearean actor 'playing with Edwin Booth in Hamlet'.

***

AFTER his fight with Sayers in 1857, Aaron Jones went to North America, where he was one of John Heenan's seconds for Sayers' future opponent in his ring debut. Heenan took on Irish-born gangster (and future US Congressman and senator) John Morrisey at Long Point, Ontario, Canada, on the north shore of Lake Eyrie.

A quarter of a million dollars was reported to have been staked on the result of the fight, which was promoted as being for the championship of America. Morrisey was the champion but it was Heenan who handed out most of the punishment before succumbing on a knockout in the eleventh round.

Morrisey's supporters had threatened to shoot Jones if Heenan were to win. As one reporter saw it,

> When Heenan appeared to have the best of it, twenty or thirty pistols were drawn, and there is no doubt that had Heenan whipped Morrisey, he would not only never have received the stakes but would have been then and there killed along with his trainer. It was a complete case of intimidation, and it could be easily seen that

163

Aaron Jones, instead of attending to his man, was looking out for stray pistol shots.[44]

Other ringsiders observed that although Morrisey was badly marked about the face, his injuries were caused by Heenan's early success and that he himself took control when Heenan tired.

But, bearing in mind that three years earlier two of Morrisey's friends had shot dead a fellow gangster who had beaten Morrisey in a prize fight, it was likely that Heenan and Jones took the threat seriously and chose to 'throw' the fight. After all, Morrisey was reported to have 'presented a most hideous spectacle, while Heenan was comparatively uninjured',

It could prove dangerous to upset rival supporters as Englishman Deaf Burke discovered when fighting in New Orleans twenty years previously; he 'was forced to fight his way out of the ring armed with a Bowie knife and escaped on horseback at full gallop'.

The reporter for the Heenan v Morrisey encounter ended his piece: 'My reasons for giving an account of this fight are to show the English P. R. that there is still a worse institution than that, namely, the American P. R.'

Although he sent a £200 challenge across the Atlantic for a third fight with Sayers, and sparred with Heenan in Montreal, Canada, it was to be another nine years, before Jones fought again in the ring.

Epitomising how prize fighters were similarly viewed on the other side of the Atlantic, a New York journalist said Jones was 'considered the most gentlemanly fighting man ever seen on this side', before a qualifying 'which, however, is not much of a compliment'.[45]

1 Bell's Life, 3 January 1858. Birmingham Daily Post, 7 January 1858.
2 Chepstow Weekly Advertiser, 16 January, 1858
3 Bell's Life, 10 January 1858
4 Birmingham Daily Post, 7 January 1858
5 Bell's Life, 24 January 1858
6 Chepstow Weekly Advertiser, 9 April 1859
7 Morning Chronicle, 5 April 1859. Bell's Life, 10 April 1859
8 Bell's Life, 10 April 1859
9 London, Such's Song Mart, 1859.
10 Bell's Life, 10 April 1859
11 Chepstow Weekly Advertiser, 9 April 1859
12 Merthyr Telegraph, 14 September 1861.
13 Bell's Life, 30 January 1859
14 Bell's Life, 10 June 1860. E. Wyn James, 'The Lame Chick and The North Star:, in Marjetka Golež (ed.), *Ballads between Tradition and Modern Times* (Lubljana, Slovenia: Slovenian Academy of Sciences & Arts, 1998), pp. 93-100
15 Evening Telegraph (Philadelphia)31 August 1867.
16 Pierce Egan's Weekly Courier, 8 Mar 1829
17 Morning Chronicle, 12 July 1826; 29 August 1827
18 Morning Chronicle, 16 January 1828. Bell's Life, 20 January 1828
19 Morning Chronicle, 16 Jan 1828
20 Morning Chronicle, 16 January 1828
21 Egan's Weekly Courier, 24 January 1829
22 Morning Chronicle, 4 March 1829
23 Morning Chronicle, 15 October 1824. Bell's Life, 17 October 1824
24 Morning Post, 25 December 1828
25 Bell's Life, 1 Feb 1829
26 Bell's Life, 27 February 1831
27 Bell's Life, 10 Feb 1828.
28 *Era*, 20 December 1846
29 Bell's Life, 14 October 1827
30 Bristol Mercury, 15 October 1827
31 Bell's Life, 15 October 1827
32 Bell's Life, 3 Feb, 1828.
33 Bell's Life,3 February 1828
34 Monmouthshire Merlin, 9 June 1832
35 Bristol Mercury, 9 June 1832. Monmouthshire Merlin, 9 June 1832
36 Bell's Life, 23 March 1828
37 Merthyr Telegraph, 4 February 1860.
38 Welsh Dictionary of National Biography, Robert Jenkins.
39 Welsh Gazette, 24 January 1901
40 Henry Tobit Evans, *Rebecca and her Daughters, being the History of the Agrarian Disturbances in Wales, 1843-1844, known as the Rebecca Riots* (Cardiff, Educational Publishing Company, Ltd., 1910).
41 Bell's Life, 27 January 1833.
42 York Herald, 30 April 1859.
43 Morning Call, 20 September 1893
44 Era, 14 November 1858.
45 Era, 28 November 1858.

7

Revival? 1861 - 1900

The fight in 1860 for the Championship between Tom Sayers (who had beaten Welshman Bill Benjamin the previous year) and the American, John Heenan, was hailed as the beginning of a revival of the prize ring in Britain. It was the major topic of conversation, overshadowing political reform at home and abroad as well as unrest in Europe. There was considerable interest in the USA as well, with 150 fans crossing the Atlantic to support their man.

The contest had been rumoured to take place 'within twenty miles of Newport', but the only connection to the Monmouthshire port was with the driver of the train carrying the fight party, John Williams, who later kept the *Trout Inn*, in Market Street, Newport.[1]

The pair came together in Hampshire, and the next day, sports papers sold hundreds of thousands of copies; Press coverage of prize fighting increased, and a sporting daily was started up to report the activity.

***

BUT did the event really presage the restoration of the ring's 'faded glories' or was there 'only a momentary forgetfulness of the conditions of our being' because national pride was at stake?[2]

After all, it was ostensibly a challenge to England's world supremacy in prize-fighting (the English champion was effectively champion of the world), but it was also a symbolic assault on England as a leading political and military power from a country with which it had fought two wars and was not far off a third.

Forecasts of a revival were encouraged by the authorities' perceived timidity in tackling the issue, and by renewed upper class support. The Government appeared to be 'a direct patron of the ring'; when anti-prize fight spokesman George Hadfield, MP drew the attention of the House of Commons to the forthcoming match, labelling it 'brutal' and 'demoralising', he was met with shouts of 'nonsense' from government benches, and Sir George Lewis raised a laugh at the expense of opponents.[3]

Prize fighting flourished in prison, as it had fifty years before. This time, a former Dartmoor convict disclosed in a letter to a newspaper that it was

> a very common thing to see two ruffians stripped to the trousers fighting a pitched battle, which lasted for a considerable part of an hour. They had their seconds and backers, while betting – in tobacco – went on briskly on all hands. In few instances did the officers intervene.[4]

And a punch-up in Parliament, reminiscent of the fight between two MPs outside the Palace of Westminster forty years before, proved that the use of fists remained popular with the country's leaders. Members were debating the Irish Home Rule question when

> some twenty or thirty were at once struggling and pushing and wrestling together. Blows were exchanged and for some moments the scene in that part of the House was that of a free and indiscriminate fight.[5]

***

PREDICTIONS of the sport's demise, on the other hand, were fuelled by continued corruption surrounding the London ring, increased denunciation in the Press, interference by the law and by the eventual banning of excursion trains to fights.

Revival? 1861-1900

In Wales the main reason given for the sport's claimed passing was that people were simply not interested in its 'evils', the activity supposedly having become rare by 1883. By 1889, the country was free of the prize ring, thanks to the influence of Nonconformism, campaigners for the disestablishment of the Church of England in Wales told a sceptical House of Commons.

The Sunday Closing Act of 1881, which shut down public houses on that day in most counties in Wales, was claimed to have damaged prize fighting in north of the country. Bala police said that the 'lower classes' now attended work at the beginning of the week, whereas previously, 'It was nothing to see crowds of people... going to witness a prize fight in Caemawr or on the Green when people were going to attend afternoon and evening services'.[6]

The sport was 'rapidly' dying out even in its South Wales mining stronghold, where, it was said, colliers now enjoyed eisteddfod competitions which the spread of education had made more compatible with the collier's mind.[7] Welsh people had a genuine delight in the intellectual excitements at eisteddfodau by exercises in oratory, poetry and music competitions, whereas it was the English who took delight in pugilism.[8]

This sentiment was part of the continuing attempts to portray Welsh people in a better light after the 'Treason of the Blue Books' in the middle of the century. Accordingly, according to the *Western Mail*, which was replying to references by presumably England-based journals to prize fights and cock fights taking place in Wales, 'Nowhere within the realm is the population more inoffensive, less criminal, or attached in a higher degree to innocent pastimes and intellectual pursuits'.[9]

***

HOWEVER, casting doubt on the alleged Welsh aversion to prize fighting, a magistrate lamented in 1863 that advertising for a boxing show at

Aberdare on the same night was more attractive than that for his lecture (on Ireland) at the town's Temperance Hall. Likewise, further west, attendances at a public hall at Morriston for 'meetings of real intellect, real pleasure and profit-no matter whether the admission be free or merely nominal... were comparatively deserted', while 'hundreds of people walked and drove to Morriston, through pouring rain and thick mud, and paid, some 5s. and none less than 2s.' to see a fight at the venue.[10]

Prize-fighting's being a furtive activity meant that nobody could be certain of the state of its health, but it certainly appeared to be thriving in Wales, where a victorious Sayers was handed a purse of gold in Cardiff after a public subscription.

Indeed, if there was ever a golden age in Wales, this was it, with plenty of fighters – in this period more than five hundred were identified in this research and probably many more went unreported - and no shortage of people keen to watch them.

South Wales, which boasted the biggest towns, was a leading area for the sport. Popularity reached its peak during the later decades of the century, the boom coinciding with the growth in in-migration, industrialisation and the opening-up of the south Wales coal mining valleys and the ports serving them. The *Cardiff and Merthyr Guardian* claimed in 1870 'If Cardiff bids fair to become notorious for wife-beating, stabbing and manslaughter, the sister town of Merthyr seems bent upon achieving pugilistic renown'.

Newport was a particularly violent place. Its claim to fame was its drunken mobs, a common and highly dangerous hazard, the combination of alcohol and political passions a toxic mix, with election nights providing most drunken, violent and bloody affrays.

Revival? 1861-1900

Riots at the 1868 election were second in intensity only to the Chartist troubles of thirty years earlier. Soldiers with fixed bayonets chased a several thousand strong mob along the main street, past the Westgate hotel (the scene of the Chartists confrontation) and into a side street where a woman was bayoneted to death on her own doorstep. At the next election, the mayor was beaten up and robbed, and troops again chased rioters at bayonet point, while on the following November 5, a policeman was stoned to death by a crowd of drunks.

Two pub landlords took part in a prize fight in Swansea in 1874, 'Cabs were hired; seconds selected; a wager agreed on, £5', both choosing well-known exponents, 'Shonny Shrag' and 'Cloggy' as their seconds.

> All arranged, money down, the nerves properly attuned, the toilette of the ring performed, a friendly shake of the hand duly indulged in, and – fight commenced.....It was not until the ninth round that the fight ended with the 'sponge thrown up' and the younger man the winner.[11]

Prize fighting flourished in North Wales as well. A much-heralded clash in 1865 involving Richard Owens, from Llanidloes, enabled police to lie in wait at two favourite venues, so the organisers decided on board the train out of Liverpool to plump for Collins Green, Warrington, twenty miles away. There, Owens, having his second outing, beat Harry Neville in 84 rounds over two hours and 24 minutes, Neville being disqualified for repeatedly falling to escape punishment.

Neville's handlers complained that the referee had bets on the fight, but *Bell's Life* said that was irrelevant; once he had accepted the job of referee, any bets he had made were void.[12]

Twice in as many weeks in 1871 men fought for the Championship of Wrexham. The first was between Bill Lawrence (the Gipsy Tinker) and

Williams (Bill the Coal), who fought for two hours before calling it a draw. Lawrence, however, still thought he was the top man and challenged next in line Charles Jones, better known as 'Charley the Well'. In this fight, when Lawrence began to tire, his brother, who was one of his seconds, punched Jones twice in the face. But this didn't make any difference, Jones' body punches forcing Lawrence to concede defeat.

In south Wales, unlike in the north of the country, the Sunday Closing Act appears to have given the sport a boost. Glamorgan was dry and Rumney was on the wet side of the Sunday drinking border with Monmouthshire, and prize fighting people took advantage of the village's easy access. Under headlines of 'The blessings of Sunday Closing' and 'The Border Nuisance', a local paper reported that John Giles, a dock labourer of Cardiff, was fined 20s at Newport in 1892 for taking part in a prize fight at Rumney on a Sunday.[13]

***

MINERS were in the majority among Welsh pugilists in this period, comprising roughly two thirds of those identified in the present research. They usually fought locally or within their home county while retaining their jobs. The magistrates' clerk at Aberdare at a hearing following one night-time battle in 1894 wondered what light the men had to fight by, and inquired whether they carried lamps in their hats so that they could see each other, and one of the fighters replied, equally seriously or not, that he did not know who he was fighting because it was so dark.

Prize fighting at Aberdare prompted a surprise vitriolic attack on the area from a Scottish newspaper. A question in the House of Commons about a fatal fight in 1894 referred to Aberdare, but a printing error in the official report of *Hansard* resulted in Aberdeen being named, leading to the pronouncement

> the people of Aberdeen are cast in a different mould from those of Aberdare, and no wonder. The brave blithe town of Aberdeen is in every respect the very antipodes, morally and physically, of Aberdare, which is a district of the Merthyr Tydvil [sic] Parliamentary borough, as also is Dowlais – making together the largest colliery constituency in the United Kingdom. But the whole region is a black, barren, wretched district, with scarcely as blade of grass to be seen, or indeed anything but desolate heaps of pit refuse.[14]

Impressive attendances were reported, at least 4,000 estimated at the fight in the Tondu and Maesteg area in 1884 between Shoni Engineer (Treorchy) and Thomas Davies (Pentre), more than 2,000 on Rhymney Hill above Tredegar in 1860, when Edwards met Stevens, and a similar number when Richards and Ryan battled in the Penderyn area of Merthyr in 1866, while Charles Collins and James Fitzgerald, met on the Rumney moors in front of a 'respectable' crowd of between 500-600.

The necessary secrecy limited attendances, though, for most bare-knuckle contests, and, while there were hundreds of participants, more often their battles took place in front of a select company.

In 1893, only 'twelve or fourteen' watched a fight near Cardiff, 'about forty backers and friends' saw 'well-known bruisers' Tom Israel and William Jones at Glyncorrwg, a 'little party of selected men' were present for Jack Northey versus Joe Mitchell on Maindy Mountain, and thirty for Thomas Shaw and William Rees near Llwynypia Station.[15] For an encounter on the canal side at Fourteen Locks, Newport, 'only nineteen people in all were present, and some of these were on the high ground as outposts looking out for the police'.[16]

***

THE public were interested in anything to do with the sport. They flocked to see exhibitions by the top men of the era at fairs, in theatres and even in circuses. English champion Jem Mace toured regularly throughout South Wales for over twenty years, while other notable visitors included Bendigo (William Abednego Thompson), the former heavyweight champion, who sparred with Bill Benjamin in Merthyr in 1861, while Dan Thomas toured South Wales towns to crowded houses that year.

A Who's Who of famous fighters trod a similar path, heavyweight champion Jem Smith at Swansea in 1888, Frank Slavin ,Australian heavyweight champion, (Merthyr 1890), scourge of Britons Frank Craig (Pontypridd, Cardiff 1894, 1895), Dick Burge British Empire lightweight champion (Cardiff 1896), and Peter Jackson, the world 'coloured' heavyweight champion as he was known at the time, (Cardiff 1896).

John. Heenan toured through Mid and South Wales with Howe's Great American Circus in 1862, and around the same time Tom Sayers and his own collection of men, horses and elephants, due to spend twelve months in Australia, journeyed through South Wales on their way to Cork and thence Down Under. Sayers' show was hardly a resounding success at Chepstow, where it was said takings did not cover expenses. The previous year, touring with Howe's and Cushing's Circus, Sayers laid a few bricks in an extension to Monmouth's old coaching inn, the *Angel Hotel*, Church Street.

John L Sullivan was reported to have received a better reception and drew a larger crowd, among them enthusiastic local councillors, in Cardiff in 1888 than had prime minister William Gladstone. Jake Kilrain, who was to challenge champion Sullivan in 1889 in the last world heavyweight championship prize fight decided with bare knuckles, and Charlie Mitchell (world heavyweight boxing title contender) were also greeted on their visit at

Cardiff station by a large crowd, and were escorted to the Park Hotel by a brass band.

The locally published *Western Mail* doubted whether prize fighting had ever had as strong a hold on the public as it promised to have in the future and credited Sullivan with having done most to make it possible. Visits by famous fighters, it was claimed, fuelled a demand for 'real' fights rather than exhibitions which had become commonplace.

Many variety acts in those same theatres had a boxing theme. Customers at Morella's Palace of Varieties in Cardiff towards the end of the century were advised 'The lovers of 'fistiana' have their fill in the exhibition given by Miss Selina Seaforth, described in the programme as the 'champion female boxer'. A regular visitor over more than a dozen years, she was described as 'the talented burlesque actress and vocalist and champion lady pugilist......the champion female boxer of the world, and her skill in the use of the gloves is astonishing'. Miss Lily Reed 'the pugilistic Amazon' performed at Andrews' New Hall, Queen Street, Cardiff.

Among other attractions were the four Pancratics (named after the Ancient Greek mixed martial arts sport) in 1888 at the Philharmonic Hall, Cardiff, whose sketch was 'exceedingly laughable and comes to a climax in a glove fight'. There were also in the last few years of the century 'the two Boxing Rams' at the Empire, 'a boxing contest between two cats' as well as a boxing kangaroo at the same theatre, while the Grand Theatre, Cardiff, presented the 'sensational melodrama' *Saturday Night in London* – which featured a prize fight in a pub.

In 1891, Ted Pritchard, billed fancifully as the 'world middleweight champion', appeared at the Philharmonic, Cardiff, other acts including 'Rags, the champion somersault dog'. Pritchard had better known and more conventional artistes alongside him at Liverpool's Grand Theatre months later – two of the biggest music hall stars of the time, singer and comedian Marie Lloyd and male impersonator Vesta Tilley.

***

THE popularity of pugilism prompted a suggestion in 1895 that the Llandudno Eisteddfod might consider adding a prize fight to the programme, 'the winner to be chaired. The implication was not as outrageous as it seemed, as spectators at the following year's gathering were accused of behaving like crowds at prize fights, and it was urged that 'elements of pugilism should disappear altogether from brass band competitions'.

Trying to explain its appeal, one newspaper stated: 'Vestiges of the old sport, lie deep down in the human strata, and come to the surface sometimes', while another pronounced.

> Many rising and prosperous towns, rapidly emerging from small hamlets to great cities, have displayed the same spirit........The restlessness and activity of trade inculcates a desire for exhibitions of the most exciting character.[17]

***

THE lower, 'rougher' classes were still said to make up the biggest part of crowds, which apparently comprised 'the most ill-looking and debased of the scum of society, ripe for any crime that would put money in their pockets.'[18] Supporting that view, Rhondda Valley men heading to a prize fight near Bridgend in 1884 'disturbed several publicans in quest of liquor, and at one inn at Brynmenin where the landlord refused them admission, they smashed the windows.'[19]

Rarely were 'respectable' men reported to have been present at prize fights. If they were in attendance, they probably tried to keep a low profile, like the twenty 'gentlemen' who paid for seats on the stage at Morriston so that they would not be 'observed by the outer world'.[20]

Newspapers scorned the adulation of prize fighters. When Jem Mace toured South Wales in 1864, local Press referred sarcastically to the 'honour' of having pugilists showing their skills on a platform which previously 'had been graced by nothing greater than an MP or the Lord Mayor of London.[21] Journals frequently placed spectators in the same category as those who enjoyed watching public executions. It was noted at such an event at Warwick that most of the early arrivals were similar in appearance, 'short, thick-set, bull-necked, full-lipped men – men who have a notable affinity to the bulldog, and who are seldom seen in great number together unless it be at a ratting match, a prize fight, or an execution'.[22]

***

THE keenest spectators were, apparently, coal miners. There were regular reports of works being left short of coal and pits left almost idle because miners had gone to see prize fights. When 'Mabon's day', named after the MP William Abraham (better known by his bardic name, Mabon), was introduced in the late 1880s, it was intended as a regular day off for colliers to improve their minds. But it turned into a popular day for attending prize fights and getting drunk.

Croll says that in 1888, Mabon skilfully deployed a highly moralized image of the miners when making a case for more leisure time; however, he adds, the drunkenness and other 'abuses' that became associated with the holiday highlighted the limitations of such a strategy.[23]

Protests from 'distressed ministers', about the interest in pubs and prize fighting among young colliers were said, however, to be 'useless'.[24] Religious organisations themselves were blamed for doing nothing to steer colliers away from such pursuits, instead denouncing 'almost every form of innocent amusement and social enjoyment – theatre, playing cards, music hall, dancing classes as sinful and ungodly.'

Ministers did not understand life outside their own limited sphere. Young colliers, it was claimed, wanted relaxation, change, excitement, brightness after working underground which they would not find in the silence of the prayer and preaching meetings. The collier had no other choice than between the negatives of the minister and the chapel and the allurements of the public- house. 'The prize fight and all its associations-are the result'.

The *South Wales Echo* put forward 'one instance of many' of this kill-joy spirit. Abertillery Sunday School Union had urged the local council not to allow a company of strolling players to put on a show in the town as the theatre was demoralising and often a nuisance. The union claimed that 'The entertainment provided was usually very low in character, and not infrequently the artistes were the scum of the earth'.[25]

***

CHURCH and chapel in Wales both regularly condemned prize-fighting as 'demoralizing', with religious leaders feeling their influence was undermined by the public's appetite for it.

As well they might. Respect for religion in Wales was claimed to be 'almost unmatched' in Britain, but, the proliferation of prize fights on Sundays late in the century –even on Christmas Day they were reported to have taken place at Morfa Mawr, near Carmarthen, on Gelli mountain, and between Llanelli and Loughor, among others - demolished that argument.

178

Sunday fights 'came off' every week near the lime-kilns at Merthyr in 1870, and also frequently among the hills behind Gilfachyrincle and Plymouth Iron Works in the town, at Penycoedcae, near Pontypridd, at Ystrad Rhondda, at New Tredegar, Milford Haven, Tonyrefail, Cwmdu, between Tredegar and Ebbw Vale, Pontypool, and Wrexham, on the moors near Cardiff, at Llantarnam and Blaina in Monmouthshire, and at Mardy.

Sunday prize fights were regarded as more reprehensible when they were held near places of worship and could be seen by the congregation. Such as within one hundred yards of Vaynor Church, surrounded by 'five places of worship' at Pentre Ystrad, Rhondda, and at the Green at Flint, when, during a Sunday morning service, a crowd gathered on the nearby green 'to witness a double fight...for a money wager. Four men stripped to the waist fought each other most savagely',[26]

A chapel minister protested that in Wrexham when a crowd watched two men 'behaving themselves as beasts' on Mayor's Sunday, a day to support the town infirmary, the town had become a centre of moral degradation.[27]

In fairness, the occurrence of Sunday fights had much to do with men avoiding losing time in their workplace, police told a court.

Some religious leaders opposed any sports, with chapel members proving sensitive to how their standing in the community would be affected by any link to pugilism. When a prominent Methodist at Nantymoel discovered that in his absence his wife had allowed a boxing booth on his land, he 'to his credit' refused payment and ordered it to be removed.[28] The report, compiled with the obvious co-operation of the minister, concluded 'It is to be hoped that these facts will vindicate [the minister] in the eyes of the residents of Nantymoel'.

Lay people could also bridle at being associated with prize-fighting. Mountain Ash residents stressed in 1883 that 'repulsive' prize fights were not indigenous to the place, but 'imported ruffianism'.

Such links worried educational establishments, too; trying to offset further criticism over a plan to set up a programme of 'manly sports and exercises' for students, the university college at Aberystwyth felt compelled to stress that these sports differed 'from the brutal prize-fight, which is a disgrace to humanity'.[29]

But the sport's fiercest critic was himself a former leading fighter. Dan Thomas, who later became a Baptist deacon, looked back on his ring days with loathing, and even threw on the fire his belt and gold watch boxing prizes

> so that my children should never see them and be tempted to take any delight in such a life. I would not, for the world, be the means of drawing anyone else to follow the path that I once trod.....I was disgusted with it.... My advice to young people is to shun pugilism. There is ruin in it; it leads to destruction.[30]

Also disenchanted, London fighter John Knifton revealed in a letter to a friend in Treorchy,

> I am thoroughly disgusted with it all. What used to be sport is now turned into swindling, and unless you row along with them they won't let you have fair play. .... there is more music and pleasure and love in singing for ten minutes than seeing all the humbugging fighting that will ever be fought, for they are nearly all swindles, and a disgrace to the fraternity of the country.[31]

Church and chapel, long-time bitter rivals for worshippers, joined forces in a 'crusade' at Swansea in 1895, promising 'vigorous action' (which never materialised) to blot out the sport. But, for all their common desire, prize fighting mostly provided a stage on which to attack each other and to promote their religious and political aims.

They did so via the Press, the *Western Mail* and the *Evening Express* supporting the Established Church (and the Conservative Party) against the Liberal and Nonconformist backers *Cardiff Times*, *South Wales Daily News*, and the radical Welsh language newspaper *Y Gweithiwr Cymreig*. Men who died in the ring were disclaimed and even used to discredit rivals, while each side blamed the other for prize fighting.

Newspapers, which continued to condemn the sport while at the same time publishing colourful reports, also turned on each other. The monthly literary publication for the English-speaking Welsh absolved Welsh weekly newspapers which were 'never given over to accounts of betting and prize fighting', and it claimed it was only the south Wales daily journals which 'dragged these 'obscenities into the literature of Wales'.[32]

Nonconformists seized in 1887 on the current Prince of Wales's 'low taste' in patronizing the sport as another reason for the disestablishment of the church in Wales. Royal support, and that of 'the highest noblemen of the realm' for prize-fighting, as one of a number of 'frivolous and immoral sports, was attacked by Calvinistic Methodists at Llanelli that year. The following year the *Times* referred to the 'unfortunate weakness' of the future King Edward VII in patronizing prize fighters and said it would be 'a serious evil' if he said or did anything to make a brutal practice more popular.[33]

The Salvation Army also opposed prize fighting, but nevertheless welcomed former pugilists into their ranks, as did the Presbyterian Church of Wales. Former fighters spoke at Army prayer meetings in the Rhondda Valley and at Flint.

The Army was always looking for converts. Shoni Castellnedd and Will Squinks turned up at a building at Ystrad in the Rhondda to answer a charge of prize fighting believing it was still a courthouse. They took a seat to wait for the magistrate to appear, but the building had for several years been used by the Salvation Army and an officer told them

> 'My dear brethren... the Saviour is the only magistrate that's coming here.....I can see you are poor sinners; if you wish to have your sins washed away, you. can have them without money or without price'.[34]

They did not take up the offer and had their fines increased for arriving late when they eventually located the courthouse.

The Army was castigated for being too inclusive. The short-lived conversion of 'notorious blackguard' Tom Maroney in the Rhondda Valley—he was gaoled after fighting in the road, led to their recruitment methods being questioned. A local newspaper remarked that the excited and emotional state men and women found themselves in at highly charged Army meetings when they converted was likely to make them lap se just as quickly. The paper added: 'as long as the converted are received in such an indiscriminate fashion…the Salvation Army will be discredited thereby'.

***

LOCAL authority opposition increased in the 1890s; Glamorgan County Council was urged to petition the Home Secretary to ban 'glove-fighting', a Newport councillor tried tohalt the teaching of 'gentlemen boxing' at the gymnasium fitted up over the public bath during the winter, and Rhondda district council only agreed to renew the theatrical licence for Porth Town hall if it would not again be used for boxing. In 1895, when Cardiff councillors were considering what use to make of wasteland at the Windsor

Esplanade, it was claimed that the land was a discredit to the town as 'Scenes of immorality and even a prize fight had taken place there'.[35]

Such was the antipathy to prize fights that to be unjustly accused of taking part in one was a serious matter. *The Sporting Life* was ordered to pay £100 libel damages in 1889 for wrongly stating that a man had been a participant.

Not everybody was in favour of the sport in the USA, either. Cardiff-born Patsy O'Leary was among a group of boxers whose sparring exhibition at Jeffersonville, Indiana, in 1867 was prevented by townspeople, a newspaper commenting 'Despite the mayor and marshal having two of the best seats in the house'.[36]

***

THE public were encouraged to turn instead to boating, cricket, pedestrianism, fencing, swimming, and cycling, which were thought more manly and acceptable, and even boxing with gloves for self-defence. Rugby was said to be 'as exciting as the prize fight, without any of the latter's disgusting brutality'.

Fight supporters, however, pointed out that other sports could be dangerous, rugby being 'far more cowardly and debasing' than the old prize fight, which was a 'fair contest of skill and endurance'. Boxing booth owner and former battler Bill Samuel hit back at criticism of the sport by suggesting that, unlike rugby, boxing was a fair one-on-one contest and was recognised as such by spectators:

> When two men are boxing, and one of them falls, the crowd is sympathetic, and he is not jumped on, but when a man is down in football people don't seem half pleased, unless there are some half-dozen men on top of him.[37]

The medical journal *The Lancet* backed boxing training for general fitness, and Llanelli and Cardiff rugby players went on to follow that advice. Thomas Hughes, the author of *Tom Brown's Schooldays*, writing on the importance of improving the body as well as the mind, believed that boxing, as opposed to prize fighting, was 'one of the best ways in which the greatest amount of exercise may be got in a very short time'.[38] He wrote this in the context of 'Most men think that sooner or later, we Englishmen are to be engaged in a life-and-death struggle with half the Continent' and when the call came, men who were not fit would be of no use.

But the 'fad of muscle worship' was dismissed as producing not healthy men but 'only superficial firmness at the expense of the constitution – No pugilists reached a healthy old age'.[39] As we have seen that final comment was not a huge exaggeration.

Likewise, with the assertion that the sport inspired British youth with 'a character of manliness and a love of fair play', and that prize fighters didn't drink or smoke, got up early, and worked hard in the open air etc. – before they entered the ring.[40] This did not tally with abundant court evidence involving pugilists in Wales.

The claim was 'utterly valueless'; any man prepared to be beaten up for money or to beat an opponent 'into a shapeless mess, could have only one virtue but that of extreme hardihood'. Evangelical clergyman Baptist Wriothesley Noel argued that pugilism made men bullies because they knew that weaker, untrained men could not fight with them.[41]

Prize fighting's qualities of courage, endurance and fair play were said, by the *Times* in 1860, to be needed, not as previously for their military usefulness, but now in the contemporary business world where 'apostles of progress' stressed that success, distinction and influence depended only on 'shrewdness and quickness, applied principally to the acquisition of wealth'.[42]

***

CROSS-BORDER forays for bare knuckle bouts continued, boosted by rail and steamer travel, regularly both ways between adjoining south Wales counties Glamorgan, Breconshire and Monmouthshire and the neighbouring English counties of Herefordshire and Gloucestershire.

An undaunted group, chased by police, crossed country and county borders to bring off a fight in South Wales early in 1867; they were disturbed twice near Bristol, then took the train and a steamer to reach Monmouthshire, then another train to St. Mellons, where police halted the late-night battle. Hostilities resumed at Llanedeyrn near Cardiff before being interrupted again. Undeterred, the party then moved on into Cardiff itself, caught a train for Bristol, alighting at the first stop, Marshfield, where the fight took place uninterrupted in a nearby field.

The area around Chepstow, on the river Wye, which forms the border between Monmouthshire and Gloucestershire and that between Wales and England, was popular for fight cruises.

Later in 1867, a steamer carrying more than one hundred supporters from Bristol and Bath, dropped anchor in the river. Monmouthshire police were stationed on the left bank, but the right bank, the Gloucestershire side, was open, so the excursionists were landed there. Two policemen kept watch on the Monmouthshire side of the river, powerless to interfere, for nearly four hours. Finally, a Gloucestershire policeman intervened, and they all got back on the steamer to Portishead, where the battle resumed.

In north Wales, Hilbre Island, at the mouth of the estuary of the River Dee, the border between Wales and England, was usually reached by fight people by steamer from Liverpool. In 1869, Birkenhead police lay in wait on the island, so the Liverpool tug carrying a fight party headed for the Point of Ayr, the northernmost point of mainland Wales at the mouth of the Dee estuary, 'where the party landed, staked their ring, and enjoyed the 'noble art' to their hearts' content.'[43]

The steamship ploy proved unsuccessful for Cardiff fighter Patsy Reardon's proposed battle with Rooke in 1863, when a vessel had been chartered to take the party from London along the Thames to the Kentish marshes. The boat took them near Dartford, but the arrival of the Kent police forced them to get back on board and travel higher up the river. Frustratingly, as they were landing, they spotted more police and returned to the vessel which then steamed up the river, 'mission unaccomplished'.[44]

Unlike in England, where special excursion trains could be chartered, in Wales spectators travelling by rail had to use the regular service, which often was not a pleasant experience for ordinary customers, who were warned 'Any respectable person' finding himself travelling back on a train with fight fans was advised to 'button up his pockets and, if possible, stop his ears in disgust'.[45]

Fight specials were banned in 1868, after more than twenty years of criticism, including from the industry's own newspaper, and from a judge who was late for assize duty after his train was 'shunted' out of the way and had to wait until a special prize fight excursion had passed'.[46]

But this restriction did not apply to other types of excursion trains, and, with London becoming 'quite a favourite place' for Welsh boxers because of the 'liberal purses given by the capital's clubs', around 150 South Wales fight fans joined a rugby excursion train for a Blackheath v Cardiff match, to support Cardiff pugilists Sam Gulliver and Evan Owen in the capital.

Revival? 1861-1900

***

THERE was still no official governing body for the sport, but *Bell's Life* administered as firmly as ever. When a fight figure assaulted one of their representatives who had been acting as a referee the newspaper reacted 'by excluding his name from their pages, and refusing to have anything to do with any match with which he was associated'.[47]

The Sporting Life took over the governing role when it acquired its rival in 1886. An employee officiated in a glove contest at the Victoria Theatre, Pontypridd, in 1890, while the journal was stakeholder and appointed the referee for prize fights at Merthyr in 1892, and in the People's Park, Pontypridd, in 1895.

The Pelican Club in London emerged in 1887 as the sport's unofficial overseer, and produced its own set of rules, modelled largely on Queensberry's. The new rules restricted the maximum number of rounds to twenty, and set the minimum weight for gloves at six ounces.

In the later years of the century, bouts, among them many involving Welsh fighters, began being promoted in England by either a single businessman, or an organization such as the Pelican Club. Fights began to be advertised for Welsh titles, (most taking place in London) although these titles were still unofficial. Men had been recognised unofficially as British professional gloved champions at middleweight and heavyweight by the 1870s, at bantam and featherweight in the 1880s, and at lightweight in the 1890s.

In 1889, two episodes damaged the Pelican's reputation and plunged the prize ring in general into greater disgrace. The events focussed greater attention on the aristocratic connections of the club and its associations with a brutal and corrupt sport.

The first lapse involved the two-round farce at the club with the Champion, Jem Smith, defeated easily by Peter Jackson, the outrage increased by the fact that a black man had managed it. The second was in a fight which took place in Belgium after being banned in England when Smith's supporters assaulted opponent Frank Slavin with sticks and knuckle dusters. A Pelican Club official was present at the fight as Smith's manager.

Shortly after, the club decided to have nothing more to do with prize fights and to instead concentrate on boxing, but that resolve did not last long, as John O'Brien, for example, won by knockout at the venue a year later.

When the Pelican club closed in 1892, the National Sporting Club became the most powerful organisation in early British boxing.

However, there remained a longing in the 1890s for the so-called natural order of things, the *Pall Mall Gazette* recalling

> the palmy days of the ring', when *Bell's Life* effectively ran the sport and fighters were blamed or praised as the editor saw fit. Fighters needed to be put back in their place, the Press having given them too much publicity and reporting every 'stupid' thing they utter.[48]

This feeling ran parallel with fears in cricket that the middle class's control was slipping as the lower classes were getting above themselves – professional cricketers had become 'unserviceable servants', 'spoiled by success and flattery' and were assertive about what they would do and not do'.[49]

***

THE major development in this period was the supplanting of the London Prize Ring Rules, which were supreme until 1867. A Welshman, John Graham Chambers, born at Llanelli, Carmarthenshire, in 1843, drew up another set which proved the foundation of the sport in its modern style.

The Queensberry Rules were named after John Sholto Douglas, the eighth Marquess, a contemporary of Chambers at Cambridge University who was persuaded to lend the new rules more authority by attaching his name to them.

This was at a time when other sports, among them golf, cricket, hockey, tennis, football and rugby, were organising themselves with

John Graham Chambers

championships, tours and regular fixtures. The Victorians aimed to control and regulate traditional sports to keep the masses occupied or transform them into efficient and muscular Christians.[50]

The forerunner of the Welsh Rugby Union, the South Wales Football Club was created in 1875. Chambers himself founded the Amateur Athletic Club in 1866, and the Queensberry Rules were designed to achieve for boxing what the establishment of amateur rules was doing for athletics, distancing the sport from the old professionalism.

The new rules stipulated the wearing of padded gloves, rounds to be of three minutes duration with a minute interval, a floored boxer to rise within ten seconds or be declared the loser, and wrestling throws to be banned.

Supporters had hoped that the rules would make their sport respectable and safe enough to be legalised, but they sowed only confusion. They were intended for the amateur sport of boxing, but were commandeered by the professionals, who began advertising their contests as competitions held under Queensberry Rules to imply that they were legal, although the rules had no legal standing.

The new rules helped professional boxing to take place indoors and the marketing of an officially sanctioned form of boxing to become easy.[51] For the middle classes, this meant that boxing events could now be held in exclusive gentlemen's clubs and for the working classes in various local halls, and for both environments the promoters could exert greater control and collect admission money, though in turn it would be easier for the police to supervise.

***

THE introduction of the Queensberry Rules resulted in four forms of pugilism as those involved tried to come to terms with an uncertain legal situation, avoid police interference, and deflect public criticism.

On offer were competing with bare knuckles, under Queensberry Rules, in a hybrid version combining old and new rules, and in so-called amateur boxing -

Men might alternate regularly between bare-knuckle and glove fights, but those used to the old style had to do more than simply don gloves and carry on as before.

They needed to alter their technique, as the Queensberry Rules had brought about major changes. In bare-knuckle fighting, the elbows and forearms were used to ward off punches, hence the unconventional stance the fighters adopted. Under Queensberry Rules, the gloves could be used to ward off punches, and so the modern stance evolved, with the classic 'squaring up' posture adopted by bare-knuckle men giving way to techniques resembling the modern stance.

Also, the old time fighters concentrated on straight punches, especially to the body, as Arthur Chambers, who fought under the London prize ring rules in Britain and in the USA, explained: 'We were afraid of cracking our hands on the skull of the other fellow'.[52] And, as the hands were now protected, a wider range of punches was seen, with hooks as well as straight punches, and punches to the head were favoured.

Some fighters welcomed the changes; one arrested for fighting with bare knuckles on a mountain at Abergavenny told police he would have preferred to have had the gloves and fight in a hall.[53]

The new rules suited the fast boxers rather than slow brawlers, since without a minute's rest between rounds, the fast-boxing style would have been exhausting. The skills of boxing were transformed from a defensive system based mainly on upper body strength to an offensive system, which encouraged chopping blows to the head.[54]

There were close links between all four forms. Harry Marks, of Cardiff Harlequins BC, who won the Amateur Boxing Association of England lightweight title in 1898, was trained by prize fighting figure 'Mangle' Hyams, and took part in exhibitions regularly with professionals such as Jem Perry and Morgan Crowther. Marks later managed world professional champion Freddie Welsh. Furthermore, professionals acted as seconds at the Welsh amateur boxing championships and sparred together in between amateur bouts.

Consequently, the distinctions between the different forms became blurred. Amateurs were even accused of helping the professional code to flourish.

The frequency of boxing contests at Cardiff prompted the town's head-constable to warn Cardiff Amateur Boxing Club in 1888 that some recent contests were for stakes, were really glove fights and should be stopped. The club claimed they were 'friendly contests', but the police argued that a contest for a stake of £25 could not be construed into a friendly one.

The same year, the Amateur Boxing Association was accused of 'systematizing an evasion of the law against prize-fighting' because staging brutal fights was more lucrative than 'artistic sparring'.[55] In 1890, the police tried several times to stop the Welsh amateur boxing championships taking place in Cardiff, but the referee refused.

The continued uncertainty had fatal consequences in the Rhondda valley in 1897. Police had previously halted a fight between Matthew Fury and Griffith Davies in a tent on the Pandy Field, Tonypandy, because, a court heard, 'they were not fighting for points, and there was no science whatever in it. The men were simply slogging each other as hard as they could'.[56]

After the defence argued that no offence had been committed because the contest was carried out strictly under the Queensberry Rules, magistrates agreed that no evidence of brutality had been adduced by the police and dismissed the case.

Consequently, the police stayed away from the venue, 'allowing the management to have their full fling'. A week later, Sam Mandry died after a fight there. A newspaper claimed that had Fury and Davies been punished, 'glove contests of the kind would have been stopped in the district permanently'.[57]

***

FAVOURITE Welsh venues for glove matches included the Victoria Theatre, Pontypridd', Merthyr's Drill Hall and *Bird in Hand* pub; the Pavilion and Drill Hall at Swansea; or outdoors at the People's Park, Pontypridd. Tickets prices ranged from two shillings for the fatal fight in May 1894, to ten shillings for reserved seats at the Drill Hall, Swansea, in 1893. A 'prohibitive' entrance fee did not prevent Merthyr Tydfil's baths being crowded for a prize fight in 1892, although around fifty 'venturesome souls' avoided the charge by climbing on to the roof and watching through the skylights.

Despite still being of uncertain legality, glove fights were advertised freely and they attracted large crowds. An estimated 1,500 saw Tom James (Aberaman) beat local man Jack Raymond in the People's Park, Pontypridd, in 1892; there were 'close on a thousand people present' in Merthyr's Drill Hall in 1893, when Patsy Perkins beat Bristol's Tom Rooney, and just over 900 spectators watched a contest at the Public-hall, Rhymney, in 1899, while in that year, monthly boxing shows attracted big crowds at Pontypridd.

***

THE impact of the Queensberry Rules was gradual, as late as 1895, for instance, Jem Perry, from Cardiff, was disqualified for throwing an opponent with a cross-buttock move.

Various compromises led to the rules being adapted into the Queensberry Rules of Endurance, the basis of the modern rules of professional boxing. A contest under the adapted rules took place in 1888 at the Lecture Theatre of the Queen-street Arcade', Cardiff. The referee was allowed under the revised rules to order an additional round to be fought if it was needed to decide a contest, which happened after six rounds of a fight at Samuel's boxing booth in Swansea in 1895.

This rule, however, was abused in the fight which led to the death of Mandry in 1897. The referee had called a halt at the end of the eighth round, reasoning that Mandry was beaten badly, and he announced Thomas as the winner. However, Mandry insisted on continuing, the crowd urged that they fight on, and it was resumed for another four rounds with a fatal result.

***

THE Queensberry Rules were originally intended to end prize fighting, but, ironically, they enabled it to survive and thrive. Author George Bernard Shaw, a keen boxing fan, argued that the process received its first boost after the introduction of the Rules from the discovery, with fight judges biased against skill and easily influenced by the crowd, that a boxer, no matter how skilful, could only make sure of the verdict by knocking his opponent out.

With boxers therefore choosing not to develop skills, the public began to take an interest again. So the skills with which the boxing glove and the Queensberry Rules were supposed to replace the old brutalities were, in fact, abolished by them. Spectators demanded more excitement, and the scoring of points was not now the aim, rather it was a finish inside the distance with more action and violence.

> Spectators did not want to see skill defeating violence; they wanted to see violence drawing blood and pounding its way to a savage and exciting victory in the shortest possible time.[58]

Shaw said the Rules ensured the survival of the prize ring in all but name. 'Boxing' became essentially the same as prize fighting, only with gloves, the two versions of the combat sport being indistinguishable in the eyes of many. He noted, 'Those who opposed prize-fighting and those who, while opposing it, nevertheless supported boxing, had feared this would happen'.

Supporters claimed that the Queensberry Rules would make the sport less dangerous, as padded gloves would deaden the blow and be unlikely to cause permanent injury. This was only partly true, however, as prize-fighters had different sorts of gloves at their disposal. Huge gloves as used in sparring would not do much damage, but with them it would be difficult to raise big enough stakes to encourage pugilists.

The *Pall Mall Gazette* argued that the real pugilistic glove was 'a great deal less innocent and pulpy. A blow with the naked fist would create only a bruise, but from a hand encased in a kid glove it would generally leave an open wound. Real fighting gloves were 'ingeniously padded'; they could appear big but the padding was in the wrong place, at the finger ends instead of where it should be, over the knuckles. The part of the hand that delivered the blows was merely enveloped in chamois leather which added to the weight and consistency of the blows.[59] Mostly the gloves would be skin-tight rather than padded, and weighed only two ounces.

There were soon calls for the rules to be amended because, it was argued, they made the sport more dangerous than under the London Prize Ring rules. Gloves were soon seen to protect the fighter's hands more than his head and to enable harder punches to be delivered than was possible with bare knuckles. Gloves, especially when soaked with sweat, in effect became clubs and allowed the fighter to hit areas of the opponent's skull, which previously were out of bounds because of the danger of breaking a knuckle or fingers.[60] Campaigners contended that wounds inflicted by bare fists, 'though very much more disgusting to behold, were more on the surface, and though they may have bled profusely they seldom left a permanent injury behind'.[61]

The other safety issue was the time break after a knockdown, ten seconds under the Queensberry rules for a boxer to regain his feet or be adjudged the loser. Under the London Prize Ring rules, if he dropped down he had thirty seconds to recover plus another eight seconds to walk unaided from his corner to the middle of the ring.

Shaw believed that this made it safer because fighters could always get a half-minute break when they wanted it by pretending to be knocked down, instead of, under the Queensberry Rules, having to stagger to his feet within ten seconds in a helpless condition and be battered into insensibility before he could recover his powers of self-defence. Shaw's argument ignored, however, that under the London rules, the fighter could 'recover' sufficiently several times and take a succession of beatings in the same fight.

Peter Jackson thought it unfair that fighters under the London rules could go to the floor when they felt like it without endangering their chances of success. The rule on this point was open to abuse. It said that if a man 'wilfully' throws himself down without receiving a blow, he will be deemed t to have lost, but this does not apply if he slips from the grasp of his opponent or from obvious accident or weakness.

It was claimed that in knuckle fighting, with the thirty-second rule, knockouts were so rare that fighters thought they were not worth trying for. It was almost impossible to knock someone out with the bare fist, but far easier with gloves. The glove fighter tried for nothing else. Gloves and the ten-second rule explained the development of the Queensberry Rules into the modern 'desperate and dangerous' knockout match or glove fight by encouraging heavy blows.

A glove fight was generally terminated in minutes. Prize fights with bare knuckles often lasted for several hours. Under the London Prize Ring Rules, rounds could be of extremely short duration, or, as in the case of one fight, provide an extremely long and boring exercise. Two men 'fought' at Beachley, near Chepstow, in 1866 for 2 hrs. 8min. Several times they stood in the ring looking at each other with their arms folded for at least five minutes. The 33rd and last round was 'the most remarkable round ever witnessed in any prize fight', as

> for thirteen minutes the men faced each other in the ring, neither attempting to put up his fists until the patience of the spectators being exhausted they became clamorous, and the referee then repeated the caution he had previously given. It was agreed to call it a draw.[62]

An argument about the respective merits of glove and bare fist fighters became physical at Swansea, resulting in a clash on the local beach.[63] Bare knuckle man Morgan Grey had sneered that glove fighter Billy Morgan was a 'showman and not a rough-and-tumble fighter', and boasted that Morgan could not knock him out in ten rounds with the gloves whereas he could 'settle' Morgan in four rounds with bare knuckles. In the event, they proceeded to the Swansea foreshore, to a spot illuminated by the harbour's electric lights, where at midnight a 'decent crowd' saw Morgan knock Grey out.

***

PRIZE fighting reinvented itself in the latter decades of the century, attempting to polish its image as it struggled for greater public acceptance, as well as for legality.

Using the fact that gloves were worn, it began calling itself 'boxing'. Supporters did not try to claim that the men were engaged in a contest of skill for points (as in boxing), and they insisted their 'boxing' was different from prize fighting, although they agreed that men were still fighting for money (as in prize fighting), and that the main aim was to batter an opponent into submission (as in prize fighting).

They relied on claims that ring personnel and spectators were now well-behaved, in contrast to the unruly prize fight scenes of the past, combatants were brave and to be admired, whereas previously they had been despised. They also claimed and that fight arrangements were no longer corrupt and slip-shod, but instead were 'admirable'.

Opponents were not won over, though. Many, including H. W. Thomas, a former pugilist from Swansea, believed 'boxing' had simply become prize-fighting with gloves, whatever people now chose to call their activity. There had previously been big differences between boxing and prize fighting, and there still were.

The distinction had been acknowledged at the beginning of the century when famous pugilist Mendoza refused a challenge because of his 'having retired from the business of a public prize-fighter to that of a private tutor in the polite art of boxing'.[64] And the same point was made frequently in the final years of the century.

A public protest meeting at Tonypandy expressed their 'disgust at the performances of prize-fighting (erroneously termed boxing)', while, after a fight at Morriston, *Cambrian* stated: 'There is a vast difference between a glove fight of this description and the manly art of boxing'.[65] The *Cardiff Times* commented: 'It is certainly not easy to see the difference between the 'knockout' and the old prize fight. Yet one is legal [sic], and the other not'.[66] It was widely believed that the gloves, often merely skin gloves or two-ounce gloves, were 'only a sham' and were used 'with a view to keeping within the law'.

In 1891, an MP, noting that prize fights were on the increase and that blows with the gloves were more damaging than with the naked fist, urged the Government to ban these fights and to punish not only the principals but all those who promoted or attended them.

He was wasting his breath. The Government reiterated that boxing contests were lawful when they were merely an exercise of skill, choosing to go along with the assertion that the new 'boxing' and prize fighting were different.

And just as calls in mid-century for the Government to legislate on the legality of prize fighting went unanswered, so did appeals in the final years that it was 'about time that the legislation which forbade savage prize fighting with bare knuckles should condemn its revival in a form not less degrading' fell on deaf ears.[67]

---

[1] Star of Gwent, cited in *Cheshire Observer*, 14 April, 1860. Weekly Mail, 24 May 1902.
[2] Times, 19 April 1860; Bury and Norwich Post, 1 May 1860; Manchester Times, 21 April 1860
[3] Bury and Norwich Post, 28 February 1860.
[4] Times, 9 December 1862.
[5] South Wales Daily News, 28 July 1893.
[6] Cambrian News, 5 July 1889
[7] Weekly Mail, 3 July 1897
[8] Morning Star, cited in Merthyr Telegraph, 26 March 1866. Pontypridd Chronicle, 26 April 1889. Rhyl Journal, 15 August 1891. Western Mail, 11 December 1873. South Wales Daily Post, 5 June 1895. Western Mail, 18 September 1899.
[9] Western Mail, 13 December 1873
[10] Cambrian, 9 December 1898.
[11] Western Mail, 18 August 1874.
[12] Bell's Life, 4 March 1865.
[13] Evening Express, 5 November 1892
[14] Aberdeen Weekly Journal, 4 June 1894.
[15] Western Mail, 16 January; 29 November 1893; 6 June 1894; 6 September 1894.
[16] Western Mail, 19 November 1900
[17] Western Mail, 7 Sept. 1874. Cardiff Times, 28 January 1888
[18] Bell's Life, 22 January 1860. Merthyr Telegraph, 11 May 1861. Cardiff Times, 7 January 1888. Cardiff and Merthyr Guardian, 17 June 1871
[19] Cardiff Times, 22 March 1884
[20] Evening Express, 6 December 1898
[21] Aberdare Times, 28 May 1864. Cardiff Times, 10 June 1864.
[22] Birmingham Daily Post, 31 December 1861.
[23] Andy Croll, 'Mabon's Day: The rise and fall of a Lib-Lab holiday in the South Wales coalfield, 1888-1898', *Labour History Review*, Vol. 72, No. 1, April 2007, p. 49.
[24] South Wales Echo, 27, 30 August; 3 September 1897. Cardiff Times, 4 September 1897
[25] South Wales Echo, 10 September 1897.
[26] Llangollen Advertiser, 19 December 1884.
[27] Llangollen Advertiser, 23 December 1887
[28] South Wales Star, 18 September 1891

[29] Aberystwyth Observer, 28 March 1881
[30] South Wales Daily News, 25 April 1895
[31] South Wales Echo, 16 March 1888.
[32] Wales, 7 November 1894.
[33] Cardigan Observer, 24 December 1887. Times, 10 March 1888.
[34] South Wales Daily News, 21 March 1888.
[35] Western Mail, 8 October 1895.
[36] Daily Evening Bulletin (Maysville, Ky.) 17 August 1887.
[37] Western Mail, 16 Mar 1895.
[38] Quoted in the Cardiff and Merthyr Guardian, 28 January 1861.
[39] Lancet, cited in Birmingham Daily Post, 8 May 1860. Daily News, 3 September 1862.
[40] Manchester Times, 31 March 1860
[41] Daily News, cited in Birmingham Daily Post 10 May 1860.
[42] Times, 19 April 1860
[43] Cheshire Observer, 31 July 1869
[44] Daily News, 25 November 1863
[45] Aberdare Times, 1 February 1862
[46] Railway Times, cited in Bury & Norwich Post, 13 March 1844. North Wales Chronicle, 22 December 1855.
[47] North Wales Chronicle, 9 December 1865.
[48] Pall Mall Gazette, 18 November 1893
[49] Illustrated Sporting News, 8 February 1866, cited in Mike Huggins, The Victorians and Sport (London, Hambledon and London, 2004), p. 56.
[50] Jack Anderson, 'Pugilistic Prosecutions: Prize fighting and the courts in nineteenth century Britain', *The Sports Historian* No. 21 (2) (November 2001). P.46.
[51] Anderson, Pugilistic Prosecutions, p. 46.
[52] Evening Express, 11 October 1898
[53] Evening Telegraph, 17 February 1898
[54] Anderson, Pugilistic Prosecutions, p.46.
[55] Pall Mall Gazette, 20 April 1888
[56] South Wales Echo, 20 August 1897.
[57] South Wales Daily News, 25 August 1897.
[58] Shaw, Cashel Byron's Profession.
[59] Pall Mall Gazette, 30 March 1882
[60] Anderson, Pugilistic Prosecutions, p.46.
[61] Standard, cited in Aberdeen Weekly Journal, 18 August 1877. Daily News, cited in Evening Express, 9 December 1897
[62] Monmouthshire Beacon, 9 November 1866
[63] Evening Express, 3 April 1897.
[64] Morning Post, 18 January 1807
[65] Glamorgan Free Press, 28 August 1897. Cambrian, 9 December 1898.
[66] Cardiff Times, 27 March 1896
[67] Western Mail, 18 November 1898

8

Fighters to 1900

Wales produced many outstanding prize fighters in the later decades of the century, some recognised as British champions, and others finding considerable success in the USA and challenging for world titles. John O'Brien, for example, was good enough to earn the chance of a fight with world champion Bob Fitzsimmons in the USA.

Sadly, ill-health, heavy drinking, bad luck, or a lack of commitment prevented most from reaching the top of their profession. Cardiff-born O'Brien's ring career was affected by all those factors. When fit, O'Brien was a match for most middleweights – and heavyweights, too.

Born in the Roath area of the town, he took up the sport seriously after leaving the Guards and returning to his home town. His ring career began brightly with a handful of victories, but his London debut proved a disaster, a 'fluke' punch from Arthur Morris knocking him out in the first round.

All of O'Brien's subsequent reported fights were in the capital, where he embarked on an impressive winning run, 'easily disposing' of former English amateur heavyweight champion Ted White, Alf Ball, and fellow Cardiffian Alf Mitchell, whom he knocked down seven times before stopping him in the eighth round in 1891.

The prize for the winner of the Mitchell contest was to be matched with Ted Pritchard for the middleweight championship of England. O'Brien said that he was willing to meet Pritchard for a purse of £500 and the middleweight championship belt, now held by him (O'Brien)....a £200 side stake was also offered.

Pritchard replied that he would fight O'Brien at any weight he liked, said as far as he was aware, highlighting the lack of an organisational structure in the sport, there was no such thing as a championship belt; if there was any sort of belt then, as he himself was the champion, O'Brien must have been given it or had bought it in Cardiff.

The pair were due to meet at the National Sporting Club, London, but O'Brien caught a chill, which confined him to his bed. His illness proved more serious than was first thought, for, later seen in a Cardiff street, he was reported to be

> absolutely a cripple, and with his feet encased in a pair of list shoes, hobbles around like a man of 70. Another month or six weeks must elapse before the Cardiffian can hope to be anything like firm on his pins.[1]

O'Brien also had to withdraw from a fight with Fitzsimmons in New Orleans because the weak state in which the recent attack of sciatica had left him ruled him out of training for more than three months.

It was to be another two years before O'Brien returned to the ring, at the National Sporting Club, for the 'Championship of Wales', against heavyweight David St. John, of Resolven. St. John was confident, claiming that the second-round knockout he suffered against O'Brien four years previously was down to youth and inexperience. He insisted: 'I am now 23 and have had more practice, and better able in every way to meet the Irishman'.[2]

St. John had all the physical advantages; he was six years younger, 5 inches taller at 6ft. 3ins., and two stones heavier at 13st. 12 lbs.

In a short but explosive fight, St. John was nearly out for the count after taking a left to the neck in round two, before a right to the head knocked O'Brien 'clean off his feet in the third', when he broke his arm. Another right to the head put O'Brien down in the fourth, before O'Brien in round five 'brought the right across in very neat fashion, and St. John dropped as though shot'.[3]

When unfit, O'Brien was an embarrassment. He took on Frank Craig (USA) in London in 1894 after leaving himself with only a month to sweat off 3st. 6lbs, and, in a weak state, was knocked down three times in the second round, the third time for the count.

Subsequently, O'Brien was reported to have started 'taking care of himself' and looking for another fight. That duly arrived in April 1895 – and proved an even bigger disaster. Craig was to have fought Pritchard, who pulled out through illness, and O'Brien stepped in as a last-minute substitute. For all his talk of 'looking after himself', O'Brien was in a nearby pub when the call came, and when he stepped into the London ring, it was obvious he had been drinking there for some time.

The common verdict of the Press was that

> Anything more deplorable than Saturday night's fiasco at the Central-hall, Holborn, it would be difficult to imagine. A well-trained man fit to fight for a kingdom and an untrained opponent, fat as an alderman and hopelessly drunk to boot, do not present a picture particularly edifying to the athletic minded amongst us. O'Brien was manifestly as drunk as the proverbial fiddler.[4]

Another journal described the 'fight' in detail.

> O'Brien sat in the opposite corner fat and flabby, and with a vacant stare that made everyone near aware of his condition. While the gloves were being put on [there were calls that O'Brien was not fit to fight' and that the fight would last only one round.] Johnny

wandered listlessly to the centre and put up his hands in a mechanical manner. He was all abroad and quite unsteady on his feet, and Craig promptly shot out left and right and knocked his opponent down....{O'Brien] was knocked down five times without landing a blow in return....It was a melancholy business which should never have disgraced the annals of boxing.[5]

On the lowest of notes, O'Brien's ring career ended.

***

PRITCHARD was, like Tom Spring seventy years earlier, said to have had Welsh links. Indeed, some record books state that he originated in Merthyr Tydfil. However, contemporary sources, among them census reports and his own marriage certificate, refer to him as being born in the Lambeth district of London. The nearest Welsh connection for Pritchard so far discovered was that his paternal grandfather was almost certainly born in Monmouthshire. That would have been good enough for Pritchard to be regarded as Welsh as far as modern national rugby selectors were concerned let alone those of his own era whose teams depended on English-born players with no relevant pedigree.

Pritchard came to prominence in 1889 at the Lambeth School of Arms, London, knocking Jem Hayes down four times in the early rounds and once more in the last round. Hayes' supporters, hoping to save their man from defeat, broke into the ring and started several fights which prompted an intervention by police. The referee later awarded the stakes and bets to Pritchard.

Pritchard stopped Alec Burns, his next opponent, in the second round and then made short work of Alf Mitchell, in a match billed for the 'middleweight championship', punishing him heavily before Mitchell's seconds entered the ring during the fourth round causing the referee to call a halt.

Pritchard, now referred to as the English middleweight champion, knocked Jack Burke down three times before winning on a third-round stoppage, and was straightaway described as the world middleweight champion, albeit only in an advertisement for an engagement at the Philharmonic, Cardiff. Next, Pritchard met Jem Smith for the (heavyweight) Championship in 1891. Despite conceding more than two stones, Pritchard recovered from a first-round knockdown to force a third round stoppage, with Smith left hanging over the ropes.

Pritchard accepted an offer of $12,000 from the New Orleans Olympic Club to fight 'world' middleweight champion Bob Fitzsimmons in September of the following year, but that was one of two big fights that failed to materialise.

He was matched with O'Brien for the English middleweight championship, only for O'Brien to pull out through illness, and another setback was Pritchard being knocked out in four rounds by Australian fighter Jem Hall, a result which ruled out a meeting with Fitzsimmons.

Pritchard was absent from the ring for the next two years, instead showing off his skills in variety halls throughout. He returned for three short fights, a two round win over the one stone heavier Dick Burge, a first round knockout at the hands of Frank Craig, and a two rounds defeat by Smith, who, as in their first meeting, was two stones heavier, in a match advertised as for the championship of England.

***

DAVID St. John had a short and undistinguished ring career. One of only a few Welsh fighters over six feet tall, he fought Tom James (Aberaman) three times. At Merthyr in 1892, he won on a fourth round knockout, at Pontypridd in 1893 for what was billed as for the heavyweight championship of Wales, he pummelled James to defeat in six rounds, and (after losing to O'Brien), at Neath in 1895, his last reported fight, when James was considered to have got the better of the draw.

David St. John
(Western Mail, 28 November 1899)

St. John later joined Peter Jackson (Virgin Islands) as a sparring partner, appearing at the Folies Bergere nightclub in Paris and at music halls in Britain, and also at a Pontypridd venue.

Afterwards, he joined the army, making an inauspicious start to his military career by going absent without leave just months after joining the Grenadier Guards. During his five days at large, St. John took part in a Nazareth House charity event, which boasted 'the four best boxers in the British Army', St. John accompanied by three Cardiff men who were army champions - Drummer Collins being the holder of the light, his brother, Sergeant Collins, the middle, and Private Leahy the heavyweight honours.

But St. John proved a hero outside the ring, winning a medal during the Battle of Omdurman in Sudan in 1898 and also acclaim at the Battle of Belmont during the second Boer War. The latter action took place on 23 November 1899, when the British attacked a hill under heavy rifle fire from the Boers entrenched on the crest. St. John, credited with killing between ten and twelve Boers in the battle, was among the 75 British fatalities.

A fellow Welshman in a letter to his parents at Swansea, described his final moments.

> We fought hand to hand. I was just behind David St. John when he was hit. He stuck his bayonet right through a Boer but could not get it out again. He tried to throw the man over his shoulder to get him off, but then another Boer came up and shot him through the head. Then another of our men put the bayonet through that Boer's heart.[6]

St. John's actions echoed those of another pugilist war hero, Jack Shaw, a corporal in the Life Guards, from Nottinghamshire, during the Battle of Waterloo on 18 June 1815. Shaw, also a heavyweight, over 6 ft tall and weighing 15 stone, killed eight enemy soldiers with the sword before succumbing himself.

***

BEN Lloyd, after successive knockout victories, fled the Rhondda Valley in 1897 while awaiting trial and fearing gaol for taking part in a prize fight. He was next heard of two years later in a series of letters from South Africa, where he apparently had joined up to fight for the Boers.

Lloyd was not the only Welshman to fight against the British army. It was reported that two men from a village in Caernarvonshire who went out years previously to try their fortune as miners in the Transvaal, had written home to say that they had joined the army of the Transvaal.

The first Boer War of 1880-1881 left the two Dutch Boer republics of the Transvaal and the Orange Free State self-government under British suzerainty, but the discovery of gold in the Rand led to significant British immigration which resulted in the immigrants (uitlanders) becoming a majority in some areas. Keen to protect their society, religion and language from the immigrant influx, the Boer governments denied the uitlanders political rights, and the uitlanders appealed to the British government for assistance.

The Liberal-supporting Welsh press tended to adopt an anti-war tone, and most of the Welsh-language publications were strongly hostile to the war, primarily because of their support for nonconformity. Scholars have argued that the Welsh-language press showed support for the Boers because they saw them as 'almost as fellow victims of English colonialism'.

This was the view of Lloyd, who wrote from Johannesburg in one letter accusing Britain of lying about the background to the war. Lloyd wrote:

> I am writing this letter to you now, as very likely I shall be shot in the course of a few days. I suppose you see the accounts in the papers about the dispute between the Transvaal and the English Government. It is the biggest fraud that ever happened. The English pretend that the Uitlanders want the franchise. They want nothing of the sort. We are perfectly satisfied as we are. When I say that I mean the working men – not the capitalists. It is they that have made all this trouble, and now the cowardly --- have left the country until the fighting is over. After the English Government get this country, which they have been thirsting for ever since gold was discovered here, the capitalists will do as they like with us, the same as they do with the free slaves in England to-day. This is admitted to be absolutely the best Government in the world for the working man. Every working man will tell you the same. That is the reason

the capitalists are against it. They want all their own way, the same as they have got in Free England.[7]

The following month, writing from Mooi River, between Johannesburg and Durban, Lloyd predicted a quick end to the war. The English outnumbered the Boers four to one and the Boers had poor ammunition, their shells made in Germany only one in twelve of which worked.

Several months later, Lloyd was identified among Boer prisoners at the Green Point Common transit camp, Cape Town, by a former fellow member of the 3rd Welsh Militia Battalion in which he had served at Cardiff. Lloyd claimed to have been 'commandeered' by the Boers.

Boer prisoners, including Welsh, English and Scots, were shipped in 1900 from such camps to remote islands, and later that month Lloyd was reported among the prisoners on the island of St. Helena.

***

PATSY Reardon, Dan Thomas's protégé, had been based in Cardiff from 1858 and was often referred to as 'the Welshman', but he was born in south west Ireland. When Reardon appeared at a sparring exhibition in a Dublin theatre, he was advertised fancifully as 'the renowned Irish champion of the world lightweights'.

Many Wales-based fighters had a strong Irish background arising out of the exodus from around the middle of the century. O'Brien was referred to as 'the Irish Welshman', and 'the Irishman', while Redmond Coleman, of Merthyr, also born in Wales to Irish parents, gave his nationality in the 1911 census as 'Irish'.

Irish migrants in Wales identified closely with those pugilists. Jem Mace would have testified to that. In 1862, the former champion of England needed to be smuggled by police through the streets of Cardiff from the railway station to the town's Music Hall, because of the threat of violence from 'hundreds of Irish' eager to avenge an alleged slight which Reardon had recently suffered from English spectators. And when Peter Burns, better known as Dublin Tom, was beaten by Shoni Engineer, is was reported that 'The news spread rapidly on returning to Cardiff, and the Irish are much annoyed at Burns' defeat by the Welshman'.[8]

After two wins in Wales, Reardon made his debut in the London ring in 1860, when he forced William Smith, of Brighton, to retire after eight rounds in 1hr. and 5 minutes.

Reardon's short career was blighted by police interference, which forced two matches against John Rooke and one with Tom 'Shocker' Shipp to end as draws and caused two more fights to be interrupted several times. The clash against Bob Travers lasted four hours and five minutes spread over two days because of a persistent police presence, and his meeting with Jem Dillon, which took place on both sides of the Thames, ended prematurely after police interfered twice.

Reardon was due to have a return fight with Shipp, but the Bristol man was taken ill and died while training. A newspaper added to its report, presumably for the benefit of readers who had not fully appreciated the significance of what had occurred, 'Of course, under the circumstances, the match is off'.

***

MORGAN Crowther, born near Crumlin, Monmouthshire, in 1869, and discovered by Billy Leahy, who kept an oyster bar in Newport, and Billy Morgan, a Cardiff bookie. was a tough little fighter. In 1889, Crowther challenged 'anybody in the world with 2oz. gloves at 8st. 8lbs for £100 a-side'.

In January, 1890, after a loss to Bill Baxter in London, a reporter commented: 'A gamer youth than the loser never doffed shirt', while another rated him a good prospect, particularly with the knuckles.

> With a little polishing up it will be difficult to find a man his weight and inches capable of lowering his colours, whilst on the turf [bare knuckles] we should say the Welshman would prove a still harder nut to crack at 8st. 7lb. [9]

Successive victories against Arthur Wilkinson at the Kensington Social Club, London, put Crowther into championship contention. The first contest lasted 45 rounds in three hours; The ring was encroached upon, and the struggle came to an end without any decision having been arrived at, but the referee later awarded the fight to Crowther. Their second fight in 1891 lasted more than 2 ¾ hours, with Crowther well on top throughout to win on a 42nd round knockout.

It could have been a different ending, however.

> In round fourteen the man from Newport scored the first knock-out blow, and the event created the wildest excitement. As Crowther was waiting for his opponent to rise one of Wilkinson's backers deliberately kicked him on the ankle, a dastardly act which called forth the loudest cries from all sides, the event showed to what extent the Cockneys would go to pull the fight out of the fire.....Crowther did not recover from this kick for several rounds.[10]

Another newspaper commented that Crowther was 'not far from being the best fighter at his weight in England'. A surprise punch which forced him to retire in the 28th round against Tom Wilson at the Kennington Club when he had been on top failed to halt his progress.

His next fight, a year later, was advertised as being for the 8st. 4lbs. championship of England against Fred Johnson (London) at the Goodwin Club, Kingsland-road, London. For seven rounds they were level, but then

Johnson took a commanding lead. Crowther was knocked down in round 16, and in round twenty Johnson was having matters all his own way but was staggered by a right-hander and was then knocked down three times, the third time for the count.

Crowther's victory formed part of a triple celebration for Newport, prompting the newspaper comment that the town 'has got a bit of a swell head at present in matters athletic'. His triumph followed those of the town's gymnastic club which won Two Hundred Guinea Challenge Shield offered by the National Physical Recreation Society at Liverpool and Newport rugby team, invincible the previous season, who, with another excellent campaign, earned 'the unquestionable right to the title of the champion Rugby players of the kingdom'.

After this success, Crowther received offers in 1893 to fight in the USA against George Dixon, for the claimed bantamweight championship of the world', but could not follow through because he was unable to obtain backing for side stakes.

Crowther fought only twice more, losing on points to Tom Merrin in 'a hurriedly arranged affair......got up for the delectation of a party of gentlemen who had just returned from a shooting exhibition' in Devon, and four years later in 1897 he came out of retirement to face Dave Wallace at the National Sporting Club and was beaten over twenty rounds.

***

ALF Mitchell, was another ex-Guardsman, who returned to Cardiff after leaving the Army at the close of the Sudan campaign. Mitchell's biggest fights were against Pritchard for the middleweight championship in 1890 and a year later, against O'Brien at the National Sporting Club, London, with the winner to be matched against Pritchard for the title. He was outclassed in both. Mitchell proved more successful against Alf Ball, meeting him six times with the gloves, each winning three times, but in a bare knuckle fight Mitchell was the winner after 64 rounds.

***

PATSY Perkins, born at Newport in 1862, had six fights, winning four and losing two, in London before returning to South Wales at the beginning of the 1890s.

Perkins styled himself the 10st 8lb champion of Wales but that appears to be on the strength of nobody having accepted his challenge to fight for that 'title' rather than winning it in the ring. Stewardship of the title remained uncertain for a couple of years, highlighting the absence of any governing body. Perkins beat Bristol's Tom Rooney at Merthyr for what was billed as the ten-stone championship of Wales and the West of England, and beat Bob Wiltshire (Cardiff) in a 'title' match in London.

After retiring from the ring Perkins moved to live at Southampton and was reported to have been the last to shake the hand of good friend David St. John before his regiment sailed to South Africa.

***

PERKINS' rival claimant Wiltshire had beaten Sam (Butcher)Thomas and Sam Gulliver for the same 'title', so Perkins' victory over Wiltshire seemed to have ended any doubts as to who was the rightful champion, but as both men were allowed 2lbs overweight, this was not the case.

Wiltshire trained at the Shirenewton premises of Bill Benjamin before his fight with Sam Thomas in London in 1892 and employed Mitchell as one of his seconds. He stopped Thomas, who had Shoni Engineer in his corner, in the fifth round, a right to the jaw dropping Thomas for the count. Wiltshire defended successfully against Sam Gulliver the following year, again halting his man in the fifth round, but was dethroned in 1895 by Perkins.

He ran a successful boxing class in Cardiff before having his final contest at St. Mellons in 1900 when Londoner Dave Wallace stopped him in the tenth round.

***

MERTHYR-BORN Arthur Locke was also active in the London ring, impressing many judges by winning his first two fights before being reported to have 'not been taking care of himself', as the saying went, and winning just one of the remaining nine.

***

BILLY Morgan was one of many fighters who might have achieved more had it not been for exploits outside the ring. A clever boxer with a heavy punch, his ring appearances were interspersed with those in court for drunken violence.

He lost his first fight in 1895 when he was too exhausted to continue against Tom Hooligan at Swansea. Morgan, 'generally regarded as one of the best at 10 stone', announced his retirement after the ring death of Thomas Davies, and appears to have kept to his word for three years, not counting a midnight bare knuckle fight on Swansea beach He won all seven subsequent fights, six by stoppage.

Described as 'probably one of, if not the finest boxer at his weight ever turned out in Wales', he sparked rumours of a comeback in 1914 when, at the age of 39 he fought ten rounds in Alf Harry's booth on Swansea Sands. A return to the prize ring did not materialise, but Morgan had more than his share of fighting in the next few years – in the First World War trenches while serving with the 2nd Worcester Regiment.

The former 'blackguard and pest', shot by a frightened club steward in Swansea a dozen years previously, was wounded twice and became a battlefield hero. A veteran in the Welch Regiment said that he had never come across a finer soldier than Morgan, who was 'absolutely oblivious to danger and will either come through unscathed or with great distinction'.

In a letter home Morgan told of a lucky escape early in the conflict. His unit was digging trenches when the Germans sent over what British soldiers called a 'Jack Johnson', a howitzer shell which on impact sent up a greasy black smoke. 'I was very lucky' Morgan said. 'I was sent into a house for some timber. If I had not been sent I should have met my doom. I can see I am not going to be killed by shells'.[11]

Three months later, the *South Wales Weekly Post* headlined a story about 'a hero of the Richebourg charge, of which Morgan said

> This was the biggest 'battle' I have ever been in. We made a charge on Saturday night at Richebourg. It was the biggest bombardment ever known before we made the charge. We lay flat on the ground between our line and the German line, raining hundreds of shells. We lay for two hours before we had the order to get on with the business. We captured three lines oi trenches. We had to give up the third one because we could not get our reinforcements up in time; they were shelled so much.[12]

Morgan, who received the first of his wounds in this action, had told his wife

> I got a bullet in the muscle of the left arm. and it came out in the forearm so I am lucky to be here. We lost about 400 of our fellows in the charge and lost a lot in the reserve trenches. Thank God I am here; I never thought of seeing you and our little chicken anymore.

Morgan had been in action at Richebourg, Ypres, Festubert, and Givenchy. In an interview he said he had been in street fights in La Bassee, a bayonet in one hand and his rifle in the other 'because rifles were not much use at close quarters'.[13]

Five months later he was wounded again, this time in the forehead. The Germans had blown the parapet on top of him and other soldiers and buried them in the trench for 2 ½ hours.

Morgan made one more ring appearance. While on leave in Plymouth after his first injury, he won the Southern Command middleweight title

***

REDMOND Coleman, the fierce-punching lightweight from Merthyr, could boast a short but impressive career inside the ropes. He won nine local fights in a row, usually by knockout, before making a spectacular London debut in 1894 when he knocked out his opponent inside two minutes.

At the age of 22, Coleman might have been heading for a glittering career, but his regular court appearances and spells in prison for drunkenness and violence, restricted him to three more reported fights in the next six years, two of which he won.

With his police record, Coleman might have been expected to have fallen foul of army discipline after joining up in World War One (at the age of 42). He served as a loader and packer for a few months in the middle of the war (two months of which was spent in France) before being discharged because of 'indigestion' with a (surprising) character rating of 'good'.

***

SHONI Engineer, at 5ft. 10ins and around 10 ½ stones, had been a colliery blacksmith. He had seven reported fights, bare knuckles and gloves, between 1884 and 1890, winning four and losing three. He was knocked out in three rounds by Bill Samuel on the Corporation Field, Neath, after being hit over the ropes. The fight report commented 'The gloves were large ones, and luckily for Shoni they were not 4oz, for he would then have been knocked out in the first round'.[14]

***

SAM and Ivor Thomas (also known as Butcher) were the sons of a Treorchy butcher. Sam was a booth and bareknuckle fighter, who weighed around ten stones and had eight reported fights, winning five, losing two and drawing one. He broke his wrist early against Dai Davies but still managed to win by knockout- although Davies had fallen to his knees at the time and claimed, unsuccessfully, a foul. Thomas later became a second and a referee.

Ivor was a similar tough specimen, who overcame a 20 pounds weight disadvantage and survived three knockdowns in the first round to knock out D. Jones (alias Tom Cochin, Hafod) in the second round at the People's Park, Pontypridd.

***

RICHARD Ambrose, a dock labourer had a few fights in the 1890s, winning two and losing three. He was also a Swansea RFC forward, and an indication of how average height and weight has increased, particularly in a rugby context, can be seen by the fact that Ambrose was 5.ft. 9ins and 10 stones which would have made him too small for any position, forward or back, in a top rugby team today.

Notwithstanding his size, Ambrose was big and strong enough to twice wrestle with a bear at the Swansea Empire theatre in 1896.

***

A HOST of tough fighters of this period included Bob Dunbar, apparently originally from Birmingham and also known as Young Lane, who settled in Newport. He was referred to as a 'clever and game boxer' when as a young man he was outweighed and outgunned by Bill Samuel at

217

Haverfordwest. In the early 1880s he lost an eye in a gun accident, but nevertheless continued in the ring.

Sam Gulliver, Jack Hitchings, Richard James (Dick Sion James), Jack Northey, and Daniel Desmond, were also larger than life characters who fought mostly at a local level. Another was Merthyr-based Delhi Lucknow Thomas, who was born in 1857 at Llandovery, Carmarthenshire, his forenames commemorating the recent relief of those besieged cities during the Indian Rebellion.

Enoch Morrison, Felix Scott and Tom Rooney who also operated in Wales, were, like fellow black contemporaries, treated in a disturbing way by newspapers late in the century. Almost without exception their names in the Press, national and Wales-based, were accompanied by references to their colour, 'coon', 'darkie' and what is now termed 'the n-word' were used regularly, presumably to drum up interest although there were enough black boxers for there to be little novelty value in their fights. The manner in which they were described gave a clear impression that they were somehow regarded as comic characters.

***

A number of Welshmen fought in the USA, none making a bigger impression than Tommy West, born in Cardiff, where he was known as Tich Morgan.[15] He emigrated as a boy, served in the USA navy, and fought for the world welterweight and middleweight titles in a 14-year career.

After a mediocre early record spread over four years, West rose to prominence in his twentieth fight with a rousing performance as a last-minute substitute in New York against the highly regarded Joe Walcott. The crowd booed and many left the building when he was announced as the opponent, because he was considered 'a third-rater, having been defeated by many good welterweights', and 'little better than a pick-up'.[16]

But West, dominating the closing rounds against a tiring Walcott, might have snatched a shock victory had not the timekeeper mistakenly called time a round early, at the end of the 19th, and the referee ruled a draw.[17] The pair met again three months later in New York, and this time there was no doubt about the outcome, West 'clearly' winning over twenty rounds with no 'dissentient voice among the 3,000 crowd.'[18] Walcott, although an admirer of West, remembered him as having 'a disconcerting habit of biting chunks from his scalp in the bloody battles'.[19]

West fought Tommy Ryan in New York in June 1898 for what was billed as the world welterweight championship and was comprehensively beaten, the referee halting it in the 14th of the twenty-round contest.

West's clash with Jack Bonner in New York the following year ended in accusations of skulduggery. *The Sun*, published in the city, described the lead-up

> When the men toed the scratch for the eighth round a peculiar odour was noticed around the ring…..as Bonner thrust out his left hand Tommy was seen to reel. Both of his hands dropped to his side, and he gazed about him vacantly….He fairly groped toward the further end of the ring, and in a muffled voice shouted to Referee White: 'Charley, Charley, I can't see. There's some stuff on that glove'. Then he sank into his chair and his handlers went to his aid. [referee White then complained of something in his own eyes that had blinded him.] Then he said: 'I knew it. That fellow Bonner wanted to lose and has put something on his gloves'. The fumes of the stuff, which afterward proved to be oil of mustard, pervaded the atmosphere, and everyone within reach began to cough and pull their hats down over their foreheads.[20]

The fight was stopped and awarded to West. Spectators and police then jumped into the ring, one policeman slapped Bonner's face, some of the crowd who had lost money on the favourite Bonner threatened to whip him, and the referee punched Bonner on the jaw.[21]

Later in 1899 in New York, West beat Frank Craig, the scourge of British boxers, knocking him down no fewer than 16 times in 14 rounds.[22] In April 1900, West had a return match against Bonner in New York and forced him into a 14th round retirement after a savage beating.

West had nine fights in the final year of the century, losing just one, and rounding off with another victory over Bonner.

***

SEVERAL other Welsh fighters in the USA found additional excitement outside the ring. James 'Jem' Bayton, reported as being born in 1837 in Monmouthshire, acted as a second in a prize fight at Covington, Kentucky, in 1868. The fight party had journeyed down river from Cincinnati on a barge that was being towed and were pelted with stones by fight fans who couldn't afford the $5 tickets, until someone on board scattered them by emptying three chambers of a revolver at them.[23]

Later that year, Bayton, 5ft 5 ½ in, and 9st. 4lb, was beaten in Kentucky by Johnny Lafferty, formerly of New Orleans, his second retiring him after 17 rounds, over 39 minutes.

***

PATSY O'Leary was born in Mary-Ann Street, Cardiff, in 1865, to parents from Ireland, and before going to the USA he worked at the Dowlais Ironworks. He built an impressive record of victories before challenging Tommy Warren, of Louisville, for the featherweight championship of the USA in November 1886.

Fighters to -1900

Tommy West

The fight was for $1,000 dollars a-side, with kid gloves and under the Queensberry Rules.[24] A special train with over 1,000 spectators left Louisville early in the morning, paying $5 a head to for the privilege. The pair fought near Muldraugh Hill, Meade County, Kentucky, in front of a

221

tough and unruly crowd, nearly all armed, who spent the preceding hours in target shooting.

In the seventh round, when time was called, Warren struck O'Leary in the face and a foul was claimed, but Warren did not hear the instruction and the foul was not allowed, so the fight went on.

In the twelfth and last round, they were ordered to break, and as they did so, Warren struck O'Leary a heavy swinging blow with his right to the jaw. A foul was again claimed by O'Leary's backers and he passed under the ropes and out of the ring. The referee did not allow a foul this time either and O'Leary was brought back. The referee then spent 15 minutes in reading rules, before deciding that O'Leary had committed a foul in leaving the ring and awarded the fight to Warren.[25]

O'Leary, based in Cincinnati, wanted another fight with Warren, and complained that the referee called foul after repeated breaches by Warren, but gave way to crowd threats and reversed his decision. He believed he would never have won' even with a Gatling gun' (a forerunner of the machine gun).[26]

Just before signing the articles for a rematch in 1887, the pair quarrelled and set out for a site five miles away to settle their differences. On the way, they came to blows and Warren chewed O'Leary's face severely, biting his cheek clean through.[27]

The fight was then called off because both sides believed they could not find a suitable place at that time of year. Instead, O'Leary took on J. Stephens at Dayton, Ohio, early in 1888 and, although sixteen pounds lighter, knocked him out in twenty minutes to take the stake money and 70 per cent of the gate.

Hours after his fight with Stephens, O'Leary was arrested for theft, and the resultant legal process kept him out of the ring for the rest of the year. He faced a charge of grand larceny of a diamond stud from a man's shirt, an offence which guaranteed a gaol term.[28] He was gaoled in default of $1,500 bail to await the action of the grand jury.

Six weeks later, O'Leary escaped from Dayton gaol while the sheriff was absent and a new warder was in charge. He had attached himself to a party of visitors who were inspecting the building and walked out with them unnoticed and not challenged by the turnkey. His escape was not discovered until the sheriff returned more than two days later.[29] O'Leary, who faced a year's gaol for theft, was recaptured six weeks later in St. Louis.

He returned to Britain and was back in the ring at Newcastle at the beginning of 1890 when he was beaten by a local fighter in eight rounds. The local newspaper remarked that he looked pale as if he had trained hurriedly.

O'Leary went back across the Atlantic straight after the fight and, weeks later was knocked out in the fifth round at the Arlington club, Buffalo, New York.

***

PATSY Reardon also spent time behind bars in the USA, one month in the county gaol in Illinois in 1868 after his opponent, Thomas McCann, died in the ring. In the following twelve months, he was reported to be giving sparring exhibitions and acting as a second around St. Louis, where he died of consumption aged 34 in 1871.

***

AARON Jones was said to be running a bar, gymnasium, and billiards-rooms in Philadelphia at the outbreak of American Civil War in 1861. He was then, supposedly conscripted into the Union army before being taken prisoner by the Confederates. But an escaped prisoner revealed that Jones was, in fact, a captain in a Louisiana regiment of the Confederate army which obviously was not received very well in the north. A newspaper commented

> it would appear that Jones is a sort of leading rebel instead of the pressed conscript we supposed him to be. There has generally existed a feeling of pity for Aaron simply because it was thought he could not help himself; now that people learn otherwise, public sympathy will be removed, and Mr. Jones will be remembered only as a rebel from choice instead of necessity.[30]

After the war Jones said he had no choice about joining the Confederates. At the outbreak he had been penniless in the South, unable to afford to go north 'and was therefore compelled to stay where was and make the best of a bad bargain'.[31]

Jones served as a field orderly to General Beauregard of Fort Sumter fame. The Battle of Fort Sumter opened on April 12, 1861, when Confederate artillery, under Beauregard, fired on the Union garrison, the first shots of the war. Later that year, Jones was based at Mobile, Alabama, 'where he officiates in some connection with the city troops or home guards'.[32]

Jones settled in Columbia, South Carolina, after the civil war and toured the southern states giving exhibitions, also opening a gymnasium in Charleston.[33]

He returned to the ring in 1867 against Mike McCool at Buesenbark's Station, Butler County, Ohio, 31 miles from Cincinnati.[34] He was in a determined mood, judging by his training routine.

> The daily work is divided between walking, rowing, exercises with weights and bags, and rubbing down. The hardest portion of it is the walking to strengthen legs and reduce flesh that is superfluous. A walk of ten miles and return, incased [sic] in three flannel shirts and a winter coat, with a morning sun pouring down 90 degrees of heat from an unclouded sky, with perspiration running in streams

from face, head. Limbs and body, is hard work, and well calculated to make a man 'strong on his pins!'[35]

Sixty-one reporters covered the fight, which was for $5,000 a-side, and between them and the 3,500 crowd, most of whom had arrived on a 32-carriage train, was 'a cordon of ring keepers armed with heavy cudgels'. Patsy Reardon was among the host of well-known fighters at ringside.

At the request of Irish-born McCool, one of Morrisey's successors as American champion, Jones sucked his knuckles, which were a deep walnut colour, to show that no poisonous drug had been used in dying them.

Jones was beaten in the 34th round of a brutal, bloody fight over 25 minutes. Those numbers indicate there must have been many very short-lived rounds, and indeed there were. The longest session lasted 24 seconds, nine lasted fewer than ten seconds, the shortest being two seconds, most of the rounds ending when Jones went down to avoid punishment or immediately after landing a blow of his own. That was the last appearance in the ring for Jones, who for ten minutes lay on the field insensible, no doctor appearing to be present.

At the end, fighting broke out in the crowd with fists and knives being used freely, but when it was announced that the train was about to leave it ended quickly.

Jones died 18 months later, still only in his thirties. He had been found ill and destitute in New Orleans and a friend had taken him to a farm at Leavenworth, Indiana, to recuperate. A month later, however, married man Jones, complaining that he had been poisoned a few months earlier by a girlfriend whom he had jilted, died and was buried on the farm.[36]

***

SWANSEA'S Thomas Davies lived in Pittsburgh, USA, for seven or eight years from the late 1880s, showing 'promise as a boxer' and served as a corporal in the United States army, before returning to Wales late in 1894.

Cardiff boxer James 'Jem' Perry claimed two wins and a defeat, all unverified, before migrating to the USA, where he claimed five victories, again none of which were reported. In 1894 he was back in Britain, taking on Arthur Valentine in front of a 5,000 crowd at the Central Hall, Holborn, London. Perry, who had twice been warned for holding, was disqualified in the fifth round after throwing Valentine with a cross-buttock.[37]

The reason for Perry's move to the USA became evident the following year when he was arrested for having deserted from the Royal Navy in 1892. Perry's discomfort was soon over, however, as just a week later the Admiralty said it had no further use for him.

Billy Morgan, from Swansea, made a fleeting trip to the USA in 1898 as an able seaman, but was found hiding in the hold as a stowaway when it ran aground off Fire Island, New York, and returned home immediately, working his passage on a cattle boat.[38]

Probably the most travelled Welsh fighter was Jem Hucker, another Royal Navy man, who managed both careers simultaneously and competed in places as distant as British Columbia and Honolulu. The Swansea-born petty officer on board Her Majesty's ship *Cambridge* at Devonport, fought with 4 oz. gloves at the People's Palace, Plymouth, in 1893. Hucker lost controversially to Tom Merrin and a disturbance followed, although neither fighter was involved. A woman rushed one of the seconds, and began scratching and kicking him, explaining afterwards the man had 'made reflection upon her character, which, as a married woman, she was bound to defend'.

Fighters to -1900

***

DAI Dolling, from Swansea, was reported in an article in his later years to have had thirty bare knuckle fights and one hundred with boxing gloves in the later decades of the nineteenth century, suffering only one defeat, at the hands of Morgan Crowther.

However, such an outstanding record was surprisingly not remarked upon at the time, neither was he the celebrity he apparently deserved to be, which raises doubts as to its veracity.

Rare references to his involvement in a prize fight came in 1896 when he was a second for Dick Ambrose in his fatal fight with Tom Davies at Swansea and the following year when he was one of Billy Morgan's seconds in the clash with Morgan Grey on Swansea sands. Dolling, said in a newspaper report to be 'well-known in local boxing circles, had been punched by Grey during the fight, and afterwards the pair had a 'set-to' themselves.

Whatever the truth of his own record in the ring, Dolling would go on to became world famous by helping other sportsmen to excel.

---

[1] Evening Express, 7 July 1892.
[2] Evening Express, 14 March 1894
[3] Western Mail, Birmingham Daily Post 24 Apr 1894.
[4] Licensed Victuallers' Mirror, cited in Evening Express, 20 April 1895.
[5] Sportsman, cited in South Wales Daily Post, 15 April 1895.
[6] North Eastern Daily Gazette, 28 December 1899
[7] Western Mail, 29 December 1899
[8] North Eastern Daily Gazette, 3 January 1887
[9] Western Mail, 28 Jan 1890. Sportsman, cited in Western Mail, 29 January 1890.
[10] Western Mail, 3 Dec 1891.
[11] Cambria Daily Leader, 1 February 1915.
[12] South Wales Weekly Post, 29 May 1915.
[13] South Wales Weekly Post, 16 June 1915.
[14] Western Mail, 15 Sept 1890
[15] South Wales Daily News, 24 June 1902
[16] The Sun (New York), 10 December 1896; Omaha Daily Bee, 13 December 1896.

[17] Record-Union (Sacramento, Calif.)10 December 1896. Saint-Paul Globe, 10 December 1896.
[18] Evening Times (Washington), 4 March 1897.
[19] Bismark Tribune (N.D.), 21 January 1930.
[20] Sun (New York), 1 March 1899.
[21] Western Mail, 3 Mar 1899.
[22] Western Mail, 27 Nov 1899.
[23] Daily Ohio Statesman, 28 April 1868.
[24] St. Paul Daily Globe, 8 November 1886.
[25] Wichita Eagle, 9 November 1886.
[26] St. Paul Daily Globe, 6 November 1887.
[27] Sacramento Daily Record-Union, 5 November 1887.
[28] St. Paul Daily Globe, 21 January 1888; 8 February 1888. Barton County Democrat (Ky.) 26 January 1888
[29] St. Paul Daily Globe, 14 March 1888
[30] New York Clipper, October 1862 cited in Evening Despatch, 14 November 1916.
[31] New York Clipper, cited in Sporting Life, 24 June 1865.
[32] Daily Intelligencer (Wheeling, Va.) 16 December 1861.
[33] New York Clipper, cited in Sporting Life, 24 June 1865.
[34] Era, 24 April 1859; 2 December 1860. Evening Tel. (Philadelphia), 31 August 1867.
[35] Evening Tel. (Philadelphia)19 July 1867.
[36] Charleston Daily News, 1 March 1869. Evening Despatch, 14 November 1916.
[37] Western Mail, 4 Mar 1895.
[38] Evening Express, 31 May 1898. South Wales Daily Post, 23 June 1898

9

Female fighters

Prize fighting among women had been well-established in Britain from the 18th century and was reported on regularly throughout the following one hundred years.

But female pugilists were rare in Wales, where women had mainly minor roles in prize fights, usually as spectators. They enjoyed the violence; sparring matches were 'much admired by ladies', it was claimed in 1874. And they were more open about it than some of their English counterparts. In England, fights were customarily held on racecourses on the last day of a meeting and provided women, or at least those of the upper classes, with a discreet viewing opportunity. At one set-to after the Epsom Races, it was reported that 'Several elegantly dressed females were peeping from barouches'. At Wrexham's March Fair in 1861, females were 'flocking in almost as thickly as males' at the customary boxing booth.

In Wales, women were in the midst of crowds of spectators at Cwmddu in the Swansea area, also in Adam Street, Cardiff, while in Graig Lane at Bangor in north Wales, women, including the wife of one of the pugilists, were part of a 'great crowd' enjoying the action. Several were among a large audience at the Philharmonic Hall, Cardiff, in 1897 watching film of the world title fight between Corbett and Fitzsimmons.

The Welsh strove to project a pure image of their women after the 'Treason of the Blue Books', so for them to be seen to be associated with prize fights was considered more reprehensible than it was for men.

In the Rhondda Valley, women could be doubly damned for attending such an event. Two women, and several men, living at Blaenrhondda, went before Rhondda Valley police court after being arrested on the local mountain. The stipendiary declared "I am ashamed of the two women – going to the mountains to see a fight, and on a Sunday, too!"[1] On another occasion, the local newspaper reported reprovingly that 'young women, who seemed temporarily devoid of any decency', ran to and from a nearby stream with towels to staunch the blood from one of the participants in a prize fight near Vaynor church on a Sunday afternoon.[2]

Women frequently incited contests. The inquest on a ring death at Porth in 1886 heard that the challenge leading to the fight had been issued by the landlady of the surviving fighter. The coroner said not only the boxer but the seconds and those who encouraged the fight were liable, 'especially that truculent old lady'.

On Mardy Mountain in 1885, it was reported that 'the mothers of the two fighters were doing everything to urge their men on'. A Rhondda wife encouraged her collier husband to fight at Gelli, telling him to give his prospective opponent 'a jolly good hiding'.

Occasionally, women acted as seconds. When two butchers met in the Blue Boar field at Pontypool in 1846, the father and two sisters of one of the combatants were engaged in what was called 'keeping the ring' during the encounter. And when two hawkers fought at Tenby in 1889 for five shillings a-side, the wife of one acted as his second.

Female Fighters

Not all women supported their battling offspring, however. While John Towers was sitting in Newport police court in 1841 his mother

> a lady of the Falstaff and Jem Ward school combined in her lovely and effeminate person toddled into court, approached the place where her ungracious son was sitting with closed eyes in musing melancholy, and at once, despite her unwieldly proportions, and with true "boxiana" spirit, clenched her 'mauleys', and 'went in' about her son's head — right and left, left and right, before and behind, and all around, like 'a good 'un'.[3]

Prize fights often had female lookouts. A crowd of women who had followed the lighted lamps of colliers to the field on Pembrey Mountain near Llanelli in 1898, raised the cry of 'Police' to aid the escape of those involved.

But women were not always trusted in this capacity. The site for a contest in 1887 in the dell at the foot of a Merthyr quarry was completely hidden from view, except on one side, and women pickets were stationed at the top of the quarry. Some of them shouted that the police were coming, but the pugilists and their seconds thought this was only a ruse to make them postpone the battle and the fight continued. However, it ended soon after when police dashed into the middle of the crowd.

***

THE small number of female prize fighters belied the existence of a vast untapped pool of pugilistic talent in the country. It was common to see female neighbours brawling in the less fashionable areas of major towns.

Two, one 66 and the other 88, swapped punches in the street at Lampeter in Cardiganshire in 1810.

> after nearly an hour's hard fighting, the younger heroine seemed to have the advantage; and, if the civil power had not opportunely interfered, would most certainly have killed her antagonist.[4]

Prize fighting figure Jack Matthews's wife, Ellen, 'remarkably muscular and vigorous', punched a woman in a Cardiff pub in 1859 and the woman died minutes later. The incident took place in a 'house of ill-repute', the *Forester's Arms* beer house run by Matthews' husband and sparked a riot. A mob, 'numbering some thousands' destroyed five adjoining houses which were leased by Jack Matthews and operated as brothels. Ellen, 32, was found guilty of manslaughter, and gaoled for three months with hard labour.

Susan Davies, referred to euphemistically as 'a lady of the lane', displayed her own punching power by knocking a man out of his chair in a Cardiff beer house in 1852, and followed up by nearly knocking out the front teeth of the landlady, who had not ordered her out because she 'was in bodily fear of her'.[5] Weeks later, Davies, 'very violent at the police station', was fined with the alternative of a month's gaol for assaulting the landlady of the *Jolly Sailor* beer-house in the town.

Another proficient pugilist was a Wrexham teenager Sarah Ann Davies, who, a court was told in 1890, 'proved herself a first-rate boxer' when she punched a neighbour on the nose.

In the 1890s, 'Ladies of the pave', including a Merthyr woman 'the heroine of a hundred brawls', had truly formidable reputations as fighters, and they often appeared in court charged with attacking each other'.[6]

Welsh women often became involved in industrial disputes but were usually on the fringes of any violence. Their main role was to intimidate strikebreakers and their families with the 'rough music serenade', a cacophony created by beating together kitchen utensils as the blacklegs went to and from work.[7] But during a coal dispute at Cwmbach in 1850, when Welsh miners clashed with strike breakers from the Forest of Dean, women were in the thick of the fray. The first policeman to arrive at the scene of a battle between the two sides reported

> A girl came out through the window. She stood half in and half out and then fell on the paving. Four of five Welsh women fell on her and kicked and beat her. I went and caught her by the arm. She said;' Oh…for God's sake, save my life.[8]

Ann Forecast, described by *The Welshman* in 1835 as the best female fighter in London, was said to have never had an objection, when in liquor, to fight a man.[9] But some fierce Welsh women did not appear to need a drink to fire them up.

During the Rebecca riots in the 1840s, at Cwm Cille in the parish of Llangyfelach, Glamorgan's chief constable, Captain Charles Frederick Napier, was attacked by five members of the family of a suspect he was trying to arrest. A newspaper reported: 'The women during the whole of the time fought with frantic violence'.

Napier said that the mother 'jumped on my back, scratched my face and bit my ear', [she then] 'took an iron bar from the fire and struck me two or three times on the head with it'. The sister 'having struck me with a stick, took a saucepanful of hot water off the fire, and threw the water over me, which compelled me to let [the son] go. As the struggle with the family continued; the sister cut Napier's head with a reaping hook.[10]

The mother of a prize fighter put her fist in the face of an inspector when he tried to arrest her son at the scene at Ruthin in north Wales in 1882, and when officers followed them home, she again prevented his arrest.

When police went to Redmond Coleman's home in Merthyr in 1896 to arrest the fighter for being drunk and disorderly, they were attacked by the women of the house. As one officer looked under a bed for him, Coleman's mother, Ann, hit him with a poker, and a sister, Charlotte, tried to hit him with a fender. Charlotte and another sister, Annie, then followed the officer into the kitchen, throwing knives, cups and saucers and plates at him and at the other policeman. Charlotte then knocked his helmet off with a tin.

A week later, as frequent miscreant Coleman was being marched in a group of prisoners to Merthyr railway station *en route* to Swansea gaol, a woman grabbed him and tried to help him escape.

***

WHEN they stepped into the ring, women tended to observe the same rituals as the men, contrary to the jibe in the satirical *Punch* magazine that 'a female fight would be a very scratch performance'.[11]

The aforementioned Susan Davies and Martha Watkins, from Newport, met in front of at least five hundred spectators early one morning on the moors near Cardiff, when

> they both stripped to the waist, each of the combatants having her clothes tied up round her by a handkerchief of a colour they had previously agreed upon, that each party might distinguish 'the favourite' more easily. Having chosen their seconds, who rested the principals on their knees, wiped their foreheads, and supplied them with drink, exactly after the manner of 'the profession', they proceeded to battle.[12]

They fought 'eighteen rounds in the course of an hour – not scratching, mauling, or pulling each other's hair; but a real fair stand-up fight'.[13]

In 1881 'a regular stand-up fight' was reported between women near the Newbridge railway station in Monmouthshire. Two colliers had previously come to blows, and the loser, wanting revenge but not confident enough to attempt it himself, consulted his wife who fought with the winner's spouse. The published fight report read

In the space of a few minutes these two determined specimens of feminine humanity were making it warm for each other, not scratching each other's optics out and tearing each other's chignons, as is the wont of furious womanhood, but letting fly with their fists *a la* Tom Sayers and Heenan. A ring was formed by a crowd of admiring bystanders, and the two went at it fast and furious for some 20 minutes or half an hour, when victory crowned the efforts of [the loser's wife], whose opponent was decidedly used np, and the honour of the male .....was redeemed by his gentle help-meet in life. [14]

In 1886, Sarah Ann Williams and Mary Ann Carter, of Wattstown, battled for three quarters of an hour on a Saturday night in a Rhondda pub, the *Butchers Arms*, with their husbands seconding. 'The evidence revealed shocking depravity', the *Cardiff Times* reported.[15] The women, who said they had been incited to fight by their husbands, were charged with riotousness, and were bound over, their husbands being fined 20 shillings each for abetting.

Recognition of female fighting skills was unusual, Huggins explaining: 'The sporting press usually reinforced gender ideas' and ridiculed the performances of women.[16] However, the Cardiff fighter, Davies, who 'severely maltreated' her opponent, even impressed the officers who turned up to arrest them, with her skill; she had 'displayed a great deal of science', according to a police inspector.[17]

Similarly, two female servants fought between 35 and 40 rounds in 1855 in the mansion of a Pembrokeshire magistrate, who was unable to stop them and was forced to remain 'an unwilling spectator of the match' but was, nevertheless, impressed.[18]

The magistrate, 'in consideration of the consummate science in the pugilistic art, the bravery they had displayed and the punishment they had inflicted on each other', decided not to send them 'to the tread-mill', but would only desire them to quit his service. The servants' prize fight was looked on 'one of the best and most gallantly contested 'stand-up fights' that has been recorded for many a day.'

A similar skilful display was provided by two women living near Broadmoor Colliery, Pembrokeshire, who quarrelled over a young man and decided to settle things with a prize fight, when 'The time and place were named and the necessary attendants on each side chosen.....seven rounds passed off in a most scientific manner'.[19]

Accomplished female fighters appeared in fairground boxing booths, one being the wife of the man who founded Taylor's boxing booth of Cardiff in 1861. The last owner of the booth, Ron Taylor, said his grandmother boxed. 'But she was so fast,' he remembered, 'that no-one could hit her, anyway.'[20]

At the end of the nineteenth century, it was reported that 'a prominent feature' of a boxing booth at the Treorchy fair was 'the presence of a famous 'lady boxer'. She could show 'points', and naturally loud was the praise bestowed.'[21]

The 'present mania for pugilism' in South Wales in 1888 wasn't confined to the men; a Mrs. Gray, of Cardiff, offered to box any other lady, or to spar three rounds with her husband to raise money for victims of a recent fire.

Not everyone was impressed, with female fighters, though. They were part of a 'satanic contagion', a Welsh newspaper reported in 1895.[22] Quoting a diatribe from an American clergyman, the newspaper said that the increasing 'intrusion' of women into a man's world of politics, preaching, lecturing, law, medicine, bicycling and pugilism would leave the world not worth the saving.'

***

Female Fighters

FEMALE pugilists had to wait until the closing years of the twentieth century to gain official acceptance. In 1997, they were allowed to compete at amateur level, and to take out professional boxing licenses in 1998. Abergavenny-born Ashley Brace made her professional boxing debut in 2015 at the Newport Centre and won eight of nine fights, the other a draw, winning the WBC international female bantamweight title at Ebbw Vale two years later and the EBY European super-flyweight title in Cardiff in 2018.

***

POLICE used the fact that the presence of women at a prize fight was nothing out of the ordinary to halt a battle on Senghenydd mountain. The local newspaper reported:

> Whilst the thirty-fifth round was in progress a couple of women were observed approaching, but little notice was taken of them, as it was considered that mere feminine curiosity attracted them to the spot. When the two fair ones came nearer, however, they were seen to be of remarkably fine physique for members of the gentler sex, and before the little band of "sports" could decamp they were all "under arrest. The police-for the two women were stalwart officers disguised in female attire, took the names and addresses of all the members of the party, none of whom tried to escape at the last moment. The disguised officers were Police sergeant Jenkins and Police-constable King.[23]

---

[1] *Western Mail*, 28 November 1876
[2] *Merthyr Telegraph*, 7 May 1875
[3] Monmouthshire Merlin, 15 May 1841.
[4] *Chester Chronicle*, 6 April 1810.
[5] *Cardiff & Merthyr Guardian*, 27 March 1852
[6] David J. V. Jones, Crime in 19th Century Wales (Cardiff, Univ. of Wales Press, 1992), p. 95.
[7] Rosemary A. N. Jones 'Women, Community and Collective Action: The Ceffyl Pren Tradition', in Anegla V. John (ed.), *Our Mother's Land: Chapters in Welsh Women's History 1830-1939* (Cardiff, University of Wales Press, 1991), p. 35.
[8] *Cardiff and Merthyr Guardian*, 11 May 1850.
[9] *Welshman*, 3 July 1835.
[10] *Monmouthshire Merlin*, 29 July 1843
[11] *Bury & Norwich Post*, 22 August 1804. *Punch*, cited in *Aberystwyth Observer*, 21 April 1888.
[12] *Cardiff and Merthyr Guardian*, 4 September 1852

[13] *Cardiff and Merthyr Guardian*, 4 September 1852.
[14] *South Wales Daily News*, 11 July 1881
[15] *Cardiff Times*, 16 October 1886
[16] Mike Huggins, The Victorians and Sport (Hambleden & London, London, 2004), p. 81.
[17] *Cardiff and Merthyr Guardian*, 4 September 1852
[18] *Pembrokeshire Herald*, 29 June 1855
[19] *Pembrokeshire Herald*, 8 October 1858.
[20] *Daily Telegraph*, 26 July 2006
[21] *Rhondda Leader*, 23 June 1900
[22] *South Wales Daily Post*, 19 August 1895
[23] *Evening Express*, 4 March 1902

10
Fairground boxing booths

Fairground boxing booths were an integral part of the prize fighting scene. Operated mostly by people involved in the wider sport, they brought the ring to the neighbourhood, providing a cheap and convenient way to see a glove fight (fighters and challengers wore gloves years before the Queensberry Rules were instigated).

For the admission fee of a few pence, spectators could cram into a large tent and get a taste of the action, watching pugilists display their skills against each other or, more likely, against volunteers from the crowd. Those who stepped forward would be promised money if they could survive a few rounds against a house fighter.

Booths provided regular employment between ring bouts for seasoned men who, as well as using the establishment to remain in shape, picked up fights on their travels. They gave veteran fighters a job when their ring careers ended, and were also nurseries for aspiring fighters, as these men passed on their knowledge to the younger boxers.

Fighters travelled with the booth from town to town, erecting and dismantling it. They were given food and lodgings and received a small wage, usually a share of the takings, most of their money coming from coins thrown into the ring by spectators as a show of appreciation after they had fought.

As well as enticing men out of the crowd, booth operators regularly advertised open competitions, inviting men to forward their names days in advance. Advertising his forthcoming show at Pontycymmer, Felix Scott coaxed 'Now all you champions of the Valleys You can pay your debts what you owe each other in Scott's show while he is in the Valley'.[1]

When in urgent need of fighters Scott advertised regularly in the local Press. He had a 'vacancy for a tidy boxer' while at Aberdare in 1897, while his advert for men for his booth at Pontypool two years later stipulated 'No chicken-hearted men need apply'.

World champion Jimmy Wilde, himself a former booth employee, enthused: 'A boxing booth is the finest training ground for a fighter. He's *got* to win to last'.[2] Later Welsh hero Tommy Farr fought as a teenager in ' the University of Joe Gess's boxing booth'.[3] He concurred with Wilde.

> As a means to learn the trade of fighting it is beyond price. To every fight-minded youngster I strongly recommend the boxing-booth as the best teacher of all, an unholy grind it is to be sure. A cracking, crunching, smashing thing. But it does teach all that is demanded of a pugilist – the will to win no matter the opposition or the odds.[4]

Another booth fighter was Cardiff boxing preacher Harry Condie, who acquired his ring skills in the closing years of the nineteenth century, set up Bute Athletic Club, toured with a boxing booth and worked as a pavement artist. He became an evangelical preacher at the time of Evan Roberts religious revival in Wales.

***

BOOTHS had been popular attractions since the Restoration and continued to be well-patronised throughout the nineteenth century. They were part of the regular hiring and agricultural fairs held throughout Wales, or rather at the 'pleasure fairs' which operated in tandem with them. Booths were also on site when circuses visited a locality, and at Welsh race meetings.

Fairground boxing booths

The fairs included Newport's Stow Fair, the Llandaff Fair, the annual spring fair at Wrexham, the annual Blossoms Fair at Denbigh, the Portfield hiring fair at Haverfordwest, and the annual hiring fair at Kidwelly. The Ffair Llangyfelach became one of the largest in Wales with thousands attending it from all over South Wales. It was first held in the early part of the eighteenth century – in the churchyard at Llangyfelach but was soon moved to a different venue.

> Booths which were erected there, flat tomb-stones used for displaying wares, oil-flares with their soot and pungent smells, And the raucous voices of stall-holders, caused the righteous indignation of the curate and parishioners of Llangyfelach. The result was that future fairs were held in a big field opposite the church.[5]

The fair lasted three days. The first day was the hiring fair, the second day was flannel fair and the third was a pleasure fair which included boxing booths.

The Midsummer Fair at Presteigne, sometimes called the Cherry Fair because of the large quantities of that fruit on sale, gained a widespread reputation for its prize fights.

Fairs adapted to the changing conditions of the industrial revolution by increasingly aiming for the new coal mining communities instead of the traditional hiring and pleasure fairs. In the Rhondda Valley the usual round began the week after Whitsun at Treorchy, moving on to Porth, Tonypandy and Ferndale.

Visits by the fair would be timed to coincide with colliery pay-days, and on one visit to Treorchy when this did not happen, the showmen waited another week until the people had money to spend. In contrast, Llantwit Major in the Vale of Glamorgan gave a reminder of the old-time Welsh Fair. Surrounded by fields, with 'No coal-pit or slate quarry within sight', the fair would last only a day or two, with little business done in the day. 'Away from the coal away from the money' was true of Wales as far as the showmen were concerned.[6]

The importance of the mining communities to fairground business was highlighted by the coalfield dispute in 1898 involving the colliers of South Wales and Monmouthshire, which turned into a lockout lasting for six months. In the early part of the year fairground takings were poor because the colliers were out of work. Business at a boxing booth at Abergavenny Fair in May was 'unusually quiet, owing to the dislocation of trade by the terrible dispute in the Welsh coalfields', and most showmen abandoned the Welsh season in favour of English and Scottish Whitsun sites'.[7]

Pleasure fairs eventually supplanted the hiring and agricultural fairs. By 1896, the Cardigan Hiring Fair, for instance, had 'become mainly one of pleasure; shows were not numerous, but there was a boxing booth'.[8]

The popularity of booths (and beer) spread across the English Channel, proving one of the 'sights' at the Paris Exhibition in 1867, inspiring the comment

> Assuredly our volatile neighbours over the water are going ahead. *Le boxe* and *le bittere bier* are making rapid strides amongst them, and I should not be surprised if, before long, they become 'more *English* than the *English* themselves.[9]

Booths competed for fair-goers' money at these fairs with circuses, menageries and peep shows, shooting galleries, children's roundabouts, waxworks, and 'wild Indian shows'. Other regular attractions, included 'gambling (alias spinning) tables, where, with a small expenditure of time, the art of losing money with facility might be picked up' while 'drinking booths were always a feature of the Presteigne fair'.[10] In addition, customers might be treated to a tattooed lady, Madame Salva's fine art show, and John Studt's fairground rides which included the 'Channel Tunnel Railway'.[11] Pilot tunnels had been begun on both sides of the English Channel in 1881, but the project was abandoned the following year, owing to concerns over Britain's national defences.

In the final years of the century, moving pictures became a major fairground attraction. Boxing booth operator Bill Samuel also had a Cinematograph 'with living pictures' at the Llanelli fair and at Welsh Hay in the early part of 1898. At the Troedyrhiw Fair in 1900, Jack Scarrott's boxing booth faced competition from an 'electric bioscope, with a splendid range of war pictures'.

Despite competing entertainments and considerable opposition arising out of their sleazy image, association with undesirables and potential for encouraging crowd disorder, for ordinary members of the public, boxing booths were the main attraction at fairgrounds.

The Llangyfelach Fair would not be complete without Samuel and his 'pugilistic exhibitions', it was claimed in 1891. A booth at the fair in Pontypool in 1863 drew the only crowd; an acrobat collected just 1½ d after he passed round his cap and he threw it back. The boxing booth appeared to be the most popular attraction at Denbigh's annual Blossoms Fair in 1880 'if perhaps we except the roundabouts among the youngsters'.

***

A tent used in the Rhondda valley in the 1890s was a typical booth. It was 'about 12 yards long by about 7 yards wide and 8ft. high, having a sloping roof, the canvas bearing red stripes throughout'.[12] The structure might be fronted by a gaudily-painted canvas, bearing representations of famous fighters.

Out front, the proprietor, usually a former pugilist, would beat a gong to attract attention, and after a crowd had gathered, a barker, probably the same man and flanked by his current fighters, would stand on a platform or on a cart, attempting, with a 'bawling voice', to entice customers into the tent. At Usk's Trinity Fair, the barker

> expatiates on the valorous exploits of 'Ben the Bruiser', and 'Plucky Joe' the probable cognomens of the aforesaid notabilities, and expresses the pleasure that they would feel in 'having a set to with the gloves,' with any gentleman who may aspire to the honor [sic].[13]

Bill Samuel's spiel may have sounded discouraging,

> Come in,' he would say, 'and have your head punched until you don't know whether it's your head or your heels. But mind you, we don't *kill* people in here – we only leave them so that they *won't live*!

But it was 'well-calculated to rouse the mettle of any strong man'.[14]

At Llandaff Fair in 1860, admission was three pence to watch 'the great and renowned novice… try his hand with Young Slasher of Brighton', while twenty years later, the entrance fee for Samuel's booth at Llangyfelach Fair was just 2d 'to witness the doughty deeds of the veteran 'Shoni Shuroi'. the 'Aberdare Chicken', the 'Swansea Champion,' and the courteous, but agile and hard-hitting, William Samuel himself.'[15]

Such tents were not the sturdiest of structures. A slight breeze sprang up and upset a booth operating alongside Abergavenny races in 1888; the owners hung on to the ropes and tried to keep the booth up but it collapsed 'to the delight of the crowd, who volunteered gratuitous advice freely'.[16]

Neither were tents the safest of arenas. When the referee failed to turn up at a boxing booth in the centre of Cardiff in 1902 angry customers demanded their money back and while the proprietor was duly obliging at the door, disorder broke out inside, oil lamps were disturbed and the front of the crowded booth was set alight. Fortunately, the fire brigade arrived promptly. In Tom Thomas' boxing booth on the Neath Corporation Field on a Saturday night in 1905 a brawl broke out when one of the boxers objected to interference by his opponent's second and swapped punches with him. The crowd rushed on to the platform and joined in, causing the platform to collapse.

Once 'challengers' had been recruited, customers would file into the tent, paying an entrance fee on the way. If no challengers stepped up, house fighters would face each other, or a 'plant' hidden within the crowd would challenge the said fighter and the pair would perform a staged bout, unbeknown to most onlookers.

The ring, on a platform raised five feet above the ground, occupied most of the space inside the Rhondda booth, with spectators having only standing room of about four feet all around it.

A newspaper reporter gave an atmospheric account of what went on inside a booth mid-century at Newport, where between fifty and sixty spectators were 'huddled together', and

> the atmosphere which pervades it is odoriferous, but not, if I must speak the truth, sweet, nor cool, nor refreshing. The majority of us are boys, and smoke rank tobacco with short pipes. Low scowling, brutal looks have they, and much foul language issues from their lips with their smoke. Civilised-looking beings some, but bull-necks and belchers mostly.[17]

Waiting for something to happen he continued,

> At first, we did not perceive that there *was* a ring, but now order is restored, and the space for those mighty champions, the Pet and Bruiser, is well preserved. They step into the sacred circle, put on the gloves, shake hands, which now have the appearance of being

poulticed and begin the evening's entertainment...The Bristol bruiser plants – I think I use the right expression? – a hit on the nose of the Newport pet, which seems to disgust that gentleman most profoundly, and pleases the audience beyond measure. Both the belligerents look very red in the face, and anger begins to burn within them. They give each other 'smellers' and are almost pounded up to jellies. Suddenly a rush is made by the inhabitant of Newport at he of Bristol, and the former aims a fierce blow, which the latter eludes by falling to the ground.

The venue for Bob Dunbar's fight with Jockey Saunders in Newport in 1888 was a 'canvas booth lit by naptha lamps ... crowded almost to suffocation', a spectator recalled years later.[18]

In those days the onlookers claimed - and fully exercised their claim - the right to shout every kind of terrifying and intimidating imprecation at the contestants and also at the referee. Many of them went further, leaving the frail sitting accommodation in the booth and advancing to the ringside with angry threats and uplifted fists. There was an orgy of swaying terrorism.

Booth fighters were obliged to take on all-comers. Most challengers, although perhaps tough men themselves, and often much bigger than the resident fighters, would be unskilled and perhaps emboldened by alcohol.

Faced with these experienced campaigners - among those who featured in the 1890s were Cardiff's John O'Brien, the Welsh champion, heavyweight David St. John and another seasoned man, Sam (Butcher)Thomas (Aberaman), who both toured the Rhondda with Samuel's establishment - men from the crowd might need to be carried by the booth fighter (in most cases only until near to the end of the agreed distance to avoid handing over money) to ensure a worthwhile spectacle.

Challengers would have as much chance of success as they would at any of the fairground stalls, but it would not be good for business if they were treated too harshly as others would be discouraged from following them. Such lack of care might rebound on booth personnel and hit them in more than just the pocket.

Fighters from a Cardiff booth operating at the annual Lydney fair in 1885 took advantage of unskilled customers and the next night they were attacked by a mob of local toughs, who surrounded the tent and meted out 'retribution of a most complete and brutal character' to three of the boxers whose faces were beaten 'beyond recognition'.[19] One booth boxer crawled under the canvas and was chased by the 'maddened' locals for two miles through fields before jumping into a canal and escaping.

Booth fighters had to look out for their own safety on other occasions, too. Colliers, some of them experienced mountain fighters, tended to have a group of followers with them when they took up the challenge, and booth owner Scarrott recalled 'Very often, when you were boxing one of them and you were backing before his punches, watching out for a chance to get in the KO. you'd get a punch from behind from one of his pals'.[20]

***

SAMUEL, from Swansea, was the most colourful of the booth owners. He claimed a long and successful ring career, and to be the 'Welsh champion', referring often in his later years to his successes –26 bare-knuckle fights without defeat, he said.[21]

However, his own words are the only available evidence of this. He mentioned 14 fights in the ring, 12 wins and two draws, including a draw against Dan Thomas, in an interview but, apart from a handful of fights, corroborative evidence is lacking. Samuel never provided details, surprisingly so for an avid self-publicist who accepted a challenge to spar three rounds with the great John L. Sullivan and once walked alone into the lion's den at a circus.

This latter 'deed of daring' had never been performed since the circus had been started in 1805, the ringmaster claimed.[22] Entering the lion's den had been a regular feature of this particular circus, it had been so at Merthyr and at Cardiff earlier in the year and would be again at Pontypridd the next month. But Samuel would be the first to go in alone, without the lion-tamer. Clad in his fighting gear and armed with a cudgel, Samuel 'boldly entered the cage......walked amongst the animals and made them fly right and left before him. This he did several times'.

Newspapers referred to Samuel as the 'self-proclaimed champion fighter', but, while his accounts might well have been the exaggerations of a showman, as those publications implied, he was unquestionably formidable with his fists, as a few displays leading up to his seventies attest.

Bill Samuel
(Herald of Wales, 11 March 1916)

Fairground boxing booths

In 1890, a glove fight between 51 year-old Samuel and 'Shoni Engineer' in a circus tent on the Corporation Field, Neath, ended in round three, when Engineer was knocked over the ropes, the *Western Mail* reporting: 'The gloves were large ones, and luckily for Shoni they were not 4oz, for he would then have been knocked out in the first round'.

In 1892 at Neath, when a proposed bout failed to materialise, Samuel took on the aggrieved combatant himself, and after breaking his own right arm in the first round, tucked the hand into his pocket and carried on one-handed, knocking his opponent down and forcing him to retire in the fourth round.

Samuel, at the age of 55, put on the gloves again to rescue another of his shows. His boxing booth at the Cardiff World's Fair in 1894 was the scene of a benefit night for prize fighter Sam Hughes. Tom Ball, an Australian, was announced to box John O'Brien, but, as Ball would not meet O'Brien, Samuel took O'Brien's place, floored Ball in the first round and twice more in the second, after which Ball claimed he was injured and unable to continue.

Samuel's battles that made the newspapers in his younger days took place outside the ring. In 1865, he challenged prize fighter Thomas Pearson in Swansea's High Street and after Pearson declined to accept because he had just spent ten days in gaol for fighting and did not want 'to go down again', Samuel struck him several times in the face. In 1882, Samuel and Bob Dunbar, another prize fighter, clashed in the same Swansea street, after Dunbar's friends had claimed he had earlier bettered Samuel at Llanelli.

Five years later, Samuel applied to take over a hotel in Swansea, the local newspaper, under the headline 'FROM BRUISER TO BONIFACE', the reference relating to the name of the jovial innkeeper in George Farquhar's

1707 play 'The Beaux Stratagem', commenting 'He is now desirous not of knocking people silly, but of selling them that which often makes them so'.[23]

Samuel claimed he was now 'desirous of hanging up his gloves for good and living in peace and quiet', but his serenity was not to last, for, in the following years, he assaulted a dealer at Bridgend in a row over a horse, brawled in the street, and, up until his sixtieth year, continued to issue challenges. He offered Llansamlet fighter Tom Harris £5 to meet him over 6x3-minute rounds in his Cardiff booth – and a further inducement was that Samuel would fight with just one hand.

***

NEWPORT-BORN Scarrott was a former booth fighter who, in his early twenties, set up a travelling establishment in the last decades of the century

Wilde, in his autobiography remembered Scarrott fondly as

> a grand fellow and for 50 years and more he carried his booth throughout the mountains and valleys of south Wales. Among boxing enthusiasts he was wholeheartedly popular, and he had some of the finest boxers in the world through his hands.[24]

Operators such as Scarrott, said Wilde, were unsung heroes and the booths were under-valued.

> Scarrott in the early days had helped to make me, as he had helped to make many other champions. Little known, hard-working, certainly not wealthy, it is Jack and his fellow booth owners who prepare the champions of the boxing world. I have always believed that booths get too little attention.[25]

Scarrott died in 1947 after collapsing in the showground at Caldicot.

Felix Scott was born in Bermuda around 1857 and served in the Royal Navy before settling in Liverpool in 1880. He had a few fights in his adopted city before starting in 1888 an 18-month prison term for biting off part of a policeman's ear. Fresh out of gaol, or, as the *South Wales Echo* put it delicately, having 'been absent from public view' he was knocked out in three rounds by John O'Brien in Liverpool.

He once lost twice on the same night at the National Sporting Club to the same opponent, losing on a disqualification and then, after his supporters put up the money for an immediate chance of revenge, being knocked out in quick time.

In the early 1890s he began operating a boxing booth and, echoes of Samuel in the lion's den, helped to capture an escaped lion at the Halifax Fair. He had a booth at Barry Docks in the middle of the decade and, again, in the Samuel manner, was involved in a fist fight in the street, his opponent being local boxer Jack Williams, who had enraged him by ignoring a public challenge.

Scott took his booth the length and breadth of Wales and when based at Pontypool supplemented his earnings by selling firewood and giving self-defence lessons.

Enoch Morrison was born at Atcham, Shropshire, in 1862 and moved to South Wales in the early 1880s. His career in the ring lasted a dozen years, eventually he combined being the manager of a workmen's club in Barry and the operator of a small boxing booth. He died at Barry in 1896 aged 33.

Other booth operators included John Matchett (Wrexham), John Stokes (Barry), James Tolley (Tonypandy), Samuel Roper (Wrexham), Davies (Caerphilly), Charlie North (Chepstow), James Day, William Carder (Aberdare), Martin Fury, Lloyd Davies (Swansea), Harris (Flint), Joe & Frank Gess, Smith, Hughes, Harry Cullis, Hurst, Lloyd, and Danter. The Cardiff-based Taylor's Boxing Emporium travelled throughout Wales and the rest of the United Kingdom for well over one hundred years from the middle of the 19th century.

Among the active fighters/showmen were Dunbar (Newport), Lloyd Roberts (Pontypridd), and Patsy Perkins, who operated booths at Aberdare and at Neath.

Perkins' first booth job was at the age of twelve when he joined showman Jack Steward at Newport for 5s. a week plus board, rising to 10s. at the age of 18. He stayed 12 years with Steward, who used to offer £1 a round to anyone of Perkins' weight who fancied his chances. The £1 was said never to have been claimed.

There followed a 12-month spell with Alf Ball's booth where Perkins would be backed against all comers for £5 over six or ten rounds. Again, it was claimed the money never needed to be handed over.

He next joined Harry Hughes' booth at Canning Town, and when that partnership ended Perkins returned to Wales in 1892 to begin another stage in his ring career. In between fights and running his booth, Perkins acted as trainer, second, and as master of ceremonies on fight nights.

Perkins later returned to the booths and for years he fought for several weeks every winter at London's Royal Agricultural Hall. He was promoting fights in Yorkshire when the First World War broke out, and, concealing his age, he was 53, he enlisted in the Army Service Corps, spending two years in Salonika. His last fight was against Sergeant Saunders, of the Royal Engineers whom he knocked out in ten rounds.

***

THE life of a booth owner had its difficulties. James Day, summoned in 1891 for neglecting to maintain his wife, said a broken arm left him unable to follow his occupation, while had also had to sell his show to maintain himself during the winter. The travelling involved led to complications in Samuel's day job as a pub landlord. His application in 1890 for a renewal of the licence for the *King's Arms*, Swansea, was held up after police claimed the pub was not properly conducted owing to the landlord's frequent absence from home with his booth.

***

SAMUEL cut down on his travels later in the century, when, buoyed by the legal uncertainty surrounding the sport, booth owners increasingly promoted matches between independent fighters in permanent and semi-permanent structures, popularly referred to as saloons. Admission prices for these shows were shillings rather than pence.

Samuel's establishment in Alexandra Road in 1895 was referred to as Mrs. Samuel's saloon, probably because of her husband's bankruptcy, in 1891 caused, he said, by depression in the licensing trade and very heavy legal expenses. One of those costly financial setbacks came when he lost a county court case concerning payment for a consignment of cocoanuts for one of his booths. An employee said the nuts were all bad and some people threw them back at him.[26]

In 1895, Mrs. Samuel was forced to demolish the premises and rebuild and 'the new and spacious boxing saloon was well filled, the reserve seats containing not a few of the gentlemen of Swansea'.[27] The next month, Perkins opened his establishment, the Old Gloucester School of Arms, in the Strand, Swansea, the local paper reporting supportively

> his shows deserve patronage, for Patsy has been at great expenses in fitting up seats, etc. In the centre is a 16-ft. ring and from each end seats are placed tier above tier, so that all who pay for a seat may be certain of a good view of the contests.[28]

Samuel and Perkins featured as 'friendly rivals' in Jack Jones' novel of turn-of-the-century Merthyr, a rivalry restricted to jibes about each other's booth in the town. But with competing saloons in the centre of Swansea their real-life relationship was far from amiable, instead it turned violent.

Just after Perkins had opened for business, they had a brawl in Swansea High Street after it was suspected that Samuel had bribed a boxer not to appear at Perkins's venue. The pair ignored a police officer nearby and fought 'for all they were worth' and, after followers of both 'gathered in a menacing way', it needed two more officers to prevent a riot and bundle them into the Goat-street Police-station, 'a huge crowd following them and blocking up Goat-street for some time'.[29]

Perkins' venture lasted only a few months, despite its being the 'scene or many a stiff encounter', before Samuel's wife, Elizabeth, took over the running. And she nearly had an even shorter occupancy, because a fire broke out on one fight night that threatened to turn into 'one of the most terrible catastrophes ever known in Swansea.'[30]

The saloon formed part of an old building and was approached through another room which had been divided off to form a sort of corridor, which was hung with pictures of famous fights of the past and illuminated by oil lamps and Chinese lanterns. Between the entrance corridor and the saloon were hung a pair of curtains, and close by them was one of the Chinese lanterns.

Near the end of the fifth round between Hooligan, of Swansea, and Osborne, from the West of England, a continued murmur was heard from the doorway and 'a great tongue of flame flashed up to the roof'. The curtains in the doorway were blazing. Two police-constables managed to beat out the flames, and the crowd resumed their seats to watch the rest of the fight, which was considerably delayed owing to the volumes of smoke that had poured into the room.

***

BOOTHS experienced the same opposition as regular prize fighting. While other fairground attractions were seen as having the sole purpose of relieving simple people of their money by sharp practice, boxing booths were regarded as brutal, disreputable providers of puerile entertainment, 'degrading and demoralizing'.[31]

In the early decades of the century, the Llandaff Fair 'became the scene of such licence that it was a disgrace to the countryside. The boxing or fighting booths were notorious'.[32] Reporting that the booth at the Mold pleasure fair in 1871 attracted only 'an audience of six', a local newspaper said the days of such occasions were nearly over, 'and we say sooner the better'.[33]

Newspapers drew attention to the brutish appearance of booth personnel. The owners were 'gentlemen of refined feelings, whose bull necks, short prison-cropped hair, and muscular development form the theme of admiration among semi-intoxicated blackguards'.[34] Of one, it was reported that

> His face, on some luckless day, has run into collision with a harder substance, and his nose has sustained serious damage therefrom. It is dreadfully flattened and bruised, and its fair proportions are distorted for ever.[35]

A fighter was identified by the same physical features and, in addition, was thought to be stupid, 'a perfect specimen of the genus homo, possessing 'brawn without brain'.[36] The platform at a booth in Merthyr's Market Square comprised 'half a dozen of the most murderous looking countenances we ever saw'.[37] One writer commented on such a line-up: 'I should not much like to meet them in a lonely lane of a dark night, after receiving my month's salary'.[38]

Booth people were looked on as thieves, thugs and drunkards, which was a reputation difficult to dispel as some tried hard to live up to it. One report stated

> They are none of them afflicted with conscientious scruples none of them are above helping his neighbour to dispose of his superfluous property, and few of them know accurately the distinction between mine and thine.[39]

George Williams, employed in Harris's boxing booth, was in court at Flint for stealing a gold twenty dollar piece from a man who had just returned from the California gold diggings, Sidney Smith, a booth fighter on his way to Aberavon fair, knocked an old man unconscious outside a pub at Bridgend, Martin Fury, a tinker, was before Merthyr Police Court for giving a woman a 'terribly blackened eye', and two booth employees, were ordered out of the town of Brynmawr for fighting in the street.[40]

As well as employing minor criminals, booths were said to attract more of them, with pickpockets invariably operating where spectators would be engrossed in what was happening in the ring. The Presteigne May Fair was 'notorious' for the gangs of pickpockets and cardsharpers it attracted. Seven pickpockets arrested there in 1824 were transported for life, and as late as 1874, the town crier was sent round the town to warn people of the arrival of a noted gang.

Following Newport's Stow Fair in 1857, the line-up at the local court included a pickpocket, someone who stole a side of bacon from a stall, and 'an atrocious-looking Londoner' who was handed a 21-day sentence for gambling. He operated a fairground scam called 'pricking the garter' which

Fairground boxing booths

involved the dupe trying to secure the loop in a rolled-up belt. This was impossible to do as its location would change depending on which end of the belt the trickster pulled. A collier handed his coat and waistcoat to other spectators while he had a 'spar' in a boxing booth at Abertillery in 1901 and afterwards he discovered a sovereign had been stolen from his garments, just one of several instances of pocket picking at the fair.

***

FAIRS were considered more peaceful without boxing booths, which were said to incite disorder. Booths were absent from the annual two-day Llangyfelach Fair in 1879, and it was noted that 'the whole appearance of the gathering was more orderly than of yore'.

There was more than enough evidence to justify that feeling. After customers had been in the booth at the Llandaff Fair in 1860, they were said to have spent the evening 'practising upon each other', while a mass brawl between 'town roughs' and boxing booth employees occurred at the Ruthin March Fair in 1870, 'which ended in the infliction of serious wounds from 'boxes' and kicks to both parties. It took a few police officers, among them the chief constable, to sort it out.

Booth operator Scarrott said that crowds supporting fighting colliers would often 'turn up half drunk, and I've known them try and break into the caravans'. He reckoned that Ferndale was 'about the roughest place in the valleys in those days.' Recalling a 'riot' in his booth, he said

> It was only over a shilling which somebody put in the cup when we made a collection for an old mountain fighter and which somebody else took out, but before you could say Jack Robinson everybody was fighting through and through… Two mountain fighters started it…..One they called Shoni Engineer…and the other Dai Brawd.[41]

Another fracas occurred during a contest in Stokes' booth at Porth involving Sam (Butcher) Thomas (Ynyshir) in front of about 500 spectators. In the second round, with opponent Malloy (Wolverhampton) handing out stiff punishment, the crowd 'being evidently in favour of the Welshman', broke into the ring and the round ended in chaos. Malloy had the better of the third round, and, describing what followed, a local newspaper noted he 'had to fight his man and the crowd, who 'rushed over him and trampled upon the poor fellow. So ended a long-looked-for event, much to the disgust of every lover of fair-play'.[42]

Booth owners often caused trouble themselves by brawling with each other, as the main counter attraction in the fairground was often another such business.

Samuel was usually involved when rivalry between showmen turned violent. Charlie North took Samuel to Brynmawr police court in 1886 for threatening him after a previous charge of assault by Samuel had been dismissed. The court heard that the day after the Brynmawr Fair, Samuel, who had attacked North at the Neath Eisteddfod, put up his fists and told North he could kill him in a minute. The case was dismissed with North ordered to pay all costs, including Samuels's railway fare from Pembrokeshire. In 1900, Samuel and Scarrott had a fist fight on the Neath Fair Field. Scarrott, who had summoned Samuel for assault, told a court that Samuel had attacked him and when getting the worst of it, enlisted his wife, his son and an employee to help him. Samuel was bound over but boasted: 'He is 26 and I am 63 and I satisfied him in two rounds'.[43]

Neither were the wives of booth proprietors averse to a set-to. Rival owners were boxing at Caldicot in 1889 when one suggested they should continue 'without the gloves'; their wives, Milly Dunbar and Annie Roberts, decided to do just that and, as a result, ended up in court where they were bound over.[44]

Boxing booth proprietors often came to blows with the owners of dissimilar fairground attractions as well.

The families of North, who described himself as a 'teacher of the noble art of self-defence and champion sparrer of the kingdom', and of rival showman Studt, who operated fairground rides, were involved in an affray in the early hours at Chepstow in 1890, when tent poles, ends of rifles, sticks and stones, and anything handy were improvised as weapons.

Champion or not, North seems to have come off worst, with a cut on his head about two inches long, the middle finger of his left hand split, apparently with a knife, a black eye, bruises about his body generally, and a fractured rib.

Dunbar and an employee assaulted William Green in 1890 in a lane near Clarence place, Newport, where they both had booths, Green appearing in court 'with his face and head terribly battered'. William Carder assaulted William Danter, who operated a shooting gallery, at Aberdare fair in 1878, while Enoch Morrison and his wife Harriet, and Jane Danter and daughter Louisa brawled in 1894.

Proprietors even fought with spectators, Stokes' boxing emporium proving a particularly dangerous place to venture. In 1892, he had premises in the Barry's Holton-road, which attracted sailors from ships moored in Barry Docks. One night, Stokes knocked out a sailor who had challenged him, and afterwards another sailor tried to stab him. Two years later, a sailor, part of a crowd of roughs, known as the 'Liverpool gang', which was threatening other spectators in the booth, kicked a policeman in the groin and threatened to knife Stokes after being ordered to leave the booth.

When one of his fighters was beaten by a man from the crowd in 1895, Tolley, unhappy with the result, lashed out with an iron bar, knocking one man 'insensible' and striking several others.[45]

Booth owner Frank Gess knocked unconscious an amateur boxer who said he could not go ahead with a fight in the booth at Risca in 1909 because he had injured his hand. Gess was gaoled for three months four years later for causing grievous bodily harm to a man at St. Mary Hill Fair. Swansea fighter Lloyd Davies, known as Kid Davies, who had a boxing booth at St. Mary Hill Fait, on his way home threw a large stone which broke a man's jaw.[46]

Such attacks were not all one way, though. Samuel's wife, Elizabeth, was knocked unconscious by a punch on the ear from a collier at the Carmarthen fair in 1902. A disturbance took place outside their boxing booth, and Mrs. Samuel was called from her cinematograph show close by. Pictures outside the boxing booth had been destroyed by stone throwing and when speaking to a bystander about it, she was assaulted.

Samuel's employees even clashed with Salvation Army members who tried to convert the showmen and spectators.

In 1882, the Army's Pentre Old Siloh contingent marched into the site of the Treorchy Fair, stopped near the entrance to the field, and 'singing lively tunes to sacred music' proceeded with the service. The showmen approached and began to mimic the Army, when 'Suddenly a dozen fights took place between the rival throngs.' It needed the combined talents of Samuel and one of his workers to stop the brawl.

The sides met again four years later, in what was described as 'a highly amusing encounter' at Neyland, where Samuel had his show. The Army halted their march at Samuel's booth, and began a service with a song, followed by a prayer and then another song, during the singing of which Samuel made his way into their midst, turning a hurdy gurdy organ, thinking in this way to get rid of the intruding party. But he soon found he had made a mistake, for the Salvationists suited their tune to that of the organ.

> Samuel then summoned a fellow showman, who appeared flourishing a large rattle, and what with the singing, the noise of the rattle and organ, mingled with the cheers and laughter of the crowd, anything but an imposing religious ceremony went on. This lasted for fully twenty minutes, when the showman mounted a wooden box, and hat in hand, attempted to address the people. But the army captain continued to hold forth, and it was not until a collection had been made that the Army quitted the scene.[47]

Little wonder that local authorities frequently tried to discourage booths from visiting their area. The Samuel v Scarrott fracas prompted magistrates to urge that such shows, which 'sailed very near to the law' should be excluded from the Neath fair in future. On learning that a boxing booth was operating on the Market Grounds at Maesteg on Whit Monday, 1884, the local authority ordered it to be removed immediately, and residents combined with the police to have a booth dismantled at Bargoed in 1900.

It was not only on disorder charges that booth owners went before the court. Non-payment of tax sometimes brought them before the bench. Scarrott, operating at Pontypool at the time, was in court in 1925 for failing to pay entertainment tax. When challenged by customs officers, he could not produce the half tickets which he was obliged to retain from customers. He said they were knocked out of his wife's hand when the tent was rushed by eager spectators earlier that evening. The same scenario played out at his booth near Neath when he told the court that an unruly crowd rushed the booth, making it impossible for him to do anything with tickets. Stokes, who had a booth at Blackwood in 1832, also appeared in court for an identical offence, as did booth owner Albert Hall at Tredegar in 1935.

Opponents found that appealing direct to landowners rather than to the authorities was often more rewarding when trying to oust boxing booths. Residents at Ynysybwl in 1877 successfully petitioned the owner of the land on which a booth was pitched, religious leaders at Tonypandy seven years later thanked local hoteliers and land owners for not allowing 'these degrading exhibitions' on their land, and a Crumlin man refused to allow boxing booths on his land in 1897 because he believed them to be 'objectionable and detrimental to the morals of the inhabitants.

Money talked in certain places, however. Booths were permitted on fair days at Pontypool because the police made money from them, it was alleged in 1849. A reader of the *Monmouthshire Merlin* complained that the booths used to be considered by the police as 'abominations' and were speedily cleared from the fair field, but since the police began collecting tolls on market and fair days, boxing booths appeared to be looked on as 'sources of innocent recreation'.

Some Wrexham councillors thought that boxing booths at the town's Beast Market were 'a moral injury' to the community but as they brought a profit to the council, the authority decided in 1877 to keep them.

***

SALOONS were looked on as even more of a threat to the local community and faced stronger criticism than the traditional booths because, unlike the latter which made just fleeting visits to a neighbourhood, they were more or less permanent fixtures.

In 1895, religious and temperance campaigners demanded the closure of 'degrading boxing saloons which had recently sprung up in Cardiff and

Fairground boxing booths

Swansea. They urged local newspapers to ignore these shows which they claimed provoked brawls in the street and encouraged young men to lose money through betting which had "increased alarmingly'. Samuel, however, denied that gambling of any kind was allowed inside his booth and responded 'We don't keep people from church and chapel, but we do keep them from the public-houses'.

The following year, the death of Thomas Davies at Swansea prompted a further protest about the saloons of large towns; *London Kelt* stating 'their environment is always such as to repel anyone who has a moderate amount of self-respect or reverence for anything higher than a mere display of brute force'.

A fortnight later, Welsh Wesleyans and Alexandra-road neighbours complained at the police-court of the 'shocking nuisance' of noise coming from the venue. Samuel said the booth was always closed before eleven at night, was never open on Sundays nor when there was a service. If members would compensate him, he said he would find another site immediately.

***

SAMUEL claimed in 1895 that the sport was safer than rugby, adding: 'No one has ever been taken from our boxing salon to the hospital, but three Swansea footballers have been seriously injured this season'. However, his words, as well as his fairground patter, came back to haunt him when Thomas Davies died in Samuel's boxing saloon in Alexandra –road, Swansea. The fight was for seven three-minute rounds with 6oz gloves. In the second round, Davies received a blow on the jaw, which lifted him clean off his feet. He soon regained his feet and the fight was fought out to the end, but during the night he was taken ill and died.

This was one of several ring fatalities involving Welsh fight figures in boxing booths in the 1890s.

Benjamin Payne was knocked out by a punch on the jaw in a booth fight in 1894 at Torquay regatta with Tom Rooney, who had formerly spent some time in Cardiff. The following day Payne was knocked down in two other booth fights by different opponents. Payne had had a lot to drink before the fights. The inquest jury decided that death was from meningitis caused by the blows received but there was no evidence to show whose blows were responsible. However, the jury condemned a booth owner for allowing a drunken man to take part in the bouts.

In 1897, a prize fight in James Tolley's booth at the Pandy Field, Tonypandy, left Sam Mandry/Mainwaring dead. The 24-year-old haulier fought for 13 rounds under Queensberry Rules with four-ounce gloves against Ivor Thomas. Seeing Mandry was badly beaten the referee stopped the contest after eight rounds, but Mandry insisted on continuing. The pair contested four more rounds, leaving him bleeding from the nose and mouth, besides bearing marks of much violence upon various parts of the body. Tolley, who had been collecting money at the door, entered the booth during the 13th round and ordered the contest to be stopped. After the fight, the boxers drank together in a nearby pub, but Mandry, seen to have drunk more than six pints of beer, died at his lodgings hours later.

James Parsons died after boxing a professional in Perkins's booth on Southampton common on Easter Monday, 1898. He was knocked down several times, and when he arrived home complained of great pain in his head, and the next day was found dead.

William Rose died hours after a fight n 1900 at Felix Scott's booth at Westbury in Wiltshire. Rose accepted a challenge from Scott for a friendly

Fairground boxing booths

bout but in the second round fell and struck his head on the hard roadway in the town's Market Place. He died in the local hospital. The inquest jury returned a verdict of death by misadventure, adding a rider that the Market Place was not a proper site for the erection of boxing saloons, which ought to be placed where the ground was softer.

In 1951 at the Aberystwyth November Fair, 22-year-old David John Redmond, collapsed following blows to the face and later died in hospital. Booth owner Taylor told the inquest that Redmond, from Skegness, had previously knocked out his opponent in the first round. He then volunteered "to make up the show" by boxing an exhibition bout. It was in this that he was knocked out. In returning their misadventure verdict. the foreman of the jury said that no blame could be attributed to the boxing booth establishment.

***

WELSH pair John O'Brien and David St. John were involved in a booth/saloon enterprise in London in 1894. They were engaged for seven nights at the Eden Palace of Varieties, London, the proprietor offering a purse each evening to any man who could stay four rounds with either.

The two Welshmen did not make the best of starts however, O'Brien was absent from the first night after missing his train and then claiming to have had an accident and been confined to bed, and an unfit St. John tiring after two rounds and taken the distance by a much shorter and lighter opponent. St. John atoned the next night, by knocking his opponent 'senseless' in the second round.

***

BOXING booths thrived in the first half of the twentieth century, Tom Taylor, Scarrott, Scott and Wales-based Alf Harry among others, operating regularly before the First World War. Scott's was one of five such booths at the Birmingham Fair in 1901.

This continuing popularity was despite unrelenting strong opposition. In 1907 after complaints by local Methodists, Merthyr council ordered a booth in the centre of the town, described as a 'public nuisance', to be removed. Cardiff council approved a plan to convert the skating rink in Westgate Street into a temporary boxing booth for the proposed Driscoll v Welsh fight in 1910 despite a prominent member saying he was sorry to see the skating rink 'degraded into a boxing booth'. Also that year, a Llandovery councillor wanted to ban any boxing booth from the district, while church leaders at Tredegar were unhappy about booths, not so much *per se* but because of the large number of fights that had taken place *after* contests in the booths. In 1914, a Blackwood vicar complained of the harm which the booths were doing to young people by allowing youths in at half price, and East Glamorgan Baptists claimed that one booth did more harm to the young people than twenty public houses.

At the turn of the century Scott switched operations to the West of England, the Midlands, the north of England and Scotland before settling his establishment at Wigan.

Taylor had a booth on the fairground at Abertillery in 1904 and another at Brynmawr the following year when he advertised a ten-round contest for £20, £5 a-side and a purse of £10, the winner to get 75% pf the purse and the loser 25%. Jim Bayton (Brynmawr) beat Alf Rodway in the fourth of a ten-round contest in Scarrott's booth at Brynmawr in 1904. And a month later, in Scarrott's booth at the Pontypool fair, George Roach, of Rumney, fought George Dixon, of America, for a purse of gold, Roach getting the decision when Dixon refused to continue after the referee disallowed his appeal for a foul.

Scarrott pitched up at the Brecon May fair the following year, when there was also one at Newport, where Ebenezer Morgan fought James Evans for £10, Morgan taking the spoils.

Taylor and Scarrott had booths on the same weekend at Brynmawr in 1910, and local fighter Albert Bayton appeared for both operators. On the Friday night he conceded a stone in weight to Sam Johnson in Taylor's booth and won with a third-round knockout. The next night, for Scarrott, Bayton was taken the full ten rounds by Joe Atwood (Birmingham). On the Monday night Bayton met Battling Harris (Cardiff), in whose booth was not reported, and undertook to force another stoppage but his busy schedule told and he lost the ten-rounder on points.

Over the next few years booths were present at Nelson's annual fair, on a campsite at Porthcawl and at Swansea, but were 'notable absentees' from Brecon's pleasure fair in 1913.

During World War 1 a suggested solution to the manpower shortage caused by the loss of agricultural labourers to the military was to have attractions such as a cinema and a boxing booth on every sizeable farm.

An estimated one hundred booths operated during the inter-war period.

Scarrott's booth was in full flow in the 1920s throughout Glamorgan and Monmouthshire. Martin Sampson (Penyrheol) knocked Arthur Strong (Llanbradach) down four times on his way to a ten round points victory at Caerphilly in 1923, while in a six round contest Bert Hunt outpointed Arthur Knott. At Treharris the following year, Billy Ward (Pentrebach) and Teddy Boyd (Trealaw) drew over 15-two minute rounds, and Johnny Martin (Clydach Vale) outpointed Dick Terratt (Merthyr Vale) over six rounds. At

Merthyr that year, Billy Atkins (Llwynypia) retired in the 13th round of a 15-three-minute round fight against Jack Jones (Merthyr), and Terratt outpointed Young Haines (Merthyr) over six rounds.

In 1926 Johnny Edmunds (Treharris) beat Charlie Chew (Aberdare) over ten rounds, and Young Smacker (Treharris) outpointed Young Cook (Abercynon) over six rounds in Scarrott's establishment at Quaker's Yard.

The booth boom spawned *The Gypsy Vagabond*, a musical comedy revue, which played at the Cardiff Empire theatre in 1930 and included some adventures in a booth. Booths also formed the background for thirties film dramas, among them *Blue Smoke*, which featured a gipsy boxer in the fairground booths, and *Excuse My Glove*, co-starring champion boxer Len Harvey.

Booths operated at Bargoed in 1931 as well as the following year, while in 1935 in the Royal Oak booth at Abertillery, Johnny Griffiths (Abergavenny) stopped Pancho Ford (Pengam) in the eighth of a ten rounder, and Cliff Atkey (Abergavenny) stopped Sol Cook (Pengam) in the fourth round.

Among the fighters travelling with Taylor's booth, from the late 1040s was a farmhand from Ponthirwaun, between Cardigan and Newcastle Emlyn, the late Iorwerth 'Curly' Davies, father of Paul Davies, Welsh Conservative MS for Preseli Pembrokeshire.

***

OVER several years the British Boxing Board of Control varied and finally hardened their attitude towards booths. In 1947 the Board stated that most were not being run on the lines of challenges from men on the platform to the audience (but were between professional boxers) and they therefore placed them out of bounds to all licensed members of the BBB of C.

Fairground boxing booths

This was regarded as a major blow for, while there were many unlicensed boxers available, it was stressed that the booths would lose much of their glamour through the absence of champions taking on all-comers.

The ban was eased just three months later and would not now apply to booths operated by members of the Showmen's Guild, subject to conditions including that boxers appearing in booths had to work under their professional names as registered with the Board and no one under 16 years of age to be allowed to take part in a boxing beoth contest.

Later that year, the BBB of C placed out of bounds to members, boxing booths and any place where there was professional boxing for which the promoter has not been granted the Board's promoter's licence.

This decision altering the recent ruling was taken because, said the Board, there had been "flagrant breaches" of the conditions then imposed. In 1950 the Boxing Board agreed to allow licensed boxers to take part in booths subject to conditions imposed by the Board.

The Welsh Area Council consistently opposed allowing licensed boxers to take part in fair-ground booths, and strenuously opposed the granting of permission two years previously. Mr. W. J. G. Evans, chairman of the Welsh Council, said 'We believe that boxing booths are not the right places for boxers in our control'.

Under these conditions, Ron Taylor continued to operate at Aberystwyth, Llanbradach, Dowlais, Hereford, Pembridge, Horsham Park, Leicester, and Newcastle,

Recalling the boom years, Taylor lamented in 1971 'Before the war there were about 100 travelling boxing booths. Now, only five are left'. Four years later, there were just two travelling booths operating.

Taylor said in 1975 he had needed to add wrestling to his shows to cater for the female customers who had enjoyed watching it on television, but even with the wrestling it was not enough for a livelihood.[48] His current visit to Newcastle was only the boxing booth's second appearance of the year; the smaller fairs no longer wanted it.

He also had had to diversify into other ventures, the Haunted House, helter-skelter, and a striptease booth. 'It's nearly finished, you know', he conceded. 'It won't last much longer. Four generations of Taylors have run a boxing booth, but I'll be the last'.

***

Cardiff boxing manager Mac Williams tried to revive the 'virtually extinct' booths in the 1970s and had his licence suspended for his trouble.

As part of his campaign, Williams, who believed that the booths 'not only created an interest in professional boxing from the fans' perspective; it was also a good way of uncovering hidden talent, an enjoyable carnival for the audience', arranged a fight in 1977 for one of his boxers, Tony Burnett, from Caerphilly.

The fight took place in the last travelling booth in the country, operated by Cardiff-born Taylor, and was at the behest of a television company. it pitted Burnett against veteran former professional Johnny Williamson, the self-proclaimed 'King of the Booths'.

The tv producers wanted Burnett to turn up at the last boxing booth, accept the challenge and then give 'the boastful' Williamson a boxing lesson.[49] Which was what happened, but booth owner Taylor decided it was a draw, leaving Burnett disgruntled. As one scribe put it, however

> For six rounds Burnett 'knocked six different kinds of tar out of Williamson and had him on the floor twice. But Burnett forgot one thing – he was in show business not boxing and had to settle for a

draw.....While Burnett went off into the night shaking his head at the robbery, Iron Man Williamson was *en route* to hospital with two broken ribs, a punctured lung and damaged kidneys. Some draw.[50]

In 1978 the BBB of C decided that licensed professional boxers would no longer be allowed to appear in fairground boxing booths, thus ending a long-standing relationship between the official side of the sport and the booths. Eight years later the feeling that the days of the old-style booths were finally numbered was evident when Taylor, who had taken his business to Newcastle again, reported sadly

> Things aren't looking good. On Sunday night for the first time ever, I wasn't able to put on a show. I had a lovely crowd gathered to see it as well. I've been badly let down by the local boys who usually work for me. Times are meant to be hard, but not a single boxer or wrestler turned up.[51]

Taylor, the sixth generation of his family to run the booth, somehow carried on for another 16 years, though. only giving up running the attraction at fairgrounds across the country in 2002 at the age of 91.

---

[1] South Wales Echo, 17 October 1896.
[2] Wilde, Jimmy, Fighting was my business (London, Robson Books, 1990, originally publd. 1938). p. 52.
[3] Tommy Farr, Thus Farr (London, Optomen Press, 1989), p.4.
[4] Farr, Thus Farr p.18.
[5] Gower Journal of the Gower Society, Vol. 11 Ffair Llangyfelach, Jan. 1958.
[6] Era, 1 July 1905.
[7] Era, 21, 28 May 1898
[8] Cardigan Observer, 14 November 1896
[9] Isle of Wight Observer, 9 March 1867.

[10] Cheshire Observer, 7 May 1864. County Observer, 29 May 1869. Radnorshire Society transactions   - Vol. 17 1947.
[11] Era, 13 May 1900.
[12] Cardiff Times, 28 August 1897
[13] County Observer, 29 May 1869
[14] Cambrian, 4 March 1887.
[15] Cardiff Times, 16 June 1860. Notts Guardian, 14 November 1862. Cambrian, 9 March 1883.
[16] Abergavenny Chronicle, 4 May 1888.
[17] Monmouthshire Merlin, 13 June 1857
[18] Western Mail, 5 April 1927.
[19] Cardiff Times, 4 July 1885
[20] South Wales Echo and Express, 23 March 1936.
[21] Cambrian, 9 March 1883. Haverfordwest and Milford Haven Tel., 4 October 1899.
[22] Cardiff Times, 14 August 1888.
[23] South Wales Daily News, 5 February 1887.
[24] Wilde, Fighting was my business, p. 46.
[25] Wilde, Fighting was my business, p. 52.
[26] Cambrian, 23 December 1887.
[27] South Wales Daily Post, 30 March 1895.
[28] South Wales Daily Post; Western Mail, 2 April 1895.
[29] Western Mail, 18 May 1895.
[30] South Wales Daily Post, 14 December 1895.
[31] Glamorgan Free Press. 5 February 1898. Wrexham Advertiser, 18 April 1884. Monmouthshire Merlin, 9 May 1851. Cambrian, 7 March 1879.
[32] Archaeologia Cambrensis, Journal of the Cambrian Archaeological Association 6th series, Vol. 2, 1 January 1902
[33] Wrexham Advertiser, 25 March 1871
[34] Merthyr Telegraph, 4 August 1862.
[35] Monmouthshire Merlin, 13 June 1857. Flintshire Observer, 2 April 1869
[36] Merthyr Telegraph, 23 July 1870. Sheffield and Rotherham Independent, 7 June 1865. Brecon County Times, 18 May 1867
[37] Merthyr Telegraph, 4 August 1862. Cardiff Times, 16 June 1860.
[38] Brecon County Times, 18 May 1867. Monmouthshire Merlin, 13 June 1857.
[39] Monmouthshire Merlin, 13 June 1857.
[40] South Wales Daily News, 31 August 1899. Cheshire Ob. 9 April; Flintshire Observer, 14 April 1870. Merthyr Telegraph, 12 March 1875. Merthyr Times, 20 June 1895.
[41] South Wales Echo and Express, 23 March 1936
[42] South Wales Daily News, 3 April 1894
[43] South Wales Daily Post, 15 September 1900
[44] South Wales Echo, 19 June 1889.
[45] Montgomery County Times, 11 May 1895.
[46] Glamorgan Gazette, 1 September 1905.
[47] Haverfordwest and Milford Haven Telegraph, 8 September 1886.
[48] Newcastle Journal, 26 June 1975.
[49] Stephen Malcolm Williams, Big Mac and His Boys, in Wales and its Boxers: The Fighting Tradition, Peter Stead and Gareth Williams (eds.) (Cardiff, University of Wales Press, 2008).
[50] Aberdeen Evening Express, 22 October 1977.
[51] Newcastle Journal, 24June, 1986.

11

Mountain fighters

Thomas Richards, a Welsh trade union leader and MP, once suggested (ironically at a Peace Conference in Cardiff) that two rival speakers should settle their differences by taking part in 'the good old-fashioned Welsh mountain fight in the early morning with a few secret supporters'.[1]

A former miner himself, Richards was referring to the spectacle of colliers battling on a mountain top, a practice which became popular in the second half of the nineteenth century when the South Wales valleys had been opened up to the coal industry.

Mountain fighters were men who, 'Toughened by their occupations in iron and coal they became an almost uniquely Welsh breed: mountain fighters, intimidating and frightening'.[2]

The tops of the mountains which divided the narrow South Wales valleys provided ideal stages on which these men could perform as they were the only sites where such an illegal activity could proceed unhindered by the authorities. They were isolated and gave those concerned a good chance of evading police, who, climbing the steep slopes, would usually be spotted by lookouts, allowing fight people plenty of time to slip away.

Mountain fights increased in number from the 1860s, with more than half taking place in the 1890s, nearly all in the mining areas of Glamorgan and Monmouthshire in south east Wales. A newspaper claimed that they were only 'occasionally' carried on in secluded spots on the hills of the Rhondda, but a magistrate said that prize fighting was on the increase in the district.

Mountain fights were also reported to have 'come off' in the north of the country, above the road leading from Chirk to Llangollen, and as far to the west as Pembrey in Carmarthenshire.

In the latter place three brothers were beaten by one man on one night in 1898. The ring was illuminated by large colliers' lanterns as the men, stripped to the waist, got down to business. One man was soon forced to quit because of a broken leg, his brother retired with a badly cut face and another brother lasted only three rounds before retiring.

Jimmy Wilde and Tommy Farr were just two who honed their skills in such an environment. Recalling his early days at the beginning of the century, Wilde wrote in his autobiography 'Every district, too, boasted its mountain fighters, grand old fellows who fought, bare-fisted and naked to the waist, to a standstill. Gory sights many of them were, caked with blood and sweat on face and body'.

Few reliable descriptions of mountain fights have so far been available. Most information derives from hearsay and through fiction, mainly from novels featuring late nineteenth century coalminers by writers including Jack Jones and Richard Llewellyn.[3] Those fictional accounts tie in with a newspaper report of a mountain fight in 1889 in a Welsh hot-spot shortly after midnight the day before a general holiday in the Rhondda coalfield.[4] Thousands of men had climbed a hill near Treforest to watch Illtud Evans face fellow Pontypridd man Fred Bevan. Most viewed from a slope and a 'deep fringe of onlookers, principally raw youths', surrounded the ring, which was formed by ropes supported at the four corners by wooden posts, and the ground inside 'strewn thickly with sawdust'.

After setting the scene, the report described the preliminaries:

the two athletes emerged from a neighbouring building, surrounded by their trainers and principal backers. As they advanced towards the ring – each wearing a cap and an Ulster – they were loudly cheered. Two chairs were placed in the enclosure for the use of the combatants. Each went to the corner of the ring with his backer. Then a man stepped into the middle of the ring and opened a bag, from which he produced the gloves.

Then the fight atmosphere:

A wild shout now rose from the spectators. It was remarkable to witness the faces of the eager throng at this moment. Each face in the crowd was deadly pale and every eye seemed ready to spring from its socket. It was evident that the spirit of 'war' was fully roused among the spectators, and Welsh and English expletives were heard in every direction, so much so that a cry was heard to the effect that if the crowd 'kept a noise like that the cry of 'Time' could not be heard......Each man among the spectators, while the blows were being struck, seemed to move his shoulders and arms in a fighting attitude....

It was a short fight:

After exchanging several terrible blows to the head, Illtud dealt Bevan an awful blow, which sent him in a heap into his corner, where he fainted, Illtud standing over him, and the terribly excited crowd calling out the while, 'Stand back, Illtud!' (Saf yn ol, Illtud!'). Illtud was taken back to his corner, and, owing to an intimation from Bevan's seconds, Illtud's principal backer stepped into the middle of the ring, and, with the air of the master of the ceremonies, bowed to the crowd as an intimation that Illtud had been victorious.

The report is not entirely typical, however. Most mountain fights operated according to the London Prize Ring Rules, but, some, like this example, were a mixture of those constraints (a round ended when a fighter went down) and Queensberry Rules (with gloves). Five-ounce gloves were used on this occasion, and the reporter echoed the popular sentiment that they 'were little better than a make-believe that the naked fists were not used in the encounter'.

Another hybrid fight, 'with the raw 'uns', comprising two-minute rounds, with one-minute interval, to a finish, took place in 1900 on the mountain near Cwmavon between Will Lane, 'a well-known Welsh pugilist', aged 42, and Dai Rees, 21, popularly known as 'Buller' Rees, a prominent Aberavon rugby player.

Also, mountain fights tended to last considerably longer than the ten minutes of the Evans v Bevan set-to. The Lane v Rees encounter comprised 27 rounds over one hour and twenty minutes, while Edwards fought Stevens on Rhymney Hill above Tredegar in 1860 for 127 rounds. In 1862, on the Aberaman mountain, Harris and Pendry fought 97 rounds in two hours and forty minutes, in 1886 on the Cymmer, colliers Edmund Powell and Tudor Foster 'battered' each other to a standstill for two hours, and the following year, on the mountain between Tredegar and Ebbw Vale, Joseph Cecil and Richard Lloyd fought for two hours. David Thomas, alias 'Spanker', of Nantyglo, and Joseph Huish (Brynmawr) fought 54 rounds over two hours on Llangynidir mountain in 1893 before Huish was forced to retire with cramp in his legs.

However, although fights could continue for hours over tens of rounds, those under London Prize Ring Rules, where a round was over when one man went down, might contain considerably fewer minutes of actual fighting.

If bouts lasted only minutes, notwithstanding the Evans v Bevan encounter, this was usually because they had been halted by the police. In 1866 two men fought five rounds on Dowlais mountain before police were spied 'looming in the distance', whereupon all concerned 'skedaddled', and the following year James Macdonald and Cornelius Crowley could manage only three rounds on the Twynygwaun mountain before law officers arrived.

A prize fight on Blorenge mountain, Abergavenny, in 1898 was interrupted by a pack of fox hounds, which 'were clearing the Blorenge when Reynard made a run along the breast of the of the mountain, and to the surprise of the fighters, ran into their midst, followed by the huntsmen'.[5] Police, in the area to watch the hounds, followed them in and made arrests.

As uncertainty persisted over the legal position of glove fighting, even pure Queensberry Rules fights took place on mountains. Colliers James Thomas and William Howells, charged with taking part in a prize fight on Llanwonno mountain in 1896, asserted innocence in court, saying they had fought under the Queensberry Rules over eight rounds with 5oz. gloves, but they were found guilty because the magistrate reiterated that using gloves did not make their actions legal.

Fights could draw substantial crowds. At least two thousand spectators were reported to be on Rhymney Hill above Tredegar in 1860 when Edwards fought Stevens, and 'at least 1,500 watched a Sunday morning fight on Llanwonno mountain between W. D. Rees, of Treherbert, and Morgan Davies, of Port Talbot. several hundred were estimated when John Cahill, fought on Aberdare mountain 'covered in blood', when Seth Smith and William Thomas fought on the Aberdare Mountain, and in 1898, and when Alfred Rodway, of Ebbw Vale, and David Thomas, alias 'Spanker', from Brynmawr, punched away on the Blorenge mountain.

They could be savage affairs, even allowing for the hyperbole common in contemporary newspaper reports. Accounts regularly described men 'covered in blood, with black eyes, bruised and swollen faces, eyes blood shot and nearly closed. Fighters ended up with broken arms or severe cuts on the head, while Twm Clump's eyes were badly damaged and one side of his face was 'hammered into a jelly' after 33 rounds on the top of Lledrddu Mountain in 1896.

In Jones' *Black Parade*, the seconds 'were stopping up the horrible gashes over their man's eyes with handfuls of shag tobacco before sending him up for some more of the terrible punishment'. Their remedy was on the basis that nicotine in the tobacco caused narrowing of the blood vessels, meaning less blood flow and oxygen to the tissues.

The rules, such as they were, were not always adhered to rigidly, least of all by ring officials. In the fifth round of a battle on Llanwonno Mountain in 1896, between Williams and Roberts, both of Mountain Ash, Williams rushed in, and just as he was trying to get out of the way Roberts raised his right knee which came in contact with Williams's stomach, and they fell with Williams underneath. Williams failed to respond to the call of time, and the referee awarded the fight to Roberts.

In a fight on Maindy Mountain in 1894 between Rhondda pugilists Jack Northey and Joe Mitchell it was reported that Northey 'would have been ordered out of the ring in any properly-managed encounter for foul play', instead of a draw being decided after 64 rounds over one and a half hours.

***

EVEN more so under such uncontrolled circumstances, deaths were not uncommon, and, like prize fights in general, more fatalities were likely to have gone unreported or not attributed to prize fighting. After ten rounds on Cefncilsanws mountain above Merthyr in 1858, David Thomas

> became almost helpless, his eyes had a vacant stare, consciousness left him, yet, goaded by a brutal mob, he fought for four more rounds, though to all appearance he was in a dying state. He was then struck so violently that he fell down, never to rise again.[6]

Mountain fighters

Spectators used a makeshift stretcher to carry Thomas to his home from which a few hours earlier he had emerged 'in the full vigour of health, a lifeless corpse, the victim of a brutal passion'.

David Richards died on the mountain called the Blanau, between Chirk and Llangollen in 1861 after more than forty rounds spread over an hour against Thomas Pugh. Pugh was severely punished about the face, arms, and body, but he struck Richards in the face and both fell. Richards tried to rise but fell back to the ground and he was carried to a nearby house where he died shortly after. Rowland Thomas battled 75 rounds over two and a half hours against Thomas Beynon at Giant's Cave before dying on the mountain between Merthyr and Aberdare in 1868. Beynon was so badly injured that he had to be carried into the police station.

Isaac Latcham's death came after twenty rounds in three quarters of an hour on the mountain near Pentwyn at Abertillery in 1873. John James, 'bleeding fearfully from the nose and mouth', was so severely punished after fighting for seventy five minutes on the mountain side near Clifton-row, between Porth and Hafod in the Rhondda Valley in 1886 that he had to be carried home in a chair and died soon after. John Hopkins lay motionless after a fight with Cornelius Collins on Llanwonno mountain in 1890 and was picked up and put into a passing milk cart and taken to a nearby barn where he died.

Edward Augustus Collard died on Penrhys mountain midway between Ferndale and Pentre after fighting thirty rounds in more than one hour in 1897. After twenty rounds, Collard weakened, but, with a lack of compassion, common among ringsiders and commented on by newspapers,

'His backers urged him on, but each time he was 'knocked out' he had to be picked up by his supporters'.[7]

After receiving the 'terrible blow' which ended the fight, Collard was carried to a hillside cottage, the men who carried him there leaving and saying they were going to fetch a doctor. But a quarter of an hour later he died.

***

SOMEONE introduced as a 'mountain fighter' would be granted immediate respect and might be feared, with the brand so strong that men would often claim such a status to intimidate others. During a brawl in Newport's Market Street in 1908, Thomas Leader, of Crumlin, was heard to boast: 'I am a mountain fighter'. The local newspaper commented: 'Whether this was an attempt to overawe the other man with his claim of prowess was not stated'.

But, while many have heard of mountain fighters, they remain semi-mythical figures. Williams visualises them 'with their scarred faces, broken teeth and misshapen noses', and Llewellyn provides a fuller description, Dai Bando's features betraying his calling, with 'one tooth to the side of his mouth' and 'his face was covered with little punch cuts, all dyed blue with coal dust, and his eyes were almost closed by skin which had been cut and healed time and time again'.[8]

Bando cut an imposing figure. According to main character Huw,

> His skin was pinkish with cold, and with muscle to make you doubt your sight. His arm muscles were bigger than my thigh, and over the top of his trews, six squares, each as big as my two fists together, stood out so that you could have rattled a stick over them. His shoulders had great fat fingers of muscle leading down to the tops of his arms like opening a fan, and behind his shoulders, bunches of muscle lay about the blades, with two great cords going down on each side of his backbone.[9]

However, it is not known if he developed that physique by following the diet of Williams' 'fearsome individuals'.

Such uncompromisingly rugged specimens supplemented their industrial-strength durability with raw meat and eggs, reckoned to give them ferocity and stamina, draughts of sour buttermilk (llaeth enwyn) and, during fights, swigs of something stronger.[10]

Mountain fighters appear to have started young, like the two boys in their mid-teens, Ernest Pugh, and Francis Jones, who fought 'with all the formalities of the ring' on the mountainside near Pontypridd in 1890, some then moving on to the booths and thence to the prize ring.

There are no reports available of the reputed mountain fights of John Jones, better known as 'Shoni Engineer', but the Treorchy man could hold his own in the regular ring with the raw 'uns as well as wearing gloves. He beat Peter Burns, of Cardiff, in 1887 in a bare-knuckle fight over one hour and three quarters and 48 rounds. With the gloves and weighing 10 stone 13 lbs, he overcame the one stone heavier Morris Tobin, 31, in seven rounds at the Fair Field, Treorchy, in 1885, knocking down the coal trimmer from Cardiff three times in the sixth round and once in the seventh.

Likewise, Sam Thomas appeared in recorded fights with gloves in the booths, in permanent local venues and in the National Sporting Club, London. He knocked out David Davies (Mardy) at Merthyr after breaking a wrist halfway through a fight, and also halted at Merthyr heavyweight Tom James (Aberaman), who at 6ft and over 13 stones, towered 4 ½ ins over him and outweighed him by three stones.

Thomas' younger brother, Ivor, refereed a prize fight on a mountain, but his own recorded battles were on lower ground, where, just as tough and an equally hard puncher as Sam, in 1896 he knocked out an opponent who was 20 lbs heavier.

Redmond Coleman, who had one mountain fight that was reported, on the Brecon road near Merthyr, could certainly do himself justice in more organised fights, as we have seen.

***

MOUNTAIN fights were reported regularly in the first decade of the twentieth century.

The year 1902 was a particularly busy time. James Harris (Ton) beat Edward Davies, alias Ned Diendaid, (Ton) for £5 a-side after several rounds 'in a secluded spot' on Maindy Mountain. Everybody had dispersed by the time the police arrived, but both men were arrested at their homes shortly after, Davies' face and eyes being 'greatly discoloured' and Harris' right hand 'swollen to such an extent that he could hardly close it'.

Police who found William Watkins and Joseph Huish, both of Brynmawr, fighting on the mountain near Nantyglo in front of a 200-strong crowd at five o'clock in the morning, asked Abertillery magistrates to help them in stopping such practices, claiming 'They had enough to do in their own division without having interlopers from Breconshire'. Police discovered W. Norris and John Jones at Clydach Vale on a Sunday morning, stripped to the waist and sitting on the knees of their seconds who were sponging them. Law officers also intervened on Penrhys mountain where a crowd had gathered before any blows had been struck by William Jones or William John Davies, of Tylorstown, and they interrupted a prize fight for £1 a-side between William Meredith and Joseph Watkins on the mountain near Blaina.

Mountain fighters

Late in 1903 a fight on the mountain between Glyncorrwg and Resolven was reported to have been with 'the raw 'uns' under Queensberry Rules involving three-minute rounds and a minute interval between.[11] Watching Dai Jenkins (Maesteg) fight Tom Culley, a Wales-based Londoner, for £25 a-side were 'A number of sports who were fortunate enough to be invited' and were treated to a 'severe struggle' with Culley triumphant after 'twelve hard rounds'. Herbert King and Oliver Robinson, of Ferndale, contested a few rounds for £2 a-side on Ferndale mountain before police arrived. All concerned scattered but fighters and officials were later arrested. Also in 1903 Mark Scott, 19, was arrested at the scene on the mountain between Pontypridd and Ynysybwl and fellow collier Albert Thomas, also from Coedpenmaen, was collared later in the day. They had fought for 'a full of beer'.

Collier David Jones and haulier Charles Silver had gone twenty rounds with bare knuckles before police arrived on Penrhys mountain to halt their £1 a=side Sunday morning contest in 1904.[12] Other Sunday scrappers were Gelli colliers Samuel Fear and Frank Maggs who fought over eight rounds for £1 a-side on Gelli mountain in 1903, and Nantyglo colliers Philip Evans and William Cornick, who met on Nantyglo mountain the following year.

Police found Lewis John Evans, an Aberbargoed collier, stripped to the waist and fighting on the mountain near New Tredegar in 1909, and a few months later, colliers Joseph Tregening and Ernest Lewis, of Resolven, fought 25 rounds with bare fists on a mountain near Resolven.[13]

Greater secrecy prevailed after the opening decade of the twentieth century, but there is no doubt, boosted by much anecdotal evidence, that mountain fights continued well after this time. One, in 1919, pitted William

283

Williams (Ystrad) against Victor Evans (Cwmparc) for £5 a-side in the neighbourhood on a Sunday.

***

MOUNTAIN fighters were hard men without a doubt, but were they an elite breed as folklore would have us believe, more fearsome than prize fighters who operated nearer sea level?

Scarrott admitted he and his booth boxers were afraid of these men.

> They used to come to the fairgrounds from the collieries with their gangs with them, most of 'em half drunk, and the very sight of them was enough to freeze the heart out of a bull terrier. Broken noses, black eyes, cauliflower ears, lumps knocked off 'em. If they heard that there was a well-known champion in a boxing booth at a particular fair they'd walk 50 miles to have a go at him.[14]

However, skill usually triumphed against these fearsome-looking battlers in fiction as well as in real-life.

Characters in Jones' *Black Parade* were confident of the superiority of bare-knuckle mountain fighters. In the lead-up to a booth fight, they were certain that the opponent was 'an easy mark for Harry, who was 'the unbeaten champion at his weight, and stones over his weight, of the five mining valleys'.[15]

But the fight was under Queensberry Rules, meaning gloves not bare fists, and it was soon clear that the opponent was a trained boxer. Without having a glove laid on him, he knocked Harry 'senseless' in the third round.

A spectator in *How Green Was My Valley* summed up a mountain fight as 'no science, no brains….a boxer would have put both in their graves'.[16] Jimmy Wilde agreed; although admiring the courage of those men, he remarked on their 'clumsy fighting' and how he 'could never picture himself being laid out as easily as many of the unfortunate combatants'.[17]

Mountain fighters

Shoni Engineer was well-beaten by John O'Brien when they fought nineteen rounds with bare knuckles at Marshfield, near Cardiff, in 1889. Shoni wanted to quit after six rounds but his backers would not allow him to, 'Shoni going down repeatedly before throwing up the sponge'.[18] Likewise, Sam Thomas was 'completely outclassed' in a glove fight with Bob Wiltshire three years later at the Ormonde Club, London, losing in five rounds.[19]

The fearsome reputations enjoyed by mountain fighters look to have been in a local context. For instance, Merthyr man Dai Vaughan was described as 'one of the great mountain fighters of his time and at the peak of his powers was considered to be the undisputed champion of the Merthyr Valley, but he made no impact on the wider stage.[20] Even more so, Pontypridd-born Frank Moody, a British and Empire middleweight boxing champion in the 1920s, recalled that his father 'was not a glove fighter and he never boxed in a ring, but as a mountain scrapper he had a reputation that caused him to be highly respected in the locality'.[21]

Mountain fighters were not generally prominent on the national scene, the most successful and the best-known fighters continuing to be based in the major coastal towns.

***

BUT should we be talking about 'mountain' fighters at all? Did they even fight on mountains? The short answer is 'No'.

There is no universally accepted standard definition for the height of a mountain or a hill, but in England and Wales any landform over 2,000 feet is considered a mountain and below 2,000 feet a hill. By this definition, Wales has 190 mountains. However, only three - Pen y Fan in Powys at 2907ft., Fan Foel in Carmarthenshire (2526), and Chwarel y Fan in Monmouthshire

(2228) are anywhere near the prize-fighting heartland of south Wales. Thus, the mountains referred to in most fight reports might be considered to be hills, the 'hills' being what the south Wales mining areas were called before they became known as the 'valleys'.

It might be more accurate, then, to call these battlers 'hill' fighters. But as the words 'mountain' and 'hill' were interchangeable in contemporary usage, often in the same sentence in newspaper reports, it is understandable if 'mountain' is the choice, particularly as 'mountain fighters' has the cachet, with its suggestion of wild, rugged masculinity, of epic brawling and drinking, not forgetting its link to the 'long-bearded mountaineers of Wales stereotype.

---

[1] Llais Lafur, 25 November 1916.
[2] Williams, 'A Brutal Passion', p. 13.
[3] Jones, Black Parade, pp. 52-60. Llewellyn, *How Green Was My Valley*, pp. 329-335.
[4] Western Mail, 5 November 1889
[5] Evening Express, 11 February 1898.
[6] Merthyr Telegraph, 25 September 1858
[7] Western Mail, 17 May 1897
[8] Williams, 'A Brutal Passion', p. 13. Llewellyn, How Green Was My Valley, p. 167.
[9] Llewellyn, How Green Was My Valley, p. 169
[10] Williams, 'A Brutal Passion', p. 13.
[11] Western Mail, 17 October 1902.
[12] South Wales Daily News, 19 December 1904.
[13] Evening Express, 6 August 1909. South Wales Daily News, 4 January 1910.
[14] South Wales Echo and Express, 23 March 1936.
[15] Jones, Black Parade, pp. 189-193.
[16] Llewellyn, *How Green Was My Valley*, p. 330.
[17] Wilde, Fighting was my business, p.18.
[18] Western Mail, 2 May 1889.
[19] South Wales Echo, 10 March 1892.
[20] Davies, Mountain Fighters, p. 169.
[21] Davies, Mountain Fighters, p. 167.

EPILOGUE

The Ring is dead?

Did the prize ring finally expire at the turn of the twentieth century? Some newspapers claimed that the glory days of bare-knuckle prize fighting were either long gone – they had 'disappeared, it was said, along with Heenan and Sayers' forty years previously – or that they were becoming rarer. Which was it?

Well, prize fights hadn't disappeared at all. Encounters continued to be frequent and popular, to the extent that they were said to be 'the craze of the time', sweeping over South Wales like a 'fatal epidemic', and rendering many churches 'comparatively empty'.[1]

Dai Jenkins and Harry Ainsworth worked hard at proving the doom-mongers wrong by battling each other three times in the space of four months; Jenkins fitted in another fight in that spell as well.

Their first contest, 'under old style rules', took place in the early hours in the Duffryn Valley near Maesteg in 1902, when a 'limited attendance' saw Jenkins, of Maesteg, take on his Ebbw Vale opponent for a 'modest' £10 a-side. The stakes, it was said, were not as high as they used to be when prize fighting was common in the mining districts of Glamorgan but a newspaper added, the winner (who turned out to be Ainsworth in the 13th round) knew he would receive a purse from a well-known 'sport' whose identity was guarantee it was well-stocked with gold.

Later that month the pair had a return match, for £30 a-side, near Rhigos in the upper part of the Glynneath Valley where about fifty 'sportsmen' saw Jenkins gain revenge with a sixteenth-round stoppage. A confident Jenkins, who had promised to knock out his opponent inside ten rounds, for £60-£30 a-side, won the decider three months later with a ninth round KO. In between the second and third fights, Jenkins knocked out Alf King (Bristol) in nine rounds near Westbury in Wiltshire.

Jenkins was in action in 1903, this time among the sand dunes between Pyle and Porthcawl. Fighting 'with the raw 'uns' two-minute rounds 'under the Marquess of Queensberry Rules. he showed his punching power 'in front of a large gathering of sports from all parts of the Principality', by stopping John Thomas, (Rhondda Valley) in the eleventh round of the hybrid bout. Jenkins took home £140 in all, including £30 out of the £40 purse, Thomas, receiving the remaining £10.

But the next year began on a low note for Jenkins, who was beaten in seven rounds by the 'much heavier' Tibby Wade, from Birmingham, the fight in the Neath Valley being with bare knuckles to the finish for £100. Things were back to normal for him, though, two months later, when in a bareknuckle fight for £50 a-side near Rhigos, Jenkins felled Bernard Platt (Lewisham) 'like a log' in the eleventh round.

Two months further on, Jenkins and Platt had a return fight on the mountain between Resolven and Cymmer. Jenkins' handlers backed him to win in twelve rounds and justifying their confidence, he landed a right to the stomach and 'Platt turned pale and dropped as though in convulsions'.[2]

In 1901 two colliers, James Phillips, 21, and Abraham Evans, 19, fought 17 rounds for a sovereign in a Treorchy field at six in the morning. Among other fights in 1902, Cardiff pair J. Connors and J. Burke fought for £10 a-

Epilogue – The Ring is dead?

side near the town, Burke taking the honours and the money, 'a swinging right hand punch to the jaw' knocking Connors out in the ninth round, while a barn a few miles from Brecon was the scene for a clash between a Londoner and an American for £120 a-side.

Several bareknuckle fights were reported in 1904. Tom Davies beat fellow Penrhiwceiber man Tom Rees over 21 rounds in the wood near Castell Coch, giving him a broken jaw into the bargain, two Cardiff teenagers battled 13 rounds on the outskirts of the town. In a field near Maesteg another Sunday fight involved Sydney Davies (Maesteg) and fellow collier John Price (Pontycymmer), while there was also a prize fight in the early hours in a field at Sully.

In 1905 a bareknuckle fight where 'a lady was said to be involved although a large amount of money was wagered' came about in the Cardiff area.[3] The following year prize fights 'came off' at Brynmawr and on wasteland at Maesteg, the latter watched by more than fifty people. A Sunday clash at Cymmer featured collier David John James (Cymmer) against a man named Rooke, while Andrew Baker and William James, of Ystradgynlais, fought on colliery tips.

***

THERE would have been more such battles had it not been for increased police activity with stations now connected by telephone, making it difficult for a crowd to assemble without officers knowing about it.

In 1901 police were busy breaking up fights in the Rhondda Valley and at Merthyr and on more occasions at Merthyr the following year. In 1903 they halted a set-to in a brickyard at Glynneath; where 'everybody absconded', but the fighters, Richard Phillips, a collier, and labourer William Davies.

In 1906 arrangements for a contest were completed in the *Rolling Mill* pub, Abertillery, but police stopped it happening out in the street. Those concerned then walked to Abertillery Park where the combatants 'went at each other in fine style' until officers intervened again and managed to arrest one of the fighters, William Ford. That year, police on horseback prevented a prize fight for £10 a-side in the early hours of a Monday morning near Porth between colliers Thomas Price (Ynyshir) and William Henry Gregor (Wattstown), disappointing a 550-strong crowd.[4]

Police arrived too late to prevent the action near Cowbridge racecourse in 1909, but they arrested two men, haulier Daniel Bowen (Clydach Vale) and labourer Morris Hughes (Blaenclydach) 'whose personal appearance seemed to indicate that they had been engaged in a pugilistic encounter'.[5] However, they managed to halt a fight in woods near Maesteg on a Sunday morning between John Hopkins and George Price for £1 a-side.

***

RELIGIOUS leaders, ratepayers and local councillors continued to speak out against prize fighting. With young Welshmen drinking, gambling and attending fights and football matches in preference to chapels, Congregationalists conceded that it wasn't enough for preachers 'to fire away at the devil' in pulpits on Sundays.[6] They needed 'to get to close quarters with him the other six days and thunder away until we are heard'. Congregational ministers protested at the prominence given by daily newspapers to the sport, as did Monmouthshire Baptist Association, who complained that advance publicity made it easier for gambling. Members of Aberdare Free Churches protested about the forthcoming Freddie Welsh 'prize fight' in the town in 1913 and called for such events to be made illegal.

Epilogue – The Ring is dead?

Following pressure from ratepayers, prize fights on land at Pontypridd were banned in 1902 and Swansea watch committee members spoke about their in 1908.

***

ANY golden age was over for bare knuckle prize fighting, though, and its days were inevitably numbered. At the same time, what was now popularly known as 'boxing', went from strength to strength.

A contest which could be said to span the two eras –took place in 1905. It was a scheduled 15 round fight at the Queen Street Hall, Cardiff, for £25 a-side a purse of £40, with the *Sporting Life* supplying the referee.

The contest pitted in his final fight Ivor Thomas, who took severe punishment and was knocked out by a right to the jaw in the third round. That was no disgrace, however, as his opponent was the future 'Peerless' Jim Driscoll.

In the early years of the new century in the USA, Welshmen spanned the two eras as well. Tommy West had five more contests, all endning in defeat, including challenges for world middleweight and welterweight titles. West's seconds retired him after 17 rounds of a 20-round contest, 'the bloodiest and most desperate ever seen' in Louisville, Kentucky, the Cardiff-born man having fought from the seventh round with a broken nose, right eye closed, his forehead laid open in two places and his cheek split, the newspaper report commenting: 'West's corner looked like a slaughterhouse, and the fighter's attaches actually had to wipe the blood from the floor with a mop'.[7]

In 1906 West was supervising a group of plasterers in San Francisco when the earthquake occurred. He told the local paper after arriving in Salt Lake City days after the disaster that he been woken by being thrown violently from his bed on to the floor. His hotel room was in a six-storey building.

The sensation he said that followed strongly resembled running over a rough railroad bed at rapid speed. He left with just enough money to take him to Salt Lake; he had a bankbook showing a good deposit, but the bank had burned down.[8]

Dai Dolling enjoyed a later career as an outstanding boxing trainer on both sides of the Atlantic. He looked after Tom Thomas when the Cardiganshire man won the British middleweight title in 1909, bantamweight champion Digger Stanley and featherweight champion Ted Kid Lewis before moving to the USA, where for several decades his work with fighters and young trainers earned him the title of the 'patriarch of pugilism'. Dolling trained world champion swimmers, runners, and top wrestlers as well as world champion boxers such as Gene Tunney and Al Brown.

***

EARLY in the First World War it was reported that Rhymney, was 'a hotbed of blackguardess' as for a month the area had 'been the scene of one continual round of fights and pugilistic encounters'.[9]

But after the conflict, prize fighting, in the old sense of the word, went into sharp decline. Indeed, it seemed to become a topic of historical interest, even nostalgia. Most newspaper references dealt with reminisces in obituaries of those formerly involved, including those of Tom Fletcher (1929), Crowther (1832) and Patsy Perkins (1933).

Crowther's name had cropped up often in this respect, bringing rehashes of his ring career n the news pages on a few occasions after he retired from the sport In 1904 bookmaker Crowther saw his eight-year-old chaser Nahillah among nine finishers from a 26-horse field in the Grand National, the following year Crowther was stabbed outside his home and a year later his brother Richard was gaoled for manslaughter.

Epilogue – The Ring is dead?

Memories were also jogged by the 'Fifty Years Ago' columns of Welsh newspapers, and by feature films offering a glimpse of what used to be. The 1913 novel *White Hope* (by W.R.H. Trowbridge), had echoes of the Johnson-Wells aborted fight, and was turned into a British silent film of the same name in 1915 which had a remake seven years later. Johnson's story was also the basis of the play and subsequent 1970 movie *The Great White Hope*.

At the Pavilion cinema, Abertillery, in 1924 the silent film comedy *The Great White Way* included a 'realistic' prize fight scene, the Palace Cinema, (Abertillery), advertised in 1926 that 'a championship prize-fight, in which will be seen the most realistic battle ever screened, is but one of the big scenes in *His People*', and in 1928, an American silent comedy film *Good Morning Judge* showing at Cardiff's Park Hall cinema featured a prize fight.

A three round prize fight, the reward for the winner being a village maiden, even featured in an opera, *Hugh the Drover*, by Ralph Vaughan Williams which opened in 1924. Williams had apparently revealed years previously that he wanted to set a prize fight to music.

***

LIKE the old-style prize fighting, the newly-polished version referred to as 'boxing', was in surprisingly good shape at the beginning of the twentieth century. The difference, though, was that, rather than then wilting, it blossomed.

In Wales, boxing was popular at Llandovery public school, their magazine reporting in 1910 that 'The Juniors have also startled us not a little by giving exhibitions of 'hurricane hitting' in boxing matches, which, however, have rarely been extended to a second round'.

Famous visiting boxers continued to show off their skills, Charles 'Kid' McCoy, former world middleweight champion, and Charley Mitchell, world heavyweight title challenger at Cardiff in 1902, and ten years later at Llanelly McCoy, Mitchell, and Matt Wells, who had defeated Freddie Welsh for the British title. On the latter occasion the entrance to the hall was approached via a bridge over a river. A crowd gathered on the bridge awaiting the doors to open when it collapsed, plunging scores of men into the water, which, fortunately, was only four feet deep and nobody was seriously injured.

In 1914, Sam Langford attracted a crowd of 1,500 to watch him in exhibition bouts at Swansea, but a much-heralded visit to the town by controversial American heavyweight Jack Johnson was called off amid protests which also ruled out appearances in other parts of Britain.

Instead of contests being clandestine affairs, in the new century they were now able to go ahead increasingly in permanent indoor venues and were seldom halted by police.

The sport's healthy state was despite its legal position remaining in doubt, and without a governing body or health and safety rules.

The surge in popularity was down to an image makeover, according to the report of a fight at Mountain Ash.[10] The sport had been discredited in the past because of its 'unsavoury associations', but its recent revival had been accompanied by a better class of supporter and also by better exponents, making it no longer brutal, but skilful.

**

ITS health had improved after it had received the implied backing of the law in a controversial trial in 1901.

The 'Billy Smith case' at the Old Bailey was a landmark in the sport. Smith, real name Murray Livingstone, was a 25-year-old American, who died from a brain injury received during a glove fight at the National Sporting Club in London. Ten men, Smith's opponent Jack Roberts and others

Epilogue – The Ring is dead?

involved in varying capacities in the fight, including Merthyr-born fighter Arthur Locke who was one of Smith's seconds, pleaded not guilty at the Central Criminal Court to manslaughter.

The court heard that in the seventh round Smith fell with the back of his head on the lower of the two ropes which surrounded the ring, and his head bumped off the rope on to the padded floor. He got up, and immediately time was called for the end of the round. Smith was helped to his corner and remained there for the regulation time – a minute – and then stood up to continue the contest. Seconds after the round began, he sank down to his knees, taking hold of the rope, and there he remained until he was counted out after ten seconds. He was carried out of the room and taken to Charing-cross Hospital, where he remained unconscious and died.

The prosecution contended it was an unlawful fight because of the rule which enabled it to be won by the injury or exhaustion of one of the combatants. If a contestant was knocked down and did not get up unassisted within ten seconds and renew the contest, he would be considered defeated.

Under the ten-seconds rule a contest would, in fact, be a fight; and if death was caused in the course of a fight it was manslaughter, however fair the fight may be. The ten-seconds rule was the antithesis of sport. That rule also said that the decision would be given to the contestant who obtained the greatest number of points. A man who was winning by points in 14 out of 15 rounds might by the operation of that rule lose in the 15th round by being unable to rise after the expiration of ten seconds.

The contest's being fought according to rules did not make it lawful. The English law did not permit rules to be made which were contrary to the common law of the country and games to be played according to those rules.

It had also been decided previously that wearing gloves did not make it other than a prize fight.

Defence counsel argued that all exhibitions of strength and skill in sports or recreations were lawful and if death took place during them it was accidental homicide. A boxing match was lawful. This contest was one of skill to be decided by the number of points made. It was not a prize fight; there was no knockout blow in this case. The death was accidental; Smith had slipped before any blows were struck.

Mr. Justice Channell said the question was 'Was this a fight? If it was a simple boxing contest, in which the object was not to administer blows, but merely to show how it could be done, it was lawful; but if it was a prize fight under the disguise of a boxing competition it was illegal. If it was a mere contest of skill in which there was no intention by one party to injure the other, it was lawful and the defendants would be entitled to be acquitted. The jury, after an absence of an hour and a half, said there was no possibility of their being able to agree.

At the retrial, before Mr. Justice Grantham, prosecuting counsel said the case was undertaken rather with a view to putting a stop to future competitions of a like kind than to get any punishment inflicted upon the defendants.[11]

A surgeon said the death was caused either by a blow on the head from a fist or a fall on the ropes or on the floor.

Giving evidence, a club member said that in the penultimate round Smith, in avoiding a punch, fell into the ropes and struck his head on one of them. In the final round, Smith went down; Roberts threw a very light punch and Smith was struck and was counted out. Another member said towards the end of the seventh round both boxers fell, Roberts on top; Smith's head was

Epilogue – The Ring is dead?

on the rope then slipped to the floor. He also said Smith appeared to be dragging one foot behind him. In the eighth Smith did not fall as if he had been struck. The referee said he did not notice anything the matter with Smith until the start of the eighth round and then thought he was pretending but before he could form a definite opinion Smith sank to his knees.

Speaking in support of the rules operated by the club were the president of the ABA, and club members Lord Lonsdale, Admiral Victor Montague, and the Earl of Kingston.

The judge said the evidence pointed very strongly to the fact that Smith met his death from falling on the ropes and that he was not struck at all. There was no evidence that it was a fight. The jury, without leaving the box, found the death was accidental, and that it was a boxing match; the defendants were not guilty.

The verdict caused raised eyebrows in the legal profession. A barrister claimed that the prosecution, by not calling two reporters who were eye-witnesses, did not seem to have wanted a conviction on what appeared to have been strong evidence of a prize fight, while the judge appeared to have directed the jury away from the idea that it was a prize fight.[12] The *Sporting Life* newspaper had given a different version of the ending of the fight, reporting that Roberts had knocked Smith down twice in the eighth round with blows to the side of the head, Smith remaining in a sitting position until counted out.[13]

***

THE sport was now *considered* lawful, and emboldened by the Smith verdict, began to organise itself in Britain. There was still no official governing body; but the NSC, which had assumed control in the 1890s, administered until 1929 when the British Boxing Board of Control was formed. The Welsh Boxing Association and Control Board had been established as a regulating body in Wales the previous year.

Safety concerns were addressed by increasing the size of gloves, the last fight with two-ounce gloves taking place in 1903. Today, the weight of gloves has increased, for safety reasons, and now varies between eight and 10 ounces.

Another safety measure was the introduction of weight divisions. During the nineteenth century there had generally been no weight restrictions between fighters. In 1909, eight weight divisions were set up officially by the NSC. They comprised – flyweight, bantamweight, featherweight, lightweight, welterweight, middleweight, light-heavyweight and heavyweight. Over the years, to reduce weight discrepancies, nine in-between divisions were added - minimumweight, light flyweight, super flyweight, super bantamweight, super featherweight, super lightweight, super welterweight, super middleweight, and cruiserweight.

For most of the previous century there was just one champion, and that only by popular acclaim. But that aspect of the sport also changed rapidly, as at the same time the equivalent number of championship belts was established.

The first champion's belt, transferable between successive champions, had been tied around Ben Caunt after his victory over Nick Ward in 1841. Made of purple velvet and silver, it included designs of the rose, shamrock and thistle, but, as Wales was considered officially part of England, like the Union flag, it sported no Welsh emblem![14]

In recent years there has been concern that the number of in-between weights increases the danger of fighters weakening themselves by losing an excessive amount of weight immediately before a fight to fit into a lower

Epilogue – The Ring is dead?

weight category and thereby making themselves more susceptible to brain damage.

∗∗∗

ON the wider scene, for over half of the twentieth century there was one effective governing body for world title fights, the USA-based National Boxing Association, and with just one champion at each of eight weights, there was only a limited opportunity for a fighter to become world champion. During this time, the feat was managed by four Welshmen - Percy Jones, flyweight (Porth) 1914, Freddie Welsh, lightweight (Pontypridd) 1914 - 1917, Jimmy Wilde flyweight (Merthyr Tydfil) 1916 - 1923, and Howard Winston featherweight (Merthyr) Tydfil 1968.

There are now four major world sanction bodies - the International Boxing Federation, World Boxing Association, World Boxing Organisation and World Boxing Council - so in all 17 weight divisions there can be four different world champions, a total of 68– and counting, because of a strong feeling that the weight disparity among heavyweights can be so big that a super-heavyweight class should be introduced.

With the proliferation of world sanctioning bodies plus travel improvements, world title opportunities increased greatly. Eight fighters, again all from south Wales, have benefited - Steve Robinson featherweight WBO (Cardiff) Apr 1993 - Sep 1995, Robbie Regan bantamweight WBO (Caerphilly) Apr 1996 – 1996, Joe Calzaghe super-middleweight WBO, IBF, WBA, WBC (Newbridge) Oct 1997 - Jun 2008, Barry Jones super-featherweight WBO (Cardiff) Dec 1997 – 1998, Enzo Maccarinelli cruiserweight WBO (Swansea) Sep 2006 - Mar 2008, Gavin Rees light-welterweight WBA (Newbridge) Jul 2007 - Mar 2008, Nathan Cleverly light-heavyweight WBO (Cefn Fforest) May 2011 - Aug 2013, Lee Selby featherweight IBF (Barry) May 2015- May 2018.

***

LINKS between amateurs and professionals which grew in the latter part of the nineteenth century before waning over the next one hundred years, revived in the early years of the 21st century.

In 2008, AIBA, the International Amateur Boxing Association, presented the World Series of Boxing (WSB) which enabled teams of amateurs to compete without headguards and using the AIBA Ten Points-Must scoring system, providing a bridge between Olympic Boxing and professional boxing.

In 2016 AIBA voted to allow professionals to box at the Olympic Games.

One could ponder what changes in the future will there be before amateurs and professionals are indistinguishable.

**

IN addition to those now competing in the ring, women began to write authoritatively on the sport. Chief among them were Joyce Carol Oates, from the USA, publishing *On Boxing* in 1987, and British academic Kasia Boddy, whose *Boxing: A Cultural History* was published in 2008.

Women voiced strong opinions on its future as well. Women MPs were in opposite corners on the issue. Dr. Edith Summerskill campaigned for boxing to be banned, while Mrs. E. M. 'Bessie' Braddock supported it. A later supporter, Charlotte Leslie MP was chair of the All-Party Parliamentary Group on boxing.

***

PROTESTERS did not hold back after the fading away of old-fashioned prize fighting, but turned their attention to 'boxing' which they insisted, in

Epilogue – The Ring is dead?

the modern use of the word, and 'prize fighting', now popularly used synonymously, were indeed the same thing and as such were brutal and barbaric.

A Welsh journal referred to a 'prize fight under the guise of a boxing contest' at Mountain Ash in the opening decade of the twentieth century, and four years later in 1913 Haverfordwest town council prohibited boxing shows at the Market Hall after a member claimed they were not as innocent as colleagues had been led to believe, having many of the elements of the prize fight.

In 1934 a Welshman had announced he was setting up 'The Anti-Pugilistic Movement' to abolish all pugilistic contests and appealed for support from 'all lovers of clean sport'. He said that fighters were urged to live a pure life, have temperate habits and to train hard, but it was all 'for the purpose of battering and bruising a fellow being'.[15]

A Cardiff alderman and the Welsh Boxing Board of Control argued the point in 1935 as had a counterpart at Abertillery two years before who said that 'boxing' in the old sense of the term, 'became tainted when people tried to beat each other for money'.

And in 1936 churchgoers at Brynmawr protested against the British Broadcasting Corporation for broadcasting prize fights which were 'inhuman, cruel, barbaric, a disgrace to a Christian country, and a foul blot on civilisation'.

***

MOST contemporary commentators believed that what had come to be called 'boxing' was different from prize fighting.

According to Boddy, as the Queensberry Rules took over, 'it became clear that the new sport of gloved boxing was entirely different from the old bare-knuckle prize-fighting'.[16]

Among a minority of modern commentators, the American novelist Oates, a respected writer on the sport, accepted the old-time view, stating

> It should be understood that 'boxing' and 'fighting' though always combined in the greatest of boxers, can be entirely different and even unrelated activities. Amateur boxers are trained to win their matches on points; professionals usually try for knockouts.[17]

Boxing, she maintained, was 'a highly complex and refined skill belonging solely to civilisation', while 'fighting....belongs to something pre-dating civilisation'.

Today, those involved in the professional code use 'boxing' and 'prize-fighting' interchangeably.

Fight people and spectators, bearing out Shaw's claim, prefer men who can hand out savage punishment – have a finishing punch - over those who rely on sheer skill. Welsh fight fans proved the point at the end of another immaculate display in 1956 by clever Cardiffian Joe Erskine.

> Erskine clearly and convincingly outpointed his Belgian opponent. Marcel Limage in his home town of Cardiff. yet when the referee announced the verdict the crowd booed Erskine. who has never been beaten as a professional. No one could have denied that Erskine won well, but he had failed to put his man down and that seems to be the only thing which counts with present day boxing followers. They don't want skill nowadays. That apparently does not mean a thing. All the majority want to see is swinging fists and a man crashing to the canvas.[18]

Attitudes have not changed. World heavyweight champion Anthony Joshua explained in 2017:

Epilogue – The Ring is dead?

People want to see the fighters I fight unconscious every time. I was delivering. I put him down. I hurt him, I slashed both of his eyes, he was bleeding. My shorts and boots were pure white, and now they're pink. People wanted to see him unconscious and I was trying.

***

BOXING'S dangers were highlighted in 1913 when Newport man Johnny Basham knocked out Harry Price in Liverpool and the South African died hours later without regaining consciousness. Basham was charged with manslaughter but was released after medical evidence that death was due to a brain injury more consistent with a fall than with a blow. The inquest jury protested, however, against the practice of a knockout blow counting as a win.

Further questions about the sport's regulations were raised in 1948 when Ebbw Vale boxer Mickey Markey, 17 years old, died after being knocked out in the sixth round of a fight at Willenhall in the Midlands. It was only his second professional fight. In his professional debut just weeks before Markey had been knocked out in the first round. Markey's previous experience of the ring amounted to a mere eight amateur bouts.

Another Monmouthshire man, Newport's David Pearce, saw his ring career cut short in 1984 when the ruling body acted on brain scan irregularities and suspended him, also stripping him of his British heavyweight championship belt.

***

INFLUENTIAL boxing figures questioned their own attachment to the sport after the death of James Murray in 1995 which created, according to the secretary of the BBB. of C, John Morris, 'the biggest crisis there has ever been in boxing'.[19]

Harry Mullan, long-serving editor of the *Boxing News*, said 'I think anyone with half a conscience or a heart or an ounce of compassion has to wonder what he's doing in boxing', veteran national boxing writer John Rodda stated 'the drip, drip, drip on my conscience has taken me close to the point where I believe it [boxing[should be banned,' and fight promoter Frank Warren, confided: 'I've spent a long time defending boxing and trying to justify it and I'm not doing it anymore'.[20]

***

THE medical profession was, and remains, divided on whether professional boxing should be abolished.

In 1959, the British Medical Society said it had no official policy on the matter and this subject had never come up for discussion in the council. At the same time, *The Lancet* medical journal urged doctors to fight for the total abolition of boxing. In 1982, the doctors' trade union, the British Medical Association, called for a campaign to abolish professional boxing, later produced a report and in 1986, renewed calls for a ban after the death in London of Steve Watt, the Scottish welterweight less than three days after collapsing in the ring.

In 1996, the BMA renewed its call for a ban in the light of evidence that boxing caused lasting brain damage. Nurses rejected a ban, opening a split within the medical profession. The Royal College of Nursing said that a ban would be an unreasonable infringement on personal liberty, and the best way to protect boxers was to allow the sport to continue with safeguards.

Two years later, with Englishman Spencer Oliver fighting for his life after being knocked out, Sports Minister Tony Banks turned down calls for a ban, urging critics to recognise boxing's benefits. The BMA rejected the suggestion that boxing was beneficial, claiming 'The idea that if boxing did

Epilogue – The Ring is dead?

not exist, these youngsters would be on the streets or committing crime is false'.[21]

In 2000, Paul Ingle, 28, suffered a blood clot during his IBF featherweight title fight at the Sheffield Arena. He was stretchered out of the ring and spent four weeks in intensive care before recovering.

That year the BMA reiterated its long-standing opposition to the sport, finding

> it impossible to justify deliberately causing damage to the brain and the eye. The effects are cumulative, so the more often you fight the more chance you have of being injured.[22]

The organisation wanted ultimately to see it banned but believed that would only happen if there was a change in the law and in public opinion. More people being turned off boxing was what it would take to see it banned.

In 2016 Scottish boxer Mike Towell died in hospital after he was injured in a bout against Welsh fighter Dale Evans in Glasgow.

***

THERE might easily have been a ban early in the twentieth century. The court's controversial decision in the Billy Smith case was tacit approval only, and it was feared a ban was likely in the wake of a colour bar issue being fought out ten years later.

There had been slow progress in the treatment of black fighters during a time of great change in the sport.

Previously, Enoch Morrison had ended up in court after reacting physically against racial abuse in the street and the same applied to Lloyd 'Kid' Davies, an American who settled in Swansea, in the early years of the new century. Their names and those of others, including Wales-based Felix Scott, were almost always accompanied in newspaper boxing articles by the word 'coloured' and regularly by 'coon', 'darkey', 'the black' and what we now refer to as 'the n-word'.

An unofficial barrier left these boxers to fight for so-called 'coloured' championships', one such contest, billed for 'the coloured championship of Wales', taking place at the Badminton Club, Cardiff, in 1908. The participants were named as Jim Nepor (of Boston), who knocked out J. G. Nelson (of the West Indies) in the eighth round.

The colour bar became official in 1909 when the self-appointed governing body, the National Sporting Club, banned black boxers from fighting for British titles.

The NSC's stance was backed by the Government two years later during an intense campaign to prevent a fight going ahead between English heavyweight Bombardier Billy Wells and the imposing black American Jack Johnson.

A variety of arguments was put forward for the ban, including that it was a prize fight and thus illegal, commercialism in the sport (which had always been its major component), and that it was a mismatch for comparative novice Wells.

However, the main (understated) reason was that a high-profile fight between a white and a black fighter would aggravate racial feelings, or, rather, should Johnson, as widely expected, triumph, expose as a fallacy the supposed racial superiority of white over black which underpinned Britain's colonial empire,

That was exactly what had happened to the myth in the USA the year before when the heavyweight championship took place in Reno, Nevada. Reigning champion Johnson knocked out former holder James J. Jeffries, a white American, in the fifteenth round of a one-sided fight. The defeat of

Epilogue – The Ring is dead?

the 'Great White Hope' Jeffries led to race riots and proved to be the last such big fight in the USA for years.

A similar win for Johnson was forecast in England - Lord Lonsdale said Wells had 'no chance'. Another humiliating defeat was thus on the cards for a white boxer against a black opponent this side of the Atlantic after West Indian Peter Jackson's two-round defeat of 'the champion of England', Jem Smith, at the Pelican Club, London, in 1889 and, early in 1911, Sam Langford's easy sixth-round victory over the Australian champion Jem Lang at London's Olympia.

The latter result dashed the hopes of the English boxing establishment which had hoped the fight would give Lang's supporters 'an opportunity of demonstrating whether their man is really that champion of the white race who is destined to snatch the laurels from the dusky brow of Jack Johnson'.[23]

To make matters worse, unlike with the Smith debacle where the audience was restricted to the rich and powerful with aristocrats acting as ring officials, there were plenty of pictures of Langford v Lang in the newspapers showing 'The 'Black eclipse of a white boxer' so thousands could see the white boxer sprawled on the canvas with the black man looming over him.[24]

Responding to calls to prevent the clash between Wells and Johnson, the Home Secretary, Winston Churchill, said the fight was illegal and that if it was not prevented voluntarily, he would issue a summons for it to be stopped. It was not spelled out whether the contest was illegal because it was a prize fight, the stance adopted by government ministers in the 19th century or was illegal because it was a contest between a white man and a black man. Churchill's declaration indicated that the authorities, in fact, saw no difference between prize fighting and boxing and intervened only when it suited them - in this instance over the colour issue.

In the event, the owners of the venue gained an injunction preventing the staging of the fight, and with all concerned agreeing that it would not take place the magistrate adjourned the summons sine die and agreed not to make a statement on whether the fight was illegal or not.[25]

Although 'coloured' was still used regularly in press reports, the other epithets all but disappeared. When they were used by spectators at a fight such language could anger others in the crowd. After some ringsiders at a Frank Moody contest in Merthyr directed such language towards his West Indian opponent, Rocky Knight, the *Merthyr Express* reported that 'the unsportsmanlike spirit...... provoked the resentment of others among the crowd resulting the fight being waged to an accompaniment of quarrelling voices'.[26]

But although there was an improvement in crowd behaviour, the colour bar persisted. It continued to be supported by the Government, which forbade a fight in London in 1922 between Joe Beckett and the Senegalese Battling Siki, claiming that 'in contests between men of colour and white men the temperaments of the contestants are incompatible'.[27]

Weeks later Siki was even barred from Britain where he was due to engage in a series of exhibition bouts. Siki's promoter said he had no objection to black boxers having exhibition bouts, but he was opposed in principle to black v white contests. He had organised the aborted fight with Beckett because it provided a chance for 'making a white man once again the champion'.[28] For their part the NSC said in 1929 that it had 'no objection to two black men being in opposition in the ring at the club, but we bar contests between black men and white men'.[29]

Epilogue – The Ring is dead?

With the Government of the same mind as their predecessors, it was only to be expected that the newly-formed British Boxing Board of Control, a number of whose members were members of the NSC, would continue the bar and they passed a rule that only fighters born of white parents were eligible to fight for British titles.

The 'colour bar' ended in 1947 following a concerted Press campaign combined with pressure from MP John Lewis. One newspaper called the bar 'a filthy reflection on the sportsmanship of our legislators and an affront to all true sportsmen'.[30]

In an unconvincing defence of the Board's stance, BBB of C secretary Charles Domnall, a strong opponent of any change in the rule, said coloured fighters could fight for British titles [that is] Empire titles which are far more important than our home championships'.[31]

The new, reforming Labour government, recognising that the Empire was changing to the Commonwealth, leaned on the BBB of C to effect a change.

The *Western Mail* commented that the bar, which even applied to boxers born in Britain, even to those who had served their country had been 'a sore which has been festering on the side of British sport for too long'.[32]

The first Welshman to benefit from the change in the rule was Joe Erskine, who won the vacant British heavyweight title in 1956. Erskine, whose grandfather was a Jamaican seaman, outpointed Johnny Williams in Cardiff. It was a triple celebration because it was also the first all-Welsh fight for the British heavyweight title and the first time such title fight was held in Wales. Erskine's neighbourhood supporters were quick to congratulate him, the *Western Mail* reporting 'Policemen had to clear the ring of coloured folk from Bute Town, anxious to acclaim him'.[33]

309

Despite the successful campaign to prevent the Wells v Johnson fight not amounting to a legal precedent, for a time it looked as if the action taken over the colour bar would now encourage action against fights where there was no colour issue. This was feared as certain to threaten the whole future of boxing.

After Churchill's statement, the fight promoter said that the court would provide the biggest test case ever in the sport. If the decision was upheld no other boxing contest could take place in England as they were all held under the same conditions. It did not come to a court ruling, however, so the question was left hanging and the fear persisted.

The first sequel to the Wells v Johnson affair was the preventing of the Georges Carpentier -Young Joseph fight with the venue's owners also saying it risked their licence. This was followed by the prevention of the Wells-Gunner Moir contest because owners of venues would not take the risk either.

According to the fight promoter

> There is no doubt that boxing is in danger until the law clearly defines what is legal and what is illegal. Until this is done owners of halls will not know whether they are incurring the displeasure of the London County Council or any other authority and will not allow their premises to be used for boxing contests.[34]

When police took steps in 1911 to stop a fight for the British title between Welshman Jim Driscoll and Owen Moran (Birmingham), it was feared that the 'campaign against boxing....threatens to put an end to 'big money' boxing contests'.[35]

The summonses for an intended breach of the peace was a surprise as there was no colour issue involved. The promoter said they would probably try to make a test case on the legality of professional boxing contests.

Epilogue – The Ring is dead?

The new Home secretary, Reginald McKenna, reiterated the long-established legal position of boxing/prize fighting. After the court heard familiar arguments over whether it was boxing or prize fighting, the stipendiary said what was intended was a prize fight and ordered the parties to be bound over to keep the peace. Soon after, Moran gave up hope of fighting Driscoll and booked passage to the USA for fights.

Weeks later, after Cardiff police explained the law on boxing to them, the local Badminton Club postponed a boxing show so as not to commit an offence while they sought legal advice. The *Western Mail* called it a 'nervous reaction' by the club as the police had no power to ban such shows. The officer 'was just giving the usual warning'.[36]

The Home Secretary and the stipendiary had appeared to confirm that '"boxing' was the same as the old prize fighting and therefore illegal, but no further action was taken, and the sport's legal position is still indeterminate.

No court has ever been asked to rule directly on the legality of 'boxing'. Juries have been left to decide themselves whether the fight before them was more a sparring contest of regulated limitations, thus tolerable, rather than an unregulated and illegal prize fight.

Anderson states: 'It remains the case that on this dubious thread of policy and distinction does the legality of boxing hang'.[37] It was unsatisfactory that the courts themselves abdicated responsibility for the decision by leaving the matter to the jury. Furthermore, a fundamental problem of resting the legality of boxing on the distinction between sparring and a prize fight was that the modern professional bout was - the wearing of gloves apart - the direct descendant of the prize fight where the fighters box for money and often do so to the point of near exhaustion.

Commentators were forced to conclude, he added, that the apparent immunity of boxing from the sanction of the law defied rational explanation; all one could surmise was that boxing remained outside the ordinary law of violence because society chose to tolerate it.

***

THE first of several attempts in Parliament to ban boxing was made in 1950. Opponents claimed it was 'brutalising' to spectators, 'degrading', was virtually prize fighting and not a sport but a business, and caused brain damage, the primary objective being to render your opponent insensible.[38]

Boxing had a stout defender in Mrs. Braddock, who sought financial help from the government to prevent the sport becoming extinct and defended it against attacks by arguing that no pne was compelled to box, it was a completely voluntary matter and there were many other activities more dangerous that should be looked at.[39]

In 1964, after Lyn James (Pontypridd), died in hospital in London from a brain injury (his opponent Colin Lake was born in Newport, Wales, and raised in Holloway, London), Dr. Summerskill urged the BBB of C to examine all boxers at least a month before a fight. She told Parliament that a month before the fight, James' own doctor said he was not fit to take part. He was examined before the fight, but these doctors were not independent as they were employed by the boxing business.

Lord Morrison said in view of the brutal elements of this sport Parliament should prohibit boxing altogether. The reply was that the Government felt it would not be right to interfere in the existing regulations which stipulated examinations when applying for a professional licence and on the day of a fight.

Epilogue – The Ring is dead?

Another attempt followed the death in a world title fight in Los Angeles in 1980 of Merthyr bantamweight Johnny Owen. After being knocked out by the Mexican Lupe Pintor, Owen never regained consciousness and died on 4 November 1980, aged twenty-four. Dr. Summerskill asked the Secretary of State for the Environment whether, in the light of the death of Owen he would establish strong regulations covering the conduct of professional boxing in the United Kingdom. The reply was that there were already firm regulations and boxing, like every other sport, should run its own affairs with minimum interference from the Government.

In 2000, Labour MP for Newport West Paul Flynn tried to get a ban on head blows in the sport.

***

DESPITE Churchill's warning, the Government and Parliament consistently refused to entertain a ban, contending that professional boxing was different from illegal prize fighting. There was a risk, accepted by all participants, of injury or death in almost every sport, there was no evidence that the British public 'had any wish to become a nation of pansies', a ban impinged on individual freedom, and the sport's benefits should be recognised.[40]

***

IT has been argued, though, that it would not need a test case in court or action by the Government to put an end to the sport.[41] Doctors could achieve that outcome. With medical cover a legal requirement for all boxing, doctors could make boxing illegal in Britain by withdrawing their support and refusing to attend bouts.

A test case, Government action, an end to society's tolerance, medical intervention - which, if any, is likely to deal a knockout blow?

[1] Merthyr Express, 24 July 1909.
[9] Western Mail, 14 May 1904.
[3] Western Mail, 5 September 1905.
[4] Western Mail, 25 December 1906.
[5] South Wales Daily News, 10 August 1909
[6] North Wales Times, 19 October 1901.
[7] The San Francisco Call., 5 March 1901.
[8] Salt Lake Tribune, 22 April 1906
[9] Merthyr Express, 23 January 1915.
[10] Cambrian, 27 August 1909.
[11] Times, 29 June 1901
[12] Times, 19 July 1901
[13] Sporting Life, 23 April 1901.
[14] Era, 16 May 1841.
[15] Western Mail, 1 March 1934.
[16] Kasia Boddy, Boxing, a cultural history (London, Reaktion Books, 2008),.p.106
[17] Joyce Carol Oates, On Boxing (London, Bloomsbury, 1987), p. 49.
[18] Liverpool Echo, 19 January 1956
[19] Guardian, 16 November 1994, cited in Neil Carter, Medicine, Sport and the Body: A Historical Perspective (London, Bloomsbury, 2004), p, 190.
[20] Guardian, 16 October, 1995, 15 March 1996, 24 October 1995, cited in Carter, Medicine, Sport and the Body, p. 191.
[21] Times, 5 May 1998.
[22] Guardian, 18 December 2000.
[23] Sporting Life, 2 January 1911.
[24] The Tatler, 1 March 1911.
[25] Halesworth Times, 3 October 1911.
[26] Merthyr Express, 21 July 1923.
[27] Yorkshire Evening Post, 9 November 1922.
[28] Western Mail, 30 January 1923.
[29] Edinburgh Evening News, 9 January 1929.
[30] Sunday Mirror, 23 March 1947.
[31] Belfast News Letter, 27 March 1947.
[32] Western Mail, 3 April 1948.
[33] Western Mail, 28 August 1956.
[34] Globe, 10 October 1911.
[35] Lloyds Weekly Newspaper, 5 November 1911.
[36] Western Mail, 9 January 1912.
[37] Jack Anderson, PUGILISTIC PROSECUTIONS: PRIZE FIGHTING AND THE COURTS IN NINETEENTH CENTURY BRITAIN, The Sports Historian No. 21 (2), November 2001.
[38] Times, 10 July, 29 November 1950; 21 May 1953. Hansard : HL Deb 28 March 1962 vol 238 cc961-3.
[39] HC Deb 21 July 1953 vol 518 cc192-3; 18 June 1959 vol 607 cc646-8.
[40] Times, 27 November 1950. Hansard : HL Deb 28 March 1962 vol 238 cc961-3. Times, 5 May 1998. Guardian, 18 December 2000. Daily Telegraph, 28 March 2016.
[41] BBC on-line network. Friday, June 12, 1998 Published at 12:13 GMT 13:13 UK.

Index

A

Aaron, Barney, **94**
Aberaman, **47**, **76**, **193**, **206**, **246**, **276**, **281**
Aberavon, **13**, **256**, **276**
Aberbargoed, **283**
Abercanaid, **20**, **159**
Abercwmboi, **91**
Aber-cwm-y-bwcci, **90**
Aberdare, **12**, **13**, **16**, **19**, **28**, **32**, **35**, **63**, **64**, **71**, **80**, **90**, **170**, **172**, **244**, **251**, **252**, **259**, **277**
Aberdare Free Churches, **290**
Aberdeen, **173**
Abergavenny, **31**, **158**, **191**, **242**, **277**
Abersychan, **18**, **32**, **45**
Abertillery, **63**, **279**, **282**, **290**, **293**, **301**
Abertillery Sunday School Union, **178**
Aberystwyth, **180**
Abraham, William M. P., **177**
Ainsworth, Harry, **287**
Alcohol, **49–56**
Amateur Athletic Club, **189**
Amateur Boxing Association, **192**
Amateur Boxing Association of England, **191**
Ambrose, Richard, **34**, **35**, **43**, **47**, **54**, **217**
American Civil War, **223**
Amesbury, William, **34**
Amlwch, **128**
Andrews, Ben, **159**
Angel Hotel, Monmouth, **174**
Anthony, William, **70**
Anti-Pugilistic Movement, **301**
ap Rees, Gruffydd, **86**
Apreece, Sir Thomas, **86**
Arundel, Thomas, **29**
Ashford, **144**
assault at arms, **16**
Atkey, Cliff, **268**
Atkins, Billy, **268**
Atlantic Ocean, **162**, **167**, **223**
Australia, **174**

B

Badminton Club, Cardiff, **306**, **311**
Bailey, Jem, **135**, **138**, **155**, **156**
Baker, Andrew, **289**
Bala, **169**
Ball, Alf, **201**, **213**, **252**
Ball. Tom, **249**
Bando, Dai, **280**
Bando, or bandy, **94**
Bangor, **89**, **229**
Banks, Tony, Sports Minister, **304**
Bargoed, **261**
Barlow, John, **92**
Barry, **251**, **259**
Barry Nursing Association and Accident Hospital, **49**
Barry, Tom, King of Clowns, **130**
Basham, Edward, **44**
Basham, Johnny, **45**, **303**
Batch, Henry, **70**
Bath, **16**, **25**, **185**
Battle Bridge, **152**
Battle of Belmont, **207**
Battle of Fort Sumter, **224**
Battle of Waterloo, **207**
Battling Siki, **308**
Baulch, John, **103**
Bayton, Albert, **267**
Bayton, James 'Jem', **220**
Bayton, Jim, **266**
Beachley, **196**
Beachley to Aust ferries, **139**
Beaufort Arms, Aberaman, **47**
Beauregard, General, **224**
Beckett, Joe, **308**
Bedwas, **14**

315

Bedwellty, **31**, **32**
Beerhouse Act 1830, **50**
Belcher, Jem, **78**, **111**
Belgium, **188**
Bell Inn, Merthyr, **11**, **119**
Bell's Life, **5**, **109**, **115**, **132**, **136**, **142**, **143**, **146**, **151**, **153**, **154**, **156**, **158**, **187**, **188**
Ben, champion Yorkshire fighter, **78**
Benbow, James, **59**
Bendigo, **2**, **144**, **174**
benefit of clergy, **37**
Benjamin, Bill, **5**, **42**, **73**, **80**, **132**, **139**, **141**, **142**, **143**, **144**, **146**, **148**, **167**, **174**
Berkeley Hospital, **18**
Bevan, Fred, **274**
Bevan, John, **76**
Beynon, Thomas, **34**, **279**
Billy Smith case, **294**, **305**
Birchell, Harris, **129**
Bird in Hand, Merthyr, **192**
Birkenhead, **186**
Birmingham, **153**, **217**
Black Parade, **63**, **278**, **284**
Blackett, **104**
Blackheath, **186**
Blaenavon, **21**, **24**, **159**
Blaencaerau, **14**
Blaenclydach, **290**
Blaenrhondda, **230**
Blaina, **282**
Blanau, **279**
Bloody Fields, **12**
Bloody Island', **64**
Blorenge mountain, **277**
Blossoms Fair, Denbigh, **241**
Boddy, Kasia, **300**, **302**
Boer_War, **205–9**
Bonner, Jack, **219**
Booth, Edwin, **163**
Booth, General, **78**
Borrow, George, **25**, **41**, **89**
Bowen, Daniel, **290**
Bowen, John, **20**

Bowling, John, **43**
Boxiana, **124**, **136**
boxing booths, **5**, **77**, **239**, **242**, **243**, **255**, **257**, **262**, **264**
Boyd, Teddy, **267**
Brace, Glau, **1**
Braddock, Mrs. E. M. 'Bessie', **300**, **312**
Brailsford, **138**
Brawd, Dai, **257**
Brecon, **129**, **160**, **289**
Brecon Beacons, **15**
Breconshire, **15**, **114**, **185**, **282**
Bridgend, **176**, **250**, **256**
Brighton, **147**, **210**
Bristol, **2**, **74**, **78**, **95**, **103**, **111**, **117**, **127**, **128**, **135**, **138**, **147**, **155**, **185**, **193**, **210**, **213**, **246**
Bristol Channel, **74**, **127**, **138**
Britannia, **162**
Brithwaunydd, **21**
British and Foreign Temperance Society, **132**
British Boxing Board of Control, **297**, **303**, **309**
British Broadcasting Corporation, **301**
British Columbia, **226**
British Medical Association, **304**
British Medical Society, **304**
Broad Oak, **94**
Broadmoor Colliery, **236**
Brookes, Jack, **147**
Broome, Harry, **142**, **143**
Broughton, Jack, **96**
Broughton's rules, **96**, **98**, **99**, **135**
Brown, George, **29**
Brumingham, John, **129**
Brymbo, **22**
Brynmawr, **256**, **258**, **277**, **289**, **301**
Brynmenin, **176**
Buffalo, **44**
Buffalo, New York, **223**
Burge, Dick, **174**, **205**
Burke, Deaf, **25**, **137**, **153**, **158**
Burke, J., **288**
Burke, Jack, **205**

316

Index

Burnett, Tony, **270**
Burns, Alec, **204**
Burns, Peter, alias Dublin Tom, **76**, **80**, **210**, **281**
Butchers Arms, Monmouth, **11**
Butchers Arms, Shirenewton, **73**, **80**
Butchers Arms, Wattstown, **235**
Bute Arms, Cardiff, **68**
Butler County, Ohio, **224**
Butler Johnstone, Henry, MP, **123**

C

Caemawr, **169**
Caerleon racecourse, **12**
Caernarvon, **163**
Caernarvonshire, **207**
Caerphilly, **16**, **138**, **158**, **159**, **251**, **299**
Cahill, John, **277**
Caldicot, **258**
California, **256**
Calzaghe, Joe, **299**
Cambrian Hotel, Cardiff, **80**
Cambrian, The, **117**
Cambridge University, **124**, **189**
Canada, **163**, **164**
Canning, George, **4**
Capcoch, **90**
Cape Town, **209**
Carder, William, **251**, **259**
Cardiff, **7**, **10**, **11**, **12**, **13**, **16**, **21**, **23**, **26**, **32**, **37**, **39**, **44**, **46**, **47**, **49**, **50**, **52**, **54**, **61**, **68**, **71**, **73**, **79**, **80**, **81**, **82**, **94**, **126**, **129**, **130**, **132**, **158**, **170**, **172**, **173**, **174**, **175**, **179**, **181**, **184**, **185**, **186**, **191**, **193**, **198**, **201**, **202**, **205**, **206**, **209**, **210**, **212**, **213**, **218**, **220**, **226**, **229**, **232**, **234**, **235**, **236**, **246**, **247**, **249**, **250**, **262**, **273**, **281**, **285**, **288**, **289**, **291**, **294**, **299**, **301**
Cardiff Amateur Boxing Club, **191**
Cardiff Boat, Cardiff, **26**
Cardiff Harlequins BC, **191**
Cardiff Times, **181**
Cardigan gaol, **44**

Cardigan Hiring Fair, **242**
Cardiganshire, **292**
Carmarthen, **178**
Carmarthen Journal, **117**
Carmarthenshire, **188**, **274**, **285**
Carpentier, Georges, **310**
Carruthers, James, **141**, **143**
Carter, Mary Ann, **235**
Castell Coch, **289**
Castle, Newport, **68**
Caunt, Ben, **155**, **298**
Cecil, Joseph, **276**
Cefncilsanws, **278**
Central Criminal Court, popularly known as the Old Bailey, **105**, **294**, **295**
Central-Hall, Holborn, **203**, **226**
Chambers, Arthur, **191**
Chambers, John Graham, **127**, **188**
Chambers, William, **127**
Champion, **2**, **109**, **114**, **146**, **154**, **159**, **244**, **259**
Channell, Mr. Justice, **296**
Charing-cross Hospital, **295**
Charles, Bill, **11**, **51**, **116**, **128**, **135**, **137**, **138**, **155**, **157**
Chartist uprising, **126**
Chepstow, **28**, **32**, **56**, **80**, **128**, **174**, **185**, **196**, **251**, **259**
Cherry Fair, Presteigne, **241**
Cheshire, **15**, **161**
Chester, **15**, **79**
Chew, Charlie, **268**
China, **20**, **43**
Chipping Sodbury, **157**
Chirk, **274**, **279**
Christmas Day fights, **178**
Church, **169**, **178–81**
Churchill, Winston, **307**
Chwarel y Fan, **285**
Cincinnati, **220**, **222**, **224**
Clarke, Nobby, **155**
Cleverly, Nathan, **299**
Cloddiau, **1**
Cloggy, **171**

317

Clydach Vale, **20, 267, 282, 290, 336**
Coedpenmaen, **283**
Cole, William, **160**
Coleman, Ann, **234**
Coleman, Annie, **234**
Coleman, Charlotte, **234**
Coleman, Redmond, **29, 41, 42, 44, 52, 82, 209, 216, 233, 234, 282**
Collard, Edward Augustus, **34, 36, 63, 74, 279**
Collins, Charles, **173**
Collins, Cornelius, **34, 279**
Collins, Drummer, **207**
Collins, John, **56**
Collins, Michael, **14**
Collins, Sergeant, **207**
Colour bar, **305**
Commissioners for Education Report, **126, 131**
Condie, Harry, **240**
Confederate army, **224**
Connors, J., **288**
Conwy, **91**
Cook, David, **29, 31**
Cook, Sol, **268**
Cook, Thomas, **138**
Cooper's Fields, Cardiff, **12, 17**
Copleston, Edward, Bishop of Llandaff, **95**
Corbett, James J., **229**
Cornick, William, **283**
Courts, **7, 8, 33, 60, 98**
Covington, Kentucky, **220**
Cowbridge, **8, 158, 290**
Craddock, Edward, **34**
Craig, Frank, **174, 203, 205, 220**
Crawley Hurst, **106**
Cribb, Tom, **79**
Crimes, **42–50**
Cropley, Alex, **130**
Cross Vane, **29**
Crowley, Cornelius, **277**
Crowther, Morgan, **8, 16, 25, 31, 41, 42, 43, 54, 68, 72, 73, 75, 80, 81, 191, 210, 211, 212**

Crowther, Richard, **43, 292**
Crumlin, **210, 262, 280**
Culley, Tom, **283**
Cullis, Harry, **251**
Cummings, Patsy, **82**
Curtis, John, **34, 60, 62, 104**
Cwmavon, **276**
Cwmbach, **232**
Cwmbargoed, **15**
Cwmddu, **229**
Cwmdu, **179**
Cwmparc, **284**
Cymmer, **14, 276, 288, 289**
Cynon Valley, **90**

D

Daffy's Elixir, **51**
Daniels, **21**
Danter, Jane, **259**
Danter, Louisa, **259**
Danter, William, **259**
Dartford, **186**
Dartmoor prison, **168**
Davies (Caerphilly), **251**
Davies, Aaron, **58**
Davies, Dai, **217**
Davies, Daniel, **76**
Davies, David, **281**
Davies, Edward, alias Ned Diendaid, **282**
Davies, Enoch, **34**
Davies, Griffith, **192**
Davies, Iorwerth 'Curly', **268**
Davies, John (2), **158**
Davies, John (3), **34**
Davies, John, 'The Lame Chick', *148*
Davies, Joseph, **14**
Davies, Lloyd 'Kid', **260, 305**
Davies, Mary, **115**
Davies, Morgan, **277**
Davies, Paul, **268**
Davies, Richard, **34**
Davies, Sam, **59**
Davies, Sarah Ann, **232**

Index

Davies, Susan, **232**, **234**, **235**
Davies, Sydney, **289**
Davies, Thomas, **34**, **35**, **55**, **61**, **62**, **214**, **226**, **263**
Davies, Thomas (2), **14**, **31**, **173**
Davies, Thomas (3), **29**, **76**
Davies, Tom, **289**
Davies, William, **34**
Davies, William (2), **289**
Davies, William John, **282**
Davis, Bill, **129**
Davis, Cyrus, **106**, **107**
Davis, David 'Welsh', **25**, **137**, **153**
Davis, George, **57**, **97**, **113**
Davis, Tom, **162**
Day, James, **251**, **252**
Dayton, Ohio, **222**
Denbigh, **56**, **119**, **241**, **243**
Denbighshire, **15**
Desmond, Daniel, **45**, **82**, **218**
Deutschland, **162**
Devon, **212**
Devonport, **226**
Digger Stanley, **292**
Dillon, Jem, **23**, **210**
Dixon, George, **56**
Dixon, George (2), **212**, **266**
Dixon, Phillip, **78**
Doctors, **108**, **313**
Dolling, Dai, **227**, **292**
Domnall, Charles, **309**
Donovan, Pat, **78**
Dougie, 'Tubby', **13**
Douglas, John Sholto, Marquess of Queensberry, **189**
Dover, **144**
Dowlais, **29**, **146**, **220**, **276**
Drill Hall, Swansea, **193**
Driscoll, 'Peerless' Jim, **1**, **291**, **310**
Drunkenness, **2**, **49**, **50**, **53**, **134**, **138**, **216**
Duffryn Valley, **287**
Dukestown, Sirhowy, **36**
Dunbar, Bob, **23**, **47**, **52**, **59**, **82**, **217**, **246**, **249**, **252**, **259**

Dunbar, Milly, **258**
Durban, **209**
Dynover Arms, Pontypridd, **11**

E

Earl of Essex, **148**
Earl of Kingston, **297**
Earnings, **67–82**
Ebbw Vale, **79**, **96**, **146**, **179**, **276**, **277**
Ebbw Vale., **287**
Edmunds, Johnny, **268**
Edwards, **173**, **276**, **277**
Edwards, Thomas, **59**
Edwards, Thomas (2), **34**
Edwards, Watkin, **13**
Edwards, William, alias 'Will Gwas y Doctor', **43**
Ellery, Samiel, **69**
Empire Theatre, Cardiff, **175**
Empire theatre, Swansea, **217**
Engineer, Shoni, see John Jones, **18**
Epsom Races, **229**
Erskine, Joe, **302**, **309**
Eton public school, **89**
Evans, Abraham, **20**, **288**
Evans, Dale, **305**
Evans, David, **14**
Evans, Evan, **34**
Evans, Harry, **57**
Evans, Illtud, **274**
Evans, Lewis John, **283**
Evans, Philip, **283**
Evans, Richard (2), **92**
Evans, Richard., **52**, **75**
Evans, the Welch collier., **161**
Evans, Thomas, **34**, **64**
Evans, Thomas (2), **34**
Evans, Victor, **284**
Evans, W. J. G., **269**
Evasions, **10–16**
Evening Express, **181**

319

F

Fair Play Club, **125**, **152**
Fan Foel, **285**
Farquhar, George, **249**
Farr, Tommy, **240**, **274**
Fear, Samuel, **283**
Ferndale, **55**, **63**, **241**, **257**, **279**, **283**
Ferry Side, **130**
Fiddler's Green, **15**, **159**
Fire Island, New York, **226**
Fishguard, **88**
Fitzgerald, James, **173**
Fitzsimmons, Bob, **202**, **205**, **229**
Flemingstone, **95**
Fletcher, Robert, **62**
Fletcher, Tom, **292**
Flint, **179**, **181**, **256**
Flintshire, **9**, **15**
Flying Eagle, Cardiff, **80**
Flynn, Mike, **58**
Flynn, Paddy, **151**
Flynn, Paul, **313**
Flynn, Tom, **59**
Fochrhiw, **17**
Folies Bergere, **5**, **206**
Forch, **20**
Ford, Pancho, **268**
Ford, William, **290**
Forecast, Ann, **233**
Forest of Dean, **232**
Forester's Arms, Cardiff, **80**, **232**
Foster, Tudor, **276**
Foulkes, **137**
Fourteen Locks, **12**, **173**
Fownhope, **114**
Freeman, Charles, **160**
Fury, Martin, **251**, **256**
Fury, Matthew, **192**

G

Gambling, **71–74**, **118**
Gardiner, Bill, **128**, **136**, **137**, **158**
Garndiffaith, **56**, **159**
Gas, **128**
Gatewen, **28**
Gatling gun', **222**
Gelli, 230, **283**
Gelligaer, **14**, **31**, **55**
Gelliwion, **18**
George the Sailor, **93**, **94**
Germany, **209**
Gess, Frank, **251**, **260**
Gess, Joe, **251**
Giants' Cave, **12**, **279**
Gibb, Tom, **91**
Giles, John, **172**
Gilfach, **29**
Gilfachyrincle, **179**
Gillam, Bill, **147**
Gillan, **67**
Gimlet, William, **21**
Gladstone. William, **174**
Glamorgan, **12**, **15**, **35**, **37**, **49**, **50**, **148**, **182**, **185**, **233**, **241**, **273**
Glancy, Richard, **44**
Glascoed Common, **156**
Glasgow, **103**, **305**
Glatchen, Yanto, **15**
Gloucester, **117**, **139**
Gloucestershire, **156**, **159**, **185**
Glyn Ponds, **14**
Glyncorrwg, **173**, **283**
Glynneath, **289**
Glynneath Valley, **288**
Goitre pond, 12
Gold Tops, 12
Golden Lion, Swansea, **32**
Good Morning Judge, **293**
Goodwin Club, London, **211**
Gow, **151**
Gower, **91**
Grand Duke Nicholas, of Russia, **90**
Grand National, **292**
Grand Theatre, Cardiff, **175**
Grand Theatre, Liverpool, **176**
Grant, Jack, alias Henry Williams, **44**
Grantham, Mr. Justice, **296**
Gray, Mrs., **236**

Index

Greek George, **54**
Green Meadows, **113**
Green Point Common, **209**
Green, Bill, **129**
Green, William, **259**
Greenhill, **43**
Gregor, William Henry, **290**
Grenadier Guards, **206**
Grey, Morgan, **197**
Greyhound, Cowbridge, **158**
Griffiths, **151**
Griffiths, (2), **114**
Griffiths, Johnny, **268**
Gruffyth ap Rees, **86**
Gulliver, Sam, **52**, **54**, **186**, **213**, **218**
Gun and Tent, London, **80**
Gwaunfarren, 12

H

Hadfield, George M.P., **168**
Hafod, **279**
Haines, William, **57**
Hall, Albert, **262**
Hall, Jem, **205**
Hamlet, Thomas, **161**
Hampshire, **167**
Hands, Dick, **129**
Hare and Greyhound, Newport, **45**
Harewood End, **94**
Harp Tavern, London, **107**
Harris, **276**
Harris (Flint), **251**
Harris, ?, **77**
Harris, Battling, **267**
Harris, James, **282**
Harris, John Henry, **45**
Harris, Tom, **250**
Haverfordwest, **93**, **218**, **241**, **301**
Hay, **34**, **243**
Hayes, Jem, **204**
Hayman, Chaffy, **25**, **72**
Health, **57**, **58**, **60**, **61**, **62**, **99**, **107**, **170**, **201**

Heenan, John, **23**, **163**, **164**, **167**, **174**, **235**, **287**
Henllys, **29**
Hereford, **15**, **117**
Herefordshire, **15**, **94**, **114**, **158**, **161**, **185**
Hertfordshire, **105**, **137**
Heycock, George, **120**
Hilbre Island, **185**
Hirwaun, **16**, **73**
His People, **293**
Hitchings, Jack, **218**
HMS Cambridge, **226**
Hoddell, W., **135**, **159**, **160**
Holt, **133**
Holt Castle Green, **15**
Holwell, Bill, **161**
Hooligan, Tom, **47**, 214, **254**
Hooligan, William, **48**
Hope and Anchor Tavern, Swansea, **69**
Hopkin, Rees, **34**, **76**
Hopkins, John, **34**, **63**, **279**, **290**
Horner, Luke, **78**
Horton, **93**
House of Commons, **81**, **169**
How Green Was My Valley, **284**
Howard, Jack, **129**
Howe's and Cushing's Circus, **174**
Howe's Great American Circus, **174**
Howell, David, **160**
Howells, William, **277**
Hucker, Jem, **226**
Huddersfield, **135**, **162**
Hugh the Drover, **293**
Hughes, Edwin, **119**
Hughes, Harry, **252**
Hughes, Morris, **290**
Hughes, Sam, **249**
Hughes, Thomas, **91**
Hughes, Thomas (2), **184**
Hughes, William, **13**
Huish, Joseph, **276**, **282**
Humphreys, Richard, **34**, **60**, **128**, **135**, **159**
Humphries, **65**

321

Hunt, Bert, **267**
Huntsman and Hounds,London, **103**
Hyams, 'Mangle', **191**
Hyde Park, London, **85**

I

Ilfracombe, **74**
Illinois county gaol, **223**
Indian Rebellion, **218**
Ingle, Paul, **305**
Inglis, Peace, **107**, **108**
Ingram, David, **128**, **147**
Injuries, **57–62**
International Amateur Boxing Association, AIBA, **300**
International Boxing Federation, **299**
Ireland, **43**, **106**, **170**, **209**, **220**
Irish, **130**, **135**, **157**, **163**, **168**, **209**
Irving, Washington, **90**
Isaac, John, **76**
Isaacs, Shony, **15**
Isle of Grain, **142**
Israel, Tom, **173**

J

Jack of Finchley, **151**
Jack of the Wern, **1**, **91**
Jackson, **161**
Jackson, Peter, **174**, **188**, **196**, **206**, **307**
James, David John, **289**
James, Evan, **160**
James, John, **279**
James, John Jenkin, **34**, **63**
James, Lyn, **312**
James, Richard, **47**, **80**, **146**, **218**
James, Sam, **13**
James, Tom, **47**, **78**, **193**, **206**, **281**
James, William, **18**, **289**
James, William (2), **55**
Jeffersonville, Indiana, **183**
Jeffries, James J., **306**
Jenkins, Dai, **56**, **283**, **287**, **288**
Jenkins, David, **129**

Jenkins, Jack, **59**
Jenkins, Police sergeant, **237**
Johannesburg, **208**
John, Edmund, **20**
Johnson, Fred, **211**
Johnson, Jack, **294**, **306**
Johnson, Sam, **267**
Jolly Sailor, Cardiff, **232**
Jones, **34**
Jones (the Welch Champion), **22**, **72**, **137**, **162**
Jones, Aaron, **19**, **55**, **57**, **75**, **80**, **148**, **149**, **163**, **164**, **223**
Jones, Albert, **18**
Jones, Andrew, **69**, **129**
Jones, Barry, **299**
Jones, Charles, 'Charley the Well', **76**, **172**
Jones, D., **113**, **116**, **217**
Jones, David, **283**
Jones, Francis, **281**
Jones, George (Punch), **29**, **54**
Jones, Harry, **78**, **152**
Jones, Harry (2), **128**
Jones, Henry, **48**
Jones, Hugh, alias Huwcyn Twyrch, **119**
Jones, Jack, **63**, **163**, **164**, **254**, **274**, **284**
Jones, Jack (2), **268**
Jones, John, **282**
Jones, John, alias Shoni Engineer, **47**, **76**, **173**, **210**, **216**, **249**, **257**, **281**, **285**
Jones, Morgan, **114**
Jones, Percy, **1**, **299**
Jones, Robert, **120**
Jones, Sampson, **159**
Jones, Stephen, **38**
Jones, Thomas 'Paddington', **111**
Jones, Tom, **159**, **161**
Jones, Welsh, **135**
Jones, William, **44**, **173**, **282**
Jones, William (2), **114**
Jones, William (3), **14**
Jordan, **154**, **155**
Joshua, Anthony, **302**

Index

Judges, **9**, **25**, **33**, **56**, **108**, **194**
Judson, John, **44**, **48**, **59**
Justices praised, **22**

K

Kensington Social Club, **211**
Kent, **142**, **144**, **186**
Kentucky, **220**
Kenyon, Lloyd, **9**
Kerigkadarn, **114**
Kilrain, Jake, **174**
King Edward VII, **181**
King George 1, **85**
King George IV, **78**, **85**, **86**
King, Herbert, **283**
King, Police-constable, **237**
King's Arms, Blaenavon, **32**
King's Arms, Swansea, **81**, **253**
Kings Head, Chepstow, **80**
Kirkman, Jem, **150**, **151**
Knifton, John, **49**, **180**
Knight, John Henry, **45**
Knight, Rocky, **308**
Knott, Arthur, **267**

L

Lache-Eyes, **15**
Lafferty, Johnny, **220**
Lake Eyrie, **163**
Lake, Colin, **312**
Lake, Edward, **57**
Lambert, Tom, **56**
Lambeth, **204**
Lambeth School of Arms, **204**
Lancashire 'up and down fighting', **61**
Lancet, **184**, **304**
Lane, Will, **276**
Lang, Jem, **307**
Langan, Jack, **100**
Langford, Sam, **294**, **307**
Langham, Nat, **144**
Latcham, Isaac, **34**, **63**, **279**
Lawrence, Bill, the Gipsy Tinker, **171**

Leader, Thomas, **280**
Leahy, Billy, **210**
Leahy, Private, **207**
Leavenworth, Indiana, **225**
Lecture Theatre, Cardiff, **193**
Lenton, the India-rubber Clown, **130**
Leslie, Charlotte, **300**
Lewis, a Welshman', **113**
Lewis, Edward, **34**
Lewis, Ernest, **283**
Lewis, Henry, **34**
Lewis, Henry (2), **34**
Lewis, John, **43**, **48**, **113**
Lewis, John M.P., **309**
Lewis, Philip, **68**
Lewis, Richard, **131**
Lewis, Roderick, **92**
Lewis, Sir George, **9**, **168**
Lewis, Ted Kid, **292**
Liability, **7–10**
Life Guards, **207**
Lisvane, **21**
Little Ireland', **43**
Liverpool, **68**, **138**, **176**, **186**, **259**
Livingstone, Murray, **294**
Llanbadarn Fynydd, **34**, **128**
Llandaff, **55**, **71**, **93**, **94**, **95**, **241**, **244**, **255**, **257**
Llandovery, **20**, **218**
Llandovery public school, **293**
Llandrindod Wells, **108**
Llandudno Eisteddfod, **176**
Llanedeyrn, **185**
Llanelli, **127**, **178**, **181**, **184**, **188**, **231**, **243**, **249**
Llangollen, **59**, **129**, **158**, **274**, **279**
Llangyfelach, **233**, **243**, **244**, **257**
Llangynidir, **276**
Llansamlet, **250**
Llantwit Fardre, **27**
Llantwit Major, **241**
Llanwonno, **29**, **38**, **63**, **277**, **278**, **279**
Lledrddu, **278**
Llewellyn, Evan, **13**
Llewellyn, Ned, **16**

323

Llewellyn, Richard, **274**
Lloyd, Ben, **41, 207, 208**
Lloyd, Marie, **176**
Lloyd, Richard, **276**
Llwynypia, **173**
Locke, Arthur, **214, 295**
London, **5, 7, 10, 23, 33, 46, 51, 54, 68, 70, 73, 80, 85, 86, 87, 88, 90, 94, 103, 104, 105, 107, 111, 112, 113, 115, 116, 117, 118, 123, 124, 125, 134, 144, 147, 148, 149, 153, 154, 155, 157, 158, 161, 168, 175, 180, 186, 187, 188, 191, 195, 196, 201, 202, 203, 204, 210, 211, 212, 213, 214, 216, 226, 233, 275, 276, 281, 285, 294**
London Prize Ring Rules, **135, 136, 188, 195, 196, 275, 276**
Long Point, Ontario, **163**
Lord Ellenborough, **60**
Lord Gwydir, **85**
Lord Lonsdale, **297, 307**
Lord Morrison, **312**
Lord Palmerston, **4**
Lord Raglan Inn, Aberdare, **80**
Lord Raglan, Newport, **45**
Los Angeles, **313**
Loughor, **178**
Louisiana, **224**
Louisville, Kentucky, **220, 291**
Lushington, **107**
Lydney, **17, 247**
Lynch, Charles, **147**

M

Mabon's day', **177**
Macarte's American Circus, **130**
Maccarinelli, Enzo, **299**
Macdonald, James, **277**
Mace, Jem, **22, 146, 174, 177, 209**
Maesteg, **14, 31, 173, 261, 283, 287, 289, 290, 342, 357**
Maggs, Frank, **283**
Magistrates, **15**

Magor, **146**
Mahers, John, **113**
Maindy, **278, 282**
Manchester, **138**
Manchester ruling, **10**
Mandry, Sam, **34, 36, 55, 192, 193, 194, 264**
Manning, **153**
Mardy, 230, **281**
Markey, Mickey, **303**
Marks, Harry, **191**
Marlborough, **95**
Maroney, Thomas, **48, 182**
Marquis of Westminster, **15**
Marshfield, **185, 285**
Martin, **87**
Martin, John, **106**
Martin, Johnny, **267**
Mason's Arms, Swansea, **32**
Matchett, John, **251**
Matthews, Ellen, **232**
Matthews, Henry, **9**
Matthews, Jack, **26, 46, 80, 81, 232**
Matthias, Richard, **75**
Maxfield, Thomas, **148**
Mazey, Rees, **55**
McCann, Thomas, **64, 223**
McCool, Mike, **224**
McCoy, Charles 'Kid', **293**
McIntyre,, **129**
McKenna, Reginald, **311**
Meade County, Kentucky, **221**
Mendoza, Daniel, **65, 93, 97, 198**
Meredith, William, **282**
Merrin, Tom, **212, 226**
Merthyr, **11, 12, 15, 17, 20, 29, 41, 43, 44, 49, 52, 55, 62, 63, 64, 68, 82, 94, 146, 173, 174, 179, 187, 192, 193, 204, 206, 209, 213, 216, 218, 231, 232, 233, 234, 254, 255, 256, 278, 279, 281, 282, 285, 289, 295, 299, 313**
Merthyr Drill Hall, **193**
Merthyr Riots, **43, 126**
Merthyr Tydfil baths, **193**

Index

Merthyr Tydfil baths, **193**
Merthyr Tydfil Orpheus Society, **49**
Middlesex, **137**
Millbank prison, **151**
Mitchell, Alf, **68, 80, 201, 204, 212**
Mitchell, Charley, **293**
Mitchell, Charlie, **174**
Mitchell, Joe, **173, 278**
Mitchell, Peter, **34**
Mobile, Alabama, **224**
Mochdre, **91**
Moir, Gunner, **310**
Moira, Cardiff, **80**
Mold, **255**
Molineaux, **86, 93**
Monmouth, **8, 15, 94, 128, 157, 174**
Monmouth Cap, **15, 128, 157**
Monmouthshire, **2, 5, 11, 14, 16, 19, 24, 27, 29, 68, 77, 93, 94, 141, 142, 147, 155, 156, 159, 167, 179, 185, 204, 210, 220, 234, 242, 262, 273, 285**
Monmouthshire Baptist Association, **290**
Montague, Admiral Victor, **297**
Montgomeryshire, **15, 22, 60, 67, 92, 103, 111, 112**
Montreal, **164**
Moody, Frank, **285, 308**
Mooi River, **209**
Moran, Owen, **310**
Morella's Palace of Varieties, Cardiff, **175**
Morfa Mawr, **178**
Morgan, Billy, **49, 52, 197, 210, 214**
Morgan, David, **129**
Morgan, David (2), **154**
Morgan, James, **159**
Morgan, Jenkin, **34**
Morgan, Jerry, **80, 81**
Morgan, John, **14, 25**
Morgan, Thomas, **76**
Morgan, Walter, **34, 64**
Morgan, William, **55**
Morganwg, Iolo, **95**

Morris, Arthur, **201**
Morris, John, **303**
Morrisey, John, **163, 164**
Morrison, Enoch, **47, 59, 251, 259, 305**
Morrison, Harriet, **259**
Morriston, **170, 177, 198**
Moseley, Solomon, **93**
Moulders Arms, Newport, **80**
Mountain Air Inn, Penyrheol, **14**
Mountain Ash, **180, 278, 294, 301**
Mr. Noon, **145**
Mullan, Harry, **304**
Mynachlog-ddu, Pembrokeshire, **160**

N

Nahillah, **292**
Nantyglo, **283**
Nantymoel, **179**
Napier, Capt.Charles Frederick, **233**
Napoleon, **89**
National Boxing Association, **299**
National Sporting Club, **68, 188, 202, 212, 281, 294, 297, 298**
Nazareth House, **49, 206**
Neat, Bill, **115**
Neath, **13, 22, 93, 159, 206, 216, 249, 252, 258, 261**
Neath Valley, **288**
Ned of the Green Hills, **119**
Nelson, J. G., **306**
Nepor, Jim, **306**
New Jersey State prison, **163**
New Market Street, Usk, **13**
New Orleans, **202, 220, 225**
New Orleans Olympic Club, **205**
New Tredegar, **179, 283**
New York, **163, 164, 218, 219**
Newbridge, **16, 234, 299**
Newcastle, **104, 223**
Newcastle racecourse, **103**
Newgate prison, **89**
Newnom, John, **158**
Newport, **11, 12, 17, 20, 22, 23, 26, 28, 44, 45, 51, 52, 57, 59, 73, 78, 80,**

325

93, 94, **128, 129, 132, 133, 146,
155, 158, 167, 172, 173, 182, 210,
211, 213, 217, 234, 241, 245, 246,
252, 259, 280, 312**
Newport Gymnastic Club, **212**
Newport Rugby Club, **212**
Newspaper Stamp Act, 1855, **155**
Newspapers, **5, 42, 52, 62, 63, 117,
118, 155, 263**
Newton hero, **129**
Newtown, Montgomeryshire, **103, 107,
108, 160**
Neyland, **260**
Nicholas, Philip, **34**
Nick-names, **76**
Noah's Ark Inn, Newport, **131**
Noel, Baptist Wriothesley, **184**
Nolan, Joe, **147**
Norris, W., **282**
North America, **163**
North Wales Gazette, **117**
North, Charlie, **80, 251, 258, 259**
Northey, Jack, **29, 44, 48, 72, 173, 218,
278**
Nottinghamshire, **207**

O

O'Brien, John, **47, 54, 68, 72, 74, 80,
188, 201, 202, 203, 205, 209, 212,
216, 246, 249, 285**
O'Leary, Patsy, **183, 220, 222**
O'Shea, Donoghue (Dennis), **55**
Oates, Joyce Carol, **300, 302**
Occupations, **74–82**
Offences Against the Persons Act 1861, **9**
Ogmore Vale, **58**
Old Gloucester School of Arms,
Swansea, **253**
Old Pine Apple, Cardiff, **11, 80**
Old Red Cow, Newport, **11**
Oliveira, Benjamin, MP, **123**
Oliver, Spencer, **304**
Olympia, London, **307**
Olympic Games, **96, 300**

Orange Free State, **208**
Orme, Harry, **149**
Ormonde Club, London, **285**
Osborne, **254**
Osborne, George, alias Captain Marco,
79
Owen, Billy, **99, 117**
Owen, Evan, **186**
Owen, John, **54**
Owen, Johnny, **313**
Owens, Richard, **171**
Oxford, **95**
Oxford Arms, Presteigne, **160**
Oxwich, **91**

P

Palmer, Pedlar, **13**
Pancratics, **175**
Pandy Field, **192, 264**
Pankration, **96**
Pannwr, Ellis, **91**
Paris, **5, 206, 242**
Paris Exhibition, **242**
Parrot Inn, Merthyr, **53**
Parry, Robert, **94, 100**
Parsons, James, **264**
Pea, Bill, **129**
Peak, Thomas, **33, 92**
Pearson, Thomas, **47, 75, 249**
Peckham Fields, London, **112**
Pedestrianism, **183**
Pelican Club, **23, 187, 307**
Pembrey, **274**
Pembrokeshire, **235**
Pen y Fan, **285**
Pencoed, **19**
Penderyn, Dic, **43**
Pendry, ?, **77, 276**
Pengam, **14**
Pengarnddu, **18**
Penhow, **132**
Penrhiwceiber, **289**
Penrhys, **279, 282, 283**
Penrice Fair, **91**

Pentre, **279**
Penydarren Park, **12**
Penyrheol, **14**
People's Palace, Plymouth, **226**
People's Park, Pontypridd, **187**, **192**, **217**
Perkins, Patsy, **47**, **68**, **74**, **193**, **213**, **252**, **253**, **254**, **264**, **292**
Perks, Jack, **129**
Perrott Inn, Quaker's Yard, **12**
Perry, James 'Jem', **191**, **193**, **226**
Persia, **162**
Peterstone, **22**
Philadelphia, **80**, **223**
Philharmonic Hall, Cardiff, **175**, **229**
Phillips, James, **288**
Phillips, Richard, **289**
Pick, **152**
Pick, George, **161**
Pierce, David, **13**
Pike, **129**
Pintor, Lupe, **313**
Pittsburgh, **226**
Platt, Abraham, **93**
Pleasant View, **32**
Pleasant View Inn, Aberdare Hill, **32**
Plymouth Iron Works, Merthyr, **179**
Plymouth works, **15**
Point of Ayr, **186**
Police, **7**, **8**, **10**, **11**, **12**, **14**, **15**, **16**, **17**, **18**, **19**, **20**, **21**, **22**, **23**, **24**, **25**, **26**, **27**, **28**, **29**, **31**, **45**, **46**, **68**, **72**, **74**, **80**, **81**, **147**, **150**, **154**, **169**, **173**, **179**, **185**, **186**, **190**, **191**, **192**, **209**, **210**, **220**, **230**, **231**, **232**, **233**, **235**, **237**, **253**, **254**, **257**, **258**, **261**, **262**, **263**, **273**, **276**, **294**
Pontnewynydd, **2**, *See* Wintle
Pontsarn, **132**
Pontycymmer, **289**
Pontypool, **14**, **17**, **25**, **52**, **82**, **159**, **179**, **230**, **243**, **262**
Pontypridd, **18**, **19**, **45**, **47**, **56**, **80**, **146**, **148**, **174**, **179**, **187**, **192**, **193**, **206**, **217**, **252**, **274**, **281**, **283**, **285**, **291**, **299**, **312**
Port Talbot, **277**
Porth, **34**, **63**, **74**, **182**, **230**, **241**, **258**, **279**, **290**, **299**, **356**, **365**
Porthcawl, **45**, **288**
Portishead, **185**
Portobello, Jack, **16**
Powell, Edmund, **276**
Powell, Thomas, **94**, **100**
Powys, **285**
Presbyterian Church of Wales, **181**
Press gangs, **88**
Presteigne, **34**, **160**, **241**, **242**, **256**
Preston, **154**
Price, **137**
Price, George, **290**
Price, Harry, **303**
Price, John, **289**
Price, Lewis, **34**
Price, Thomas, **34**, **128**, **290**
Price, William, **34**
Prince of Wales, **86**, **181**
Prior, **162**
Pritchard, Ted, **45**, **72**, **74**, **175**, **201**, **203**, **205**, **212**
Pugh, **137**
Pugh Smith, John, **131**
Pugh, Ernest, **281**
Pugh, Thomas, **33**, **34**, **279**
Pugilistic Benevolent Society, **60**
Punch Bowl, Blaenavon, **14**
Punch-up in Parliament, **168**
Purcell, Luke, **160**
Pyle, **288**

Q

Quaker's Yard, **14**, **64**
Queen Caroline, **85**
Queensbury Rules, **189**, **190**, **193**, **194**, **221**, **239**, **264**, **275**, **277**, **284**, **288**, **302**
Queensbury Rules of Endurance, **193**

R

R. v Coney, **7**, **32**
R. v Hunt, **8**
Radnorshire, **9**, **15**, **34**, **60**, **128**, **159**, **160**
Raglan, **45**, **80**, **128**, **137**, **158**
Railway Inn, Aberdare, **8**
Railway Inn, Abersychan,, **32**
Rand, **208**
Randall 'the giant', **160**
Randall, Jack, **71**, **106**, **111**
Rasher, Jack, **112**
Raymond, Jack, **193**
Reardon, Patsy, **23**, **42**, **55**, **64**, **136**, **186**, **209**, **210**, **223**
Rebecca riots, **95**, **126**, **160**, **233**
Red Lion, Cardiff, **80**
Redbrook, **14**
Redmond, David John, **265**
Rees, Dai 'Buller', **54**, **59**, **276**
Rees, David, **34**, **35**, **64**
Rees, Gavin, **299**
Rees, Thomas. Twm Carnabwth, **160**
Rees, Tom, **289**
Rees, W. D., **277**
Rees, William, **173**
Regan, Robbie, **299**
Resolven, **29**, **202**, **283**, **288**
Rhigos, **288**
Rhondda, **29**, **41**, **48**, **52**, **58**, **74**, **80**, **176**, **179**, **181**, **182**, **192**, **207**, **230**, **235**, **241**, **243**, **245**, **246**, **273**, **278**, **279**
Rhondda Valley, **52**, **176**, **181**, **182**, **207**, **230**, **241**, **279**, **288**, **289**
Rhydycar Tips, **12**
Rhyl, **132**
Rhymney, **12**, **14**, **19**, **56**, **77**, **173**, **193**, **276**, **277**, **292**, **356**, **363**, **378**
Rhymney Public-hall, **193**
Richards, **173**
Richards, Bill, **78**
Richards, David, **35**, **279**
Richards, John, **34**, **36**, **59**, **80**

Richards, M., **131**
Richards, Thomas, **273**
Ring deaths, **33**, **41**, **62**, **63**
Riot Act, **7**, **10**
Risca, **28**
River Brent, **137**
River Dee, **185**
River Mersey, **138**
Roach, George, **266**
Roath, **201**
Roberts, Annie, **258**
Roberts, Jack, **294**, **296**, **297**
Roberts, John, **91**
Roberts, Lloyd, **252**
Roberts, Trevor, **34**
Roberts, Walter, **34**
Robinson, Jemmy, **56**
Robinson, John, **34**
Robinson, Oliver, **283**
Robinson, Steve, **299**
Rock and Fountain, Penhow, **73**, **128**
Rodda, John, **304**
Rodway, Alfred, **277**
Rogers, Luke, **78**
Rolling Mill, Abertillery, **290**
Rooke, ?, **289**
Rooke, John, **23**, **186**, **210**
Rooke, Morris, **76**
Rooney, Tom, **193**, **213**
Roper, Samuel, **251**
Rose, William, **264**
Ross, **158**
Rowlands, George, alias Gipsy George, **54**, **82**
Royal Albert-hall, **23**
Royal College of Nursing, **304**
Royal Cornwall Gazette, **127**
Royal Navy, **226**
Rumney, **16**, **28**, **61**, **130**, **172**, **173**
Ruthin, **233**, **257**
Ryan, **173**
Ryan, Tommy, **219**

Index

S

Sacheverell riots, **10**
Sage, Smith, **56**, **159**
Salt Lake City, **291**
Salvation Army, **78**, **182**, **260**
Sampson, Martin, **267**
Samuel, Bill, **47**, **61**, **62**, **80**, **81**, **183**, **216**, **217**, **243**, **244**, **246**, **247**, **249**, **250**, **251**, **253**, **254**, **258**, **260**, **261**, **263**
Samuel, Elizabeth, **253**, **254**, **260**
San Francisco earthquake, **291**
Saunders, Jockey, **246**
Savage brothers, **70**, **152**, **153**
Savage, Bill, **149**, **151**
Savage, Edward, **46**, **61**, **69**, **70**, **123**, **124**, **135**, **137**, **150**, **153**, **154**
Savannah, **162**
Sawbridgeworth, **105**
Sayers, Tom, **23**, **42**, **44**, **139**, **141**, **142**, **143**, **144**, **145**, **148**, **149**, **163**, **164**, **167**, **170**, **174**, **235**, **287**
Scarrott, Jack, **243**, **250**, **257**, **258**, **261**, **265**, **266**, **268**, **284**
Scotch Cattle, **95**, **126**
Scott, Felix, **22**, **46**, **68**, **239**, **250**, **251**, **264**, **266**, **305**
Scott, Mark, **283**
Scroggins the Welch champion, **129**
Scroggins, Jack, **97**, **98**, **105**, **106**, **118**
Seaforth, Selina, **175**
Selby, Lee, **300**
Senghenydd, **237**
Seren Gomer, **117**
Shaw, **129**
Shaw, George Bernard, **2**, **194**, **196**, **302**
Shaw, Jack, **207**
Shaw, Thomas, **173**
Sheffield Arena, **305**
Shenkin, Tom, **159**
Shepperton, **106**
Shields, William, **112**
Shipp, Tom 'Shocker', **210**
Shirenewton, **57**, **80**, **141**
Shonny Shrag, **171**
Shony Skibbor y Fawr, **49**, **128**
Showmen's Guild, **269**
Shrewsbury, **148**
Shropshire, **15**, **148**
Silver, Charles, **283**
Sirhowy, **91**
Slavin, Frank, **46**, **174**, **188**
Smith, Billy, **295**, **296**, **297**
Smith, Cornelius', **69**
Smith, Jem, **174**, **188**, **205**, **307**
Smith, Seth, **277**
Smith, Sidney, **256**
Smith, Thomas Assheston, **89**
Smith, William, **210**
Smout, Robert, **112**, **116**
South Africa, **41**, **207**
South Wales Daily News, **181**
South Wales Football Club, **189**
Southampton, **264**
Sowhill, **14**
Spectators, **7**, **8**, **10**, **18**, **22**, **23**, **28**, **32**, **60**, **70**, **86**, **97**, **157**, **176**, **177**, **186**, **193**, **197**, **210**, **229**, **234**, **239**, **245**, **256**, **258**, **259**, **275**, **277**
Spencer, **129**
Sporting Life, **183**, **187**, **297**
Spring the Conjuror, **61**, **150**, **153**
Spring, Tom, **57**, **59**, **79**, **100**, **109**, **114**, **115**, **135**, **136**, **204**
Squinks, Will, **182**
Squire Harrison, **92**
St. Asaph, **82**
St. Helena, **209**
St. Ives Inn, Neath, **11**, **80**
St. John, David, **46**, **47**, **72**, **202**, **206**, **207**
St. Louis, **223**
St. Mellons, **21**, **185**
Stephens, Frederick, **34**
Stephens, Henry, **7**
Stephens, J., **222**
Stevens, **173**, **276**, **277**
Steward, Jack, **252**
Stokes, John, **251**, **258**, **259**

329

Stow Fair, Newport, **241**
Strawhat, Dai, **159**
Strong, Arthur, **267**
Strood, **142**
Studt, John, **243**, **259**
Sullivan, John L, **65**, **174**
Sully, **289**
Summerskill, Dr. Edith, **300**, **312**, **313**
Sunday Closing Act, **6**, **169**, **172**
Sunday prize fights, **17**, **133**, **169**, **178**, **230**, **263**, **277**
Sunderland Bridge, Cardiff, **32**
Sussex, **106**
Swan, Cardiff, **7**
Swansea, **10**, **12**, **27**, **29**, **32**, **35**, **43**, **47**, **48**, **49**, **52**, **55**, **61**, **62**, **72**, **76**, **78**, **80**, **81**, **94**, **117**, **126**, **127**, **129**, **160**, **171**, **180**, **192**, **193**, **197**, **198**, **207**, **214**, **217**, **226**, **229**, **234**, **244**, **247**, **249**, **253**, **254**, **263**, **291**, **299**
Swansea Sands, **12**
Sweeney, Peter, **69**, **125**, **150**, **151**
Sweeney, Tom, **150**
Swift, Owen, **80**, **139**, **140**, **148**

T

Taff Vale, **16**
Talgarth, 129
Tamplin, John, **159**
Tar, **21**
Taylor, Ron, **236**
Taylor's Boxing Emporium, **251**
Teague, Joseph, **17**
Tenby, **20**, **230**
Terratt, Dick, **267**
Thames, **27**, **137**, **186**, **210**
The four Pancratics, **175**
The Great White Hope, **293**
The Great White Way, **293**
Thomas, Albert, **283**
Thomas, Charles, **28**
Thomas, Dan, **19**, **42**, **51**, **80**, **81**, **128**, **146**, **147**, **148**, **174**, **180**, **209**, **247**
Thomas, David, **14**, **31**, **34**, **278**

Thomas, David (2), **63**
Thomas, David (3), **34**
Thomas, David, alias 'Spanker', **276**, **277**
Thomas, Delhi Lucknow, **218**
Thomas, H. W., **198**
Thomas, Ivor, **34**, **217**, **264**, **281**, **291**
Thomas, James, **277**
Thomas, John, **34**, **37**
Thomas, John (2), **118**
Thomas, John (3), **288**
Thomas, Joseph, **21**
Thomas, Richard, **13**
Thomas, Robert, **91**
Thomas, Rowland, **34**, **64**, **279**
Thomas, Sam (Butcher), **47**, **213**, **246**, **258**, **281**, **285**
Thomas, Thomas, **34**
Thomas, Thomas (2), **72**, **76**
Thomas, Tom, **245**, **292**
Thomas, William, **277**
Thomas, William, alias 'Crib', **43**
Thorn, Thomas, **27**
Three Horseshoes, Newport, **69**
Tilley, Vesta, **176**
Tirphil, **261**
Tobin, Morris, **281**
Tolley, James, **251**, **264**
Tondu, **76**, **173**
Tonypandy, **36**, **192**, **198**, **241**, **251**, **262**, **264**
Tonyrefail, **24**, **179**
Towell, Mike, **305**
Trainer, Mike, **163**
Trainor, Stephen, **128**, **157**
Tram-road champion, **129**
transatlantic cable, **162**
Transvaal, **208**
Travel, **95**, **142**
Travers, Bob, **210**
Trealaw, **21**
Treason of the Blue Books, **126**, **131**, **169**, **230**
Tredegar, **24**, **45**, **91**, **92**, **129**, **173**, **179**, **276**, **277**
Tregening, Joseph, **283**

Index

Treherbert, **277**
Treorchy, **20**, **173**, **180**, **217**, **236**, **241**, **260**, **281**, **288**
Trout Inn, Newport, **167**
Trowbridge, W. R. H., **293**
Turner, Edward, **7**, **34**, **37**, **41**, **47**, *55*, *56*, *57*, *59*, *60*, *62*, **70**, **71**, *75*, *79*, *82*, **87**, *97*, *98*, **103**, *104*, *105*, *106*, *107*, *108*, *109*, *110*, *111*, *115*, *116*, *117*, *118*, *148*, *149*, *152*
Twm Clump, **278**
Tylorstown, **56**, **282**

U

Ufton, **95**
Uitlanders, **208**
Union army, **223**
United States army, **226**
USA, **163**, **167**, **191**, **201**, **212**, **218–26**, **299**
USA navy, **218**
Usk, **2**, **13**, **27**, **132**, **146**, **159**, **244**
Usk prison, **146**

V

Valentine, Arthur, **226**
Variety acts, **175**
Vaughan Williams, Ralph, **293**
Vaughan, ?, **34**
Vaughan, Arthur, **34**, **63**
Vaughan, Dai, **285**
Vaughan, Patsy, **56**
Vaughan, Samuel, **34**
Vauneg, **158**
Vaynol estate, **89**
Vaynor, **63**, **179**, **230**
Victoria Theatre, Pontypridd, **187**, **192**

W

Walcott, Joe, **218**
Wallace, Dave, **212**
Wallace, Jem, **150**
Ward, Billy, **267**
Ward, Nick, **298**
Warner, Shamus, **47**, **56**
Warren, Frank, **304**
Warren, Tommy, **220**, **222**
Warwick racecourse, **67**
Warwickshire, **95**
Watkins, Griffith, **7**
Watkins, Joseph, **282**
Watkins, Martha, **234**
Watkins, Thomas, **34**
Watkins, William, **282**
Watt, Steve, **304**
Wattstown, **235**, **290**
Welchman, **33**, **113**, **118**, **153**
Wells, Bombardier Billy, **306**, **310**
Wells, Matt, **294**
Welsh Area Council, **269**
Welsh Boxing Association and Control Board, **298**
Welsh Harp, Flintshire, **92**
Welsh Militia Battalion, **209**
Welsh Rugby Union, **189**
Welsh, Freddie, **1**, **191**, **290**, **294**, **299**
Welshman, **162**
Welshpool, **1**, **112**
West, Tommy, **138**, **139**, **213**, **218**, **219**, **220**, **254**, **291**, **395**
Westbury, **288**
White Hart Hotel, Pontypridd, **80**
White Hart Inn, Pentwynmawr, **43**
White Hope, **293**
White Swan, Monmouth, **11**, **68**, **100**
White, Ted, **201**
Wilde, Jimmy, **1**, **240**, **250**, **274**, **284**, **299**
Wilde, John, **43**
Wilkinson, Arthur, **68**, **211**
Williams, ?, **34**
Williams, Bill the Coal, **172**
Williams, Charles, **113**
Williams, Daniel, **129**
Williams, Edward, **76**
Williams, George, **256**
Williams, Jack, **251**

331

Williams, John, **1**
Williams, John (2), **167**
Williams, John (3), **34**
Williams, John (4), **18**
Williams, Johnny, **309**
Williams, Jonathan, **68**
Williams, M., **34**
Williams, Mac, **270**
Williams, R. G., **163**
Williams, Roger, **34**, **36**, **64**
Williams, Sarah Ann, **235**
Williams, Thomas, **20**
Williams, Thomas, alias Tom the Welchman, **131**, **161**, **162**
Williams, W., **129**
Williams, William, **76**, **284**
Williamson, Johnny, **270**
Wills, John, **18**
Wilson, Tom, **211**
Wiltshire, **95**, **288**
Wiltshire, Bob, **68**, **73**, **213**, **285**
Wimbledon Common, **30**
Wind Street, Neath, **13**
Winstone, Howard, **299**
Winter, Joseph, **115**
Wintle, Thomas Morgan, **2**
Woking Common, **149**
Wolverhampton racecourse, **153**
Worcester, **117**

World Boxing Association, **299**
World Boxing Council, **299**
World Boxing Organisation, **299**
World Series of Boxing, **300**
Wrenn, Supt Henry, **20**
Wrexham, **10**, **28**, **33**, **44**, **52**, **77**, **137**, **149**, **171**, **179**, **232**, **241**, **251**, **262**
Wye, **185**

Y

Y Gweithiwr Cymreig, **181**
Ynyshir, **258**, **290**, **356**, **365**
Ynysybwl, **13**, **18**, **262**, **283**
Yorkshire, **135**, **161**
Youler, 'Davenport's Jew', **104**
Young Bloody, **92**
Young Brag, **22**, **137**, **162**
Young Cook, **268**
Young Haines, **268**
Young Joseph, **310**
Young Smacker, **268**
Ystrad, **284**
Ystrad Rhondda, **179**
Ystradgynlais, **289**

Z

Zacharias, Thomas, **34**

Fight records

Almost one thousand Welsh prize fighters have been identified in this research, but there were likely to have been many more who were active. Several factors ensure that the precise total must remain unknown.

With the sport regarded as illegal, fights tended to take place in secret, and there was no official organisation nor records kept. Many fight reports did manage to make it into the Press, increasingly as the century progressed, but a small number of recorded fights for many and long gaps between fights for others suggest there were many more.

Published information about prize fights was not always reliable, most reports were incomplete, often not including what one would reasonably regard as vital information such as forenames and/or surnames, respective weights, the fighters' places of residence, fight venues and even fight results often with most of these essential pieces missing, or the combatants merely referred to as 'two well-known pugilists'. When fighters' names were published, their spellings often varied considerably in rival newspapers and in many instances completely different names were reported, or merely nicknames, or aliases. Not only did different names present a problem identical names proved a major difficulty as well. There may have been, for example, five individuals named William Jones and four named Tom or Thomas Jones fighting in the 1890s; or there may have been just one of each, we cannot be certain. Similarly, for fighters with other popular

Welsh surnames such as Davies/Davis, Evans, James, Thomas and Williams. Another obstacle to identification was that if one fighter was known to be in a particular weight class, it did not follow that his opponent was of a similar weight; he could have been considerably heavier or lighter.

It was often only when fighters appeared in court after being caught in the act and their real names revealed that it was possible to cross-check with contests which had been reported days earlier.

'The Admiral' alias 'Brass Buttons'
1866
Aug. (Pontypool) v 'Tallow' L 16

Harrty Ainsworth (Ebbw Vale)
1902
Sep. Maesteg v Dai Jenkins W 13
Sep. Rhigos v Dai Jenkins L 16
Dec. v Dai Jenkins L 9

Jack Allen (Neath)
12 st.
1894
Sep. (Neath) v Ned Flynn (Neath) L3

…..Allsopp (Cardiff)
1888
Jun. Brynmawr v Tom Collier (Nantyglo) D 14

Richard Ambrose (Swansea)
1871- 1904
5ft. 9ins. 10st.
1893
Feb. (Gower) v Bob Wiltshire (Cardiff) L 3 disq
1894
Dec. (Swansea) v Jim O'Brien W KO 1
1895
Jul. Swansea v Charley Palmer/Johnson (USA) L rtd 7
1896
Mar. Swansea v Tom Davies W pts. 7
1899

Oct. Swansea v William Grey (Swansea) L KO 3

William Amesbury (Dowlais)
1890
Jul. v Delhi Lucknow Thomas W
(same day) v John Davies W
1891
Apr. Dowlais v John Davies (Dowlais)

Ben Andrews
1860
Jan Blaenavon v Dai Strawhat D
William Anthony
1864
Nov. Swansea v Henry Batch police halted 12

Thomas Arundell (Aberdare)
1886
Sep Henllys v John Felton police halted

William Atkins
1869
Jun. Cardiff v George Gwinn police halted

'Auguste' (Foxhole)
1895
Apr Swansea v Thomas Harries (Llansamlet) W pts
Apr Swansea v … Jenkins W 5

'Stitcher Bach'
1863

334

Fight Records

Aug. Pontypool v 'Butcher Boy' W

James 'Jem' Bainton/Baynton/Bayton (Monmouthshire)
B. 1837 5ft. 5 ½ ins 9st. 4lbs.
1868
Dec. Kentucky v Johnny Lafferty L 17

Andrew Baker (Ystradgynlais)
1910
Aug. v William James

Richard Ball (Newbridge)
1891
Mar. Newbridge v George Perry (Newbridge) police halted

Joe Ballinbrook
1886
Apr. Glasgow v Patsy Roy L 17

John Barlow
1794
Mar. Wrexham v Thomas Peak L KO

W. Barron (Cardiff)
1899
Jan. Pontypridd v Rees (Trealaw) L 4
Feb. Cardiff v J. Moore (Cardiff) W KO 10

Charles Barry (Swansea)
1896
Jan. 20 Swansea v Tom Harris (Llansamlet) L 10

William Barry (Swansea)
1895
Jun. Swansea v Thomas Harries (Llansamlet) abandoned 3

Edward Basham (Newport)
1899
Jun. Llantarnam v Henry Sweet (Newport)

Henry Batch
1864
Nov. Swansea v William Anthony police halted 12

John Batt
1863
Dec. Pontypool v John Daniels

John Beavan 'Shone Castellnedd' (Neath)
1883
Mar. Penrhiwceiber v Thomas Morgan police halted 4
1888
Mar. v Will Squink Police halted

James 'Admiral' Benbow
9 st.
1827
Sep. Llangollen v Thomas Edwards W 4

Bill Benjamin (Shirenewton)
(1824- 1906) 5ft. 10 ½ ins, 12 stone
1858
Jan. Isle of Grain v Tom Sayers L 3
1859
Apr. Ashford v Tom Sayers L 11
1861
Jul. London v Dick James (Aberdare) W 2

William Bennett (Norton Bridge)
1894
Apr. Pontypridd v Dan Evans 'Dan Matthews' Police halted

Evan Bevan (Aberdare)
1896
Jul. Craig mountain v Robert Davies (Aberdare) Police halted

Fred Bevan (Pontypridd)
1887
    v David Howell (Treforest) W
1888
Oct. Treforest v Lloyd Roberts L 3
1889
Nov. Treforest v Illtud Evans (Pontypridd) L

….Bevan

335

1888
Sep. Pontypridd v unknown

Joseph Beynon
1893
Nov. Cwmdare v Evan Llewellyn

Morgan Beynon (Capcoch)
1889
Sep. Aberdare mountain v David Howells (Mountain Ash) W

Seth Beynon (Blaenavon)
(1840-1876)
1864
May Llanfoist v William Taylor 'Billo Bach' (Blaenavon) L 32

Thomas Beynon (Merthyr)
1868
Apr. Merthyr v Rowland Thomas 75

Joseph Birch
1875
May Maesycwmmer v Benjamin Dodd L 30+ rounds

Harris Birchell
1844
Jun. Ormes Head, Caerns. v McIntyre W 65

'Joe the Black' (Swansea)
1863
Jun. Swansea v 'Joe Cloggy' (Swansea) L 17

'Blanche' (Hopkinstown)
1895
Aug. Llanwonno mountain v 'Gwynne' (Treforest) L KO

Charley Bolton
1844
Sep. v Bill Jones (Monmouth) W

.... Booth
1873
Jan. Wrexham v Charles Stevens W

Daniel Bowen (Clydach Vale)
1909
Aug. Cowbridge v Morris Hughes

John Boyes (Bagillt)
1891
Jul. Bagillt v Patrick Brown (Flint) police halted

'Butcher Boy'
1863
Aug. Pontypool v 'Stitcher Bach' L

Bill Brecon
1892
Dec. Merthyr v Arthur Watkins abandoned 3

Michael Brenon
1851
Jan. Cardiff v John Ryan

George Britton 'Cockney' (Wattstown)
1895
Mar. Ynyshir v Jack Hitchins (Ynyshir) police halted 4

Patrick Brown (Flint)
1891
Jun. Bagillt v John Boyes (Bagillt) police halted

......Brown (Bridgend)
1875
Nov. Bridgend v....Collins Brown died

.....Brown (Ebbw Vale)
1889
Mar. Ebbw Vale v unknown W

'Bruiser' (Swansea)
1891
Jun. Swansea v Young Fellow' L 3

John Brumingham
1856
Dec. Swansea v unknown

336

Fight Records

John Bryan
1881
Aug. Cardiff v Patrick Crimmins police halted

R. Bryn (Cardiff)
1888
Oct. Llandaff v W. Dwyer (Cardiff) W 13

..... Bumford
1891
Jun. Cadoxton v ....Harley L 11

'Bunt'
1896
Aug. Lledyddu mountain v 'Twm Clump' W 33

J. Burke
1902
Sep. Cardiff v |J. Connors W 0

Peter Burns 'Dublin Tom' (Cardiff)
(1862 -) 5ft. 7ins.
1887
Jan. Pencoed v John Jones 'Shoni Engineer' L 48

George Butcher
1895
Jul. Cardiff v Charles Lewis W KO 6

John Cahill
1866
May Aberdare mountain v unknown

Nicholas Cahill (Merthyr)
1897
Nov. Merthyr v Redmond Coleman

Richard Callagh (Cardiff)
1858
Jul. Rumney v William Williams (Cardiff) abandoned

Edward Calwell (Treherbert)
1900
Sep. Treherbert mountain v Edward Jeffreys

Patsy Cane (Cardiff)
1893
May Cardiff v J. Griffiths (Cardiff) L 10

.... Carey
1899
Jan Pontypridd v .... Miller W 4

Joe Cecil
1887
May Tredegar mountain v Richard Lloyd D

Bill Charles (Newport)
D, 1837 5ft. 7 ½ 12st. 13lbs.
1827
Oct. Newport v Jem Bailey W 8
Oct. Glascoed v Jem Bailey L 117
1828
Feb. Kingswood Hill v Jem Bailey W 100
1832
Jun. Monmouth Cap v Stephen Trainor W 9
1833
Apr. Raglan v William Gardiner L 38

John Charles
1866
Jun Dowlais mountain v John Edwards police halted 5

'Sowhill Chicken' (*poss, William Jones*)
1863
Jul. Llanhilleth v 'Tredegar Infant'

Henry Chidingworth
1856
Mar. Abersychan v John Jenkins

.... Chink (Newport)
B, 1877
1896
Aug. Marshfield v Sydney Morgan (Newport) L 11

'Chips'

1864
Jun. v 'Tallow' W16

P. Cleary (Rhondda)
1889
Jul. Ystrad Rhondda v J. Morgans police halted

'Joe Cloggy' (Swansea)
1863
Jun. Swansea v 'Joe the Black' (Swansea) W 17

'Twm Clump'
1896
Aug. Lledyddu mountain v 'Bunt' L 33

Redmond Coleman (Merthyr Tydfil)
(1872-1927)
5ft. 4ins. 8st. 4lbs.
1880s
beat ? Watkins over 5 rounds
Beat Rees Mazey in 7 rounds
Beat Jack Murphy in 6 rounds
1892
Nov. Tylorstown v Thomas Jones
Dec. Merthyr v Dan Evans (P'pridd) W KO 5
1893
Mar. Merthyr v Jack Sullivan (Dowlais) W 6
    Mount Pleasant v Tom Curnew (Troedirhiw) W 2
    v Charlie Mann W 1
    v Hugh Lloyd D 38
1894
Apr. 23 NSC London v Curley Howell W 1
1895
Apr. 5 Swansea v Rees Mazey ND
.. 25 Swansea v Rees Mazey ND
May 10 Swansea v Rees Mazey L 8
1897
Nov. Merthyr v Nicholas Cahill
1900
Jun. 22 Merthyr v Jack Murphy W retd. 12
Jun. Merthyr v Jack Murphy W 3
    v George Jones L
1901
Feb. 1 Merthyr v Billy Ross L KO
1902
Dec. 15 Swansea v Dai Morgan L KO
1903
Jan. 26 Cardiff v P. Burke L KO
1917
Pontypridd v Danny Plumpton ND
1919
Ynysybwl v Dai Hafod W

Edward Augustus Collard (Mardy)
1897
May Rhondda v John Thomas (Mardy) L 30

Tom Collier (Nantyglo)
1888
Jun. Brynmawr v ....Alllsopp (Cardiff) D 14

Charley Collings (Cardiff)
1861
May Rumney v Dan Davies 'Swansea Dan' W 25
May Rumney v James Fitzgerald D 117

Cornelius Collins (Mountain Ash)
1890
Apr Llanwonno mountain v John Hopkins (Miskin)
Michael Collins
1868
May Blaenavon v David Evans

....Collins (Bridgend)
1875
Nov. Bridgend v ...Brown

...Collins (Rhondda)
1895
Dec. Ferndale v Joe Knight W

Dan Connell (Cardiff)
1899
May Cardiff v ....Tamplin W retd. 6

Jack Connelly (Cardiff)

338

Fight Records

1897
Aug. Cardiff v M. Jenks W retd. 5

Will Constantine (Cardiff)
1895
Mar. Swansea v Jack Cooke (Landore) L 1
1898
Jan. Pontypridd v ….Evans (Pontypridd) L retd. 6

J. Connors (Cardiff)
1902
Sep. Cardiff v J. Burke L 9

John Conyers
1897
Oct. Resolven v Evan Hopkins police halted 5

Archie Cooke (Penygraig)
1890
Feb. Treforest v P. Coughlin (Trealaw) W 12
1893
v Tom Israel L 1
1899
Jan. Porth v Albert Jones W
Jan. Porth v J. Farleigh L

David Cooke (Abertillery)
B, 1865
1888
Aug. Tredegar v Morgan Crowther L 14

Jack Cooke (Landore)
1895
Mar. Swansea v Will Constantine W 1

William Cornick (Nantyglo)
1904
Jun. Nantyglo Mountain v Philip Evans

P. Coughlin (Trealaw)
1890
Feb. Treforest v Archie Cooke (Trealaw) L 12

Edward Craddock (Merthyr)

1897
Sep. Merthyr v Thomas Evans.

Patrick Crimmins
1881
Aug. Cardiff v John Bryan police halted

George Crithey (Ferndale)
1884
Feb. Cwmaman v Richard Mort (Mardy)

Cornelius Crowley (Merthyr)
1867
Feb. Merthyr v James MacDonald police halted 3

Morgan Crowther (Newbridge/Newport)
(1869-1932)
5ft. 3 ½ ins 8st. 4lbs.
1887
v Seth Smith (Mountain Ash) W
v Cook W
v Charley Hopkiss W
v Elly Jones W
1888
Aug. Tredegar v David Cooke W 14
Oct. Usk v
1889
Feb. Cardiff v Tom Withers (Dudley) L 22 foul
May Cardiff v Ikey John (Cardiff) D 5
Jun. Lydney v James 'Chaffy' Hayman police halted 12
Aug. 9 Cardiff v Tom 'Pawdy' McCarthy (Cardiff) W 6
Sep. 19 Cheltenham v Jack Hicks W 4
Oct 9 Newmarket v Edwin 'Nunc' Wallace W 6
1890
Jan. London v Bill Baxter (Shoreditch) L17
Mar. Hereford v … Hickman (Hereford) W 5
May. Bath v James 'Chaffy' Hayman police halted 17
Oct. Bampton v Bill Johnson (Bristol) L 5
1891

339

Feb. London v Arthur Wilkinson (Islington) W 45
Dec. London v Arthur Wilkinson W KO 42
1892
Apr. London v Tom Wilson (Leicester) L 28
1893
Apr. London v Fred Johnson W KO 20
Oct. Exeter v Tom Merrin (Plymouth) L 20
1897
Mar. London v Dave Wallace L 20

Richard Crowther (Newbridge)
1865
1898
Nov. Abercarn v ….Hopkins
1899
Oct. Cardiff v Thomas Davies (Rhondda) W 14

William Crowther (Tonyrefail)
1888
May Tonyrefail v Ivor Davies police halted

…. Crutchley
1869
Jul. Point of Ayr v …. Kenny L
Tom Culley
1902
 Pct. Resolven v Dai Jenkins W 12

Patsy Cummings
(1819- 1896)
@**1840-1870**
@**1876**
Flintshire v Mel Gibney (USA) W

Tom Curnew (Troedirhiw)
1893
Mount Pleasant v Redmond Coleman L 2

William Curran
1865
Oct. Swansea v unknown police halted 60

Eugene Currin (Newport)
1867
Feb. Newport v Tom Power (Newport) halted

Thomas Daley (Aberdare)
1874
Sep. Abernant tunnel v Ebby Welsh (Lewis) (Aberdare) W

T. Daley (Cardiff)
1896
Dec. Cardiff v W. Jinks (Cardiff) D 6

Ishmael Daniel (Cwmtillery)
1894
Jul. Blaenavon mountain v Eli Tar (Cwmtillery) L 7

John Daniels
1863
Dec. Pontypool v John Batt

John Davey
1884
Maesteg v Thomas Davies L

Aaron Davies (Rhondda)
1898
Aug. Cardiff v Mike Flynn (Ogmore Vale) D 7
Benjamin Davies
1894
Apr. Neath v David Davies (Neath) W KO 3

Charlie Davies
1844
Nov. Milborne v Bill 'Monmouth' Jones W KO 27

Dan Davies 'Swansea Dan'
1861
May Rumney v Charley Collings (Cardiff) L 25
@**1865**
            v Patsy Vaughan L

David Davies (Mardy)

1888
May Glynneath v Dai Howells (Pontypridd) W 32
1889
Mar. Pontypridd v Sam (Butcher) Thomas L KO 8

David Davies (Neath)
1894
Apr. Neath v Benjamin Davies L KO 3

Edward Davies 'Ned Diendaid' (Ton)
1902
May Maindy Mountain v James Harris L

Enoch Davies
1819
Jun. Southwark v ….Jones

George Davies (Cardiff)
14st.
1894
Jul. Cardiff v Jim Driscoll (Cardiff) L 4

Griffith Davies (Tonypandy)
B. 1876
1897
Aug. Rhondda v Matthew 'Mat' Fury police halted 6

Howell Davies (Gelli)
1900
Apr. Ystrad v William Fry Police halted

Ivor Davies (Tonyrefail)
1888
May Tonyrefail v William Crowther police halted

Jack Davies (Swansea)
1892
Sep. Swansea v Shamus Warner (Swansea) L 27

John Davies (Cowbridge)
10 ½ st.
1828
Mar. Cowbridge v John Newnom (Cowbridge) W 79

John Davies (Merthyr)
1857
v Walter Morgan

John Davies
1884
Mar. Aberkenfig v Thomas Davis L

John Davies 'Shoni Sailor' (Dowlais)
1890
Jul.. v Wm. Amesbury (Dowlais) L
1891
Apr. Dowlais v Wm Amesbury (Dowlais)

Joseph Davies
1865
Nov. Aberdare mountain v Thomas James police halted
Joseph 'Punch' Davies (Aberdare)
1892
Apr. Caerphilly v Joseph Jones (Cwmpaek) L 9

Morgan Davies (Port Talbot)
1896
May Llanwonno mountain v W. D. Rees (Treherbert) L 28

?? Davies (Mountain Ash)
1895
Jun. Llantrisant v Jack Northey W 18

Richard Davies (Presteigne)
1818
Jan. v Thomas Watkins

Robert Davies (Aberdare)
1896
Jul. Craig mountain v Evan Bevan (Aberdare) Police halted

Sam Davies
10st.
1889
Pencoedene v Llew Herbert 26 rounds
1895

Sep. Neath v Tom Flynn L 5

Susan Davies (Cardiff)
1852
Sep. Cardiff v Martha Watkins (Newport) police halted 18

Sydney Davies (Maesteg)
1904
Nov. Maesteg v John Price

Thomas Davies (Cwmpark)
1888
Oct. Garth Mountain v John Northey (Pentre) police halted 7

Thomas Davies
1884
Maesteg v John Davey W

Thomas Davies (Pentre Ystrad)
1884
Mar. Aberkenfig v John Jones (Shoni Engineer) W 28
Oct. Blaencaerau mountain v David Thomas (Bryncenin) police halted

Tom Davies 'Tom Books' (Ystrad)
1880s
v George Jones L

Tom Davies (Swansea)
(1868-1896) 5ft. 8ins. 13st. 7lbs.
1896
Mar. Swansea v Dick Ambrose L pts. 7

Thomas Davies (Rhondda)
1899
Oct. Cardiff v Richard Crowther L 14

T. Davies
1866
Apr. Flintshire v J. Roberts L 13

Tom Davies (Penrhiwceiber)
1904
Apr. Tongwynlais v Tom Rees W 21

William Davies 'Penwin'

1869
May New Tredegar v Peter Mitchell (New Tredegar). .

William Davies (Pontypridd)
1888
Nov. Pontypridd v Frederick Stephens Honeychurch 'John Stephens'

William Davies (Ton Ystrad)
1889
Jan. Ystrad Rhondda v John Northey (Ton Ystrad) L rtd 43

William Davies
1903
Mar. Glynneath v Richard Phillips police halted

William John Davies (Tylorstown)
1902
Sep. Penrhys Mountain v William Jones – police halted

Bill Davis
1840
Nov. Cardiff v David Jenkins D

David (Birmingham 'Welsh') Davis
12 ½ st.
1828
Dec. Wolverhampton v …. Manning W 18
1831
Feb. Maidenhead v Deaf Burke L 12
1833
Nov. – v Preston D 18
1835
Jun. Staffs. v Preston L 22

George Davis
1822
Jun. Stanmore v unknown W 6

…. Davis
1828
Nov. Hull v Tom the Nailer L 17

Thomas Davis

342

Fight Records

1884
Mar. Aberkenfig v John Davies W

Tom Davis
1845
Oct. Liverpool v Keeney Malone W 54

Charley Dawson (Monmouth)
1843
v Jack Perks (Brecon) L 27

T. Day
1846
Jan, Flintshire v F. Grossage W 8

Daniel Desmond (**Pontnewynydd**)
(1845-1894)
1864
May Pontypool v Thomas Walsh (Pontnewynydd) W 46
1872
Nov. Goytre v Thomas Fletcher D 101

Dick the Devil
1870s
v William Francis L

.... Didds
1891
Jun. Cadoxton v (unknown) 16

Will. Dixon (**Seven Sisters**)
1895
May. Neath v David Williams (Seven Sisters) police halted

Jack Doad (**Penygraig**)
1890
Aug. Pontypridd v Jack Raymond (Pontypridd) L

Benjamin Dodd
1875
May Maesycwmmer v Joseph Birch W 30+ rounds

Jim Dolby (**Cardiff**)
1892
Dec. Plymouth v Jack Ferris (Ivybridge) W 7

Charles Donoghue (**Cardiff**)
1898
Nov. Cardiff v Dick Murphy L 9

John Donovan (**Cardiff**)
1887
Feb. Cardiff v Robert Moon L
1889
Apr. Cardiff v Hannahan (Cardiff) D 27

Tubby Dougie (**Sandfields**)
1899
Apr. Swansea v Pedlar Palmer L

Jim Driscoll (**Cardiff**)
14st.
1894
Jul. Cardiff v George Davies (Cardiff) W 4

'Peerless' Jim Driscoll (**Cardiff**)
1900
Pontypridd v Dai Stevens (Treorchy) W
1905
Jun. – Cardiff v Ivor (Butcher) Thomas – W 3

Bob Dunbar 'Young Lane' (**Birmingham/Newport**)
B. 1855. 10st.
1882
Oct. Haverfordwest v Bill Samuel (Swansea) L
1888
Mar. Newport v Jockey Saunders (Birmingham) W 5 disq

W. Dwyer (**Cardiff**)
1888
Oct. Llandaff v R. Bryn (Cardiff) L 13

Morgan Edmunds (**Ystrad**)
1896
Jun. Ystrad v Tom Smith (Ystrad) Police halted

343

Tom Edmunds (Ogmore Valley)
1895
Jul. Cardiff v Phil Thomas (Ogmore Valley) W KO 25

Evan Edwards 'Yanto Glatchen' (Abertillery)
1860
Feb. Rhymney v Richard Stevens L 117

George Edwards
1863
Aug. Pontypool v 'Paper Morris'

Jim Edwards (Ferndale)
1896
Sep. Ferndale mountain v George Rogers W 24

John Edwards
1866
Jun. Dowlais mountain v John Charles police halted 5
T. R. Edwards (Aberaman)
1893
Jun. Pontypridd v Thomas Morgan (Treharris) L KO 7
v George Jones L

Thomas Edwards
17st.
1827
Sep. Llangollen v James 'Admiral' Benbow L 4

Thomas Edwards
1831
Apr. Caerphilly v William Gibbon L 10

Thomas Edwards (Troedyrhiw)
B. 1869. 11st. 2lbs.
1893
Apr. Merthyr v Tom Prosser (Merthyr Vale) L KO 3
1894
May Aberdare v David Rees (Aberdare) W7

Watkin Edwards (Aberdare)

1894
Jun. Aberdare v Evan Llewellyn (Aberdare) Police halted

? Edwards (Aberdare)
1891
Aug. Cardiff v ? Rees (Aberdare)

Aaron Evans (Bargoed)
5ft. 10ins. 10st. 6lbs.
1896
Jul. Llanishen v H. Iles (Bristol) W 10

Abraham Evans (Treorchy)
1900
Sep. Forch mountain v Thomas Williams
1901
Sep. Treorchy

Daniel Evans 'Dan Matthews' (Pontypridd)
B. 1871. 5ft. 4ins. 8st. 2lbs.
1892
Dec. Merthyr v Redmond Coleman (Merthyr) L KO 5
1894
Apr. Pontypridd v William Bennett Police halted
1895
Apr. Pontypridd v David Evans W 4
Sep. Pontypridd v Llew. Herbert W 5

David Evans
1868
May Blaenavon v Michael Collins

Evan Evans (Porth)
1886
Aug. Porth v John Jenkin James W32
1894
Jun. Porth v Fred Smith (Porth) Police halted

E. Evans
1848
Jan. Vaunog v J. Jutson L 11

... Evans (Pontypridd)

1899
Jan. Pontypridd v Will Constantine W 6

Harry Evans (Shirenewton)
1860
Feb. Gloucester v Edward Lake (Newport) L retd. 20

Ieuan Evans
1864
V Richard Owens L

Illtyd Evans (Pontypridd)
1889
Nov. Treforest v Fred Bevan (Pontypridd) W
1890
Oct. Llanwonno mountain v Jack Hitchings (Ynyshir) L KO 7

Joseph Evans (Aberdare)
1888
May Aberaman mountain v David Rees (Aberdare) 32

Philip Evans (Nantyglo)
1904
Jun. Nantyglo Mountain v William Cornick

Richard Evans (Cwmbargoed)
1876
June Cwmbargoed v Lewis Griffiths Police halted.

Thomas Evans
1859
 - Aberystruth v William Price

Thomas Evans (Merthyr)
1897
Sep. Merthyr v Edward Craddock

William Evans (Tonypandy)
1893
Jul. Pontypridd v Tom Israel (Pontypridd) L 2

…. Evans 'the Welch collier'
1833
Jan. nr. Hanley v ….Jackson W 61

….Evans
1862
Mar. Monmouth & Redbrook v Bob Fletcher (Monmouth) D 32

J. Farleigh
1899
Jan. Porth v Archie Cooke (Penygraig) W

Samuel Fear (Ystrad)
1899
Nov. Ystrad v William Jenkins (Ystrad)
1903
Dec. Gelli Mountain v Frank Maggs

'Young Fellow' (Swansea)
1891
Jun. Swansea v 'Bruiser' W 3

John Felton
1886
Sep. Henllys v Thomas Arundell (Aberdare) police halted

Tom Finn (Cardiff)
1892
Apr. Cardiff v James Cox (Bristol) W 5

? Finnery (Blaina)
1890
Oct. Blaina v ? Sullivan

James Fitzgerald
1861
May Rumney v ….Collins D 117

…. Fitzpatrick (Bridgend)
1897
Dec. Bridgend v J. D. Russell (Barry) W 10

Bob Fletcher (Monmouth)
1837
May Rockfield v Thomas Meredith 47 rounds

Bob Fletcher (Monmouth)
1841-1869
1862
Mar. Monmouth & Redbrook v ....
Evans D
1865
Aug. Blaenavon mountain v James Vaughan
1867
Feb. Chepstow v William 'Young' Godwin (Newport) police halted

G. Fletcher
1870
Oct. Prestatyn v Arthur Chambers L 56

Thomas Fletcher
1845 -1929
1872
Nov. Goytre v Daniel Desmond (Pontypool) D 101

.... Flowers
1887
Apr. Bedwas v .... Prosser L

Mike Flynn (Ogmore Vale)
1898
Aug. Cardiff v Aaron Davies (Rhondda) D 7

Morris Flynn (Swansea)
B. 1871
1894
Dec. Swansea v unknown Police halted

Edward 'Ned' Flynn (Neath)
13st.
1894
Sep. Neath v Jack Allen (Neath) W3

Tom Flynn
7st. 8lbs.
1895
Sep. Neath v Sam Davies W 5

Mike Ford (Roath)
1899
Aug. Rumney v. T. Morgan (Cardiff), Cardiff, L KO 3

.... Ford (Cardiff)
10st.
1894
Sep. v ... Morgan ('Mulduggie') (Cardiff) L 6

William Ford
1906
Mar/ Abertillery v ? police halted

Tudor Foster (Penygraig)
1886
Cymmer Mountain v Edmund Powell– police halted.

William Foster (Cardiff)
1895
Mar. Swansea v Tom Hooligan (Swansea) L disq 2

.... Foulkes (Wrexham)
1841
Mar. Wrexham v ... Pugh (Wrexham) L

William Francis (Aberdare)
1870s
V Dick the Devil W

.... Freer (Wrexham)
1844
Oct v Fred Latham L

Sam Fry (New Tredegar)
1892
Oct. New Tredegar v D. J. Morgan (New Tredegar)

William Fry (Gelli)
1900
Apr. Ystrad v Howell Davies (Ystrad) Police halted

Martin Fury (Brynmawr)
1876
Sep. Cardiff v Phil Reardon police halted.

Fight Records

Matthew Fury (Tonypandy)
B. 1878
1897
Aug. Tonypandy v Griffith Davies Police halted 6
28

Alfred Gag (Cardiff)
1868
Jun. Penarth v Cornelius Leary (Penarth) L

....Gazer (Pontypridd)
1866
May Pontypridd v McCue L

George the Sailor
1812
Feb. Newport v unknown L 13

William Gibbon
1831
Apr. Caerphilly v Thomas Edwards W 10

Steve Giblin (Penarth)
1889
May Cardiff v 'Princy' (Penarth) police halted

John/ Jack Giles (Cardiff)
1892
Nov. Rumney v (unknown)
1896
Jul. Cardiff v Patsy Healey (Cardiff) L 23

.... Gillan (Montgomery)
1820
Oct. Hants. v unknown (Devon) L 10

William Gimlet (Trealaw)
1891
May Pontypridd v Joseph Thomas police halted

William Gilmore
1871
Nov. Coedcae v Thomas Williams police halted 4

William Gittings (Tredegar)
1888
Aug. Tredegar v Charles Pearce (Tredegar)

William 'Young' Godwin (Newport)
1867
Feb. Chepstow v Bob Fletcher (Monmouth) police halted

Joseph Goodwin (Merthyr)
1881
Feb. Merthyr v Walter Ward (Merthyr) L 10

John Gough (Cwmpark
1894
Apr. v ... Sweet

Bill Green
1843
Apr. Llangollen v Andrew Jones W 36

.....Green (Canton)
1888
Mar. Canton v ....Royle (Gloucester) W 10

William Henry Gregor (Wattstown)
1906
Dec. Porth v Thomas Price police halted

Morgan Grey (Swansea)
1897
Apr. Swansea v Billy Morgan L KO

William Grey (Swansea)
1899
Oct. v Dick Ambrose (Swansea) WKO 3

Michael Griffin
1885
Dec. Merthyr v John McGrath police halted 7

Bob Griffiths (New Tredegar)

1895
May Treharris v W. H. Williams (Gellligaer) police halted

David Griffiths
1870
May Sguborwen v Peter Morris police halted

Johnny Griffiths (Maesteg)
1897
v Thomas Thomas L 4

J. Griffiths (Cardiff)
1893
May Cardiff v Patsy Cane (Cardiff) W 10

Lewis Griffiths (Cwmbargoed)
1876
June Cwmbargoed v Richard Evans Police halted.

Will Griffiths (New Tredegar)
1899
Dec. Rhymney v Pedlar McMahon (Swansea) L KO 8
1900
Dec. Tirphil v Rees Owen W KO 14

Griffiths
1824
Jan. Hongeham v Rogers L 8

F, Grossage
1846
Jan. Flintshire v T. Day L 8

William Gullifer (Blaenavon)
1856
Jan. Blaenavon v John Morris (Brynmawr) W 51

Sam Gulliver (Cardiff)
9st. 8lbs – 10st.
Claimed previous wins against Pordey McCarthy, T. Evans (Cardiff) and a draw with Bob Wiltshire
1891

Oct. Bridgenorth v ....Wilkinson (Birmingham) W KO 5
Dec. London v Evan Owen (Cardiff) W 16
1893
Apr. London v Bob Wiltshire (Cardiff) L KO 5

George Gwinn
1869
Jun. Cardiff v William Atkins police halted

'Gwynne' (Treforest)
1895
Aug. Llanwonno mountain v 'Blanche' (Hopkinstown) W KO

.... Gwyer
1858
Apr. Cwmdu v ...... Wheeler. Police halted.

David Hagerton
1894
Nov. Gorseinon v T. Stock (Gorseinon) W 4

Bill Haggerty/Eggerty (Treherbert)
1895
Sep. Rhondda v David Williams (Treherbert) police halted

Thomas Hamlet
1831
Mar. Bristol b John Callaghan L 27

Dick Hands
1840
Jul. Pontypool v Jack Howard W 9

.....Hannahan (Cardiff)
1880-
1889
Apr. Cardiff v John Donovan (Cardiff) D 27

.... Harley
1891

348

Fight Records

Jun. Cadoxton v .... Bumford W 11

Benjamin Harries (Ynysybwl)
1896
Aug. Llanwonno mountain v Samuel Jones (Ynysybwl)

Thomas Harries (Llansamlet)
1895
Jan. Swansea v Dan Thomas (Hafod) L 7
Apr. Swansea v Auguste L pts
Jun. Swansea v William Barry (Greenhill) abandoned 3
Nov. ....Osborne (London) L KO 2

Bill Harris 'The Boatman' (Aberaman)
1895
Apr. Swansea v Billy Morgan (Swansea) L 4
Nov. Swansea v Osborne (London) L KO 2

James Harris
1902
May Maindy Mountain v Edward Davies W

Joseph Harris (Ferndale)
1894
May Llanwonno mountain v Basil Morris (Ferndale) 18
.... Harris
1862
May Aberaman v .... Pendry W 97

Thomas Harris (Blaenclydach)
1900
Mar. Clydach Vale v John Owen (Clydach Vale) Police halted
Tom Harris (Llansamlet)
1896
Jan. 20 Swansea v Charles Barry (Swansea) W 10

Will Harris (Tredegar)
5ft. 8ins. 9st. 7lbs.
1898

Aug. Bedwellty v Morris Taylor (Blackwood) W KO 5

.... Harrison (Porth)
1888
Jun. Aberdare mountain v ....Marshman (Ferndale) W 33

Charles Havard 'Long Charley'
1839
Monmouthshire v Bill 'Old Horse' Gardner (Ross) Magistrate halted.
William Hay
1893
Mar. Aberdare v David Williams

Patsy Healey (Cardiff)
1896
Jul. Cardiff v Jack Giles (Cardiff) W 23

Lewis Hemmings (Hopkinstown)
1889
Nov. Eglwysilan mountain v William 'Mother' Lee (Pontypridd) police halted 15
Llew. Herbert (Pontypridd)
B. 1867 5ft. 3 ½ is 8st. 6lbs.
1889
Pencoedene v Sam Davies 26 rounds
1895
Sep. Pontypridd v Daniel Evans L 5

Ivor/Jack Hitchin(g)s (Clydach Vale/Ynyshir)
1890
Sep. Pontypridd v William Nathan (Cymmer) W 12
Oct. Llanwonno mountain v Illtyd Evans (Pontypridd) W KO 7
1891
Jun. Swansea v Jack Northey (Rhondda) W 4
1893
Jun. Llanwonno v George 'Punch' Jones L
1895
Mar. Ynyshir v George Britton (Wattstown) police halted 4
1896

349

Nov. Pontypridd v Dan Matthews (Pontypridd) W 8

Fred Hobbs (Rhondda)
B. 1875. 5ft. 6ins. 9st. 8lbs.
1898
Sep. Cardiff v Charlie Snooks (Somerset) L 10

W. Hoddell
13st.
1828
Aug. Newtown v Richard Humphreys D 61

.... Hoolahan (Swansea)
1895
Jan. Swansea v ....Lewis (Swansea) abandoned 2

Tom Hooligan (Swansea)
12st. 4lbs.
1895
Jan Swansea v Billy Morgan (Swansea) W
Mar. Swansea v ... Foster (Cardiff) W disq 2
Apr. Swansea v Enoch Morrison (Cardiff) W 2
Seven successive wins
Apr Swansea v .... Horican/Horrigan (Cardiff) L disq 2

Evan Hopkins
1897
Oct. Resolven v John Conyers police halted 5

John Hopkins (Miskin)
1890
Apr Llanwonno mountain v Cornelius Collins.

Rees Hopkin (Tondu)
1846
Aug. Tondu v Jenkin Morgan.
John Hopkins (Miskin)
1890
Apr. Llanwonno mountain v Cornelius Collins (Mountain Ash)

John Hopkins (Maesteg)
1913
Dec. Maesteg v George Price – police halted

W. Hopkins (Cardiff)
11st. 11lbs.
1896
Aug. Cardiff v W. Keys L KO 9

....Hopkins
1898
Nov. Abercarn v Richard Crowther

Charley Hopkiss
1887
v Morgan Crowther (Newport) L

.... Hopton
1846
Jul. Pontypool v .... Lewis police halted

.... Horican/Horrigan (Cardiff)
1895
Apr. Swansea v .... Hooligan (Swansea) W disq 2

....Horton
1813 – Aug Chepstow v Molineux W 3

Jack Howard
1840
Jul. Pontypool v Dick Hands L 9

David Howell (Treforest)
1887
v Fred Bevan (Pontypridd) L

Dai Howells (Pontypridd)
1888
May Glynneath v Dai Davies (Mardy) L 32

David Howells (MountainAsh)
1889
Sep. Aberdare mountain v Morgan Beynon (Capcoch) L

350

Fight Records

William Howells
1896
Jul. Llanwonno mountain v James Thomas

Jem (Jimmy) Hucker (Swansea)
B, 1859. 10st. 6lbs.
Claimed wins over
Bob Hughes (Greenock) 1
Joe Field (Chatham) 12
…. Thomas (Portsmouth) 1
…. Hannon (British Columbia) 1
Thomas Lewer (Honolulu) 4
Joe Hutchey (Scotland) 3
Bob Patton (Scotland) 6
Bill Neale (RMLI Plymouth) 1
Segt. Haynes (RMLI Plymouth) 12
Beaten by Clem Hoskins (British Columbia)
1892
Nov. Plymouth v Tom Rooney L 12
1893
Feb. Plymouth v Tommy Merrin L 12

Bob Hughes (Rhondda Valley)
1895
Jul. Cardiff v Evan Lewis (Rhondda Valley) abandoned 17

J. Hughes 'Dyserth Fancy' (Dyserth)
1850
Feb. Rhyl v T. Hughes (Prestatyn) abandoned

John James Hughes (Rhondda)
1893
Jun. Pontrhondda v William Llewellyn Police halted
1896
Sep. Ystrad v William Llewellyn Police halted 25

Morgan Hughes (Cwmpark)
1894
Jul. Pencelli v Edward Meredith (Cwmpark)

Morris Hughes (Blaenclydach)
1909
Aug. Cowbridge v Daniel Bowen

T. Hughes 'Prestatyn Pet' (Prestatyn)
1850
Feb. Rhyl v J. Hughes (Dyserth) abandoned

William Hughes
1896
Sep. Ynysybwl v Richard Thomas

Joseph/Jack Huish (Brynmawr)
1893
Nov. Llangynidir mountain v D. Thomas L 54
1899
May. Llangynidir mountain v Daniel Williams – police halted 2
1902
Jun. Ebbw Vale mountain v William Watkins – police halted

Richard Humphreys (Betws Cedewain)
12st. 6lbs.
1828
Aug. Newtown v W. Hoddel D 61
1829
Llanbadarn Vynydd v Thomas Price 85

'Jem Hundred' (Rhymney)
1862
Jun. Tafarnaubach v William Taylor 'Billo Bach' L

Bob Hurd - 'Frome Bob'
1857
Jun. Newport v Jack Gillingham (Bridgwater) W 17
Aug. Newport v Jack Gillingham (Bridgwater) L foul

'Tredegar Infant'
1863
Jul. Llanhilleth v 'Sowhill Chicken' (*poss. Wm. Jones*)

John 'Shoni Sherai' Isaacs (Aberdare)
1867
Oct. Merthyr v David Lewis 'Dai Benlas' (Hirwaun) W 62

351

Tom Israel (Pontypridd)
1893
    v Archie Cook (Penygraig) W 1
Jul. Pontypridd v William Evans (Tonypandy) W 2
Nov. Glyncorrwg v William Jones (Blaina) W 7

'Jack' (Cardiff)
1896
Jul. Cardiff v 'Patsy' (Cardiff) L KO 40

David James 'Dai Rush'
B. 1874
1897
Mar. Pentre v Ben Lloyd L KO 8

David John James (Cymmer)
1908
Mar. Cymmer v ? Rooke

John Jenkin James
1886
Aug. Porth v Evan Evans (Porth) L 32

Richard James 'Dick Shon Shams' (Aberdare)
1861
Apr. Rumney v Edward Llewellyn (Pontypridd) W 23
Jul. London v Bill Benjamin (Shirenewton) L 2
1863
Dec. Pontypridd v Dick Stevens W 51

Richard James
1892
Dec. Aberdare mountain v Daniel Walters

Sam James (Glynneath)
1895
Apr. Aberavon v David Pierce (Aberaman) L 29

Thomas James
1865
Nov. Aberdare mountain v Joseph Davies police halted

Tom James (Aberaman)
B, 1873 6ft. 13 st.
1892
Jan. Merthyr v Sam (Butcher) Thomas L KO 5
May Pontypridd v Jack Raymond (Pontypridd) W 2
Nov Merthyr v David St. John (Resolven) L KO 4
1893 –
v Jack Burton W KO 4
Sep. Pontypridd v David St. John (Resolven) L rtd 6
1895
Jan. Plymouth v Tom Vincent (Plymouth) L 5
Feb. Plymouth v Tom Vincent (Plymouth) L 7 police halted
Sep. Neath v David St. John D 6
V John O'Brien?
1898
Dec. Cardiff v Fred Janes (Bristol) L 12

…. James (Ely Mill)
1811
Jan. Llandaff v …. Stephens (Llandaff) W 27

William James (Ystradgynlais)
1910
Aug. v Andrew Baker

William Jeans (Newport)
1893
May Cheltenham v George Trapp (Cheltenham) W. 14

Edward Jeffreys (Treherbert)
1900
Sep. Treherbert mountain v Edward Calwell

W. Jenks (Cardiff)
1893
Mar. Cardiff v Richard Price (Llandaff) L 12

M. Jenks (Cardiff)
1897

352

Fight Records

Aug. Cardiff v Jack Connelly (Cardiff) L retd, 5

David Jenkins
1840
Nov. Cardiff v Bill Davis D

Dai Jenkins (Maesteg)
B. 1878
5ft. 7ins. 11st. 11lbs.
1902
Sep. Maesteg v Harry Ainsworth L 13
Sep. Rhigos v Harry Ainsworth W 16
Oct. Resolven v Tom Culley L 12
Nov. Westbury v Akf King W 9
Dec. v Harry Ainsworth W 9
1903
Oct. Pyle v John Thomas W 11
(Jenkins reported to have won 12 previous fights)
1904
Jan. Neath Valley v Tibby Wade L7
Mar. Rhigos v Bernard Platt W 11
May Resolven v Bernard Platt W 9

D. Jenkins (Tirphil)
1899
Nov. Tirphil v Pedlar McMahon, , W KO 6

Jack Jenkins (Aberavon/Penycae)
8st. 13lbs.
1900
Apr. v Jack Northey, Aberavon, W KO 2
Sep. Aberavon v Dai 'Buller' Rees L retd 1

James Jenkins
1867
Jan. Tredegar v David Jones

John Jenkins
1833
Jul. Merthyr v Will Ramoon

John Jenkins
1856
Mar. Abersychan v Henry Chidingworth

John Jenkins (Treherbert)
1898
Nov. Treherbert v Daniel Jones D 10

Lewis Jenkins
1866
Feb. Blaina v Michael Wallace

Llewellyn Jenkins (Ferndale)
1889
Dec. Ferndale v Hopkin Williams

1894
Jul. Llanwonno mountain v Evan Jones
Police halted

Stephen Jenkins (Sirhowy)
1865
Mar. Sirhowy v John Luke (Sirhowy)

Tom Jenkins (Cardiff)
1894
Nov. Cardiff v Mike Sullivan (Cardiff) L4 police halted

....Jenkins (Port Talbot)
1899
Jan. Pontypridd v Ivor Thomas (Ynyshir) W 6

Wat Jenkins 'Star' (Ystrad)
1888
May Hirwain v Jim Pollard W 15

William Jenkins (Ystrad)
1899
Nov. Ystrad v Samuel Fear

.... Jenkins (Pontypridd)
1899
Jan. Pontypridd v ... Rees (Pontypridd) W 8

.... Jenkins
1895
Apr. Swansea v 'Auguste' L 5

W. Jinks/Jenks (Cardiff)
1893

Mar. Cardiff v Richard 'Dicky'. Price (Cardiff/Llandaff) L 12
1896
Dec. Cardiff v T. Daley (Cardiff) D 6

Edmund John (Hafod)
1894
May Craig Mountain v (unknown) police halted 3

Evan John (Cardiff)
1880
Mar. Cardiff v Thomas Willcox police halted

Evan John (Dinas)
1897
Jul. Dinas v Edward Thomas/Taylor 'Ned the Bell' (Dinas) L

Fred John (Ogmore Vale)
5ft. 5ins. 8st. 109ns.
1898
Oct. Cardiff v Howell Watkins D 17

Harry John
1894
Jan. Aberdare v Joe Owen L KO 3

Iley John (Cardiff)
1889
May Cardiff v Morgan Crowther D 5

John John
1897
Mar. Llanelli v Josiah Llewellyn police halted

Silas John 'Oily' (Cardiff)
1891
Mar. Gloucester v George Trapp (Cheltenham) W 10

....Johns (Abercarn)
1891
Nov. Abercarn v Owens (Newbridge) L
Aaron Jones (Shrewsbury)
1831- 1869 5ft. 11ins. 12 st.
1846

v Bill Harry W 15
v Bob Covkrell W 5
1849
Dec. Woking Common v Harry Orme L 47
1850
Sep. v Robert Wade W 43
1852
May Newmarket v Harry Orme L 10
v Harry Orme
1854
v Bob Paddock L
1855
v Bob Paddock L
1857
Jan. v Tom Sayers D 65
Feb. Sheerness v Tom Sayers L retd. 85
1867
Aug. Ohio v Mike McCoole L 34

Abraham Jones
1867
Jul. Brynmawr v John Jones police halted

Albert Jones (Cardiff)
1894
Mar. Penarth v John Williams (Cardiff) D 12
1899
Jan. Porth v Archie Cooke (Penygraig) L

Alfred Jones
1872
May Llwydycoed v Francis Mills police halted

Alf Jones (Cardiff)
1895
Jun. Porth v Tom Jones (Pontypridd) D 6
Andrew Jones
1841
Apr. Paddock, Lancs. v Jem Fitzpatrick W 96
Dec. Liverpool v Jack Hampson L 22
1843
Apr. Llangollen v Bill Green L 36

Bill Jones (Monmouth)

Fight Records

1841
Jun. Maidenhead v Johnny Walker L 35 ?
Aug. Twyford v Fred Mason L 22 ?
1844
Sep. v Charley Bolton L
Nov. Milborne v Charlie Davies L 27

Charles Jones 'Charley the Well'
1871
Jan. Wrexham v Bill Lawrence 'The Gipsy Tinker' W

Daniel Jones (Treherbert)
1898
Nov.   Treherbert v John Jenkins D 10

David Jones
1867
Jan. Tredegar v James Jenkins

David Jones (Rhondda)
1889
Jul. Pontypridd v George Morgan (Porth) W 44

David Jones (Ferndale)
1904
Dec. Penrhys Mountain v Charles Silver – police halted

D. Jones
1819
Oct. London v Joe Davis (Blechingly) W 8

D. Jones 'Tom Cochin' (Hafod)
9st. 12lbs.
1896
Dec. Pontypridd v Ivor Thomas L KO 2

Elly Jones
1887
V Morgan Crowther (Newport) L

Evan Jones (Ferndale)
1894
Jul. Llanwonno mountain v Llewellyn Jenkins Police halted

Farnham Jones (Cardiff)
1890
Apr. Cardiff v T. Smith (Cardiff) L 16 foul
1893
Nov. Cardiff v Knocker Simes L 13

Francis Jones
1890
Apr. Pontypridd v Ernest Pugh

Frank Jones
1895
Oct. Newport v ??

George 'Punch' Jones (Aberaman)
1865 - 5ft. 6ins.
1891
– v Jack Northey
??v Felix Scott W
1893
Jun. Llanwonno v Jack Hitchings W
v T. R. Edwards W
v Redmond Coleman W
v Mike O'Brien W
v Tom Davies 'Tom Books' W
1898
Dec. Aberdare v Pedlar McMahon D police halted
1900
May Merthyr v Isaiah Thomas (Cwmaman) W KO2

Gwilym Jones (Pontypridd)
1900
May Merthyr v Jack Prosser L 6
May Merthyr v Isaiah Thomas W KO 2

Harry Jones (Cardiff)
1840
Aug. Rumney v Shoni Sgubor Fawr L 12

Illtyd Jones (Pontypridd)
1890
May Pontypridd v William Lee

James Jones (Wrexham)
1869
Apr. Wrexham v T. Price (Wrexham) Jones died

355

James Jones (Aberdare)
1887
Dec. Aberdare v William Watts (Aberaman) police halted

James Parry Jones (Aberaman)
1894
Jan. Aberdare v S. Rothwell (Aberdare) L rtd 5

Jenkin Jones (Treorchy)
1895
Aug. Cardiff v Elias Morris (Blaina) W KO 19

John Jones (Rhymney)
1861
Nov. v …..Lewis (Heolgerrig) police halted

Jonathan Jones (Brynmawr)
@1860s

John Jones
1867
Jul. Brynmawr v Abraham Jones police halted
John Jones 'Shoni Engineer' (Treorchy)
1863-1894 5ft. 10ins. 10 ½ st.
1884
Mar. Aberkenfig v Thomas Davies (Pentre) L 28
1885
Jun. Treorchy v Morris Tobin (Cardiff) W 7
1887
Jan. Pencoed v Peter Burns 'Dublin Tom' W 48
1888
May Berkeley v James Goytrell/Guiderell (Bristol) L 85
1889
May Marshfield v John O'Brien (Cardiff) L 19
1890
May Pontypridd v Enoch Morrison W 5 on foul

Sep. Neath v Bill Samuel (Swansea) L KO 3

John Jones 'Shoni Scyborfawr' (S. West Wales)
@1840s

John Jones (North Wales)
@1880
North Wales v Harry Brown (Lancashire) Brown died

John Jones (Clydach)
1902
Jul. Clydach Vale v W. Norris – police halted

Joseph Jones (Cwmpaek)
1892
Apr. Caerphilly v Joseph Davies (Aberdare) W 9

Morgan Jones (Aberystwyth)
1838
Apr. Paddington v George Davison W

Morgan Jones (Merthyr)
1884
Nov. Aberdare v Thomas Williams

Morgan Jones
1896
Jun. Merthyr v William Morgan police halted 3

Peter Jones
1882
Oct. Ruthin v Robert Lewis
Rod Jones (Porth)
5ft. 9ins. 11st. 6lbs.
1889
May Llantrisant v David Robert Williams (Ynyshir) Police halted
1892
Dec. Merthyr v George Morgan (Porth) L 5 disq
Sampson Jones
1834
Oct. Gorsbrook b Branbrich L 18

Samuel Jones (Ynysybwl)
1896
Aug. Llanwonno mountain v Benjamin Harries

Thomas 'Paddington' Jones (London)
1771-1833 5ft. 7ins. 10st. 5lbs.
1785
V Blackwell W
V Burley W (in same day)
1786
Feb. Hyde Park v Jack Tar W
Feb. London v Sailor W
.. London v Sailor W
.. London v Sailor W
Dec. London v Jack Holmes W
1787
Dec. London v Ned Aldridge W
(Unknown dates)
1778
Aug. Brighton v Bob Watson L
1792
May 13 Croyden v Caleb Baldwin D
Sep. 5 Essex v Abraham Challice, W
1794
May Blackheath v Keely Lyons W
Jun. v Keely Lyons W
1795
        V Harris the Spaniard W
1797
Apr. Herts. v Chaffcutter W
1799
Apr. Wormwood Scrubbs v Jem Belcher L
1801
Jul. Wimbledon v Isaac Bitton L
1802
Mar. London v George. Nicholls W
1803
v Yokel Jew W
v George Stringer W
v Jem Smith W
1804
Jun. Edgeware Road, v Simpson W
1805
Aug. Blackheath v Keeley Lyons W

Thomas Jones
1892
Nov. Tylorstown v Redmond Coleman

Thomas Jones (Mardy)
1892
Jul. Coedcae mountain v Llewellyn Williams (Hafod) W 30

Thomas Jones
1895
May Pontypridd v Daniel Plumpton police halted

Tom Jones
1829
Dec. Pentichilin, Mgy., v Tom Shenkin W 64
1832
Feb. Cheshire v Bill Hutch L 73
1834
Mar. Cheshire v Bill Hutch L 51

Tom Jones
1842
Feb. Cheshire v Matt Harrett L 40

Tom Jones 'Tom Luse' (Pontycymmer)
1895
Jun. Porth v Alf Jones D 6
1898
Nov. Bridgend v. Will Massey L KO 4
1900
Aug. Cwmdu v 'Snowball' (Maesteg) W retd. 14

Welsh Jones
9st. 7lbs.
1833
May Huddersfield v Young Brag (police halted)

William Jones
1840
Nov. Woking Common v John Greenstreet W 10

William Jones (Monmouth)

1844
Nov. Milborne v Charley Davies L KO
27

William Jones 'Sowhill Chicken' (Pontypool)
1863
Jul. Llanhilleth v 'Tredegar Infant'
1865
Nov. Pontypool v John Morgan (Redbrook) police halted

William Jones
1889 – Dec Gelli mountain v Henry Phillips

W. Jones (Cardiff)
1891
Jul. Cardiff v Tom 'Pawdy'. McCarthy (Cardiff) W 7

William Jones (Blaina)
1893
Nov. Glyncorrwg v Tom Israel (Tonypandy) L 7

William Jones
1894
Sep. Abercanaid v Edward Richards L 8

William Jones (Ystrad)
1899
Mar. Pontrhondda v Augustus Williams L5

William Jones
1902
Sep. Penrhys mountain v William John Davies
– police halted

…. Jones
1819
Jun. Southwark v Enoch Davies

…. Jones
1833
May Huddersfield v Young Brag police halted 8

…. Jones
1851
Nov. Abergavenny v '…. Sheriff' (Nottingham) L 41

…. Jones
1848
Jan. Neath v …. Sayer L

….Jones (Cardiff)
1894
Aug. Cardiff v ..Williams (Bristol) W 7

Jordan (Monmouthshire)
1845
Mar. v Sambo
1846
Dec. London v Nobby Clarke L 15

John Judson
1864-
1887
Dec. Wrexham v Patrick Neary W KO 10

J. Jutson
1848
Jan. Vaunog v E. Evans W 11 100

Andrew Keef
1863-
1886
Mar. Cardiff v Patrick Murray

…. Kenny
1869
Jul. Point of Ayr v …. Crutchley W

W. Keys (Newport/Bristol)
10st.
1894
Jun. Bristol v Con Kezler (Newport) L 6
1896
Aug. Cardiff v W. Hopkins W KO 9

Con Kezler (Newport)
1894
Jun. Bristol v …. Keys (Newport) W 6

Fight Records

Herbert King (Ferndale)
1903
Mar. Ferndale Mountain v Oliver Robinson

Joe Knight (Abercarn)
11st. 5lbs.
1894
Dec. Ferndale v D. Collins L
1895
Dec. Ferndale v Edward Williams (Tylorstown) L 20

Edward Lake (Newport)
1860
Feb. Gloucester v Harry Evans (Shirenewton) W 20

Lodwick Lake (Aberdare)
1896
Jul. Craig mountain v Henry Rosser Police halted

Thomas Lambert
D. 1893
1889
Dec. Pontypridd v Dan Powell (Pontypridd) L 6

Will Lane (Cwmavon)
1858-
1896
Sep. Neath v Billy Morgan (Swansea) L 2
1900
Jul. Cwmavon v Dai 'Buller' Rees (Aberavon) L 37

Isaac Latcham (Abertillery)
1844-1873
1873
Feb. Aberbeeg v John Williams 'Jack the Buck'

??? Latham
1844
Oct. v Freer W

Bill Lawrence 'The Gipsy Tinker'
1871
Jan. Wrexham v William Williams 'Bill the Coal' D
Jan. Wrexham v Charles Jones 'Charley the Well' L

Robert Leah (Cardiff)
1868
May Ely v unknown police halted

Cornelius Leary (Penarth)
1868
Jun. Penarth v Alfred Gag (Cardiff) W

William 'Mother' Lee (Pontypridd)
1868 – 11st.
1889
Nov. Pontypridd v Lewis Hemmings (Hopkinstown) police halted 15
1890
May Pontypridd v Illtyd Jones
1893
Nov. Treforest v Fred Snooks (Pontypridd) L KO 3

…. Legge (Swansea)
1892
Aug. Neath v Bill Samuel (Swansea) L 4

Charles Lewis
1895
Jul. Cardiff v George But(r)cher L KO 6

Daniel Lewis
1855
Dec. Hirwaun Common v John Rosser

David Lewis 'Dai Benlas' (Hirwaun)
1864
Nov. Bedwas v William Williams (Aberdare) W 52

D. Lewis
1867
Oct. Merthyr v John Isaacs L 62

Edward Lewis (Aberstruth)
1858
Sep. Vaynor v David Thomas 15

Ernest Lewis (Resolven)
1910

359

Jan. Resolven Mountain v Joseph Tregening

Evan Lewis (Merthyr)
1869
Oct. Merthyr v William Williams (Merthyr)

Evan Lewis (Rhondda Valley)
1895
Jul. Cardiff v Bob Hughes (Rhondda Valley) abandoned 17

Henry Lewis
1895
Sep. Llanwonno mountain v Arthur Vaughan W 20

Henry Lewis
1874
Sep. Newport v Walter Roberts

John 'Jack' Lewis (London)
1823
Jul. Copenhagen Field, London v Green W 18

John Lewis
1886
Aug. Hafod v Lloyd Lewis W 20

Lloyd Lewis
1886
Aug. Hafod v John Lewis L 20

Robert Lewis
1882
Oct. Ruthin v Peter Jones

Roderick Lewis
1791
Aug. Dolgellau v Ellis Pannwr L

.... Lewis
1822
Nov. Blackheath v Gardiner
.... Lewis
1846

Jul. Pontypool v .... Hopton police halted

...Lewis (Heolgerrig)
1861
Nov. Aberdare mountain v John Jones police halted

.....Lewis (Swansea)
1885
Sep. Gower v ....Williams

.... Lewis (Swansea)
1895
Jan. Swansea v .... Hoolahan (Swansea) abandoned 2

Edward 'Ned' Llewellyn (Pontypridd)
1861
Apr. Rumney v Dick James (Aberdare) L 23

Evan Llewellyn (Aberdare)
1893
Nov. Cwmdare v Joseph Beynon
1894
Jun. Aberdare v Watkin Edwards Police halted

Josiah Llewellyn
1897
Mar. Llanelli v John John police halted

William Llewellyn 'Will Catws' (Rhondda)
1893
Jun. Pontrhondda v John James Hughes Police halted 25
1896
Sep. Ystrad v John James Hughes Police halted

Ben Lloyd (Porth)
1895
Jul. Swansea v Edward (Ted) Morgan (Treorchy) W 10
1897

Fight Records

Mar. Pentre v David James 'Dai Rush' W KO 8

Hugh Lloyd
1893
v Redmond Coleman D 38

Richard Lloyd
1887
May Tredegar mountain v Joseph Cecil D

Arthur Locke (Merthyr)
1875 - 9 st. 6lbs.
1895
Apr. London v Walter Eyles W PTS
Sept. Newmarket v Tom Ireland W PTS
Oct. London v Pat Daley L 10
1896
Feb. London v Arthur Callan L PTS
Jun. London v Jewey Cook ND
Dec. Birmingham v Maurice Greenfield L KO
1897
Sheffield Tom Causer L PTS
1898
Feb, London v Walter Eyles L PTS
Mar. Sheffield v Tom Causer L PTS
..   ..   v Tom Causer LPTS
Oct. London v Walter Eyles W PTS

John Luke (Sirhowy)
1865
Mar. Sirhowy v Stephen Jenkins (Sirhowy)

James MacDonald (Merthyr)
1867
Feb. Twynygwaun mountain, Merthyr v Cornelius Crowley police halted 3

Frank Maggs (Gelli)
1903
Dec. Gelli Mountain v Samuel Fear

....Magrath (Merthyr)
1887
Jan. Dowlais v ...Power W

Samuel Mandry/ Mainwaring
1871-
1897
Aug. Tonypandy v Ivor (Butcher) Thomas L

Charlie Mann
1893
v Redmond Coleman L1

John Mansel (Merthyr)
1885
Dec. Merthyr v John O'Neil

John Mansfield (Dowlais)
1893
Feb. Dowlais v Florence Sullivan (Dowlais) W 11

.....Mansfield (Dowlais)
1887
Jan. Dowlais v ...Power Police halted

George Marshall
1844
May v Jack Perks (Brecon)

William Marshall (Ebbw Vale)
1872
Nov. Brynmawr v John Thomas 'Jack the Lamb' (Beaufort) L 11

.... Marshman (Ferndale)
1888
Jun. Aberdare mountain v .... Harrison (Porth) L 33

Joseph Martin
1891
Nov. Gilfach Goch v William Meredith

John Mason (Merthyr)
1888
Aug. Bedwellty v Alfred Richards

Will Massey (Maesteg)
1898
Nov. Bridgend v Tom Jones 'Tom Luse' (Pontycwmmer) W KO 4

361

Feasts of Blood

Dan Matthews (aka David Evans) (Hopkinstown)
1894
Apr. Pontypridd v William Bennett (Pontypridd)
1895
Apr. Pontypridd v Daniel Evans L 4
1896
Nov. Pontypridd v Ivor Hitchings (Ynyshir) L 8
Jack May (Birkenhead/Cathays)
1899
Mar. Cardiff v Dennis Tobin (Barry) L 5

Rees Mazey (or Massey) (Swansea)
1895
Feb. 22 Swansea v Billy Morgan L KO
Apr. 5 Swansea v Redmond Coleman ND /
.. 25 Swansea v Redmond Coleman ND?
May 3 Swansea v James Day L KO
May 10 Swansea v Redmond Coleman W KO 6

Edward Meredith (Cwmpark)
1894
Jun. Pencelli v Morgan Hughes (Cwmpark). Police halted.

Thomas Meredith
1837
Rockfield v Bob Fletcher (Monmouth) 47 rounds

William Meredith (Blaina)
1891
Nov. Gilfach Goch v Joseph Martin
1902
Nov. Blaina Mountain v Joseph Watkins – police halted

Harry Millard (Rhymney Valley)
1895
Jul. Cardiff v Sam Randall (Ogmore Val) D 12

..... Miller
1899
Jan. v ... Carey Pontypridd L 4

Francis Mills
1872
May Llwydycoed v Alfred Jones police halted

Alf Mitchell (Cardiff)
1863 - 11st. 3lbs.
Middleweight
1887
Oct. Newmarket v Alec Roberts (London) police halted
Dec. London v J. Cashley (Leeds) W 3 (comptn.)
1888
Mar. London v Alf Ball D 6
Oct. Newmarket v Jack Davenport W (comptn.)
Dec. London v Jack Massey W 2 (comptn.)
Dec. London v Toff Wall (London) L (comptn.)
Dec. London v Ted Burchell L (comptn.)
1889
Jan. Liverpool v Teddy O.Neil (Lancashire) W 12
Mar. Islington v J. Richardson (Wood Green) W
Mar. Islington v C. Bartley W
Apr. Kent v Alf Ball (Deptford) W 64
1890
Dec. London v Ted Pritchard (London) L 4
1891
Dec. London v John O'Brien L KO 8

Joe Mitchell
1894
Jun. Maindy Mountain v Jack Northey D 64

Peter Mitchell (New Tredegar)
1869
May New Tredegar v William Davies 'Penwin'.

362

Tom 'Pawdy' McCarthy (Cardiff)
1889
Aug. Cardiff v Morgan Crowther (Newport) L 6
Nov. Cardiff v Bob Wiltshire (Cardiff) L 4 foul
1890
Mar. Cardiff v Bob Wiltshire (Cardiff) W 4
1891
Jul. Cardiff v W. Jones (Cardiff) L 7
1894
Feb. Aberdare v Sam Butcher (Thomas) (Aberaman) L rtd 5

…..McCue (Pontypridd)
1866
May Pontypridd v ….Gazer (Pontypridd) W

John McGrath
1885
Dec. Merthyr v Michael Griffin police halted 7

McIntyre
1844
Jul. Ormes Head, Caern. v Harris Birchell L 65

Pedlar McMahon (Cardiff/Swansea)
1874- 5ft. 6ins.
v Bob Ford (Birmingham) W KO 5
v Dick Tiddiman (Hackney)
v Billy Morgan (Swansea)
v …. Watts (Merthyr)
v Hooligan (Swansea)
v both Fury brothers W
1895
Dec. Swansea v Jack Cox W KO
1896
Feb. Swansea v 'Daddy; Yates L
Mar. Swansea v Dan Morris W 3
1898
Dec. Aberdare v George Jones Police halted D
1899
Mar. Bristol v Bill Bott W KO 3
Jul. v Frank Lowry (London) W 9
Sep. Aberavon v Frank Lowry (London) L
Nov. Tirphil v Dai. Jenkins (Tirphil) L KO 6
Dec. Rhymney v W. Griffiths (New Tredegar) W KO 8
1900
Jan. Cardiff v ? Daley W
1902
Feb. Liverpool v Frank Brierley W
Mar. Liverpool v Jim Green W
1905
Aug. Liverpool v Kid Wilson W
Sept. Birkenhead v Jim Green W
1906
Mar. Liverpool v Joe Halligan W
1908
Mar. Dublin v Billy Morgan W

Robert Moon (Cardiff)
1887
Feb. Cardiff v John Donovan (Cardiff) W

George Moore (Nantyglo)
1896
Oct. Ebbw Vale mountain v David John Price

J. Moore (Cardiff)
1899
Feb. Cardiff v W. Barron L KO 10

Bill Morgan (Rhondda)
1868-92
1891
Oct. Coity v Johnny Ritchie (Rhondda) abandoned 3

Billy Morgan (Swansea)
1876 - 5ft. 9ins. 10 st. 6lbs.
1894
Jan. Swansea v W. Squires L
Jan. Swansea v W. Squires L
1895
Jan. Swansea v Tom Hooligan (Swansea) L
Feb. Swansea v Rees Mazey W KO
Mar. Swansea v Dick Price (Cardiff) W 10

Apr. Swansea v Bill Harris (Aberaman) W 4
Apr. Swansea v ? Watts W KO
Apr. Swansea v Mike Sullivan (Cardiff) W KO 2
May Swansea v ? Leary W KO
Jun. Swansea v Young Allen W KO
Aug. Aberdare v Dick Davies W PTS
Aug. Swansea v Shamus Warner D 4
Aug. Swansea v Shamus Warner D 4
Sep. Neath v ...Lane (Cwmavon) W 2
1896
Feb. Swansea v Tom James W PTS
..   ..   v Tom James W PTS
..   ..   v E. Osborne W KO
Sept. Neath v Harry Lane W PTS
1897
Apr. Swansea v Morgan Grey W KO
May Bristol v Tom James ND
1898
Dec. Morriston v Dan Murphy W KO
1899
Jan. Bath v Harry Barrett W KO 3
Feb. Cardiff v Fred Janes ND
Jun. Stalybridge v F. Pickup (Manchester) W 6
May Stalybridge v Jim Howes W KO 3
Jun. Stalybridge v F. Pickup (Manchester) W 6
Nov. London v Jasper White W KO
..   ..   v Dave Peters W PTS
1900
Mar. Manchester v Tom Donnelly W KO
1901
Sept. Cardiff v John O'Brien ND
1902
Oct. Ton Pentre v Young Jones L PTS
1903
Jan. Swansea v Frank Reed W KO
Sept. Pontypool v Frank Reed L KO
1908
Mar. Dublin v Pedlar McMahon L. KO

David Morgan
1828
Feb. London Whetstone v Peter McBean W 27

David Morgan
1848
Sep. Merthyr v Daniel Williams police halted

David Morgan (Vaynor)
1859
v David Thomas

Dai Morgan (Swansea)
Fights 33, Won 7, Drawn 10, Lost 14, ND 2
1899
Sept. 8 Swansea v Walter 'Darkey' Thomas L TKO
Oct. 27 Swansea v Walter 'Darkey' Thomas W KO 7
Nov. 2 London v Clemenis ND

David Morgan
1894
Jun. Mountain Ash v Morgan Williams

D. J. Morgan (New Tredegar)
1892
Oct. New Tredegar v Sam Fry (New Tredegar)

Edward (Ted) Morgan (Treorchy)
1895
Jul. Swansea v Ben Lloyd L 10

George Morgan (Porth)
5ft. 7ins. 9. 11lbs.
1889
Jul. Pontypridd v David Jones (Rhondda) L 44
1892
Dec. Merthyr v Rod Jones W 5 disq

James Morgan (Monmouthshire)
1829
Jan. Usk v William Milward (Gloucs) L 43

Jenkin Morgan
1846
Aug. Tondu v Rees Hopkin

Jenkin Morgan

364

Fight Records

1874
Sep. Caerphilly v Austin Strickland L

Joseph Morgan (Cardiff)
1890
Aug. Cardiff v William Price (Cardiff) W KO 7

Rees Morgan (Aberdare)
1894
Jun. Aberaman v Isaiah Thomas (Aberdare)

Sydney Morgan (Newport)
1874
1896
Aug. Marshfield v …. Chink (Newport) W 11
1897
Mar. Marshfield v William Morgan (Cardiff) W 5

Thomas Morgan 'Twm Kitty' (|Aberdare)
1883
Mar. Penrhiwceiber v John Beavan police halted 4

Thomas Morgan (Treharris)
1893
Jun. Pontypridd v T. R. Edwards (Aberaman) W KO 7

T. Morgan (Cardiff)
1899
Aug. v Mike Ford, Cardiff, W KO 3

Walter Morgan (Merthyr)
1857
v John Davies

William Morgan (Cardiff)
1897
Mar. Marshfield v Sydney Morgan (Newport) L 5

William Morgan
1896
Jun. Merthyr v Morgan Jones police halted 3

…. Morgan 'Mulduggie' (Cardiff)
9st. 6lbs.
1894
Sep. v …. Ford (Cardiff) W 6

Morgan (Tredegar)
1864
Apr. v Stephens L 53

J. Morgans
1889
Jul. Ystrad Rhondda v P. Cleary police halted

Evan 'Yanto' Morley (Porth)
1887
Pencoed v Howel Tilary (Pontypridd) L

Basil Morris (Ferndale)
1894
May. Llanwonno mountain v Joseph Harris (Ferndale) 18

Dan Morris
1895
Apr. Swansea v Michael O'Brien L 6
1896
Mar. Swansea v Pedlar McMahon L 3

Elias Morris (Blaina)
Three previous fights incl. win v George Iles (Kingswood)
1895
Aug. Cardiff v Jenkin Jones (Treorchy) L KO 19
Aug. Cardiff v Charlie Palmer (Treforest) L KO 13

John Morris (Brynmawr)
1856
Jan. Blaenavon v William Gullifer (Blaenavon) L 51

'Paper Morris'
1863
Aug. Pontypool v George Edwards

365

Feasts of Blood

Peter Morris
1870
May Sgiborwen v David Griffiths police halted

Enoch Morrison (Cardiff)
D. 1896
1862-1896 9st. 11lbs.
1890
Mar. Merthyr v Sam (Butcher) Thomas (Ynyshir) D 12
May Pontypridd v John Jones (Shoni Engineer) (Pontypridd) L 5 foul
1894
Apr. Pontypridd v 'a stranger of Walsall' F 10
1895
Apr. Swansea v Tom Hooligan (Swansea) L 2

Richard Mort (Mardy)
1884
Feb. Cwmaman v George Crithey (Ferndale)

Solomon Moseley
1812
Jun. Haverfordwest v Abraham Pratt L 10

Daniel Murphy (Swansea)
1876- 11st. 6lbs.
1898
Dec. Swansea v Billy Morgan L KO 2

Dick Murphy (Cardiff)
1898
Nov. Cardiff v Charles Donoghue W 9

Jack Murphy
1880s
V Redmond Coleman L 6
1900
Jun. Merthyr v Redmond Coleman L retd. 12
Jun. Merthyr v Redmond Coleman L3
Patrick Murray
1862-

1886
Mar. Cardiff v Andrew Keef 79

'Jim Nagg' (Treorchy)
1894
May Treorchy v Jim Sweet Police halted
John Nash (Merthyr)
1841
Apr. Merthyr v Richard Taylor 'Shoni Scubor Fawr'

William Nathan (Cymmer)
1890
Sep. Pontypridd v Jack Hitchings (Ynyshir) L 12

Patrick Neary
1887
Dec. Wrexham v John Judson L KO 10

Welsh Ned
1833
Jun. Gloucs. V Samuel Oakey (Oakey died.

John Newnom (Cowbridge)
1828
Mar. Cowbridge v John Davies L 79

.... Nicholls (Wrexham Clogger) 9 st. 6lbs.
1843
Feb. Delamere Forest v …. Hughes W

Philip Nicholas
1836
Aug. Landilo [sic] v Thomas Thomas

W. Norris *Clydach)
1902
Jul. Clydach Vale v John Jones – police halted

Charlie North (Pontypridd)
1891
Oct. London v ….Mortimer (Claremarket) L KO 3
Oct London v ….Mortimer L ret 4

366

Fight Records

John 'Jack' Northey (Ton Ystrad)
1866-
1885
Llantrisant v Nobby Wynne (Mountain Ash) police halted
1888
Oct. Garth Mountain v Thomas Davies (Cwmpark) police halted 7
1889
Jan. Ystrad Rhondda v William Davies (Ton Ystrad) W rtd 43
1891
Jun. Swansea v Ivor/Jack Hitchins (Rhondda) L 4
v **George 'Punch' Jones** (Aberaman)
1894
Jun. Maindy Mountain v Joe Mitchell D 64
Nov. Treorchy v John Edmund Rees Police halted
1895
Jun. Llantrisant v ?? Davies (Mountain Ash) L 18
1900
Apr. v Jack Jenkins (Aberavon)Aberavon, L KO 2

'Ned the Lock' (Treherbert)
1892
Apr. Penyrheol v Jack Punch (Nantymoel) W

Jim O'Brien
1894
Dec. Swansea v Dick Ambrose L KO 1
John O'Brien (Cardiff)
1867-1911
5ft 10 ½ ins, 11st, 13lbs

Cardiff v Jem Driscoll W 6
1885
Cardiff v ..... Lyons (Bristol) W 3
v Peter Burns 'Dublin Tom' W 3
v Lloyd Roberts W
1889
May Marshfield v John Jones (Shoni Engineer) W19

1890
Feb. Liverpool v Felix Scott (Liverpool) W KO 3
Nov. London v Ted Bryant L KO 1
1891
Mar. London v Ted White (Walthamstow) W KO 9
May London v Alf Ball W KO 7
Dec. London v Alf Mitchell (Cardiff) W 8
1892
Dec. London v Dave Burke L pts.
1894
Apr. London v Dai St. John (Resolven) W KO 5
Apparently this was a return fight;no details on the first fight in 1891 in London, which O'Brien won,
Oct. London v Frank Craig (USA) L KO 2
Nov. London v Jewey Cook L pts
1895
Apr. London v Jewey Cook L pts.
Apr. London v Frank Craig (USA) L 1
v Tom James ?

Michael O'Brien
1895
Apr. Swansea v Dan Morris W 6
v George Jones L

Patsy O'Leary (Cardiff/USA)
Lightweight
1865- 8st. 9 lbs.
(Record as at 10 Dec 1887)
Cincinatti v Joe Ridge W 12
Cincinatti v Frank Murphy W 4
Cincinatti v Pete Evans W 6
Cincinatti v Tom Riley W 8
Chicago v Young Berry W KO 4
St, Louis v Pete Johnson W 3
New York v Tommy Danforth D
Philadelphia v Young Welsh W
B Martin Neary W
v Jim Peterson D
New York v Con Driscol W2
Grand Rapids v Young Carol W KO 6
Ontario v Thurston W 1
Cleveland v Bates W 6

1886
Nov. Kentucky v Tommy Warren (Louisville) L foul 12
1887
Feb. Cincinnati, Ohio v Billy Barry W 4
Jun. Grand Rapids, Michigan v Patsy Carroll (Buffalo) W KO 5
1888
Jan. Dayton, Ohio v J. Stephens W KO
1890
Jan. Newcastle, England v ?? Howe (Gateshead) L 8
Feb. Buffalo, New York v Paddy McBride (Philadelphia L KO 5

Billy Owen 'Three-fingered Jack'
1824
Feb. Scotland v unknown W 14

Evan Owen (Cardiff)
1891
Dec. London v Sam Gulliver (Cardiff) L 16

Joe Owen (Aberdare)
1894
Jan. Aberdare v Harry John W KO 3

John Owen (Clydach Vale)
1900
Mar. Clydach Vale v Thomas Harris Police halted

Rees Owen (Newbridge)
1900
Dec, Tirphil v Will Griffiths L KO 14
....Owens (Newridge)
1891
Feb. Abercarn v Johns (Abercarn) W

John Owens
1871
Apr. Bangor v Joseph Williams police halted 13

Richard Owens (Llanidloes)
1864
v Ieuan Evans W
1865
Mar. Warrington v Harry Neville W 84
Charlie Palmer (Treforest)
1895
Aug. Cardiff v Elias Morris (Blaina) W KO 13 (*pro ring debut*)
Pedlar Palmer (Greenhill)
1899
Apr. Swansea v Tubby Dougie W

Ellis Pannwr
1791
Aug. Dolgellau v Roderick Lewis W
Bob Parry
1824
Aug. Harewood's End v Thomas Powell (Broad Oak) W 103

James Thomas Parry (Porth
1899
Sep. v John Thomas (Porth/Mardy)
'Patsy' (Cardiff)
1896
Jul. Cardiff v 'Jack' (Cardiff) W KO 40

Bill Pea
1829
Ludlow v ? Coates
Knighton v George .... W 81

Thomas Peak
1794
Mar. Wrexham v John Barlow W KO

Charles Pearce (Tredegar)
1888
Aug. Tredegar v William Gittings (Tredegar)

.... Pendry
1862
May Aberaman v .... Harris L 97

George 'Patsy' Perkins (Newport)
1866- 5ft. 5 ½ ins. 10st. 8lbs.
Six previous fights including
W v Bartley London 16
W v Myers (Portsmouth)
W v Charles Woods (London)
W v Bill Tovey (London)

Fight Records

L v Dido Plumb (London)
1893
Feb. Swansea v John 'Shumack' Thomas (Cardiff) W 1
May Merthyr v Tom Rooney (Bristol) W retd 6
1895
Mar. London v Bob Wiltshire (Cardiff) (10 st. championship of Wales) W retd. 8

Jack Perks (Brecon)
1843?
v Charley Dawson (Monmouth) W 27
1844
May v George Marshall

Jem Perry (Cardiff)
1870- 5ft 5 ½ ins. 9st. 8lbs
Claimed wins over Walter Garretty, amateur champion of Australia, in four rounds, and George Johnson, of London.
Claimed wins in USA over Dick Connell (1 round), Hank Detuck (4), Hugh Cannon (6), Buck Kennedy (12), Jack Hanley (1)in USA

1892
Nov. Plymouth v Tommy Merrin L ret 6
1894
USA v unknown W KO
1895
Mar. London v Arthur Valentine L disq 5

George Perry (Newbridge)
1891
Mar. Newbridge v Richard Ball (Newbridge) police halted

Daniel Phillips (Treorchy)
1895
Nov. Treorchy v William Winter Police halted

David Phillips
1886
Jan. Nantyglo v Robert Probert

Dave Phillips (Merthyr Vale)

1892
Aug Merthyr v Thomas Prosser (Treharris) L 1
Edward Phillips (Treorchy)
1895
Jun. Treorchy v Emanuel Phillips (Treorchy) police halted

Emanuel Phillips (Treorchy)
1895
June. Treorchy v Edward Phillips (Treorchy) police halted

Henry Phillips (Rhondda)
1889
Dec. Gelli Mountain v William Jones

James Phillips
1901
Sep. v Abraham Evans
Richard Phillips
1903
Mar. Glynneath v William Davies police halted

William Phillips (Nantyglo)
1892
Sep. Ebbw Vale mountain v James Richards (Brynmawr) police halted

David Pierce (Aberaman)
1895
Apr. Aberavon v Sam James (Glynneath) W 29

.... Pike (Cardiff)
1837
Mar. Cardiff v .... Spencer (Cardiff) D 120

Daniel Plumpton (Pontypridd)
1895
May Pontypridd v Thomas Jones police halted

Jim Pollard
1888
May Hirwain v Wat Jenkins (Ystrad) L 15

369

Dan Powell (Pontypridd)
1889
Dec. Pontypridd v Thomas Lambert W 6
1890
May Pontypridd v Jack Wilks W 4

Thomas Powell (Broad Oak)
Apr. Harewood's End v Bob Parry L 103

Edmund Powell (Penygraig)
1886
Cymmer Mountain v Tudor Foster– police halted.

Tom Power (Newport)
1867
Feb. Newport v Eugene Currin (Newport) adjourned

....Power (Merthyr)
1887
Jan. Dowlais v Magrath L

.....Power (Merthyr)
1887
Jan. Dowlais v ....Mansfield police halted.

Abraham Pratt
1812
Jun. Haverfordwest v Solomon Moseley W 10

David John Price (Nantyglo)
1896
Oct. Ebbw Vale mountain v George Moore (Nantyglo)

George Price (Maesteg)
1913
Dec. v John Hopkins – police halted

John Price (Pontycymmer)
1904
Nov. Maesteg) v Sydney Davies

Lewis Price (Mountain Ash)
1890
May Aberdare v Trevor Roberts

Richard (Dicky) Price (Cardiff)
1893
Mar. Cardiff v W. Jenks (Cardiff) W 12
1894
Jan. Cardiff v Mike Sullivan (Cardiff) L 6
1895
Mar. Swansea v William. Morgan (Swansea) L 11

Thomas Price
1829
Llanbadarn Vynydd v Richard Humphreys (Betws Cedewain) 85

T. Price
1869
Apr. Wrexham v James Jones (Wrexham) Jones died

Thomas Price (Ynyshir)
1906
Dec/ Porth v William Henry Gregor police halted

William Price
1859
Aberystruth v Thomas Evans

William Price (Cardiff)
1890
Aug. Cardiff v Joseph Morgan (Cardiff) L KO 7

....Price (Ruabon)
1857
Aug. Oswestry v ....Malpas (Bilston) police halted

'Princy' (Penarth)
1889
May Cardiff v Steve Giblin (Penarth) police halted

Ted Pritchard (London)
1869-1903 5ft. 9ins 11 st.
1888

370

Fight Records

Dec. London v R. Galvin (Kentish Town) W
Dec. London v R. Leary W
Dec. London v Dave Burke (Bethnal Green) W
1889
Feb; London v Jem Hayes W5
Jun. London v Alec Burns (Battersea) W KO 2
1890
Dec. London v Alf Mitchell (Cardiff) W KO 4
1891
Mar. London v v Jack Burke W 3
Jul. London v Jem Smith W 3
1892
Aug. Brighton v Jem Hall /L KO 4
Sep. London v Jem Hall ND
1893
1894
Nov. London v Dick Burge (Newcastle) W KO 2
Dec. London v Frank Craig (USA) L KO 1
1895
May. London v Jem Smith L KO 2

Robert Probert
1886
Jan. Nantyglo v David Phillips

Jack Prosser (Pontypridd)
1900
May Merthyr v Gwilym Jones W 6

Tom Prosser (Merthyr Vale/ Treharris)
1867 - 11st.
1892
Aug. Merthyr v Dave Phillips (Merthyr Vale) W 1
1893
Apr. Merthyr v Tom Edwards (Troedyrhiw) W KO 3
…. Prosser
1887
Apr. Bedwas v …. Flowers W

Ernest Pugh (Rhondda)
1874- 1890
Apr. Pontypridd v Francis Jones

Thomas Pugh
1861
Oct. Cefn Mawr v David Richards/'Dai Matthews' W 40+

…. Pugh (Wrexham)
1841
Mar. Wrexham v … Foulkes (Wrexham) W

Jack Punch (Nantymoel)
1892
Apr. Penyrheol v 'Ned the Lock' (Treherbert) L

Will Ramoon
1833
Jul. Merthyr v John Jenkins (died)

Sam Randall (Ogmore Valley)
Had previously won three fights
1895
Jul. Cardiff v Harry Millard (Rhymney Valley) D 12

Jack Rasher (Whitechapel, London)
1820
Jan. Plaistow v Josh Hudson L
Apr. Southend v Adams W
May Epsom Downs v Charles Gyblett L 58
1821
Jun. Crawley Hurst v Joe Spencer W 70

Jack Raymond (Pontypridd)
1890
Aug. Pontypridd v Jack Doad (Penygraig) W
1892
May Pontypridd v Tom James (Aberaman) L 2

John 'Patsy' Reardon (Cardiff)
1839 – 1871 5ft. 6 ½ ins. 10 stone.
Beat ? Phillips for £5 a-s-ide

371

Beat ? Lass for £5 a-side on 29 rounds
Beat Jem Hill in 42 rounds for £25 a-side
1860
Jan. London v William Smith W 42
May London v John Rooke D 37
1861
Apr. Limpney Stoke v Tom Shipp D 27
1862
Mar. v George King D
Jul. Hampshire v Bob Travers W 53
Dec. Kent v Jem Dillon W 56
1863
Nov. Kent v John Rooke (Birmingham) police halted
1868
Jan. Illinois, USA v Thomas McCann

Phil Reardon (Cardiff)
1876
Sep. Cardiff v Martin Fury Police halted

Dai Rees(Mid Rhondda)
V Thomas Thomas L 15

Dai 'Buller' Rees (Aberavon)
12st. 6lbs.
1879-
1900
Jul. Cwmavon v Will Lane W 27
Sep. Aberavon c Jack Jenkins W retd 1

David Rees (Dowlais)
1865
Aug. Cwmynysminton/Aberdare mountsin v William Williams (Aberdare) police halted

David Rees (Aberdare)
1888
May Aberaman mountain v Joseph Evans (Aberdare) 32

David Rees (Nantyglo)
1889
Sep. Brynmawr v William Williams (Brynmawr) L 42

David Rees (Troedyrhiw)

1894
May Aberdare v Thomas Edwards (Aberdare) L 7

John Edmund Rees
1894
Nov. Treorchy v Jack Northey Police halted
Joseph Rees
1856
Jan. Blaenavon v unknown

Tom Rees (Penrhiwceiber)
1904
Apr. Tongwynlais v Tom Davies L 21

William Rees (Ystrad Rhondda)
1871-
1894
Sep. Llwnypia v Thomas Shaw (Ystrad Rhondda) W 90

W. D. Rees (Treherbert)
1896
May Llanwonno mountain v Morgan Davies W 28

? Rees (Aberdare)
1891
Aug. Cardiff v Edwards (Aberdare)

….. Rees (Trealaw)
1899
Jan. Pontypridd v W. Barron W 4

… Rees (Pontypridd)
1899
Jan. Pontypridd v ….Jenkins, Pontypridd L 8

Alfred Richards
1888
Aug. Bedwellty v John Mason

Bill Richards (Newport)
1851
Mar. Newport v John Woolfe (Tip Top Slasher) police halted

372

Fight Records

Daniel Richards (Aberdare)
1891
Jul. Mardy mountain v William Richards police halted

David Richards 'Dai Matthews'
1861
Oct. Cefn Mawr v Thomas Pugh L 40+

Edward Richards
1894
Sep. Abercanaid v William Jones W 8

James Richards (Brynmawr)
1892
Sep. Ebbw Vale mountain v William Phillips (Nantyglo) police halted

John Richards
1859
Jun. Sirhowy v Roger Williams (Williams died)

John Richards (Mardy)
1885
May Merthyr mountain v Evan Roberts (Mardy) W

William Richards (Aberdare)
1891
Jul. Mardy mountain v Daniel Richards police halted

…Richards
1865
Dec. Merthyr v …..Ryan

Johnny Ritchie (Rhondda)
1891
Oct. Coity v Bill Morgan (Rhondda) abandoned 3

John Riordon
1866
May Merthyr v unknown

Edward Roberts (Seven Sisters)
1895
Jul. Seven Sisters v Walter Stephens (Seven Sisters) police halted

Evan Roberts (Mardy)
1885
May Merthyr mountain v John Richards (Mardy) L

Jack Roberts (Aberdare)
1864
Mar. v Will Wil;liams L 42

J. Roberts
1866
Apr. Flintshire v T. Davies W 13

Lloyd Roberts
1885
V John O'Brien L
1888
v Fred Bevan (Pontypridd) W

Tom Roberts (Cardiff)
1893
Dec. Cowbridge v Joe Williams (Cardiff) W KO 6

Trevor Roberts (Penrhiwceiber)
1890
May Aberdare v Lewis Price

Walter Roberts
1853-
1874
Sep. Newport v Henry Lewis

…. Roberts (Mountain Ash)
1870-
1896
Nov. Llanwonno mountain v ….Williams (Mountain Ash) W 5

Oliver Robinson (ferndale)
1903
Mar. v Herbert King – police halted

…. Robinson
1827
Jan. Monmouth Cap v 'Gas' L 26

373

Alfred Rodway (Ebbw Vale)
1898
Feb. Blorenge mountain v David Thomas (Brynmawr) Police halted

George Rogers (Ferndale)
1896
Sep. Ferndale mountain v Jim Edwards L 24

Morris Rooke 'Morris Dido'
1866
Apr Rumney v 'Billy Woody' police halted

? Rooke
1908
<ar. Cymmer v David John James

Tom Rooney (Cardiff/Bristol)
Credited with wins over Alf Wright and George Baxter at Plymouth,
1890
Feb. Bristol v Dublin Curley W4
Jul, Bristol v Pongo W
1891
Nov. Devonport v Farmer D
1892
Apr, Plymouth v Sam Kendall W
Nov. Plymouth v Jem Hucker (Swansea) W 12
1893
May Merthyr v Patsy Perkins (Merthyr) L retd. 6
Sep. Plymouth v Jem Brown (Bristol) L 9
1895
Dec. Devonport v Alf Wright L4
1896
Nov. Plymouth v Sam Bentley L 20
1904
Jan. Plymouth v Sam Bwnrlwy L retd. 4
Mar. Falmouth v Gunner Vickers L 15
Apr. Penzance v Gunner Vickers D 10
1905
Jan. Plymouth v Alf Glanfield D 15

Henry Rosser (Aberdare)

1896
Jul. Craig mountain v Lodwick Lake Police halted

John Rosser
1855
Dec. Hirwaun Common v Daniel Lewis

S. Rothwell (Aberdare)
1894
Jan. Aberdare v James Parry Jones (Aberaman) W rtd 5

Jack Rough
1866 - 9st. 10lbs.
1888
Sep. King's Norton v William Farmer (Birmingham) L 27

Rowland Rowlands
1832
Nov. Thornhill v Rowland Thomas W

'Rufus'
1865
Jul. Pontypool v 'Blackfriars Tom' W 5

William Russ (Cardiff)
1866
May Rumney v unknown

J. D. Russell (Barry)
1897
Dec. Bridgend v Fitzpatrick (Bridgend) L 10

John Ryan
1851
Jan. Cardiff v Michael Brenon

.....Ryan
1865
Dec. Merthyr v ....Richards

Smith Sage (Pontypool)
1859
Mar. Blaenavon v John Tamplin
Bill Samuel (Swansea)

374

Fight Records

1841-1916 13st.
After (claimed) 40-plus unrecorded fights
Samuel claimed fights against Dan Thomas D, Young Sailor W, Shack Dale W, Jem Mace's Black W, Sam Lane D, Sam Lane W, Matthews W, Matthews (2) W, Ivor Wynn, W, Jacobs W, Murray W. Guidrell W, Big Pompey.
1882
Oct. Haverfordwest v Bob Dunbar 'Young Lane' (Newport) W
1890
Sep. Neath v John Jones (Shoni Engineer) WKO3
1892
Aug. Neath v …. Legge (Swansea) W 4
1894
Jan. Cardiff v Tom Ball (Australia) ND 2
      v Tom Vincent L (details unknown)

Edward Savage
1793- 12st.-
1825
Oct. Shear Mere v Kirkman L 58
1826
Jul. Noman's Land, Herts. V Kirkman W 101
1827
Mar. Whetstone v Wallace W 127
May Banstead Downs v Wallace L 61
Aug. Colney Heath v Kirkman D 93
1828
Jan. Banstead Downs v Spring the Conjuror W 120
May Epsom Downs v Kirkman L
Oct. Norwood v Peter Sweeney police halted 16
Dec. Epping Forest v Tom Sweeney L 26
1829
Mar. Sheremere v Peter Sweeney L 94
Dec. Herts v …. Gow L 23

William (Bill) Savage
11st.
1789 -
Unreported fights with Alick Reid (W), Lock the cab driver (L) and others

1827
May London v Griffiths W 23
Aug. Colney Heath v Jack Branstonn 'Jack of Finchley' W 20
1828
Jan. Banstead Downs v Paddy Flynn L 91
Mar. Chertsey v Harry Jones L 56
Sep. Battle Bridge v ….Pick L

…. Sayer
1848
Jan. Neath v …. Jones W

Felix Scott (Newport/Liverpool)
? v George Jones L
? v T. Donnelly (Birmingham)W
? v Joe Fielding (Manchester)
? v Harry Stevens (Notting Hill)
? v Ching Ghook D
Pelican Club v Davenport W
Lambeth School of Arms v 'Big Brother' McCarthy W
? v J. Hayes (Marylebone) W
1886
Dec. Liverpool v Williams W 5
1887
May Liverpool v Dick Burge (Newcastle) L 5
? v Butler's Wolf
1890
Feb. Liverpool v John O'Brien (Cardiff) L KO 3
Jun. Manchester v Tom Shawcross W 2
Dec. London
V Alfred Bowman W
V Henry Smith W
W. Robinson L
1891
Jan. London v W. Robinson L 6
Mar. London v Arthur Bobbett L retd. 2
Apr. London v W. Robinson L
May London v Alf Suffolk L disq.
May London v Alf Suffolk L KO 1 (same night)
May London v Bill Cheese W6
Jun. London v Bill Cheese L3
1892
Jun. London v Alec Young W 3

375

Jun. London v Ted Dorkings (Cambridge) L
1902
Feb. Birmingham v Walter Thomas L KO 1

Mark Scott (Coedpenmaen)
1903
Apr. Pontypridd Mountain v Albert Thomas

?? Scroggins 'the Welsh Champion'
1835
Sep. Brecon v 'the Newton hero' L
Shoni Sgubor Fawr
1840
Aug. Rumney v Harry Jones W 12

Thomas Shaw (Ystrad Rhondda)
1872-
1894
Sep. Llwnypia v William Rees (Ystrad Rhondda) L 90

James Shields (Cardiff)
1861
Nov. Ely Common v unknown

Tom Shenkin
1829
Dec. Pentichilin, Mgy., v Tom Jones L 64

Acquiline Short
1864
Oct. Pontypool v William Vernon police halted

Charles Silber (Ferndale)
1904
Dec. Penrhys Mountain v David Jones – police halted

Knocker Simes
1893
Nov. Cardiff v Farnham Jones W 13

'Slasher' (Swansea)
1895

May Swansea v Daniel Thomas (Hafod) W 4

Harry Slee (Penrhiwceiber)
1894
Mar. Llanwonno mountain v Gilbert Watson (Penrhiwceiber) police halted 23

Fred Smith (Porth)
1894
Jun. v Evan Evans (Porth)

Seth Smith (Mountain Ash)
1881
Jul. Aberdare mountain v William Thomas
1887
v Morgan Crowther (Newport) L

Tom Smith (Ystrad)
1896
Jun. Ystrad v Morgan Edmunds Police halted

T. Smith (Cardiff)
1890
Apr. Cardiff v Farnham Jones (Cardiff) W 16 foul

Robert Smout
1825
May Peckham Fields v William Shields L 12

Fred Snooks (Pontypridd)
1868 - 11st.
1893
Nov. Treforest v William 'Mother' Lee (Pontypridd) W KO 3

'Snowball' (Maesteg)
1900
Aug. Cwmdu v Tom Jones 'Tom Luce' L retd. 14

.... Spencer (Cardiff)
1837
Mar. Cardiff v .... Pike (Cardiff) D 120
Tom Spring

Fight Records

1795-1851
1812
V Hollands W
1814
v Henley W11
1817
Sep. London v Stringer W 29
1818
Apr. London v Ned Painter W31
Aug. London v Painter L
1819
May London v Carter W 71
Dec. London v Ben Burn W
1820
May London v Ben Burn W
Jun. London v Joshua Hudson W
1821
Feb. London v Tom Oliver W 26
1823
May Andover v Neal W 8
1824
Jan. Worcester v Langan W 77
Jun. v Langan W

Will Squinks
1888
Mar. v Shone Castellnedd Police halted,

W. Squires (Swansea)
1894
Jan. Swansea v W. Morgan W
Jan. Swansea v W. Morgan W

Frederick Stephens Honeychurch 'John Stephens' (Pontypridd)
1888
Nov. Pontypridd v William Davies

Richard Stephens
1860
Jan. Rhymney Hill v Evan Edwards 'Yanto Glatchen' (Abertillery) W 117

Stephen Stephens (Tredegar)
1864
Apr. Cwmbargoed & Quakers Yard v William Taylor 'Billo Bach' (Rhymney) W 60

Walter Stephens (Seven Sisters)
1895
Jul. Seven Sisters v Edward Roberts (Seven Sisters) police halted

…. Stephens (Llandaff)
1811
Jan. Llandaff v …. James (Ely Mill) L 27

Stephens (Tredegar)
1864
Apr. v Morgan W 53

Alf Stevens (Cardiff)
1895
Mar. Swansea v Shamus Warner L KO 2

Charles Stevens (Wrexham)
1873
Jan. Wrexham v …. Booth L

Dai Stevens (Treorchy)
1900
Pontypridd v Jim Driscoll (Cardiff) L

Dick Stevens
1863
Dec. Pontypridd v Dick James (Aberdare) L 51

John Stock
1879
Jul. Griffithstown v George Wood police halted

T. Stock (Gorseinon)
1894
Nov. Gorseinon v David Hagerton L 4

David St. John (Resolven)
1872 -1899
6ft. 3ins. 13st. 12lbs.
1891
London v John O'Brien L
1892
Nov. Merthyr v Tom James W KO 4
1893
Sep. Pontypridd v Tom James (Aberaman) W rtd 6

377

1894
Apr. London v John O'Brien (Cardiff) L KO 5
1895
Sep. Neath v Tom James (Aberaman) D 6

Dai Strawhat
1860
Jan. Blaenavon v Ben Andrews D

Austin Strickland
1874
Sep. Caerphilly v Jenkin Morgan W

Dan Sullivan (Merthyr)
1896
Dec. Breconshire v Tom Cromley (Birmingham) L 22

Florence Sullivan (Dowlais)
1893
Mar. Dowlais v John Mansfield (Dowlais) L 11

George Sullivan (Aberdare)
1893
Apr. Aberdare v William Williams

Jack Sullivan (Dowlais)
1893
Mar. Merthyr v Redmond Coleman (Merthyr) L 6

Mike Sullivan (Cardiff)
1894
Jan. Cardiff v Richard 'Dicky' Price (Cardiff) W 6
Aug. Cardiff v Joe Ballard (Bristol) police halted 6
Nov. Cardiff v Tom Jenkins (Cardiff) W 4 police halted
1895
Mar. Swansea v Chaffy Hayman (Bristol) W KO 9
Apr. Swansea v William {Billy) Morgan (Swansea) L KO 2

? Sullivan (Blaina)
1890
Oct. Blaina v ? Finnery
James Swales (Wrexham)
1892
Oct. Mold v unknown

Jim Sweet (Treorchy)
1894
May Treorchy v 'Jim Nagg' (Treorchy) Police halted

Henry Sweet (Newport)
1899
Jun. Llantarnam v Edward Basham (Newport)
'Tallow'
1864
Jun. v 'Chips' L 16
1866
Aug. Pontypool v 'The Admiral' W16

John Tamplin
1859
Mar. Blaenavon v SmithSage

.....Tamplin (Cardiff)
1899
May Cardiff v Dan Connell (Cardiff) L retd. 6

John Tapp
1868
Oct. Pontypool v William Towte W
'Eli Tar'(Cwmtillery)
1894
Jul. Blaenavon mountain v Ishmael Daniel (Cwmtillery) W 7

Morris Taylor (Blackwood)
5ft. 7ins. 9st. 8lbs.
1898
Aug. Bedwellty v Will Harris L KO 5

Richard Taylor 'Shoni Subor Fawr'
1841
Apr. Merthyr v John Nash

William Taylor 'Billo Bach' (Rhymney/Blaenavon)

378

Fight Records

1862 -
Jun Tafarnaubach v 'Jem Hundred' W
1864
Apr Cwmbargoed & Quakers Yard v Stephen Stephens (Tredegar) L 60
May Llanfoist v Seth Beynon (Blaenavon) W 32

Albert Thomas (Coedpenmaen)
1903
Apr. Pontypridd Mountain v Mark Scott

Alfred Thomas (Pontypridd)
1897
May Bristol v Alf Wright (Bristol) L 1

Bill Thomas (Wrexham)
1866
Mar. Orrell v Bill Stoddart (Liverpool) L 38

Charles Thomas
1868
Apr. Swansea v unknown

Dan Thomas (Pontypridd)
1828-1910 Lightweight
v Tom Evans (Dowlais)W
Dowlais v John Williams W
Dowlais v George Moule W
Dowlais Common v Tom Surrey W
Ebbw Vale v Tom Boger W
Dowlais Common v Bill Morgan W
Magor v Bill Lishon W
Merthyr Tydfil v Morgan Rees W
Pontypridd v Morgan Rees W
Newport v Ned Lewis W
1855
Jul. Machen v Jem Williams (Bristol) W 50
1856
Feb. Penhow v David Ingram (Bristol) L 35
1858
Oct. v Jack Brookes W 54
1859
Jan. v Charles Lynch W 56
1860
May London v Bill Gillam W 48

1862
Apr. v Joe Nolan (*lightweight championship*) police halted 22

Daniel Thomas (Hafod)
1895
Jan. Swansea v Thomas Harries (Llansamlet) W 7
May Swansea v 'Slasher' (Greenhill) L 4

David Thomas (Aberstruth)
1858
Sep. Vaynor v Edward Lewis

David Thomas (Vaynor)
1859
v David Morgan

David Thomas 'the Welshman' (Smethwick)
1861
Nov. Birmingham v Edmund Pardon W 7

David Thomas (Brynmenin)
1884
Oct. Blaencaerau mountain v Thomas Davies (Pentre Ystrad) police halted

David Thomas 'Spanker' (Brynmawr)
1898
Feb. Blorenge mountain v Alfred Rodway Police halted
Delhi Lucknow Thomas
1857-1924
1890
Jul. v Wm. Amesbury L

Edward Thomas/Taylor 'Ned the Bell' (Dinas)
1897
Jul. Dinas v Evan John (Dinas) W

Isaiah Thomas (Aberdare)
1894
Jun. Aberaman v Rees Morgan (Aberdare)
1900

379

May Merthyr v George 'Punch' Jones L KO 2

Ivor (Butcher) Thomas (Ynyshir)
1877- 8st. 5lbs.
1895
Jun. Swansea **v** Richard Thomas (Ynyshir) L 6
1896
Dec. Pontypridd v D. Jones 'Tom Cochin (Hafod) W KO2
1897
May Bristol v Alf Wright (Plymouth) L 1
Aug. Tonypandy v Samuel Mainwaring W (Mainwaring died)
1899
Jan.– Pontypridd v ? Jenkins (Port Talbot) L 6
Feb. London v Bill Wood - ??
1900
May London v Harry Chamberlain W 15
May Pontypridd v Harry Mansfield – L 15
Jun. Merthyr v George 'Punch' Jones W 6
1905
Jun. Cardiff v Jim Driscoll (Cardiff) L 3

James Thomas
1896
Jul. Llanwonno mountain v William Howells

Jim Thomas (Cardiff)
1899
Dec. London v Jim Kendrick L
1900
Mar. Woolwich v George Harris (Kentish Town) L

John Thomas (Jack the Lamb) (Beaufort)
1872
Nov. Brynmawr v William Marshall (Ebbw Vale) W 11

John 'Schumack' Thomas (Cardiff)
1893
Feb. Swansea v Patsy Perkins L 1

John Thomas/Rowley
1897
Dec. Trebanog mountain v Aaron Wilding W

John Thomas (Porth/Mardy)
1878-
1897
May Rhondda v Edward Augustus Collard (Mardy) W 30
1899
Sep. v James Thomas Parry (Porth) police halted

Joseph Thomas (Trealaw)
1891
May Pontypridd v William Gimlet police halted

Phil Thomas (Ogmore Valley)
1895
Jul. Cardiff v Tom Edmunds (Ogmore Valley) L KO 25

Richard Thomas (Ynyshir
1895
Jun. Swansea **v** Ivor (Butcher) Thomas W 6
1896
Sep. Ynysybwl v William Hughes

Rowland Thomas (Merthyr)
1832
Nov. Thornhill v Rowland Rowlands L 1 hour, 8 mins.

Rowland Thomas
1868
Apr. Merthyr v Thomas Beynon 75

Sam (Butcher) Thomas) (Aberaman/Ynyshir)
1864 - 5 ft. 7 ½ ins. 10 st.
v 'Portobello' W
1889
v Hopkin Williams (Ferndale) W 2
Mar. Pontypridd v Dai Davies (Mardy) W 8

380

Fight Records

1890
Feb. Pontypridd v Enoch Morrison (Cardiff) D 12
  Pontypridd v Thomas Lambert 'Bungey' (Pontypridd) W 3
1892
Jan. Merthyr v Thomas James W KO 5
Mar. London v Bob Wiltshire (Cardiff) L 5
1894
Feb. Aberdare v Tom 'Pawdy' McCarthy W rtd 5
Apr. Porth v Malloy (Wolverhampton) crowd halted
Oct. London v S. Lyons (Bristol) L ret. 9

Also (undated/unconfirmed)
v John O'Brien
v John Jones (Shoni Engineer)
v David St. John

Thomas Thomas
1836
Aug. Landilo [sic] v Philip Nicholas

Thomas Thomas 'Tom twice' (Ogmore Valley)
B. 1875- 5ft. 8ins. 9st. 11lbs.
1897
v Johnny Griffiths (Maesteg) W 4
v Dai Rees (Mid-Rhondda) W 15
1898
Jan. Cardiff v Joe Priddy (Radstock) L 9

Walter 'Darkey' Thomas (Neath)
Fights 11, Win 3, Drawn 3, Lost 5
1899
Apr. 15 London v Tom Tunstall L pts.
Sept. 8 Swansea v Dai Morgan W TKO
Oct. v David Morgan, Swansea, L KO 7

William Thomas (Mountain Ash)
1881
Jul. Aberdare mountain v Seth Smith

Thomas Thorn (Cardiff)
1869
Aug. Rumney moors v John Williams. Thorn died

Howel Tilary (Pontypridd)
1887
Sep. v Yanto Morley W

Dennis Tobin (Barry)
1899
Mar. Cardiff v Jack May (Birkenhead/Cathays) W 5

Morris Tobin (Cardiff)
1885
Jun. Treorchy v John Jones (Shoni Engineer) (Treorchy) L 7

'Blackfriars Tom'
1865
Jul. Pontypool v 'Rufus' W 5

William Towte
1868
Oct. Pontypool v John Tapp L

Joseph Tregening (Resolven)
1910
Jan. Resolven Mountain v Ernest Lewis

…..Trump (St. Mellons)
1827
Dec. Sirhowy Valley v Worcestershire Ben L 30

Edward Turner
1791-1826 5ft. 7ins. 10st. 4lbs
@1810
v John Balch W
  1813
London v 'a big Irishman' W
1814
Glasgow v McNeil W
  1816
Newcastle v Blackett W
London v Youler W
Oct. Moulsey Hurst v John Curtis W 68
1817
Mar. v Jack Scroggins; police halted
Jun. Herts. v Jack Scroggins W 33
Oct. Shepperton v Jack Scroggins W 45
1818
Dec. Crawley Hurst v Randall L 34

1819
Jun. Wallingham Green v Cyrus Davies W 30
Oct. Wallingham Common v John Martin W 42
1820
Dec. v Josh Hudson W
1821
Jun. Crawley Common v John Martin L 59
1823
Feb. Harpenden Heath v Cyrus Davies L 15
1824
Apr. v Peace Inglis L 47
Nov. Colebrook v Peace Inglis W KO 15

Arthur Vaughan
1895
Sep. Llanwonno mountain v Henry Lewis L 20

James Vaughan
1865
Aug. Blaenavon mountain v Bob Fletcher

Patsy Vaughan (Cork/Cardiff)
1844- 1869 5ft. 7ins. 9st. 8lbs.
@**1865**
V Swansea Dan W
Bristol v Davies W
1867
Feb. London v Andy Casey W 44
Nov. London v Bob Williams D

Samuel Vaughan
1833
Oct. Hay v ...Williams

William Vernon
1864
Oct. Pontypool v Acquiline Short police halted

Michael Wallace
1866
Feb. Blaina v Lewis Jenkins

Thomas Walsh (Pontnewynydd)
1864
May Pontypool v Daniel Desmond (Pontnewynydd) L 46

Daniel Walters
1892
Dec. Aberdare mountain v Richard James

Walter Ward (Merthyr)
1881
Feb. Merthyr v Joseph Goodwin (Merthyr) W 10

James (Shamus) Warner (Swansea/Cardiff)
1854- 1912
1892
Sep. Swansea v Jack Davies (Swansea) W 27
1895
Mar. Swansea v Alf Stevens (Cardiff) W KO 2
1896
Aug. Swansea v Billy Morgan D 4
Aug. Swansea v Billy Morgan D 4

Arthur Watkins
1892
Dec. Merthyr v Bill Brecon abandoned 3

Howell Watkins (Ogmore Vale)
5ft. 6 ½ ins. 8st. 10lbs.
1898
Oct. Cardiff v Fred John D 17

Joseph Watkins (Blaina)
1902
Nov. Blaina Mountain v William Meredith – police halted
Martha Watkins (Newport)
1852
Sep. Cardiff v Susan Davies (Cardiff) police halted 18

Thomas Watkins
1818
Jan. v Richard Davies (Presteigne)

Fight Records

William Watkins (Brynmawr)
1902
Jun. v Joseph Huish – police halted

..........Watkins
1880s
v Redmond Coleman L5

Gilbert Watson (Penrhiwceiber)
1894
Mar. Llanwonno mountain v Harry Slee (Penrhiwceiber) police halted 23

William Watts (Aberaman)
1887
Dec. Aberdare v James Jones (Aberdare) police halted

Ebby Welsh (Lewis)(Aberdare)
1874
Sep. Abernant tunnel v Thomas Daley (Abverdare) L

'a Welshman'
1859
Apr. Acklam, Yorkshire v ….Prior W

Tommy West (Cardiff/USA)
1870 -1929 5ft. 5 ½ ins 10st. 5lbs – 11st. 8lbs.
1892
Apr.28 Oregon v Mysterious Billy Smith D PTS 10
1893
Apr.18 Oregon v Charley Johnson D PTS 31
Dec. 22 Massachusetts v Jack Burke W TKO 3
1894
Jan 11 Massachusetts v Joe Walcott L PTS 3
Oct. 29 Illinois v Ed Pitts W KO 1
Nov. 15 Illinois v Frank O'Neil W NWS 7
1895
Feb. 15 Illinois v George Fitzgerald D NWS 15
Jul. 19 Maryland v Chris Johnson W KO 1
Oct. 4 New York v Mike Harris W TKO 7
1896
Jan. 31 New York v Charles Kid McCoy L KO 2
Feb. 29 New York v Jack Collier W KO 3
Mar. 16 New York v Scaldy Bill Quinn L PTS 10
Apr.04 New York v Billy Shadow D PTS 10
Aug. 24 New York v Max Kane NC 2
Oct. 19 New York v Tarantula Bill Smith W KO 2
Nov. 7 New York v Billy Stift W KO 7
Dec. 9 New York v Joe Walcott D PTS 19
1897
Jan. 12 New York v Charley Johnson W TKO 7
Mar. 3 New York v Joe Walcott W PTS 20
Apr. 3 New York v Jimmy Ryan W TKO 8
May 15 New York v Paddy J. Purtell W TKO 5
Oct. 28 New York v Jim Watts W KO 4
Nov. 29 New York v George Ryan W KO 15
1898
Jan. 20 Connecticut v Dan Murphy D PTS 20
Feb. 24 Connecticut v Dan Murphy W TKO 17
Mar.11 Pennsylvania v Jack Bonner D NWS 6
Apr. 22 Pennsylvania v Joe Walcott NC ND 6
Jun. 13 New York v Tommy Ryan L TKO 14
(billed for the world welterweight championship, but both men were over the weight)
Nov. 14 Connecticut v Mysterious Billy Smith D PTS 20
Dec. 2 Pennsylvania v Tommy Ryan NC NC 6

383

1899-01-21 Abe Ullman New York, U.S.A. W PTS 20
1899
Feb. 28 New York v Jack Bonner W DQ 8
Apr. 4 New York v Dan Creedon D PTS 20
Jun.12 New York v Patsy Raedy W KO 5
Sep. 4 New York v George Byers W KO 7
Oct. 21 New York v Charley Stevenson W KO 13
Nov. 24 New York v Frank Craig W TKO 14
Dec. 30 New York v James E Payne W KO 2
1900
Jan. 9 Illinois v Jack Root L PTS 6
Feb. 16 Maryland v Dick Moore W DQ 4
Feb. 26 New Jersey v Kid Lyons W PTS
Mar. 23 Maryland v Patsy Corrigan W KO 3
Apr. 6 New York v Jack Bonner W TKO 16
Jun. 19 New York v Billy Hanrahan W KO 17
Aug. 27 New York v Joe Walcott W TKO 11
Oct. 15 Pennsylvania v Philadelphia Jack O'Brien L NWS 6
Nov. 26 Pennsylvania v Jack Bonner W NWS 6
1901
Mar. 4 Kentucky v Tommy Ryan L TKO 17
(World Middleweight Title)
Mar. 29 Kentucky v Marvin Hart L TKO 16
1902
Feb. 24 Pennsylvania v Young Peter Jackson L TKO 2
Jun. 23 London v Joe Walcott L PTS 15
(World Welterweight Title)
1906
Oct. 23 Indiana v Ray Bronson L KO 4

James Westlake (Newport)

1867
Jul. v Dan Frapham (bristol) L

? Wheeler
1858
Apr. Cwmdu v ?? Gwyer. Police halted.
Aaron Wilding
1897
Dec. Trebanog mountain v John Thomas (aka Rowley) L

Jack Wilks (Merthyr)
1890
May Pontypridd v Dan Powell L 4

Thomas Willcox
1880
Mar. Cardiff v Evan John police halted

Augustus Williams (Ystrad)
1899
Mar. Pontrhondda v William Jones (Ystrad) W5
Chas. Williams
1825
Dec. Stratfield Say, Hants v John Mahers L 15

Daniel Williams
1848
Sep. Merthyr v David Morgan police halted

Daniel Williams (Brynmawr)
1899
May Llangynidir mountain v Joseph/Jack Huish – police halted 2

David Williams
1893
Mar. Aberdare v William Hay

David Williams 'Studt' (Treherbert)
1871-
1895
Sep. Rhondda v Bill Haggerty/Eggerty (Treherbert) police halted
1896

384

Fight Records

Aug. Neath mountain v Mark Williams (Treherbert) police halted 43

David Williams (Seven Sisters)
1895
May. Neath v Will Dixon (Seven Sisters) police halted

David Robert Williams (Ynyshir)
1889
May Llantrisant v Roderick Jones Police halted

Edward Williams (Tylorstown)
11st. 9lbs.
1895
Dec. Ferndale v Joe Knight (Abercarn) W 20

Edward Williams 'Ned Top of Cefn' (Broughton)
1888
Nov. Gatewen v John Wright (Poolmouth) police halted 9

Hopkin Williams (Ferndale)
1889
v Sam (Butcher) Thomas L 2
Dec. Ferndale v Llewellyn Jenkins

Joe Williams (Cardiff)
1893
Dec. Cowbridge v Tom Roberts (Cardiff) L KO 6

Joseph Williams
1871
Apr. Bangor v John Owens police halted

John Williams (Cardiff)
1869
Aug. Rumney moors v Thomas Thorn. Thorn died.
John Williams (Jack the Buck)
1873
Feb. Aberbeeg v Isaac Latcham

John Williams (Cardiff)
1894

Mar. Penarth v Albert James (Cardiff) D 12

Llewellyn Williams (Hafod)
1892
Jul. Coedcae mountain v Thomas Jones (Mardy) L 30

Mark Williams (Treherbert)
1866-
1896
Aug. Neath mountain v David Williams (Treherbert) police halted after 43

Morgan Williams
1894
Jun. Mountain Ash v David Morgan. Police halted.

M. Williams
1827
Oct. Penderyn v Thomas Zacharias

Roger Williams
1859
Jun. Sirhowy v John Richards (Williams died)

R. G. Williams (Caernavon/USA)
1850
New York v Mike Trainer W 3

Thomas Williams, 'The Welch champion'/ 'Game Welchman'
1829
Nov. Northerton v Isaac Hadley L 28
1845
Oct. v Tabberner WKO 16

Thomas Williams
1871
Nov. Coedcae v William Gilmore police halted 4

Thomas Williams
1884
Nov. Aberdare v Morgan Jones

Thomas Williams (Treorchy)

385

1900
Sep. Forch mountain v Abraham Evans

William Williams (Cardiff)
1858
Jul. Rumney v Richard Callagh (Cardiff) abandoned

William Williams 'Will o'r Ddinas' (Aberdare)
1864
Mar. v Jack Roberts W 42
Nov. Bedwas v David Lewis 'Dai Benlas' L 52
1865
Aug. Cwmynysminton/Aberdare mountain v David Rees police halted

William Williams (Merthyr)
1869
Oct. Merthyr v Evan Lewis (Merthyr)

William Williams 'Bill the Coal'
1871
Jan. Wrexham v Bill Lawrence 'The Gipsy Tinker' D

William Williams (Brynmawr)
1889
Sep. Brynmawr v David Rees (Nantyglo) W 42

William Williams
1893
Apr. Aberdare v George Sullivan

W. Williams (Newport)
10st. 8lbs.
1832
Jul. Newport v …. Shaw (Staffs.) W 58

W. H. Williams
1895
May Gelligaer v Bob \Griffiths Police halted

…..Williams
1828

Apr. Talgarth v the Traro-road champion D

…. Williams
1833
Oct. Hay v Samuel Vaughan

….Williams
1885
Sep. Gower v ….Lewis

….Williams
1888
Jul. Rhondda v unknown (Somerset) D 8

….Williams (Mountain Ash)
1857-
1896
Nov. Llanwonno mountain v ….Roberts (Mountain Ash) L 5

Bob Wiltshire (Cardiff)
1866 - 10 st.
1888
Feb. Cardiff v Sam Hughes (Birmingham) W RTD 7
1889
Nov. Cardiff v T. 'Pawdy' McCarthy (Cardiff) W 4 foul
1890
Mar. Cardiff v Tom 'Pawdy' McCarthy (Cardiff) L disq 4
1892
Mar. London v Sam (Butcher) Thomas (Pontypridd) W 5
1893
Feb. Gower v Dick Ambrose (Swansea) W 3 disq
Apr. London v Sam Gulliver (Cardiff) W KO 5
(Billed for Welsh Lightweight Title)
1895
Mar. London v Patsy Perkins (Cardiff) L RTD 8
(Welsh 10 st championship)
1900
Dec. st. Mellons **v** Dave Wallace D PTS 10 10x2

386

Fight Records

William Winter (Treorchy)
1895
Nov. Treorchy v Daniel Phillips Police halted

George Wood
1879
Jul. Griffithstown v John Stock police halted

'Billy Woody'
1866
Apr. Rumney v Morris Rooke 'Morris Dido' police halted

John Woolfe 'Tip Top Slasher' (Newport)
1851
Mar. Newport v Bill Richards police halted

Nobby Wynne (Mountain Ash)
1885
Llantrisant v Jack Northey police halted

Thomas Zacharias
1827
Oct. Penderyn v M. Williams

Others

Patsy... (Cardiff)
14st.
1896
Jul. Cardiff v Jack W KO 40

Sam ..... (Cardiff)
1892 – Sept Cardiff Docks v Jack....(Cardiff) 19 rds

No fights were recorded for the following, who were referred to as prize fighters:

Richard Bennett (Newport) @1850s, **Henry Berrett** (Aberdare) 1890s, **John Bowen** (Clydach Vale), 1897-1901, **Alfred Branch** 1890s, **Bill Brown (Cardiff)** 1890s, **George Brown (Clydach Vale)** 1890s, **William Brown** (North Wales) 1850.
William Coghlan (Cardiff) 1860s, **William Cole** (Presteigne) 1820s, **David Coleman** (Merthyr) 1902, **James Coles (Newport)** 1840s, **Alex Cropley (Haverfordwest)** 1820s.
Enoch Davies @1865, **Morgan Davies** (Merthyr) 1872, **Thomas Davies (Brecon)** 1830s, **Brusher Davis (Monmouthsire)** @1840s, **Ned Davis, 'the Wrexham champion'** 1840s, **William Davis** (N. Wales) 1840s, **James Day** 1880s, **Philip Dixon** @1840, **David Jones/ Dollings (Swansea)** 1870s-1890s **Joseph Dugmore (Pontypool)** 1860s,70s.
Joe Easton (Cardiff) 1880s, **Rees Edwards (Neath)** 1862, **William Edwards (Merthyr)** 1820s-30, **Samuel Ellery (Swansea)** 1830s, **David Evans (Merthyr)** 1870s, **Evan Evans (Aberavon)** 1860s, **Richard Evans 'Dicky Puddler' (Rhondda)** 1880s, **Richard Evans (Mountain Ash)** 1891, **William Evans (Merthyr)** 1870s,
Albert Foster (Bridgend) 1890sm **John Francis (Newport)** @1860s, **Thomas Ford 'Blue Skin' (Newport)** 1840s.
Ebenezer Gibbon (Cardiff) @1850s, **James Gibbs (Blaenycwm)** 1870s, **Richard Glancy (Newport)** 1876.
John Henry Harris)Newport) 1890s, **Richard Havard** 1890s, **William Havard (Aberaman)** 1888s, **Richard Hayes (Tonypandy)** 1897, **George 'Bruiser'**

387

Heycock (Taibach) Early 19th century, **Bill Holwell** 1840s, **William Hooligan (Swansea)** 1890s, **Luke Horner (South Wales)** @1850, **David Howell (Cardiff)** 1833, **Aaron Hughes (Merthyr)** 1860s, **Edwin Hughes (North Wales)** Early 19th century,

Evan James @ 1830, **William James (Gelligaer)** 1833, **William James (Rhondda)** 1897, **C. Jones (Mountain Ash)** 1860s, **Henry Jones (Swansea)** 1890s, **Hugh Jones 'Huwcyn Twyrch' (Denbigh)** 1820s onwards, **John Jones 'Shoni .Castell Nedd'** 1840s, **Richard Jones (Aberdare)** 1892. **Ivor Joseph (Mountain Ash)** 1891.
John Henry Knight (Tredegar) 1898.
Hopkin Lewis (Glynneath) 1890s, **Ivor Lewis 'Ivor Wynne' (Merthyr)** 1870s, **Philip Lewis 'Portobello'** 1820s, **Richard Lewis (Newport)** 1820s, **Dai Llansantfraid (South Wales)** @1855, **William Lloyd (Tirphil)** 1886, **George Long (Abergavenny)** 1830s.
John Mainwaring (Ystrad) 1890s, **Tom Maroney (Rhondda)** 1870s, **Richard Matthias 'Dick the Thief' (Merthyr)** @1850, **Pat McDonald ' the Irish Gasman' (New Town)** 1828, **James Miller (Cardiff)** 1860s, **Edwin Mitchell (Aberdare)** 1870s, **Bob Morgan (Aberdare)** 1890s, **Evan Morgan 'Yanto Clathes' (Risca)**, **Jerry Morgan (Cardiff)** 1860s, **John Morgan (Merthyr)** 1860s.
Thomas Nelson (Risca) 1860s, **John Nicholas (Cilfynydd)** @1890, **'Ned of the Green Hills (North Wales)** Early 19th century.
George Osborne (Cardiff) @1890s, **Donoghue O'Shea** 1890s, **Philip Owen** 1840s.
William Parry (Aberdare) 1870s, **Thomas Pearson 'Tom Cloggy' (Swansea)** 1870s, ...**Pearce 'the Welsh champion'** @1850 18 st, **George Pick** 1830s, **Dennis Prichard (Monmouth)** 1840s, **John Pugh Smith (Wrexham)** 1840s, **George Pugsley (Swansea)** 1893, **Luke Purcell (Brecon)**@1830.
Randall the Giant (Newtown)1840s, **Jenkin Rees (Aberdare)** 1870s, **Thomas Rees 'Twm Carnabwth'** @1830a, **Edmund Richards 'Edmund Cabbage' (Pengam)** 1886, **M Richards (Welshpool)** 1829, **Thomas Richards (Aberdare)** 1890a, **William Richards (Newport)** 1840s, **Morris Roberts (Swansea)** @1850s, **Jemmy Robinson (Denbigh)** @1840s, **John Robinson (North Wales)** @1812, **Luke Rogers** @1830, **George Rowlands 'Gipsey George'** early 1800s.
Thomas Scannell (Cardiff) 1850s, **Joe Scott (Gower)** 1830s), **Robert Shellan (Newport)** 1840s, **Shoni Shirraw (Swansea)** 1882, **Cornelius Smith** (Swansea) 1830s, **(Edwin Smith (Pontypool)** 1890s, **Henry Stephens (Cardff)** @1850s, **J. Stevens** @1865.
William Tansell 'Fiddler' (Pontypool) 1860s, 70s, **Dan Thomas (Aberaman)** 1890s, **Edward Thomas (Dowlais)** @1850s, **Evan Thomas (Ynyshir)** 1890s, **John Thomas (Merthyr)** 1826 , **John Thomas (Briton Ferry)** 1860s, **Thomas Thomas (Briton Ferry)** 1862, **William Thomas 'Crib' (Swansea)** @1830s -40s 5ft. 3 ½ ins..
Richard Vaughan (Caerphilly) 1890s.
George Walsh (Cardiff) 1870s, **Jack Walsh (Swansea)** 1860s, **Samuel Waters (Cardiff)** 1833, **Michael Welsh (Merthyr)** 1872, **John Wilde (Merthyr)** @1840s, **Adolphus Williams (Merthyr)** 1850s, **Jack Williams 'Portobello' (Pontypridd)** 1860s, **Jack Williams (Barry)** 1890s, **James Williams (Swansea)** 1850s, **Jonathan Williams 'Grog'** @1840s. **John Wills (Rhondda)** 1897.

Bibliography

Primary sources

Army Deserters 1828-1840. Category: Military, armed forces & conflict. Subcategory: Regimental & service records.
Census
Collections, historical and archaeological relating to Montgomeryshire Collections, historical & amp; archaeological relating to Montgomeryshire, Vol. 45 (1938). The National Library of Wales.
Commissioners of Enquiry 1847
Hansard
History of Pugilism (London, Oxberry, 1812)
Irving, Washington, 'John Bull', in The Sketch Book, 1820.
Proceedings of the Old Bailey. Old Bailey online'. 24th June 1901. Reference Number: t19010624-479
National Archives of Wales, Crime and Punishment Database,
http://www.llgc.org.uk/sesiwn_fawr/index_s.htm
Report to the General Board of Health on a Preliminary Enquiry into the Sewerage, Drainage and Supply of Water, and the Sanitary Conditions of the Inhabitants of the Town of Cardiff, by Thomas Webster Rammell, superintending inspector (London, HMSO, 1850)
Robert Roberts, Y Sgolor Mawr" ("The Great Scholar"),

Newspapers

Aberdare Leader
Aberdare Times
Aberdeen Weekly Journal
Aberystwyth Observer

Baner ac Amserau Cymry
Barry Dock News
Barry Herald
Belfast News Letter
Bell's Life in London
Berrow's Worcester Journal
Birmingham Daily Post
Blyth News
Bradford Observer
Brecon County Times
Bristol Mercury
Bristol Mirror
Bury and Norwich Post

Caernarvon and Denbigh Herald
Caledonian Mercury

Cambrian
Cambrian News
Cardiff and Merthyr Guardian
Cardiff Times
Cardigan Observer
Carmarthen Chronicle
Carmarthenshire Journal
Cheltenham Journal
Chepstow Weekly Advertiser
Cheshire Observer
Coatbridge Leader
County Observer

Daily News
Daily Telegraph
Denbighshire Free Press
Derby Mercury
Derby Telegraph
Dumfries Courier
Dundee Courier
Durham County Advertiser

Essex Standard
Evening Express
Evening Standard
Examiner

Flintshire Observer
Freeman's Journal

Glamorgan Free Press
Glamorgan Gazette
Glasgow Herald
Globe
Gloucester Citizen
Graphic

Halifax Evening Courier
Hampshire Telegraph
Hartlepool Northern Daily Mail
Haverfordwest and Milford Haven Tel.
Huddersfield Chronicle
Hull Packet

Illustrated Police News
Illustrated Sporting News
Illustrated Usk Observer
Ipswich Journal
Isle of Wight Observer

Jackson's Oxford Journal

Kentish Gazette

Leeds Mercury
Leicester Chronicle
Licensed Victuallers' Mirror
Liverpool Mercury
Llanelly Mercury
Llangollen Advertiser
Llais Lafur
Lloyd's Weekly Newspaper
London Gazette
London Journal
London Review

Manchester Times
Manchester Evening News
Merthyr Express
Merthyr Guardian

Merthyr Telegraph
Merthyr Times
Monmouthshire Beacon
Monmouthshire Merlin
Montgomery County Times
Morning Chronicle
Morning Herald
Morning Post
Morning Star
Music Hall and Theatre Review
Newcastle Daily Chronicle
North Eastern Daily Gazette
North Wales Chronicle
North Wales Gazette
North Wales Times
Nottinghamshire Guardian

Pall Mall Gazette
Pembrokeshire Herald
Pierce Egan's Weekly Courier
Pontypool Free Press
Pontypridd Chronicle
Potter's Electric News
Preston Chronicle
Preston Guardian
Preston Herald

Reynolds Newspaper
Rhondda Leader
Rhyl Journal
Rhyl Record
Royal Cornwall Gazette

Sheffield Independent
Silurian
South Wales Argus
South Wales Daily News
South Wales Daily Post
South Wales Echo & Express
South Wales Star
Sporting Chronicle
Sporting Life
Sporting Mirror
Sporting Times
Sportsman
Standard
Star of Gwent
Sun
Sunday Times

Bibliography

Swansea Journal

Tenby Observer
The Charter
The Era
The Racing Times
The Times
Trewman's Exeter Flying Post

Weekly Mail
Weekly Standard and Express
Welsh Gazette
Welshman
Western Daily Press
Western Mail
Wigan Observer
Worcestershire Journal
Wrexham Guardian
Wrexham Weekly Advertiser

Y Goleuad
Yorkshire Herald
Yorkshire Post

Canada
Victoria Daily Colonist

USA
Alexandria Gazette
Barton County Democrat (Ky.)
Bennington Banner (Vt.)
Bismark Tribune (N.D.),
Bridgeport Evening Farmer
Charleston Daily News
Chicago Daily Tribune
Cleveland Morning Leader
Daily Evening Bulletin (Ky.)
Daily Intelligencer (Va.)
Daily Ohio Statesman
Evening Bulletin
Evening Herald (Pa.)
Evening Star (Washington)
Evening Telegraph (Pa.)

Evening Times (Washington)
Evening World (New York)
Idaho Semi-weekly World
Indianapolis Journal
Lancaster Daily Intelligencer (Pa.)
Memphis Daily Appeal
Morning Call (San Francisco, Calif.)
Nashville Union and American
Nashville Union and Despatch
New York Clipper
New York Herald
New York Times
Omaha Daily Bee
Pittsburgh Despatch
Princeton Union (Minn.)
Sacramento Daily Record-Union (Cal.)
Saint Paul Daily Globe
Salt Lake Tribune
St. Paul Daily Globe
Sun (New York)
Wheeling Daily Intelligencer (W. Va.)
Wichita Eagle
Y Drych

France
Journal de Paris

Periodicals
Bathafarn
Fancy
Figaro in London
Lancet
Law Quarterly Review
Law Times
London Kelt
London Review
New Monthly Magazine
Sporting Magazine
The Torch
Welsh Outlook

391

Secondary sources

Books

Boddy, Kasia, Boxing, a cultural history (London, Reaktion Books, 2008).
Borrow, George, Lavengro *The Scholar, The Gypsy, The Priest* (London, Macmillan Co., 1900, First publd. 1851),
Brailsford, Dennis, Bareknuckles: A Social History of Prize-Fighting (Cambridge, Lutterworth Press, 1988).
Carter, Neil, Medicine, Sport and the Body: A Historical Perspective (London, Bloomsbury, 2004).
Charnock, Richard Stephen, Verba Nominalia, or Words Derived from Proper Names (London, Trubner, 1866).
Colley, Linda, *Britons: Forging the Nation 1707-1837* (London, Pimlico, 1994)
Copleston, William James, *Memoir of Edward Copleston (1776-1849) D. D. Bishop of Llandaff* (London, John W. Parker, 1851
Cordell, Alexander, *Rape of the Fair Country* (London, Pan, 1965).
Cordell, Alexander, Peerless Jim
Cragoe, Matthew, *Culture, Politics and National Identity in Wales 1832-1886* (Oxford, Oxford University Press, 2004)
Davies, Haydn, *The History of the Borough of Newport* (Newport, Pennyfarthing Press, 1998).
Davies, John, A History of Wales (London, Penguin, 1994).
Davies, Lawrence, Mountain Fighters: Lost Tales of Welsh Boxing (Cardiff, Peerless Press, 2011)
Davies, Percy, and Yates, Frederick, Bare Fists and Courage: The Adventures of a Welsh Prize Fighter (Risca, Starling Press, 1978).
Davies, Russell, Secret Sins: Sex, Violence and Society in Carmarthenshire 1870-1920 (Cardiff, University of Wales Press, 1996).
Davies, Russell, Hope and Heartbreak: A Social History of Wales and the Welsh, 1776 – 1871 (Cardiff, University of Wales Press, 2005).
Deakin, Fred, Welsh Warriors (Stone, Crescendo, 1990).
Doyle, Sir Arthur Conan, The Croxley Master (Charleston, Nabu Press, 2012, First publd. London, Strand Magazine, 1899)
Egan, Pierce. Boxiana or Sketches of Ancient and Modern Pugilism: A Facsimile Reprint of 1st ed., London, Smeeton, 1812 with an introduction and index by Dennis Prestidge (Leicester, Vance Harvey, 1971)
Egan, Pierce, Boxiana, from the Championship of Cribb to the present time. Vol. ii (London, Sherwood Jones, 1824)
Emsley, Clive, Hard Men: Violence in England since 1750 (London, Hambledon and London, 2005).
Evans, D. Gareth, A History of Wales 1815 – 1906 (Cardiff, University of Wales Press, 1996).
Evans, Henry Tobit. "Rebecca and her Daughters, being the History of the Agrarian Disturbances in Wales, 1843- 1844, known as the Rebecca Riots," (Cardiff, Educational Publishing Company, Ltd., 1910).
Farr, Tommy, Thus Farr (London, Optomen Press, 1989).
Foster, Brian, Eastern Valley Transportation Cases and Prize-fights (no details available).
Freeman, Anna, The Fair Fight (London, Weidenfeld & Nicholson, 2014).

Bibliography

Huggins, Mike, The Victorians and Sport (London: Hambledon, 2004)
Hurley, Jon, Tom Spring: Bare-knuckle champion of All England (Stroud, Tempus, 2007)
Johnes, Martin, A History of Sport in Wales (Cardiff, University of Wales Press, 2005)
Jones, David J. V., Crime in 19th Century Wales (Cardiff, University of Wales Press, 1992).
Jones, Emrys, (ed.) The Welsh In London (Cardiff, University of Wales Press, 2001),
Jones, Gareth, The Boxers of Wales. Volume 1: Cardiff (Cardiff, St. David's Press, 2009).
Jones, Jack, Black Parade (Cardigan, Parthian, 2009)
Jones, Tim, Rioting in North East Wales 1536-1918 (Wrexham, Bridge Books, 1997).
Kissack, Keith, Monmouth: The Making of a county town (London and Chichester, Phillimore, 1973)
Kissack, Keith, Victorian Monmouth (Monmouth, Monmouth Historical Trust, n. d. @1973.
Lambert, W. R. *Drink and Sobriety in Victorian Wales c.1820- c.1895* (Cardiff, University of Wales Press, 1983).
Livesey, Peter, *The Detective Wore Silk Drawers* (England, Chivers Press, 2000).
Lloyd, Alan, The Great Prize Fight (London, Souvenir Press, 2004; first published London, Cassell, 1977).
Lynch, John Gilbert Bohun, Knuckles and Gloves (London, Collins, 1884)
Llewellyn, Richard, *How Green Was My Valley* (London, New English Library, 1967).
Matthews, Rev. Edward, Siencyn Penhydd and George Heycock, trans. By Leslie Evans (Port Talbot Historical Society,1989).
Matthews, James, Historic Newport (Newport, Williams Press, 1910),
Manson, Iain, The Lion & the Eagle (Cheltenham, Sportsbooks, 2008).
Mee, Bob, Bare Fists (London, Collins Willow, 1998).
Miles, Henry Downes, Pugilistica: The History of British Boxing, Vols. 1, 3 (Edinburgh, John Grant, 1906).
Mingay, G. E. (ed.), The Victorian Countryside, Vol. 1 (London, Routledge & Keegan Paul, 1981).
Morgan, Kenneth O., Rebirth of a Nation: A History of Modern Wales (Oxford, Oxford University Press, 2002).
Morris, J. H. and Williams, L. J., The South Wales Coal Industry 1841-1875 (Cardiff, University of Wales Press, 1958),
Mullan, Harry, The World Encyclopedia of Boxing: The definitive illustrated guide (London, Carlton, 1999).
Oates, Joyce Carol, On Boxing (London, Bloomsbury, 1987).
Shaw, George Bernard, Cashel Byron's Profession ((Harmondsworth, Penguin, 1979; first publd. 1886).
Smith, David, and Gareth Williams, Fields of Praise (Cardiff, University of Wales Press, 1980).
Stead, Peter and Gareth Williams (eds.), Wales and its Boxers: The Fighting Tradition (Cardiff, University of Wales Press, 2008).
Strange, Keith, Merthyr Tydfil Iron Metropolis: Life in a Welsh Industrial Town (Stroud, Tempus, 2005)
Stratman, Linda, The Marquess of Queensberry: Wilde's Nemesis (Yale University Press, 2013)
Sullivan, John L., Life and Reminiscences of a 19th century gladiator (London, Routledge, 1892).
Swift, Owen, The Handbook of Boxing (London, Nicholson, 1840)

Thomas, D. J., The Temperance Movement in Newport, 1837-1937 (Newport, The Newport Printing Co., 1937).
Thompson, David, England in the nineteenth century (1815-1914) (Harmondsworth, Penguin, 1964)
Townsend Collins, W. J., Monmouthshire Writers (Newport, Johns, 1945)
Wiener, Martin J., Men of Blood: Violence, Manliness, and Criminal Justice in Victorian England (Cambridge, Cambridge University Press, 2004)
Wilde, Jimmy, Fighting was my business (London, Robson Books, 1990, originally publd. 1938).
Wilkins, Charles, The History of Merthyr Tydfil (Merthyr Tydfil, H, W. Southey, 1867).
Williams, Gareth, 1905 and all that: Essays on Rugby Football, Sport and Welsh Society (Llandysul,1991,
Williams, John, Digest of Welsh Historical Statistics, Volume I (Pontypool, Government Statistical Service, 1985.
Wilson, Ben. The Making of Victorian Values. Decency & Dissent in Britain: 1789-1837 (London, Penguin, 2007)
Woods, Robert, The population of Britain in the nineteenth century (Cambridge, Cambridge University Press, 1995),
Young, G. M. (ed.), A History of England: Victorian England (London, The Folio Society, 1999).

Articles
Anderson, Jack, 'Pugilistic Prosecutions: Prize fighting and the courts in nineteenth century Britain', *The Sports Historian* No. 21 (2) (November 2001).
Bagwell, Philip S., 'The Decline of Rural Isolation', in G. E. Mingay (ed.), *The Victorian Countryside*, Vol. 1 (London, Routledge & Keegan Paul, 1981)
Blocker, Jack S., David M. Fahey, Ian R. Tyrell, Alcohol and Temperance in Modern History: An international....., Volume 1 ( ),
Croll, Andy, 'Mabon's Day: The rise and fall of a Lib-Lab holiday in the South Wales coalfield, 1888-1898', *Labour History Review*, Vol. 72, No. 1, April 2007.
Croll, Andy, 'Street Disorder...., *Social Hustory*, 24, 3 (1999)
Evans, Neil, As rich as California…Opening and Closing the frontier: Wales 1780 – 1870, in (Gareth Elwyn Jones and Dai Smith, eds.,) *The People of Wales* (Llandysul, Gomer Press, 2000).
James, E. Wyn, 'The Lame Chick and The North Star: Some Ethnic Rivalries in Sport as Reflected in Mid-Nineteenth-Century Welsh Broadsides', in (Marjetka Golež ed.,) *Ballads between Tradition and Modern Times* (Lubljana, Slovenia: Slovenian Academy of Sciences & Arts, 1998)
Jones, Aled, 'The Nineteenth Century Media and Welsh Identity', in Laurel Brake, Bell, Bill and Finkelstein, David, (eds.,), *Nineteenth Century Media and the Construction of Identities* (2000).
Jones, D. J. V., 'The South Wales Strike of 1816', *Morgannwg, transactions of the Glamorgan Local History Society*, Vol. 11 (1967).
Jones, Rev. David, 'Memories of Old Cardiganshire', as recorded by the late the Reverend David Jones, Llangym, Ceredigion: *Journal of the Cardiganshire Antiquarian Society*, Vol, 4, nos. 1-4 1960-1963.
Jones, Ieuan Gwynedd, 1848 and 1868: 'Brad y Llyfrau Gleision' and Welsh Politics, in his Mid-Victorian Wales: *The Observers and the Observed* (Cardiff, University of Wales Press, 1992)
Jones, Ieuan Gwynedd, 'Merthyr Tydfil in 1850: Impressions and Contrasts', *Glamorgan Historian*, Vol. 4 (Cowbridge, Brown, 1967), p. 44.

Bibliography

Jones, Rosemary A. N., 'Women, Community and Collective Action: The Ceffyl Pren Tradition', in Angela V. John (ed.), *Our Mother's Land: Chapters in Welsh Women's History 1830-1939* (Cardiff, University of Wales Press, 1991)

Price, Cecil, Some Welsh Theatres, 1844 – 1870, *National Library of Wales Journal*, 1961, Winter Volume XII/2

Rees, R. D., 'Glamorgan newspapers under the Stamp Acts', *Morgannwg* transactions of the Glamorgan Local History Society, Vol 3 (1959),

Roberts, Gwyneth Tyson, 'Under the Hatches': English Parliamentary Commissioners' Views of the People and Language of Mid-Nineteenth-Century Wales, in Bill Schwartz (ed.), *The Expansion of England: Race, ethnicity and cultural history.*

Strachan, John, , 'Poets and Pugilists', History Today, Vol. 59, Issue 1 (2009).

Williams, Gareth, 'Sport and Society in Glamorgan 1750-1980', Glamorgan County History, vol. 6, ed. Prys Morgan (Cardiff: Glamorgan History Trust Ltd, 1988);

Williams, Gareth, 'A Brutal Passion', Bareknuckle Bruisers and Mountain Fighters, in Stead, Peter, and Gareth Williams (eds.) Wales and its Boxers: The Fighting Tradition (Cardiff, University of Wales Press, 2008).

Williams, Stephen Malcolm, Big Mac and His Boys, in Wales and its Boxers: The Fighting Tradition, Stead, Peter and Gareth Williams (eds.) (Cardiff, University of Wales Press, 2008).

Other sources
Crumplin, Mick, (Fight Night, Yesterday TV, October 2012).
Docklands Ancestors ref X097/224.
England, Joe, 'Merthyr's Rich Heritage' paper delivered at conference 26 November 2010
National Archives of Wales, Crime and Punishment Database,
http://www.llgc.org.uk/sesiwn_fawr/index_s.htm.
National Library of Wales catalogue File number4/1017/4 Document number7
Collections, historical and archaeological relating to Montgomeryshire Collections, historical & amp; archaeological relating to Montgomeryshire, Vol. 45 (1938), p. 183-185. The National Library of Wales.
Radnorshire Society Transactions, Vol. 58 1988
Report to the General Board of Health on a Preliminary Enquiry into the Sewerage, Drainage and Supply of Water, and the Sanitary Conditions of the Inhabitants of the Town of Cardiff, by Thomas Webster Rammell, superintending inspector (London, HMSO, 1850)
Rumney and St. Mellons. A History of Two Villages (Rumney and District Local History Society, 2005].
The Treasury: A monthly miscellany of missionary reports in connection with the Calvinstic Methodist Churches. Vol. 1, 1864, p. 122.
Welsh Dictionary of National Biography

Unpublished theses
Francis, John, 'Invisible Incomers?': Migration from the West County to Glamorgan in the mid-nineteenth century (unpublished PhD thesis, Cardiff University, 2010).
Gregory, Margaret, A Policeman's Lot: The Nature and Dynamics of the Monmouthshire Constabulary 1857 – 1914 (unpublished PhD thesis: Cardiff University, 2009).
Howard, Sharon, Crime, Communities and Authority in Early Modern Wales: Denbighshire, 1660-1730 (unpublished Ph.D. thesis, University of Wales, Aberystwyth, 2003).

Lightning Source UK Ltd.
Milton Keynes UK
UKHW021425200721
387470UK00009B/1898